Basic News Writing

SECOND EDITION

Basic News Writing

Melvin Mencher
Columbia University

wcb
Wm. C. Brown Publishers
Dubuque, Iowa

wcb group

Wm. C. Brown Chairman of the Board
Mark C. Falb President and Chief Executive Officer

wcb Wm. C. Brown Company Publishers, College Division

Lawrence E. Cremer President
James L. Romig Vice-President, Product Development
David A. Corona Vice-President, Production and Design
E. F. Jogerst Vice-President, Cost Analysis
Bob McLaughlin National Sales Manager
Catherine M. Faduska Director of Marketing Services
Craig S. Marty Director of Marketing Research
Marilyn A. Phelps Manager of Design
Eugenia M. Collins Production Editorial Manager
Mary M. Heller Photo Research Manager

Book Team **John Stout** Executive Editor
Stanley Stoga Editor
Michael Warrell Designer
Karen Slaght Production Editor
Carla D. Arnold Assistant Permissions Editor
Carol M. Schiessl Photo Research Editor

Cover photos: *upper left,* Melvin Mencher; *upper right,* George M. Cassidy—Click/Chicago; *lower left,* © James L. Shaffer; *lower right,* Dan McConnell—Click/Chicago

Library of Congress Catalog Card Number: 85–70858

ISBN 0–697–00481–3

Printed in the United States of America
10 9 8 7 6 5 4 3 2 1

Contents

v

Reporting Part 2

4 Finding Information and Gathering Facts 77

5 How Reporters Work 97

Writing Part 3

6 Planning the Story 115

Story Types Part 4

Preface

This is a how-to book. It was written to help the newcomer to journalism learn how to put words on paper that accurately and clearly describe and explain ideas and events.

Basic News Writing is designed to show the beginner how to gather information, how to analyze its importance and how to put the results of this reporting and thinking into news stories.

The techniques recommended here are those of successful news writers, men and women who have struggled to make words do their bidding. The writers who have contributed to *Basic News Writing* know that writing does not come easily. They understand how hard it is to whip words into submission so that they dance lightly or march somberly across the page. They have learned to write through patience, confidence and effort.

Patience is necessary because words have a tendency to go their own way, resisting our efforts to lock them into sentences and paragraphs. It takes time to learn to write well. Few people are born writers.

Confidence is important because sometimes it seems that the right words will never come, that the story will not blend smoothly but insists on zigzagging its way from paragraph to paragraph—no matter how patient the writer is. The newcomer should not give up. All of us possess the creative instinct. We all want to make something of our experiences, to tell others what we have seen and heard. With confidence in ourselves, we can do that.

But it does require work. The aspiring artist who seeks to transfer a sunset to canvas does not instinctively dip his brush into the precise colors on the palette. Through study and trial and error the artist learns just how much white to mix with red for the clouds. The singer cannot turn words and musical notes into a song of lost love the first time she sees the score. It takes hours, sometimes days, before everything comes together and the performance is worth recording. The journalist is no different. Beginner or experienced news writer, effort and hard work lead to well-written stories.

Unguided effort is wasted work, however. The purpose of *Basic News Writing* is to serve as compass and sextant. It provides the directions in which the student should point his or her efforts. The techniques, principles and concepts that are suggested here come from the field, from the everyday experience of journalists on the job. Every concept and principle is illustrated with a practical example from the experience of a professional.

For the student considering a career in journalism, these illustrations serve another purpose. By watching the journalist at work, the student is able to see the many faces and facets of journalism: The young woman, just out of journalism school, alone in the AP newsroom, who is called on to handle a rooming house fire that kills more than 20 people. The television network news writer who has minutes to write the story of U.S. Navy planes downing two Libyan jets. The newspaper reporter who climbs the stairs of a nearly deserted tenement to interview a family living without heat or running water.

For this second edition I have had guidance from many users of the textbook. Some wanted additional material, and others suggested the book be slimmed down. Several said the actual news writing begins too late in the book; others liked the introductory sections for their beginning students. In response, I have added and subtracted, but I have left the structure much as it was in the first edition. For those who want their students to plunge into writing at once, I suggest altering the order of the chapters in making reading assignments and using the workbook that accompanies this text. The workbook puts students to the task of writing in week one.

I have added a section on court coverage to chapter 15, and in response to several requests I have added a chapter on photojournalism.

What place has photojournalism in a textbook on news writing? The book is used by beginning students, and photojournalism is increasingly attractive to young men and women. Also, many of those who join the staffs of small dailies and weeklies will be asked to work as reporter-photographers.

The Newspaper Fund's *1985 Journalism Career and Scholarship Guide* carries advice frequently given by graduates to those still in journalism school. One bit of counsel quoted in the report is: "Know how to use a 35mm camera and develop film."

To demonstrate the power and vitality of photojournalism I have added to this edition some of the memorable pictures by well-known photographers, and I have included the work of young men and women still in school or starting on their careers. Most of their photographs are in the chapter on photojournalism; several are scattered through the text.

Another major change: "Avoiding the Wrong Word" and "Words that Need Watching" were taken from chapter 10 and placed in the workbook. Also, I clarified some of the concepts in the chapters on news values, fact gathering and writing. Several of my "nevers" became "hardly evers," and repetitions and dated material were removed.

For the second edition I had considerable assistance from friends and colleagues. Merrill Perlman of *The New York Times* clarified some vague ideas and reminded me that one word usually is better than three. Kay Ellen Krane found where I had tripped on syntax and flushed out the remnants of sexism. Ms. Krane scrutinized the proof and prepared the index. My deep appreciation to the following colleagues who also made many useful contributions to *Basic News Writing:*

Dick Haws
Iowa State University

Luke Staudacker
Marquette University

Terry Vander Heyden
Western Kentucky University

Howard L. Seeman
Humboldt State University

A number of photographers, photography instructors and photo editors contributed to the chapter on photojournalism. I would like especially to thank Claude Cookman, a photo editor for several newspapers; Walter Emerson of the University of Kansas; Michael Geissinger of the Rochester Institute of Technology; John Shearer of Columbia University; and Don Ultang of Drake University.

The philosophy of *Basic News Writing* is best summed up by Samuel Johnson's remark, "The end of writing is to enable the readers better to enjoy life, or better to endure it."

For all its practicality, this textbook recognizes that journalism is more calling than trade. Kin to teaching, cousin to preaching, journalism is much more than the sum of its techniques and the advice of its practitioners. Through its many examples, *Basic News Writing* seeks to demonstrate the moral underpinnings of journalism.

Journalism's hope and inspiration are its young men and women. This book was written for them and especially in memory of two young men who were killed in Vietnam, Ron Gallagher and Peter Bushey. Ron was editor of the *University Daily Kansan* when I was its adviser at the University of Kansas, and Peter was one of my students at Columbia University. They loved journalism and had faith in what it could accomplish. They wrote, they took pictures and they aspired to make the world a better place for us all through journalism. To them, journalism was a noble calling.

M.M.

Acknowledgments

Those who have provided help with this book include the following:

Steve Ames
Pepperdine University

Mervin Block
Free-lance television writer

Stewart Bowman
The (Louisville) *Courier-Journal*

Bonnie Britt
The Houston Chronicle

Roy Peter Clark
Poynter Institute for Media Studies

Joelle Cohen
The News Tribune (Tacoma, Wash.)

Claude Cookman
The Miami Herald

Walter Emerson
University of Kansas

Frances D'Emilio
UPI

Stuart Dim
Newsday

Mary Ann Giordano
The Daily News

Stephen Hartgen
The Anniston (Ala.) *Star*

Berkley Hudson
The Providence Journal-Bulletin

Monica Kaufman
WSB-TV (Atlanta)

Terry Keys
University of Kentucky

Dennis Love
The Anniston (Ala.) Star

Frank McCulloch
The Sacramento Bee

Avice Meehan
The Dalton (Mass.) News-Record

Mitch Mendelson
The Birmingham Post-Herald

Bill Mertens
The Hays (Kan.) *Daily News*

Mark Miller
The Berkshire (Mass.) *Eagle*

Cheyenne J. Oldham
University of Kentucky

Merrill Perlman
The New York Times

Susan J. Porter
Scripps-Howard News

Neal Robbins
UPI

Bob Rose
The Blade (Toledo, Ohio)

Christopher Scanlan
The Providence Journal-Bulletin

Howard L. Seemann
Humboldt State University

John Shearer
Columbia University

Rick Sluder
The News & Observer (Raleigh, N.C.)

Mary Voboril
The Miami Herald

Lindy Washburn
AP

Jan Wong
The Gazette (Montreal)

Charles M. Young
Rolling Stone

Journalists in Action

In the Newsroom and On the Beat

The news writer gives readers and viewers an accurate, thorough, impartial and timely account of events. The writer does this by applying skills and knowledge to the task of reporting and writing.

    The journalistic process is the same for newspapers, radio, television, newsmagazines: Facts are gathered and checked, additional information is obtained through research, the story is written and, finally, the news is produced in written or spoken form.

Looking Ahead

The lights are out in the fashionable stores along Fifth Avenue, and the tall buildings in Rockefeller Center loom over the deserted streets. Moviegoers have made their way home from Radio City Music Hall a block away on Sixth Avenue. It is well past midnight in midtown New York.

    Although the lights in one Rockefeller Center office building burn brightly, there is an unusual calm here, too. The reporters, editors and operators in the Associated Press newsroom have left for the night. The office is deserted—except for a young woman sitting at one of the desks.

    Lindy Washburn is working the early shift—11:30 p.m. to 8 a.m.—in the New York City bureau of the AP. She was hired as a summer vacation replacement after her graduation from journalism school.

    As the newcomer in the bureau, she has been taught the ropes: the need for speed, accuracy and brevity, which wires send out sports, radio, local and national news, and the method for transmitting stories she may have to write when the operators are not on duty.

    Washburn is responsible for a large area of the East Coast, and she will be on her own most of the shift. This is her first night alone on the early shift.

    As the old hands were leaving, one had stopped on his way out to reassure her. "Looks like a quiet night," he said.

On the Job. Lindy Washburn of the Associated Press takes notes on a video display terminal (VDT) for a breaking news story.
John Titchen of the *Star-Bulletin*

For a while it was quiet. Washburn handled some routine tasks. But suddenly, at 1:40 a.m., the stillness of the office is broken by the ring of the telephone. The night city editor of the *Daily News* is calling. Washburn can sense the urgency in his voice.

Handling a Big Story—Alone

"We have a tip there's a big fire in New Jersey," the *News* editor says. "Have you got anything?" No, she hasn't, she says. She asks him where the fire is. "Bradley Beach," he replies.

Washburn looks at a map and sees that Bradley Beach is a town on the Atlantic shore and is near Asbury Park, a larger city.

She calls long distance information and asks for the telephone numbers of the Bradley Beach police and fire departments and the numbers of the departments in Asbury Park. First, she calls the Bradley Beach fire department.

"Lady, we're busy," a voice says and hangs up. He sounds frantic.

She telephones the Asbury Park fire department.

"What's happening in Bradley Beach?" she asks. "I can't get anything from the department there."

"That's some fire," the dispatcher answers. "We have departments from all over the state fighting it. It looks like a big one."

"Any deaths?" Washburn asks.

"I think it was 20 last time I checked. Could be more now."

Washburn's heart picks up a few beats. This is obviously a big story. She realizes that on a slow night a fire with this many deaths will be given play around the country. She knows that at this time—nearly 2 a.m.—morning newspapers in the West are readying their front pages. She will have to hurry to catch them.

She asks the dispatcher for the address of the building, what it is used for, when the first alarm had been received. She wants to know what the building looks like—is it wood, brick, stucco? The dispatcher says it's a wooden frame building, called the Brinley Inn. No, he doesn't know the cause. Too early for that.

As she hangs up, another telephone rings. The call is from a reporter for a radio station in Asbury Park. He had called the AP's Newark bureau with information and a tape-recorded message had told him the bureau was closed for the night but that important stories should be phoned to the New York City bureau.

"Have you heard about the fire?" he asks.

"Yes," says Washburn. "How many deaths are there?" She needs the death toll. It's the key to the story. And she must have it confirmed.

"The hospital spokesman on the scene says 23," the reporter replies. She gives him the address the dispatcher had provided, and he confirms that.

He then plays a tape of the conversation he had with a doctor from the medical examiner's office who was at the scene of the fire.

Washburn now has almost all she needs. She will have to put something on the wire at once. Then she will have to alert the AP New Jersey staff to start working on the story.

She has been typing notes from her telephone conversations, and she looks them over. The death toll clearly is the heart of the story and will go into the first sentence, her lead. She rearranges her notes with this lead in mind. Then she writes her lead and is ready to file the story. She types in the code for an all-points bulletin and starts to relay the story.

Here is her story:

```
o364
    B N ZYVVYXUIV
BNBX NR07 NR05
BNBX
BC-BRADLEY BEACH FIRE
    BRADLEY BEACH, NEW JERSEY (AP)--A MAJOR
FIRE IN BRADLEY BEACH HAS KILLED 23 PEOPLE,
ACCORDING TO FIRE OFFICIALS.
    THE FIRE AT BRINLEY INN, 200 BRINLEY AVE.,
BEGAN AT 11:20 P.M. AND WAS BROUGHT UNDER CONTROL AT
MIDNIGHT, ACCORDING TO CHIEF THEODORE A. BIANCHI OF
THE BRADLEY BEACH FIRE DEPARTMENT.
```

```
THE CAUSE OF THE FIRE IS UNDETERMINED, HE SAID.
     THE BRINLEY INN, A THREE-STORY WOOD FRAME
BUILDING, WAS REPORTEDLY OCCUPIED BY 36 PEOPLE AT
THE TIME OF THE BLAZE. MANY ELDERLY PERSONS AND
TEENAGERS WERE AMONG THOSE KILLED, THE OFFICIALS
SAID.
     DEAD AND INJURED WERE TAKEN TO THE JERSEY SHORE
MEDICAL CENTER AND THE LONG BRANCH MEDICAL CENTER.

     MORE
     AP-NY-07-27 0201EDT
```

Second Lead

All of this is done in about 20 minutes, and Washburn is pleased by her ability to act quickly in a critical situation. (She later learns that she has beaten the opposition, the UPI, by 35 minutes.) But she is not pleased with her story. There are some flubs.

She sees that she should have abbreviated New Jersey in the dateline, and she realizes that the adjective *major* in the lead is extraneous. She also realizes that she should have used *said* instead of *according to* in the lead.

By the time her story has cleared the wire, Washburn is busy gathering more material. She learns that the Brinley Inn is a four-story rooming house, and she has obtained more details about the injured, where the dead had been trapped and the exact time the fire broke out.

She begins to write a new lead. Her focus will still be the most news-worthy fact she has, the 23 deaths. She will put next the new material she has gathered about those who were injured. She remembers that in stories about disasters the news with the greatest impact is almost always the number of dead and injured.

Her first story had cleared at 2:01 a.m. Her second piece clears the wire at 3:26 a.m. Here it is:

```
o365
     B N ZYVVYXWYF
AM-BEACH FIRE, 2ND LD-WRITETHRU, 400
EDS: UPDATES, CORRECTS BUILDING
TO FOUR-STORY STRUCTURE, ADDS COLOR
     BRADLEY BEACH, N.J. (AP)--AT LEAST 23
PERSONS WERE KILLED SATURDAY IN A FIRE AT A ROOMING
HOUSE IN THIS SEASIDE RESORT, HOSPITAL OFFICIALS
SAID.
     TWO OTHERS SUFFERED SMOKE INHALATION AND WERE
ADMITTED TO THE JERSEY SHORE MEDICAL CENTER, SAID
HOSPITAL ADMINISTRATOR ERNEST KOVATS. AN
ADDITIONAL 13 PEOPLE WERE EXAMINED AT THE HOSPITAL,
KOVATS SAID.
     AS MANY AS 36 PEOPLE MAY HAVE BEEN INSIDE THE
BRINLEY INN WHEN THE FIRE BROKE OUT AT 11:02 P.M.
AND WAS BROUGHT UNDER CONTROL ABOUT MIDNIGHT,
AUTHORITIES SAID.
```

WITNESSES SAID MOST OF THE VICTIMS APPEARED TO
BE ELDERLY AND APPEARED TO BE TRAPPED ON THE TOP
FLOORS OF THE FOUR-STORY WOOD-FRAME BUILDING.
     THE CAUSE OF THE FIRE WAS NOT DETERMINED, BUT
THERE WERE SOME REPORTS OF AN EXPLOSION, SAID FIRE
CHIEF THEODORE A. BIANCHI.
     AT LEAST 35 AMBULANCES FROM BRADLEY BEACH AND
SEVERAL MONMOUTH COUNTY COMMUNITIES LINED UP NEAR
THE BUILDING, WAITING TO TRANSPORT THE BODIES,
ACCORDING TO WITNESSES.
     FIREMEN REMOVED THE VICTIMS FROM A THIRD FLOOR
EXIT DOOR AT THE REAR OF THE BUILDING TO A ROOF WHERE
THEY LOWERED THE VICTIMS TO THE WAITING AMBULANCES.
     TWO DOCTORS, ONE WHO IDENTIFIED HIMSELF AS A
DOCTOR FROM THE MONMOUTH COUNTY MEDICAL EXAMINER'S
OFFICE, WERE ON THE SCENE TO BRIEFLY EXAMINE THE
BODIES BEFORE THEY WERE TRANSPORTED TO JERSEY SHORE
MEDICAL CENTER.
     KOVATS SAID SEVERAL BODIES WERE TRANSPORTED
DIRECTLY TO THE COUNTY MORGUE AT FREEHOLD AREA
HOSPITAL.
     FIREMEN SAID THE BUILDING WAS ENGULFED WHEN
THEY ARRIVED AT THE SCENE, MAKING ENTRY IMPOSSIBLE.
     THE BUILDING WAS BADLY CHARRED ON THE SOUTH AND
EAST SIDES OF THE FIRST FLOOR OF THE BUILDING.
FIREMEN SAID THE FIRE APPEARED TO HAVE STARTED ON
THE EAST SIDE OF THE BUILDING ON THE PORCH.
     LOCAL FIRE OFFICIALS, MONMOUTH COUNTY FIRE
MARSHAL FRED LEGGETT, THE STATE POLICE ARSON SQUAD
AND MONMOUTH COUNTY PROSECUTOR ALEXANDER LEHRER
WERE ON THE SCENE CONDUCTING AN INITIAL
INVESTIGATION.
     THE BRINLEY INN WAS THE SCENE OF ANOTHER FIRE IN
SEPTEMBER 1979, ACCORDING TO THE ASBURY PARK PRESS.

AP-NY-07-27 0326EDT

In the UPI's Hong Kong Bureau

A third of the world to the west, in Hong Kong, a young reporter for the UPI is going over some stories he plans to put in his files.

"Robbins," the deputy news editor calls out. He tells Neal Robbins to find a boat and track down a flotilla of Chinese junks that is approaching Hong Kong.

Chinese sneak into the British colony all the time, Robbins knows. But this is different. This is an influx by sea. It could be a big story in the United States as well as in Asia. Chinese have been leaving the mainland in small groups for political reasons. But this sounds like a large movement.

Robbins is joined by a photographer and they take off.

Soon they are cruising the Hong Kong harbor on the 30-foot *Xinhua,* looking for a cove that the Chinese supposedly are heading for. As they head out to sea, police boats pass them, spotter planes fly overhead and a helicopter slowly circles above the water.

They spot the cove. There before them are about 50 traditional Chinese sailing junks. "Their rust-color bat-wing sails make the flotilla seem a well-combed field of wheat," Robbins notes. The boats are anchored, and Robbins directs the captain toward a boat in the middle of the flotilla.

The photographer, a Hong Kong Chinese, calls out to some people in a Cantonese dialect. The boat people stare back. Robbins tries his college Mandarin. More stares.

The Unexpected

Finally, they locate a man who speaks Mandarin. The boat people come from South China, he says. There are 70 of them on the small wooden boat, all members of three families.

No, he replies in answer to a question from Robbins. They are not fleeing China for political reasons. They have come, he says, because the authorities warned them of a massive earthquake that is to strike their area soon.

Finding the people friendly, Robbins moves from boat to boat, asking questions. He boards some of the boats. The people are from a fishing area, he is told, and they have been informed that the earthquake is due in about a week. He is also told that gangsters invaded their area and stole valuables and commandeered some fishing boats.

A Final Check

In an hour, Robbins is ready to return to the bureau to write. On the way out of the cove, he stops to interview officials on the police boats. Police intercepted the junks and herded them into the cove, a police superintendent tells him. The police had counted 55 boats and were told that a hundred more were on the way. They estimate there are 2,000 people on the boats.

Robbins asks what the superintendent knows about the earthquake, the gangsters and whether the people will be fed and cared for. Finally, he wants to know whether the government will let them stay if they ask to remain.

He obtains the superintendent's exact title and the spelling of his name.

On the way back to the bureau, Robbins reads his notes. Figuring out the lead is not too hard, he thinks.

Clearly, he says to himself, the point of the story, his lead, is the fact that the boats have arrived and the reason they are here. The hard part is the wording, trying to make the lead attractive. On a story like this one, good writing is especially important.

He has arranged his notes, thought of a lead, and there is still time before they land. He starts to write his story in longhand on the boat.

In the bureau, as Robbins seats himself, the editor says, "Keep it short." Back in the States, the President has been shot, and there are ominous stirrings in Poland.

As Robbins types, his editor looks over his shoulder. He asks Robbins about the gangsters.

"That's what they told me," Robbins replies. He says that the account the people gave was a bit confused.

"Bury it," the editor advises him, meaning that it should be put deep in the story.

Robbins agrees that the fear of the earthquake is the central fact.

Here is the beginning of Robbins' story as it went out on UPI's wires from Hong Kong:

```
ZCZC XHA197 NXI
00 HUP NRS
R I
     FLOTILLA 3-31
     BY NEAL ROBBINS
     HONG KONG, MARCH 31 (UPI)--A FLOTILLA OF
CHINESE JUNKS CARRYING SOME 2,000 PEOPLE ARRIVED IN
HONG KONG TUESDAY FEARING AN IMPENDING EARTHQUAKE
IN SOUTHERN CHINA, OFFICIALS SAID.
     POLICE SUPERINTENDENT BILL RENAHAN TOLD UPI
THAT A WAVE OF 55 OF THE RICKETY WOODEN BOATS WITH
2,000 MEN, WOMEN AND CHILDREN CAME FROM HAIFENG AND
LUFENG COUNTIES IN GUANGDONG PROVINCE JUST NORTH OF
HONG KONG. THE MAKESHIFT FLOTILLA LEFT HOME SUNDAY,
HE SAID.
```

```
    ANOTHER 200 TO 400 VESSELS POWERED BY BAT-
WINGED SAILS ARE STILL OUT AT SEA CARRYING AS MANY
AS 10,000 RESIDENTS OF CHINA, RENAHAN ESTIMATED.
    BUT HONG KONG GOVERNMENT SOURCES SAID ONLY 78
BOATS HAD BEEN SIGHTED AND 48 OF THEM CONTAINING
1,800 PEOPLE ARRIVED TUESDAY.
    RENAHAN SAID THE FLOTILLA WAS THE LARGEST OF
ITS KIND TO HIT THE BRITISH COLONY, WHICH HAS BEEN
FLOODED WITH HUNDREDS OF THOUSANDS OF ILLEGAL
CHINESE IMMIGRANTS SINCE 1978.
    POLICE LAUNCHES CORRALLED THE 20-40 FOOT (7-13
METER) BOATS IN JOSS HOUSE BAY, A SMALL COVE
SURROUNDED BY UNINHABITED, GRASSY HILLS JUST IN
SIGHT OF THE TOWERING SKYSCRAPERS OF HONG KONG, BUT
OUTSIDE THE MAIN HARBOR.

    MORE
SC1755
CCCCQQE
NNNN
```

The CBS "Evening News"

In New York City, it is 5:30 p.m. according to the wall clock in the small lobby of the CBS Broadcast Center at 524 West 57th St. Through the lobby, down a long corridor and passageway, a set of double doors opens into a two-story studio. People move quickly in and out the doors.

Inside, it is almost an hour before air time for the "CBS Evening News." A large desk sits in the middle of the pale blue studio. At one side, behind large glass panels is the executive producer's room. Dan Rather, the anchorman for the Evening News, is going over the program with the producer. From time to time, Rather emerges to talk to the writers who are seated next to the central desk in the studio.

They are preparing for the 6:30 program that is shown live to viewers in some cities in the East and Midwest. Half an hour later, the videotape is broadcast for New York City and other places, and later the tape will be shown to viewers on the West Coast. When a news story is developing, new sections may be inserted live in the two later newscasts.

The Writers

The writers have been at work since 10 in the morning. Their first task is to read several newspapers—*The New York Times, The Washington Post, The Wall Street Journal* and *Daily News*. Then they scan the wires for the news. Each writer has a different area of responsibility: one handles national news; another, foreign; a third, features, disasters and obituaries.

The writers look over the major stories in the newspapers and on the wires. They are also on the lookout for the news items that make for interesting feature stories and takeouts. They are conscious of the visual possibilities of each story. A "tell" story or "reader" in which the anchorman reads from a script generally is not so interesting to viewers as a story that is accompanied by videotape.

Tell stories are written tightly. But stories with good videotape may run five or six times as long. A writer may collect several thousand words for a story and reduce it to 50 words for the anchorperson to read as a tell story. A story that involves a correspondent in the field may require a discussion with that correspondent. The writer will want to know what Lesley Stahl in Washington will stress so he or she can write an appropriate lead-in for Rather's introduction. The lead-in is a few words that capture the essence of the story without duplicating what the reporter is going to say.

By midafternoon, the writers have a good idea of the day's news, and at 3:30 the executive producer and the editor discuss the news items for the program. The editor needs to know how much time will be needed for each item and whether it will be a tell story or will be told by a reporter on videotape.

Minutes to Go

5:58 Rather leaves the executive producer's office and sits in the chair that he will use for the broadcast. He is holding a sheaf of papers, the items he will read for the Evening News. He manages to bite down on his cigar and move his lips as he reads the script. He is in his fifties, trim and vigorous. He wears a white shirt and a conservative tie. His hair, flecked with gray, is carefully combed back but rearranges itself as he moves around.

6:02 Rather turns to one of his writers and asks about an item that has been inserted in the newscast, a legal suit involving Richard Nixon. "You think we should explain this?" Rather asks a tall, middle-aged writer for the program. "If we do, we'll need 10 or 15 more seconds." The writer thinks for a few seconds, nods approval to Rather, and starts writing.

6:04 Lineup item No. 22, a tell story, displeases Rather. He discusses some of the wording with a writer. The item runs for 20 seconds and is 50 words long. They agree on new wording.

6:05 "Ten is out," someone shouts, and item 10 is scratched to make room for the additional material in the Nixon story.

6:08 The makeup woman enters the studio. The camera crew begins to position itself around the room, and the two people running the prompter machines go over the script. The machines project large type directly in front of Rather so that although he appears to the viewer to be looking directly into the camera he is reading from the script projected in front of him. A system of lenses projects the script over the lens of the camera focused on Rather.

6:10 Rather looks up from editing the lead-all, the first item in the newscast. "Very nice lead," he tells the writer. Rather resumes reading.

6:11 A woman dashes out of the executive producer's office. "We have an emergency," she says. "We need something from the archives." File footage is necessary for a news item. It may not be used, but the producer wants to have it available.

Editing the Evening News. Anchorman Dan Rather goes over the lead item minutes before going on the air. The CBS Evening News reaches 16 million homes.

6:14 Rather detects an ambiguous statement in one of the stories. The item has just been inserted in the program, and Rather wants to change some of the wording to clarify the story.
6:15 A sudden calm descends on the studio.

In the control room, there is no peace. Seven people are jammed together at a console, each one talking. In the middle front row is the director. He will cue the cameras as they focus on the anchorman and give other cues as the visuals, remotes and videotapes pop on and off the screen.

The goal of the control room staff is to have a tight program, to move neatly from Rather to a Washington correspondent without dead air, without cutting Rather off too soon; to synchronize the visuals that are the backdrop for Rather as he describes a spot in the Pacific (a map appears), a planet (a picture of Saturn looms over his left shoulder), a labor union (its emblem is shown).

6:23 Grim, Rather sits in front of a small mirror and is made up. He applies the lip rouge himself.

6:24 Rather shouts, "Sandy, you've got to pump that audio way up." Silence again.

6:25 "Five minutes," the stage manager calls out.

6:29 Rather settles into his chair, again reading the script. This time his lips are immobile.

"Thirty seconds." The deep voice booms in the studio and over a loud-speaker in the control room where the hubbub suddenly ceases. Countdowns are being prepared by the people at the various panels to cue the announcer, Rather, the videotape recorder, correspondents and the visuals. "Ten seconds."

Rather opens the program with a lead-in (introduction) to the big story of the day:

> President Reagan today signed into law his tax and spending cut bills. He called it the beginning of--quote--"a turnaround of almost half a century, marking the end of a course we have been on of excessive growth, excessive bureaucracy and excessive taxation." End of quote. In other words, a sharp turn from a course begun by the Franklin Roosevelt New Deal. Lesley Stahl reports from the Reagan ranch in California.
>
> LESLEY STAHL: What made this different from the usual Rose Garden signing ceremonies? Just about everything--casual ranch clothes, milling ranch dogs, grazing horses and the awkward signing of the budget and tax cut bills with 24 different pens. A thick mountain fog. . . .

Editing a Weekly Newspaper

North of New York City, in the small town of Dalton, Mass., Avice Meehan is the managing editor of the weekly newspaper, *The Dalton News-Record*. The newspaper serves eight communities in the area. Meehan had been working for a daily newspaper after graduating from journalism school. When the editorship of the weekly opened up, Meehan grabbed it. She liked the idea of becoming involved with a small town and its people. In her work on the daily, her coverage was limited by her beat.

For the weekly, she does everything. She covers politics, local government and Lions Club luncheons; she writes obituaries and stories about engagements and weddings. She also designs the front page and takes an occasional photo.

She is busy with the page layout but takes a minute to talk about her work.

"The hours are long, the pay is not terrific, and I generally work six or seven days a week," she says. "But I wouldn't exchange this experience for anything."

Meehan is putting an obituary in the number one spot, upper right-hand, of page one. "You couldn't do this on a daily, unless the president died." Her obituary is of a local volunteer fireman who is well-known in town. She wrote it.

"We mainly concentrate on the little things," she says. "Our readers like items about the Boy Scouts and such. We manage some hard-hitting stories, like our series on the state takeover of a local nursing home.

"You can learn on a weekly, and you can experiment. You don't have to be as conventional as you do on daily newspapers.

"People here take great stock in their children. I cover the schools and children's programs."

She needs some work done on a story, and she dashes over to a machine that feeds the small computer her paper uses in its production process.

"Everything in the paper is local," she says. She points to a story she has just written about the visit by officials of the Vietnam Era Vet Center.

"I was able to bring a national issue—the threat of loss of funds for the Center in a budget cut—to my readers," she says. Here's how she began her story:

DALTON—For many Vietnam veterans the war has not ended.

"We are the flashbacks. We are the nightmares. We want people to get a little frightened. We want the public to cry, too, but no one is crying," said Frank Penacho.

"People commonly think time heals all wounds, but it only decreases the intensity of the wounds. Time is not enough. A lot of guys in World War II are still suffering," said Robert Gillis.

Mr. Penacho and Mr. Gillis are on the staff of the only Vietnam Era Vet Center in Massachusetts. The Vet Center, located in Brockton, took to the road last week at the invitation of the American Legion for a two-day visit here.

The Vet Center opened in 1979, following passage of the Veterans Health Care Amendments Act to provide readjustment counseling to Vietnam-era veterans, a group often neglected by the Veterans Administration.

The program, with a budget of about $13 million, is threatened with elimination by the Reagan administration, although support for it has been growing. If funding continues, centers similar to the one in Brockton may open in Springfield and Albany, N.Y. The Brockton agency has a budget of $140,000. . . .

A Job Tryout

In a luncheonette in Gloucester, Mass., a young man is eating a sandwich. His name is Nicholas Trowbridge and he is recalling for a friend his first few days on the local daily, *The Gloucester Times*. He had just graduated from college where he had majored in philosophy. But he thought he had some knowledge of journalism because he had worked on his college weekly.

"I had a three-day tryout for the job," he recalls. "The editor had told me it would be two days, and by the third day the one suit I had needed cleaning.

"The first day had been a disaster. I was told to condense five stories to capsule length. After two hours at the typewriter, I had five two-page stories.

"The boss looked at them and said, 'When I said brief I meant two grafs, not two pages.'

"When the third day came and the paper's veteran reporter suggested I do a sidebar to go along with his story on a mayoral election debate at the local Legion Hall, I knew this was it.

"My assignment was to talk to people in the bar downstairs and ask them why they weren't upstairs listening to the debate. The reporter introduced me to the bartender and went upstairs.

The Wise Guys

"I talked to a few of the regulars at the bar and had the beginnings of a story. Then I ran into the wise guys.

"They were playing pool in one of the rooms off the bar, and after I identified myself, one turned to me and said, 'You're new, aren't you?'

"When I told him I hadn't even been hired yet, that I was on trial, he said, 'Well if you want the job, the big story's in the bar. Jack's his name and he set a record last week.'

"The record, they told me with complete sincerity and honesty, was for not going to the toilet. It was going to be published in the *Guinness Book of World Records,* they said.

" 'Come on, you're kidding me,' I laughed.

"They assured me it was no lie. Jack had survived on water, vitamins and beer during the long wait.

"I went into the bar and asked if Jack was in.

" 'Why do you want Jack?' one woman asked as she cradled Seven-and-Seven between her forearms.

" 'I hear he set a record, he's the one who didn't go . . . uh, forget it,' I stammered. 'Why aren't you upstairs, listening to the politicians at the debate?'

" 'One's an idiot and one's retarded,' she answered." "No, that's not it, they're both retarded.'

"I put the quote high in my story and the editor ran it on page one. The next day he told me I had the job and said I could thank the woman in the bar for it. A few days later the paper received an angry letter on my story from one of the two mayoral aspirants who claimed the story was derogatory to those with mental handicaps.

"But it's lucky my story wasn't about a mythical Jack who avoided the call of nature for a record number of days. Had it been, I'd probably still be wandering through the south in search of a job, hitching with truckers through an endless succession of roadside truck stops and hopeless interviews."

Lost in the Crowd

A few weeks later, a wiser and tougher reporter—he thought—he was assigned to journey to Boston with a busload of parishioners who were going to see the Pope during his U.S. tour. He met the people at 7 a.m. in front of a local church and a short time later in Boston they split into four groups to walk to Boston Common where the Pope was to celebrate Mass.

"I decided to stick with the largest group for the day, listen to their comments, watch their reaction to the Pope.

"On the way to the park, I ducked out for a cup of coffee. When I got out of the coffee shop, the group was gone.

"I raced to the Common. They were lost in a sea of people. After a two-hour search, I realized I was wasting my time.

"I went to a pay phone and called the boss, collect.

" 'I've lost them,' I said.

" 'Lost who, Nick?'

" 'The parishioners from St. Ann's. I went into this place to get some coffee, and when I came out they were gone, vanished,' I told him, thinking that his advice would be to continue south to look for another job.

" 'Nick lost the parishioners and he's looking for them on Boston Common,' I could hear him telling the staff.

"I could hear laughter in the newsroom.

" 'Don't worry,' he told me. 'Just get some good quotes on the bus on the way back.

" 'And don't miss the bus.'

" 'No problem,' I told him. 'I've got it under control.' "

The young reporter's self-assurance may seem to have been built on a foundation of toothpicks. But even as a beginning reporter he knew that control is essential to the journalist. When little things start slipping, the story can slide away. He continued to learn about other journalistic necessities— the need to be terse; the need to be skeptical, to always ask for proof or to verify what he is told, and the absolute necessity to be accurate.

Inside a Newsroom

If we could look in on one of the 1,700 daily newspapers a few hours before press time, we might see a picture of this kind: Telephones ringing with reporters calling in to speak to the city editor about stories they are working on. Teletype machines clacking off reams of AP and UPI copy. Copy editors reading news stories on their editing terminals, removing the word *felt* and inserting the word *said,* writing a headline for a page one story about a fatal accident.

The news editor is chatting with the managing editor about a weather story out of Florida, and reporters are writing stories on their terminals, looking up at the screen now and then to see whether the lead is just right.

A police siren pierces the evening's stillness outside, and soon the wail of an ambulance is heard. No one pays attention.

A Fatal Accident

The phone on the city editor's desk rings and he picks it up. It is a call from the police reporter at the police station. "Bad accident at an intersection with the bypass," he says. "You want me to get out there or cover from here? They think two people have been killed."

The city editor tells the reporter to sit tight, that with the rain-slick roads and the fog there may be other accidents. The editor doesn't want the reporter to lose touch with police headquarters for a while.

"Try to get a fix on it," the editor says. "If it's as bad as you say, I think you'd better get out there. I'm sending a photographer anyway."

For the next half-hour, the police beat reporter monitors the police radio. At the same time, he goes through the notes he has taken from police reports upstairs in the lieutenant's office. He spots a burglary at the First Baptist Church. He recalls that he has notes somewhere in his pad about the theft of religious scrolls from a synagogue on Maple Avenue. He decides he will put the two thefts into one story. He makes a mental note to call the lieutenant to ask whether the same people could have been involved in both burglaries.

News Center. All local news funnels through the city editor. Here, in the newsroom of *The Berkshire Eagle* in Pittsfield, Mass., city editor Bill Bell looks over local stories for the day on the screen of his editing terminal. On the left, county editor Frank McCarthy writes a headline. Day news editor Charles Bonenti, on the right, edits a reporter's copy on a terminal. In the background, reporters are at work.
Susan Plageman, *The Berkshire Eagle*

At City Hall

Three blocks away in city hall, another reporter is walking into the city council chambers. He greets the city clerk.

"Should be a good meeting tonight, Alice," he says. She nods in agreement.

"The appeal on the zoning decision on Hale's will bring them out," he says. "I'm glad you gave me the background on that one."

He turns to chat with the manager of Hale's Department Store who has entered the room, along with his lawyer. The reporter wants more background on Hale's plans to build a large store in a residential area outside the downtown area.

In the newsroom, a young reporter is bent over several sheets of paper. They are the carbon copies of obituary notices from the advertising department. One of the notices is about the death of a retired school principal. She had taught in local schools for 30 years and was a principal for 13 years. She probably has many former students in town, the reporter thinks. She decides to obtain more information about the woman.

A telephone call interrupts her thoughts. The caller is the president of the United Way. He has the results of the fund drive just completed.

"We worked all day getting the field reports together, and I'm glad to say we've set a record," he says. The reporter asks how much was raised, what accounted for the record donations. Did any particular organization or event raise an unusually large amount of money? The questions continue.

In a corner of the newsroom, the news editor is looking over some wire service stories.

"Hurricane expected to hit Florida," he tells the managing editor. "People boarding up. Worst in a decade, they think."

The managing editor tells him to put the AP and UPI stories together. It could run on page one, he says. Lots of people in town have friends and relatives who have moved to Florida.

The news for tomorrow's newspaper is being gathered in diverse ways. Some reporters are covering events. Others are taking information from sources over the telephone. News that originates outside the community is coming in on the Associated Press and United Press International news wires.

Not all the information and news being gathered will be used. The police reporter has had reports of two more accidents, and he knows that he will have little time to write up the minor burglaries, break-ins and arrests from his notes. He may do the church and synagogue thefts in a single story, but he knows that he will have to spend the few hours before deadline on the accidents, rounding them up into a single story, probably for page one.

The reporter handling the obituaries has learned that a fund drive is being planned to raise money for a memorial scholarship in honor of the retired school principal who has just died. The scholarship will be called the Rose Harriet Allen Memorial Scholarship, and some of the city's leading citizens—her former students—are serving on the committee to raise money.

The reporter intends to interview these people, not only about their plans to raise money but about their recollections of their school days in Allen's classroom.

The reporter looks at a batch of notes she has taken for several other obituaries. She shrugs. She will have no time for the calls she had planned to make for additional material for some of them. She realizes that this will displease some readers. Obituaries are one of the newspaper's best-read sections, she knows. If she can, she will spend time on the other obituaries once she has finished the Allen story. She will have to work at twice the usual pace, which is twice as fast as she thought she'd work when she was studying journalism in college.

The wire editor has handed the city editor an AP story from Phoenix about the crash of a small plane. One of the three victims had owned a chain of shoe stores in town until his retirement three years ago. The city editor calls a reporter to his desk.

"Here, rewrite this. Bill Frazier died in a plane crash in Phoenix."

The reporter understands that he will have to localize the wire story, which means putting information about Frazier into the lead. He heads for the newspaper library to dig up background—the number of stores Frazier owned, his civic activities, place of birth, and other details he will need for the combination news story and obituary.

We move from this composite picture of reporters at work on a medium-sized newspaper to the newsroom of a larger daily newspaper, *The Providence Journal*.

Confined 28 Years.
Reporter Berkley Hudson
of *The Providence
Journal-Bulletin*
interviews a man Hudson
believes has been
confined to a state mental
hospital without reason.
Bob Thayer, *The Providence
Journal-Bulletin*

Twenty-Eight Years in Confinement

Berkley Hudson is talking about a story he has just finished handling for his newspaper. The story—actually two stories, Hudson says—began one day in the newsroom. "This man had sneaked off the grounds of a state mental hospital, managed to get a bus and walked into the newspaper to tell his story." Hudson arranged to meet him later at the hospital parking lot.

The man had spent five years in the state penitentiary and 23 in a state mental hospital. Most people confined to such places believe they should be freed, but Hudson felt this story was different.

Hudson let the man talk, and the longer he spoke the more Hudson felt that there had been an injustice. Reporters often act on their hunches or intuition, which is actually a highly developed insight gained by experience.

Hudson decided to look into Chester Jefferds' story.

From examining hospital records and interviewing social workers and administrators at the hospital, Hudson concluded that neither justice nor compassion would be served by keeping Jefferds locked away.

"He doesn't belong here," a social worker told Hudson. That quote was underlined in Hudson's notes. It would have to go high up in the story. He remembered a point his journalism instructor had driven home relentlessly: Good quotes up high.

As angry as Hudson felt about the situation, he knew that the best way to tell the story would be to let it tell itself. The indignation would have to come from the reader. Hudson would lay out all the facts and let the reader reach the conclusion that Jefferds should be freed. The reporting took two weeks.

"When I had all the information I thought I needed, I decided to start writing," Hudson says. He went into the office at 10 a.m. and looked over his notes carefully. As often happens, he discovered he needed additional details.

"At 2 o'clock I had organized my notes and was ready to write." With a few breaks, he wrote until about midnight. He spent another hour with the Sunday editor, going over the story, making some changes in the copy. Here is how the story begins:

He survived inside; now he'd like to be free

By BERKLEY HUDSON
Journal-Bulletin Staff Writer

CRANSTON — Chester G. Jefferds Jr. has survived 28 years in confinement. His face has deep, bold wrinkles. His hazel eyes are murky.

He spent five years in the state prison, then 23 more in the state mental hospital. He has seen other prisoners kill themselves — and sometimes each other. His was a world of beatings and rape, strait jackets and electroshock therapy, nurse's needles and attendants' pills.

Chester Jefferds learned how a man labeled crazy stays sane in a mental institution. You keep quiet. You try to forget why you're there. You don't listen to the moans and screams around you.

"You go through the alphabet, saying the letters over and over," he says. "You go through the fraction tables. 7 into 100. 8 into 100."

He has one tooth left. The rest he lost in fights. He has a raspy voice.

"There's only one way to go in this place," he says. "You keep your mouth shut."

Those who know him call him Jeff. He is 68. It has been 28 years since he was sentenced to life imprisonment for shooting his wife to death. Now he would like his freedom.

★ ★ ★

"HE DOESN'T belong here," says David J. Arone, a social worker at the state General Hospital. "There's plenty of evidence Chester has been able to take care of himself."

Since 1973, psychiatrists, social workers and nurses have been saying what Arone says: Jefferds is not sick, mentally or physically.

The problem, Arone says, is that Jefferds is unique among the 1,400 patients at the medical center. Like others there, he is elderly and has been in a mental hospital for many years, yet he is no longer ill. What makes him different is that he is under a life sentence for murder.

"He's still here because if he weren't here, he'd be at the prison," says Frederick Young, chief of social services at the General Hospital. Jefferds, Young says, doesn't belong in prison either. Mental-health laws require the release of anyone who is not ill, but hospital officials believe that if he were released from the hospital, he would be required to go back to prison.

"Had he been at the prison all this time as a lifer, he'd probably be free now," Young says. "Most of the ques-

Six weeks after Hudson's story appeared, Jefferds was on his way to freedom. The state parole board had decided to allow Jefferds to leave the hospital for a halfway house. After three months there, he would be a free man. Hudson went out to the hospital to watch Jefferds pack. He wrote a story about Jefferds' release that began:

Chester Jefferds stood next to his suitcase. It had a rope for a handle. Inside, among his few possessions, was a card from a friend. It read, "Good luck in your new venture."

At 11:15 a.m. on Friday, Jefferds left behind him 28 years of confinement in a world of barred windows, locked wards and moans in the nights. He had spent five years in the Adult Correctional Institution, 22 more at the Institute of Mental Health and one more at the state General Hospital.

A board on March 3 had unanimously approved his request for parole of his life sentence for the murder of his wife, who was shot to death in July, 1952.

For the last eight years, psychiatrists, social workers and nurses have said he is not sick, mentally or physically. Still, he remained confined.

During the last four years, the Parole Board reviewed his case on 10 occasions. Once, in August, 1977, the board approved his removal from the locked wards for the criminally insane, but it required him to continue living at the mental institution.

The story of Chester G. Jefferds Jr., 68, was reported in the *Sunday Journal* on Feb. 8, four days after the Parole Board had considered his case once again and "continued the matter." The board wanted hospital officials to provide "concrete alternatives" on how the man could be released.

Hospital and corrections officials devised a plan to satisfy the board. As a condition of parole, Jefferds must spend at least three months in a halfway house, adjusting to his new life of freedom. . . .

Free. Six weeks after Hudson's story appeared, Chester Jefferds was released from the state hospital where he had been confined long past the time he should have been freed.
Bob Thayer, *The Providence Journal-Bulletin*

We have been talking with and watching a few of the 47,500 reporters and editors who gather, write and produce the news that is read in the 1,700 daily newspapers and 7,000 weeklies and is heard and watched on 10,000 of the country's radio and television stations.

Veterans and newcomers, young and old, they are engaged in a process that is the same, whether for a weekly in Massachusetts read by a few thousand people or for a television newscast watched by millions across the country.

From our observations, we can see that the journalistic process consists of four distinct parts:

Information gathering—Making observations, interviewing, conducting research.
Planning—Checking and verifying information, plotting the story.
Writing—Putting the story together in a form that is interesting, clear and succinct.
Production—Fitting the news into the newspaper or newscast.

In the following chapters, we will concentrate on the writing process, how reporters write accurate and clear accounts of the events we need to know about and those we enjoy hearing about. But we will not lose sight of the other parts in the process—they all bear on the writing, as we shall see.

The job of people who report and write the news is to tell those who weren't at the event what happened. The duty of the reporter is to give an accurate, complete, impartial and timely account of what has happened or what is likely to happen.

To do this requires skill and knowledge. The few words used in each of the stories on the "CBS Evening News" must be carefully chosen to reveal the essentials of the event. The writers must, as we have seen, condense thousands of words into less than a couple of hundred.

Writing the news requires clear thinking under pressure. On her first day alone on the job, Lindy Washburn was able to handle a big story. She knew what questions to ask her sources, those the reader or listener would want answered. (Chapter 15 discusses the particular information required for two dozen types of stories.)

Washburn was unable to cover the fire in New Jersey personally and had to rely on sources. She used the best she could locate. Neal Robbins was able to go to the event for firsthand reporting, which usually leads to a more interesting story since the written account will contain the observations that make a story ring true. He, too, sought out the official version of the event.

Fact gathering, which we will examine in detail in chapter 4, includes direct observation, use of sources by telephone and the use of references, documents and records. The police reporter who consulted the records in the lieutenant's office at the police station was making use of official records for his story about the break-ins at the church and the synagogue.

Before we go into any more detail about reporting and writing, let's take a closer look at the journalist. Who are these people who gather and write the news? What traits do they have in common, and what skills are they expected to have when they begin their careers? We will talk to reporters and editors for the answers to these questions.

Focus on the Journalist

The journalist is curious and seeks to share the discoveries uncovered by his or her curiosity.

Looking Ahead

In getting and telling the news, the journalist is committed to fair play, accuracy and honesty. The journalist sticks to the facts and, despite the pressures of deadlines, writes as complete a story as possible.

The journalist is interested in people but is aware of the danger of becoming too close to the individuals in his or her stories and embracing their ideas or causes. A slight distance from people and their concerns makes for objective journalism.

As he was reading a new biography of the American playwright Eugene O'Neill, the Boston University sophomore was struck by one of the scenes in the book. O'Neill is dying and he instructs his wife to burn the unfinished manuscripts of his plays in the fireplace of their Boston hotel room.

The student, Nick Gage, knew that the hotel had become a student dormitory. He was curious. What did the room look like now? He decided to walk across the campus to find out.

"To my surprise," he recalled later, "there was no evidence of a fireplace in the room. Out of curiosity, I looked up the blueprints of the building dating from its construction. Sure enough, there was no fireplace."

Gage, who was a reporter for his college newspaper, wrote a piece about his discovery. The authors of the biography heard about Gage's article and called him. Then they called O'Neill's widow who said that on second thought she might have burned the manuscripts in the basement. The authors corrected the book in its next edition.

Intrigued by the episode, Gage said he had become "bitten by the investigative bug"—so much so that 10 years later he was interviewed for a job with *The New York Times* as an investigative reporter. The man who interviewed and hired Gage was Arthur Gelb, metropolitan editor of the *Times* and the coauthor, with his wife, of the O'Neill biography Gage had read years before.

You might say that Gage's curiosity made him a natural for journalism. An inquisitive nature is fundamental to the journalist. Helen Thomas, who has covered the White House for United Press International for many years, also showed her curiosity early.

"I was an inquisitive child and was constantly reprimanded for prying into the personal lives of visitors who stopped at our home," she recalls. She also enjoyed writing.

"I've never wanted to do anything but write," Thomas says. As a youngster, she worked for her school newspaper. At Wayne State University, she majored in English and continued to write.

The desire to know and the urge to tell others what he or she has found out mark the journalist. Many choose journalism as a career because they want to have a part in the excitement of events—covering the state basketball play-offs, following the campaigns of political candidates, interviewing people who are making news in medicine, agriculture, business and music.

The journalist is there when a new spacecraft is launched from Cape Canaveral and when the Dodgers stage a comeback to beat the Yankees in the World Series. The journalist asks the mayor why drunk driving laws are not being strictly enforced and questions the president about his policy in the Middle East.

Journalism puts the journalist on the cutting edge of life, where journalists are happiest.

Commitment

Some of those who become journalists do so because they have a strong urge to set things right. They want to tell people the real story, to correct errors and misconceptions. Some want to change things. A. M. Rosenthal, managing editor of *The New York Times,* says most reporters are reformers. These reporters root for the underdog. They have a deep sense of compassion. Unlike most people who are frustrated by their inability to do something about injustice, the journalist can. In this sense, journalism is a profession—like law or medicine—because it seeks to render public service.

Listen to Mary Ann Giordano of the *Daily News* talk about the stories she wrote for her newspaper about a family caught in the coils of poverty and helplessness:

"It was cold in the eighth-floor office of the *Daily News* Brooklyn bureau. It was Sunday and the landlord doesn't usually give heat on the weekends. It was a bitter cold day—all the more painful because it was late in the winter and the freezing temperatures had been unexpected.

"As we tried to warm ourselves, my editor in Brooklyn, Bill Federici, suggested we do a story about a family without heat. Problem one was how to find one—not a very great problem since in Brooklyn that day there were untold numbers of people living without heat and hot water through the cold spell. But the easiest way, I figured, to get an address was to call the city's Heat Hotline.

"The hotline, I knew, is a city service to process complaints and press landlords into providing that essential service. In the event of an extended emergency, the city can send repairmen to fix boilers and then bill the landlord. But on that cold weekend, the calls were averaging 380 an hour, a supervisor told me.

"One of those callers was Marie Walker. She, her two daughters and their four children had been living all winter without heat and hot water in their abandoned building at 587 Gates Ave. in the Bedford-Stuyvesant section of Brooklyn.

"I called the Walker family to see if they would be interested in talking to us about their heat problem. Though surprised, they agreed and with photographer Ed Molinari I headed out there. It was midday and my deadline was about 3 p.m.

"Bedford-Stuyvesant was virtually deserted in the freeze. The stairway up to the Walker home was dark and creaky. But when I reached the Walker apartment, there was a startling warmth in the back kitchen where Marie Walker sat, water bubbling steadily around her and the stove door propped open.

"The Walkers were lively, cheerful, friendly people. Despite their hardships, they were able to joke about it. The children were well behaved, the apartment spotlessly clean.

"Through interviews with the family members and a quick check through some of their records, I was able to piece together an account of just how such nice people wound up living in an abandoned building with no heat, no hot water, no toilets, no locks on the doors—with rats and junkies as neighbors and fear an ever-present companion."

Giordano spent about two hours with the Walker family. They all sat bundled up in their coats in the front room, where a few rays of sunlight warmed the floor at their feet. She was able to develop a feel for the people and their plight.

"I could now understand how they had fallen into this situation. And I had come to like the Walkers very much."

Giordano next had to think about a story. Here, a characteristic trait of journalists—the ability to organize facts—came into play.

"Heading back to the office, I tried to organize my thoughts," she recalled. "I knew that describing the cold in the apartment was important, and showing how the Walkers coped with it was an essential ingredient of the story.

"I also knew that people would want to know why the Walkers were living that way, and I had to explain that, too.

"I had about 45 minutes to write the story when I returned to the office. The *News* ran the story as I wrote it, word for word."

Here is how Giordano's story began:

It is warm and bright in Marie Walker's kitchen. Four flames glow on the aging stove as a pot of water boils steadily. The door of the oven is open, and she sits in front of it, her sock-covered feet propped on the door as the gas heat warms her toes.

It is the only hot spot in the apartment, the only place in the entire building where warm breath does not send puffs of vapor into the air.

A thermometer in a front room, where the sun shines through a window, registers 52 degrees. That is warm, the Walker family says. Saturday it reached a high of 39 degrees inside.

It is so cold, the pipes burst in the four-story apartment building at 587 Gates Ave. in Bedford-Stuyvesant and the seven members of the Walker family must take turns drawing water from a hydrant on the street.

Giordano's complete story appears in Appendix C.

City officials responded to the Walkers' plight and promised to find public housing for them. Knowing how slowly the city wheels can turn, Giordano kept checking, and three weeks later wrote a second story that began:

The plumbing is still broken, the heat is still out, the junkies and rats still roam freely through the lower floors, and the Walker family of Bedford-Stuyvesant is still looking for decent housing.

Three weeks after an article ap-

peared in the *Daily News* detailing the plight of the seven members of the Walker family, they are still trekking through the maze of housing regulations—cruel realities that confront New Yorkers searching for livable housing.

The rest of the story is in Appendix C.

The second article brought action. "Within a short time, the Walkers were in better housing," Giordano said. "They faced last winter without fear of the cold and live today as safely as anyone does in New York."

This sense of accomplishment, the opportunity to be of service, is the greatest of all journalism's rewards.

Journalists are committed to fair play and equal treatment for all. For some, George Orwell, the British writer who sought to set things right-side-up in a topsy-turvy world, is the perfect journalist. Orwell's journalism was on the side of decency, and his commitment made his writing vivid and forceful. He knew that to reach people, he had to make his writing clear and simple, though he often wrote about complex issues.

Orwell, who wrote *Animal Farm* and *1984*—political novels that describe the horror of totalitarian governments—stressed independent thinking. He believed the journalist must never accept unquestioningly a line formulated by a party or an authority. The journalist must work things out for himself or herself.

Journalists are faithful to the facts, whatever the consequences. When he was covering the Nixon administration for CBS television, Dan Rather was under enormous pressure to let up on his dogged coverage of the president.

Integrity

He said later that the White House had a "journalistic goon squad" that pressured reporters who did not accept at face value the pronouncements from the president's office.

"The idea is to crowd you, to harass you when they can with phone calls complaining about pieces, complaining to other people during the broadcast," he said.

Although some CBS affiliates demanded Rather's resignation after he had a run-in with Nixon and viewer mail was heavily against him, CBS kept him on the job and Rather continued to demand of the president replies to questions he felt the public wanted answered.

"If a truck runs over me tomorrow," he said once, "what I really would love to have someone tell my kids is that their father wouldn't buckle—not under Lyndon Johnson, not under Richard Nixon."

Honesty for the journalist extends to the use of language. News stories should be accurate, no more exciting—through the manipulation of words—than the event itself.

Accuracy

We live in a world of exaggeration and lies. A movie reviewer writes that a new motion picture is "spectacular." We pay $5.00 and find it no better than last month's so-so movie. A president says he knows nothing about a break-in, and a vice president swears he never received payoffs in office. Lies. The television comedies we watch have laughter fed into the sound track by machine. The producers do not trust us to find the humor. They manufacture laughter when there is nothing funny. Advertisers praise their products, and we find the two-man rubber raft seats only two five-year-olds comfortably, and the four-man raft is really suitable for two. The braking mechanism on the expensive new car is faulty and the model has to be recalled.

The journalist is expected to tell truths, which requires digging beneath the surface to find the real story and then choosing appropriate words to describe it.

The journalist matches language to the event. If the meeting of the city council was routine, the news writer does not try to dramatize it with hyperactive prose.

In interviews with editors and reporters and in observations of them at work, dependability continually surfaced as an essential characteristic of the journalist. Dependability encompasses a number of desirable traits:

Dependability

Sent out on a story, the journalist works at it until it is fit for broadcast or print. The public depends on the journalist, as it does on all professionals, to do his or her best.

The journalist shows initiative in generating story ideas and is relentless and enterprising in pursuing a story. A few months after his graduation from Notre Dame, Phil Cackley was hired by *The Albuquerque Tribune* and given the University of New Mexico beat.

"When I got the beat, I didn't expect any major stories to result from it," Cackley said. "My first story was about a student who hatched a duck from an orphan egg."

But Cackley was a digger. Within a few months, he had unearthed one of the biggest sports stories in the country, an academic scandal involving the university's athletic program. Cackley's investigation disclosed that grades were faked on the transcripts of certain athletes.

The journalist does not guess or assume. Whether it is the spelling of a word, the address of someone in a story, or the charge that will be filed against a person arrested in connection with a death, the journalist checks. The public depends on the journalist to be thorough and accurate.

Readiness

President Reagan had just finished speaking in the Washington Hilton Hotel and was waving to a friendly crowd before entering his limousine.

Suddenly, six shots rang out in rapid order. Bodies were sent sprawling. The president was shoved into his car, and the car sped off. Three people were down. A crowd engulfed the husky young man who had fired the shots.

Though the situation had exploded quickly, moving from the routine to the sensational in seconds, photographers and reporters recorded the scene. Ron Edmonds, an AP photographer, took a picture of Reagan at the precise moment the first shot was fired. Holding his finger on the motor-driven shutter release, Edmonds shot a sequence of pictures in the moments immediately following the attack on the president.

Press association reporters raced to telephones and dictated stories that were used around the world. Radio and television stations interrupted their programming with the news, some of it incorrect at first. To those at the scene, the president had seemed unhurt, and this is what the first bulletins reported. They were corrected as more information became available. By being able to respond quickly to the unexpected and to write under pressure, the journalist meets the need of the public for timely information.

Deadlines The competent journalist understands the necessity of meeting deadlines. However wide the reporter's knowledge, however deep his or her talent, unless the reporter can meet deadlines, he or she is of little use in the newsroom. The deadline is an absolute demand on the journalist. For the press association reporter, there is a deadline every minute. As Lindy Washburn was writing her fire story, she was aware that some newspapers were readying their front pages for the press. At any hour of the day or night, there is a deadline for some newspaper or broadcast station.

The ability to write clear, complete and accurate stories despite the pressure of deadlines is the result of self-discipline.

Although many editors push their staff members, the journalist must provide his or her own drive. No one stands over a reporter and coaxes, begs or commands. The writer understands he or she is personally responsible for writing the story. In this sense, the journalist shares with other creative workers the drive to produce.

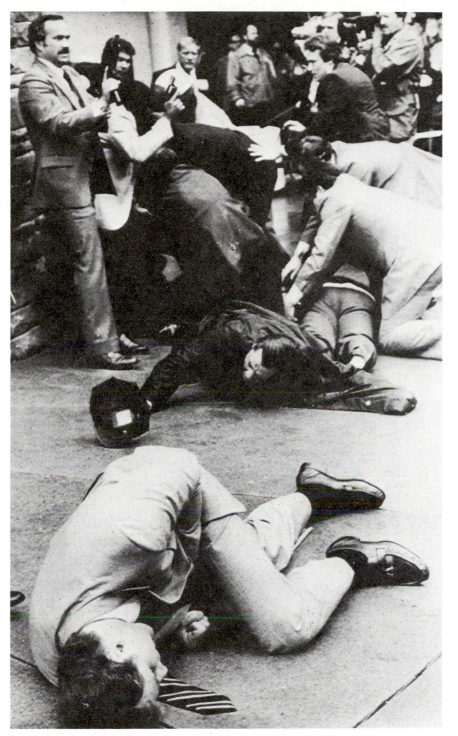

Downed by Gunman.
Caught in the fusillade that struck Reagan, three men lie in the street outside a Washington hotel. Ron Edmonds of the AP reacted quickly under pressure to snap these photographs. Edmonds' photos won the 1982 Pulitzer Prize for spot news photography.
Ron Edmonds, Wide World Photos, Inc.

Advice from the Consummate Comic

W. C. Fields, one of the greatest film comedians ever, seemed to be a natural comic. Actually, he labored at his craft.

"Show me a comic who isn't a perfectionist and I'll show you a starving man," he said. "You have to sweat and toil and practice indefinitely. A comic should suffer as much over a single line as a man with a hernia would in picking up a heavy barbell."

Discipline

The ability to work steadily at a task until it meets the highest level of a person's capabilities is another trait common to all who work creatively—writers, musicians, painters, designers, builders, dancers, actors, teachers. Ernest Hemingway labored over his sentences and paragraphs until he was satisfied. He would rewrite a paragraph time after time until it did his bidding.

For all their seeming spontaneity, musicians practice until they have their pieces sounding just right. A world-renowned pianist says that he has never missed a day's practice of at least six hours. Most singing groups are willing to work day and night to perfect their songs.

John McPhee, a *New Yorker* writer who describes himself as a "working journalist," walks into his office at 8:30 in the morning and leaves at 8:30 in the evening. He takes a 90-minute break each day for squash, tennis or racquetball.

McPhee, considered one of the finest journalists in the country, disciplines himself to write.

"People want to be writers without writing," he says. Impossible. After he graduated from college he tried to write television plays. He was learning and so the task was arduous. The temptation to leave the typewriter was so great that he even resorted to tying himself to a chair with his bathrobe sash.

Dan Rather enjoys hunting and fishing, but he has little time for recreation. "I work about 110 hours a week," he says. "It will eat you up, but if it doesn't you have a difficult time being good at it. I think you have to care that much."

In his autobiography, Anthony Trollope, the English novelist, describes how he trained himself to write every day, although he held a full-time job for many years. Once, on his way to Egypt to help set up postal service between the Middle East and England, he became violently seasick. Between bouts of nausea, he managed to write more than a thousand words a day.

Openness

The journalist is always willing to learn and is ready to experiment. Frances D'Emilio works for the Associated Press in San Francisco. Upon graduation from journalism school, she sought out wire service work to gain experience in being fast, accurate and succinct. She has learned that on the job, and she has welcomed the opportunity to learn from a variety of assignments.

All Kinds. The journalist seeks news everywhere: in classrooms, in offices and in homes. The reporter seeks out the people who toil in the fields and factories. The journalist talks to young and old, the well-to-do and the poor. In this way, the journalist is able to give readers and viewers a true cross section of the community.

Top left, Ken Elkins, *The Anniston Star; bottom left,* Ken Elkins, *The Anniston Star; right,* Joseph Noble, *The Stuart News*

She has covered a kidnapping trial and sumo wrestling. She has written weather and football stories. Every day, she says, she learns something new, either in the craft or in the subject matter of what she covers.

Creative people are always eager to enlarge their knowledge and skills. Writers read other writers for interviewing techniques, for stylistic innovations, for new ways of expressing ideas. When Tom Wolfe, Gay Talese and other journalists developed the New Journalism, their ideas were picked up by news writers all over the country.

In their openness to new ideas, journalists become involved with people of all kinds. This is not accidental. Journalists seek out a wide range of individuals because they are committed to involvement in the affairs of all people.

The news is where people are. News is found in factories and service stations, supermarkets and laundromats, unemployment offices and executive suites, schoolrooms and homes. By seeking out people with varied backgrounds, journalists can hear the heartbeat of their communities.

When Christopher Scanlan and Mark Patinkin of the *Journal-Bulletin* in Providence wanted to know about the black communities in Rhode Island, they set out on a series of interviews that took them into the offices of black lawyers and to the homes of welfare mothers. They spoke to merchants and hookers. They went to housing projects—monuments of despair to some of the tenants, models of hope to others. Here is one of their interviews:

Voices: Johnny Mitchell on the Projects

"Providence hardly knows these people exist," said Johnny Mitchell. "This project is in crisis, but nobody cares. Nobody hears what we're saying. People in here are in a crisis. A serious social crisis. They just get by. They go to sleep tonight and wake up tomorrow and don't think about the future."

Mitchell is speaking of the 734 people, mostly black, who share his home, the Roger Williams Housing Project in South Providence, perhaps the worst low-income development in the state.

He looked at the black children playing in a patch of dust and rubble and saw the teenagers darting on the glass-specked basketball court and the mothers sitting on the doorstep. For blacks here, he said, nothing has changed.

Blacks make up about 10 percent of Providence's population, but they fill well over 70 percent of the apartments in the city's six low-income family housing projects.

In Roger Williams, which is 98 percent black, all but 10 of the project's 213 families are young women who live alone with children, most on welfare.

"There's excellent hope for those kids, they're all beautiful kids," said Mitchell, "but a lot of them are going mad. No fathers, no real men. Is anybody going to get down and help? Right now, they think they're pimps. The language is unbelievable, too—little kids cussin' like men."

The people of the projects, especially of Roger Williams, are not a mirror of the state's black community. They are the extreme, the underclass. In Rhode Island, they form a big underclass.

There are about 931,000 people in Rhode Island. About 27,600, one out of every 34, is black. There are more than 50,000 Rhode Islanders on welfare. More than 8,000, about one out of every six, is black. In other words, close to a third of all blacks in the state are on welfare.

Black poverty is not limited to the inner city. In South Kingston, one out of every five welfare recipients is black. In Newport, one out of every four is black.

Welfare speaks of poverty but it does not tell the whole story. Income figures tell more. The latest U.S. Census figures show that one of every three black families in Rhode Island lives below the poverty level. They account for 11.8 percent of the state's 17,000 poor families, four times the black percentage of state population.

Poverty means other things, such as health problems. In 1976, the infant death rate for whites in Rhode Island was 13.1 deaths per 1,000 births. For non-whites, the rate was 23 deaths for every 1,000 babies born.

Poverty. It also means a higher percentage of blacks are criminals and more are victims of crime.

Scanlan said that the assignment was an educational project for him. He learned something new every day, he said.

By objectivity journalists mean reporting and writing that is free of bias. The objective journalist sees the world on the basis of factual evidence, not in terms of his or her feelings and hopes.

Objectivity

Journalists do not pass judgment on people and events; they do not say someone or something is good or bad. They do not make inferences in news stories; they do not jump from the known into the unknown.

Wrong: The student council adopted a punitive parking rule after a rambling speech in its favor by a supporter.

Right: The student council adopted a new parking rule after hearing from a supporter of the proposal. ("Punitive" is a judgment word. Quote a source using the word. "Rambling" clearly indicates the reporter's disapproval of the speech.)

Wrong: The new parking rule will cause many student motorists to park on the city's already congested streets instead of on campus.

Right: A student said, "This rule will cause. . . ." (The reporter should not make guesses about what may happen. Quote someone about the possible effects.)

Objectivity in news stories allows the reader to have the facts without the interference of the reporter's opinions, feelings, conclusions and guesswork.

Despite their involvement in the affairs of other people, journalists must be able to distance themselves from the people and the events they are observing. This distance allows for better understanding and objectivity.

Garry Trudeau, the creator of the comic strip "Doonesbury," says that he is able to develop ideas for his work by being an outsider rather than by fraternizing with important people. Like the journalist, Trudeau says he wants his strip to represent the outsider looking at the activities of people.

The journalist must be close enough—physically and emotionally—to his or her subject to understand what is being observed. At the same time, the journalist must maintain a certain distance to keep things in perspective.

Complete detachment is sometimes impossible. When six-year-old Adam Walsh disappeared from the Sears department store in Hollywood, Fla., reporter Charlie Brennan of the *Sun-Tattler* decided to stay with the story, and his newspaper agreed. A child had disappeared five years before. Her body was discovered in a canal five days later.

Brennan's first story alerted the community:

Reve Walsh usually leaves her son in the toy department at Sears while doing her shopping at the Hollywood Mall. He's always there waiting for her.

But Monday was different. Adam Walsh, six, wasn't there waiting. The Hollywood child hasn't been seen since 12:30 p.m. Monday.

"Everybody's working this one," says police spokesman Fred Barbetta. "Everybody wants this kid to show up."

Adam is the only child of John and Reve Walsh of 1801 McKinley St.

"He's very sheltered," Walsh says. "We never let him out of our sight. He even went on business trips with me."

Hollywood police, the Broward Sheriff's helicopter search team and 47 members of Citizens Crime Watch teamed up Monday night to search for the child throughout Hollywood. Their efforts so far have proven fruitless. . . .

Every day for two weeks Brennan's stories appeared on page one. In his stories, the 26-year-old reporter described the concern of the entire community and its attempts to find the child. Brennan kept in close touch with the parents, and each day he felt their grief and desperation increase.

Brennan accompanied the parents to New York for their appearance on a television show that discussed the disappearance of children throughout the country.

Three hours after the program, the telephone rang in the couple's hotel room. John Walsh took the call. It was from Hollywood. The search was over.

The remains of a child had been found floating in a canal, and the head was that of Adam Walsh.

Brennan was with Walsh when the news came.

"Oh Christ, Oh Christ, who could do this to my little boy?" the father cried. "Who could cut his head off?"

Brennan mourned with Walsh.

"It was absolutely the worst thing I've ever been associated with," Brennan said. "The parents will never be the same. I don't know if I'll ever be the same."

Of his involvement with the family and its tragedy, Brennan said, "Getting deeply involved was the only way to cover the story. To remain detached would have been inhuman."

Journalists are loyal to the facts. They believe that the relentless exposure of truths—no matter how unpleasant—will lead people to change situations for the better. This dedication to truth telling, combined with compassion, is what drove Mary Ann Giordano to speak up for the people in the tenement who were without heat or water in the winter. It led Berkley Hudson to help Chester Jefferds in his quest for freedom from a state mental hospital.

Commitment to Democratic Values   The journalist is motivated by the ideal that given the truth, people can govern themselves intelligently and will be able to live in harmony. The journalist seeks truths whatever the obstacles, and he or she presents them in language accessible to all.

The journalist is quick to point out situations that deny people the opportunities inherent in a democratic system. Some of the greatest stories in the history of American journalism have concerned abuses of people's constitutional rights, such as withholding the vote to blacks, the inequitable administration of justice—one system for the rich, another for the poor—and the persistent denial of equal opportunity to people because of their race, sex, religion or national origin.

The list of traits and qualities characteristic of the journalist may appear overwhelming. Surely, no human being can embody all of these traits. True enough, and the journalist realizes this.

No reporter ever believes he or she has gathered enough information for the story, dug deeply enough, talked to all the right people, ferreted out the whole story. Few news writers are content with what they have written.

The Struggle for Perfection   Wayne Worcester of the *Journal-Bulletin* in Providence says, "The compulsion is always there to improve, improve, to do better.

"After a while it gets to you. But that's all right. You just keep things in perspective. Waylon Jennings sings a song called, 'I've Always Been Crazy, but It's Kept Me from Going Insane.' "

Reporters must be able to laugh at themselves. They know they have a serious job to do, but they don't let the hassles and the struggles get to them. One of the reasons they are able to cope with deadlines, irascible editors, angry readers and listeners and their own admitted inadequacies is that they like what they do. For them journalism is fun.

The Pleasures of Journalism

Lew Moores of the *Cincinnati Post* likes the excitement of journalism. "There's more going on in cities, more things to look into, more successes and failures. I am intensely curious about everything and everyone," he says.

His curiosity led him to seek out some of the victims of city crime, the elderly who are preyed on by muggers.

Here is how Moores' story began:

George Prather sat in a booth at the Mecca Lounge, a bottle of Hudepohl and a glass before him alongside a portable radio tuned to the Reds game. He was joined by George McKindrick and Pete Kindle.

All three men live in apartments above the Bay Horse Saloon, located next door to the Mecca, at 625 Main St., downtown. Last Friday evening, after a Reds game broadcast, Prather walked Kindle, who is 72 years old, home. Home is 25 feet away, a side entrance on Gano Alley.

Prather had his keys out. Six youths sprang from the shadows. Prather saw them first. "Here they come," he said to Kindle, then removed his eyeglasses so they wouldn't splinter in his eyes.

Wednesday, Prather sat in the Mecca with his two friends, and pointed over his shoulder, "The bartender next door's been mugged," he said, then pointed to the end of the bar. "Herb there's been mugged, too."

There are purple commas around the sockets of Prather's eyes, and his upper lip is split and healing. Kindle, who was mugged twice last week, has a large purple welt on the right side of his face—it's becoming the aged's badge of downtown residency.

The Mecca Lounge and Bay Horse Saloon are watering spots for the old downtowners, the men and women who survive on social security checks and live above storefronts. Usually without transportation, they remain close to home, close to friends, close to the bars that appreciate their patronage. Sometimes they drink and become easy prey, sometimes they don't and become prey anyway.

And unless the police find the victims unconscious or wandering around with their wounds, the transgressions often go unreported. . . .

This story begins slowly, just a few friends sitting in a bar listening to a ball game. Swiftly it builds to a climax, then we are back in the bar, chatting with the men. Moores lets the story unfold. He does not overwrite with adjectives and adverbs. He **shows** the reader the situation, painting word pictures.

Many journalists like the action on their beats and the satisfaction they have when they can put it into words. Paul Maryniak was an avid reader of mysteries, and when the criminal courts beat opened up on the *Pittsburgh Press,* he told the executive editor he wanted the job. "I'll gladly depart with one of my limbs to get the job," he recalls saying. Nothing that drastic was necessary.

In a study of reporters on Iowa daily newspapers, these sentiments emerged as the joys of the job:

We're beholden to nobody. This place has integrity.

I'm involved in what's going on in the community.

The camaraderie of the news staff.

Independence for creative writing.

Being where the action is.

Good discipline, effective on-the-job training.

Opportunity to express opinions on the editorial page.

The freedom of adventure a small newspaper affords.

The responsibility given to me and to each reporter by management.

Charles M. Young is a worrier. He sweats and strains over his stories, never really happy about them. But his stories for *Rolling Stone* and other publications about rock groups like Kiss, Twisted Sister and Motley Crue and entertainers like Ted Nugent and Eddie Van Halen seem to flow like maple syrup over a short stack.

Despite his pain, Young enjoys writing. It is his affliction and his joy. His delight in language and his subjects is evident in his piece "Carly Simon, Life, Liberty and the Pursuit of Roast Beef Hash" that begins:

Most rock writers, it has been observed, would rather be the people they write about; that is, trade in their typewriters to scream nonsense at 20,000 rioting lude freaks while Keith Richard powerchords their brains into Cool Whip. Not me. I don't want to be Mick Jagger. Nor do I want to be Carly Simon and have millions of college students think dirty thoughts about my album covers. I don't even want to be James Taylor, who is married to Carly Simon.

I would trade it all to be Benjamin Taylor. Here is someone with a good deal in life; all Benjamin Taylor has to do is cry and Carly Simon sticks her breast in his mouth. The other 4 billion of us on earth could cry for the rest of our lives and Carly Simon would not stick her breast in our mouths.

Greater injustices have marred human history, I suppose, but I can't think of them right now, because Carly Simon has just placed her breast in Benjamin Taylor's mouth. He is having a good time. I am breaking into a cold sweat, wondering if it is obvious from ten feet away that my eyes are dropping from Carly Simon's face to her uplifted blouse every three seconds.

"This is beginning to look obscene," says Carly Simon in the living room of her huge ten-room Central Park West apartment. Benjamin, a cuter-than-hell miniature of James Taylor, is gymnastically curled around his dinner, which he is clutching with both hands and both feet, as well as his mouth.

The Extraordinary and the Routine

Some people are attracted to journalism because of the excitement of covering the big stories. Richard Dudman, who worked his way up to Washington bureau chief for the *St. Louis Post-Dispatch* from the Oroville (Calif.) *Mercury Register,* has had his share of big stories. He has covered revolutions and wars. In Vietnam, he was shot at by a terrorist at close range. The shots missed Dudman but killed a companion.

For 40 days, Dudman was a prisoner of communist guerilllas in Cambodia. Each dawn he wondered whether he would survive the day.

But he warns anyone thinking of a career in journalism to pass it by if the only attraction is excitement. The daily pursuit of news, which often involves painstaking reporting of the mundane, must interest the young man or woman planning a career, he says. The once-in-a-lifetime stories occur just that often—once in a lifetime.

"You know you have a routine to follow every day," says Pete Lee, for many years the editor of the *El Paso Herald-Post.* "But you also know that something totally unexpected will happen. You may talk to a bum one day and the president the next."

The excitement at new discovery and the willingness to adapt to routine are prerequisites for the journalist's job.

The Tough Stories

For every upbeat, enjoyable event, the journalist encounters a situation that is offensive, embarrassing, gloomy, or heartbreaking.

Sarah Booth Conroy of *The Washington Post* remembers a particularly sad story she covered as a reporter in Tennessee for *The Knoxville News-Sentinel.* She was sent out to interview a young mother who had been stricken with polio just before Christmas. The woman had been placed in an iron lung to aid her breathing. Conroy's city editor wanted a story and pictures of her three small children wishing their mother a Merry Christmas.

"I was getting along fine," Conroy recalls, "until the children, all below table height, one by one mounted steps to kiss her face, all that was left outside the iron lung."

The city editor is king of his domain, the city staff, and Conroy recalls being told by her editor in the early 1950s, when she was starting out as a reporter, to interview the young wife of Vice President Alben Barkley, who was in his 70s. The Barkleys were visiting Knoxville a few months after their wedding.

"Find out if she's pregnant," the city editor instructed Conroy.

"I went with fear and trembling," Conroy says. "But I was more afraid of Mr. Levitt (the city editor) than Mrs. Barkley.

"She looked appalled by my question," Conroy says. Mrs. Barkley asked her, "Why do you ask?"

"Because my city editor told me to," she replied.

"Go back and tell him," Mrs. Barkley said softly, "I think he must be a horrid man to send a nice little girl like you to ask a question like that."

Death in the Afternoon

In Liberia to do stories about the work of missionaries from the Southwestern Baptist Theological Seminary, the reporter-photographer team for the *Fort Worth Star-Telegram* was suddenly thrust into history's cauldron.

Liberia had erupted with savage violence. A young soldier, Master Sergeant Samuel K. Doe, had led his troops in a military coup. Under Doe's command, soldiers had assassinated the president and then set about eliminating the country's leaders.

The executions were to be carried out on a hot afternoon on a Liberian beach, and the press was invited.

Larry C. Price, the photographer, and Paul Rowan, the reporter, made their way to the beach where thick, sturdy posts 10 feet high were being placed in the white sand. As the posts were being adjusted, Price broke away from the knot of newsmen gathered 100 yards from the beach. Alone, he walked toward the posts anchored in the sand. As he walked, he snapped pictures. The heavily armed soldiers watched him but did nothing.

Rowan edged closer and took notes. The number of posts grew, Rowan noted on his pad, from four to five, from five to seven, seven to nine. In the middle of the work stood the 27-year-old photographer, snapping pictures.

The men were then brought out.

"They tied nine men, old-looking men, paunchy, gray-haired men, to the posts," Rowan wrote.

Then the shots rang out, and the bodies began to crumple into the sand. Price was so close an ejected shell casing struck him.

He continued to take pictures.

Price's photographs of the deaths of the old rulers won the 1981 Pulitzer Prize for spot news photography. The pictures are horrifying, a grim record of men calculating the death of fellow men, and the moment of death.

Price and Rowan were appalled by what they saw. But their job was to record for their readers, and for history, the momentous event.

"I'm certainly not coldhearted," Price said later. "Taking pictures of tragedy does affect me."

Journalists are witnesses to life's tragedies—sudden death in the afternoon, a youngster mangled beneath the wreckage of his motorcycle, a young mother immobilized by crippling disease and confined to an iron lung.

But the journalist endures. Journalism has been called history in a hurry. Though they laugh off such descriptions, journalists know theirs is an important and serious task that demands self-control and self-discipline.

Witness to History. Photographer Larry C. Price of the *Fort Worth Star-Telegram* stood so close to the soldiers in the firing squad on a Liberian beach that an ejected shell casing struck his cheek. ''The central thing in photo-journalism is that you have to get it when it happens,'' he said. ''There are no second chances. If you miss the shot, it's gone forever.'' Price won the 1981 Pulitzer Prize for these photographs.

© 1980 Larry C. Price/*Fort Worth Star-Telegram*

© 1980 Larry C. Price/*Fort Worth Star-Telegram*

Women, Minorities and Money

There are 49,600 reporters, copy editors, photographers, artists and news executives on daily newspapers. Of these, about one-third are women and 2,300 are members of minority groups.

Women are heavily represented on the smaller newspapers. The number of women on the larger newspapers is significantly smaller. Only 10 of every hundred editors and news executives are women, most of them on newspapers with circulations under 25,000. The same is true of radio and television stations. The situation is gradually improving, partly as the result of lawsuits brought by women journalists who charged they were discriminated against in promotions and salaries. *The New York Times* and *The Washington Post,* for example, agreed in out-of-court settlements to hire more women for managerial positions.

The number of minority journalists is small but has also been increasing. From the mid-1970s to the beginning of the 1980s, minority employment increased by 35 percent. In the 1960s, the number of minority journalists in newspaper editorial jobs was estimated at 1 in a hundred. A 1984 study of 732 dailies found minority journalists made up 5.8 percent of the total. Almost two-thirds of the nation's newspapers employ no members of minority groups, and 92 percent have none in news executive positions.

Although the number of minority journalists is small, the coverage of minority groups is a major undertaking for some newspapers. Two of the three Pulitzer Prizes for reporting in 1984 were for such coverage. *The Boston Globe* was recognized for a series of articles that investigated racial tensions in the city. The *Los Angeles Times* won the public service prize for a series on the 3 million Latin residents of Southern California. The articles analyzed the problems, achievements and changing nature of the Spanish-speaking community.

About two-thirds of all journalists are college graduates. Almost all of the newly hired reporters are college graduates, and four of every five new reporters are journalism school graduates or majored in journalism. Most new journalists who did not study journalism in college worked on their high school or college newspapers. Few of the older hands in the newsroom graduated from college.

Traditionally, many journalists came from working class homes. Dan Rather was born in Wharton, Tex. His father was a pipeliner with oil pipeline construction companies, and his mother was a waitress. He went to Sam Houston State College. Warren Phillips, who worked his way up from reporter at *The Wall Street Journal* to chairman of the vast Dow Jones operation, attended Queens College, a New York City public college, which charged no tuition to its students, the sons and daughters of shopkeepers and factory workers.

Newspaper Chains

Most newspapers and many radio and television stations are owned by companies that have several media properties. Of the 1,700 daily newspapers, 65 percent are owned by chains, the name given newspaper groups that own more than one newspaper.

The chains reach 46 million readers every day, which is 75 percent of the circulation of all daily newspapers. The chains with the largest readership are Knight-Ridder, whose 34 newspapers are read by 3.8 million readers, and the Gannett Company, which has 4.7 million readers of its 85 daily and 33 semi-weekly and weekly newspapers.

The chains are aggressive buyers of newspapers, and some press critics contend that should the trend of group ownership continue, absentee ownership will mean less sensitivity to local affairs and greater concern with profits.

Newspaper and broadcast station salaries vary according to the size of the paper or station. Usually, the larger the paper, the higher the salary. Reporters on the large metropolitan daily newspapers with contracts with the American Newspaper Guild receive upwards of $600 and $700 a week. The pay is similar at broadcast stations in the major markets.

Beginners cannot expect to land jobs immediately on large papers or stations. Usually, they find niches in small and medium-sized cities. Entry-level salaries in these communities usually range between $200 and $250 a week, sometimes more if the applicant has had some worthwhile experience. A student who has been a stringer or correspondent for a newspaper while in school or who has worked summers or part-time will command a higher starting salary.

Newspapers with Guild contracts usually pay higher salaries than non-Guild newspapers. Since not many small newspapers are organized, the Guild represents fewer than half of the 47,500 news workers.

Editors and managers of large newspapers and stations are paid around $75,000 a year. Salaries for the top people in smaller communities may be half that figure.

Big bucks Salaries for the top people on camera in television are astronomical in comparison. The CBS Evening News, the country's most-watched television newscast, reportedly pays Dan Rather more than $2 million a year. Brent Musburger, a CBS sportscaster, is paid $2 million a year, and a local sportscaster for a New York station makes $1.5 million a year.

Executives of large newspaper organizations are also well paid, by newspaper standards, earning $250,000 to $500,000 a year.

Making of the News Story

News gives us information to help us understand the world around us. Generally, newspapers and broadcast stations stress news that affects us—news of government, world affairs, business activities. We are also interested in learning about unusual events and the activities of widely known people.

The news value of an event can be judged by its impact on people, its unusual nature and the prominence of the people involved. Four additional factors also influence the newsworthiness of an event: conflict, proximity, timeliness and currency.

How the news writer applies these news values determines what people will read in their newspapers and see on television newscasts. In applying these values, the news writer considers the audience's interests and needs.

The county courthouse reporter had two piles of paper in front of her. One, much larger than the other, consisted of court documents that she had looked through for news and had rejected. The other pile included material she had set aside to take notes from for news stories.

She had gone through the day's records at a rapid pace, but the drawer in which the damage suits, pleadings and other documents were filed contained still more papers. At one sheaf of papers, she hesitated, then studied the pages closely. She tossed the document on her newsworthy pile. A companion, a young reporter learning the beat, asked her why she had decided to take a second look at the document.

"It seems to be important," she answered. "On this beat, you have to make decisions quickly or you'll be snowed under and never have time to write.

"I have two guides I use to separate material. Either the material is important or it's so unusual that I know the reader will want to know about it.

"This one is important because it is a request by a big developer to have the court force the county to issue a building permit for a shopping mall north of town."

She picked up two pages stapled together from her pile of possible news stories.

"Here's one that isn't important at all. But it will make a good little story. It's wild."

The papers described a suit for damages of several thousand dollars by a woman who accused a department store Santa Claus of slapping her six-year-old son.

"Whoever heard of someone suing Santa Claus?" she said. "This is the kind of story readers enjoy."

What Is News?

That evening, the novice reporter thought about what the courthouse reporter had told him. He had recently graduated from college and was being given a tryout by the newspaper. He realized that all his training in how to write would not amount to much unless he could distinguish between what was newsworthy and what wasn't.

He wrote down two definitions:

1. News is material that the public must have because it's important.
2. News is material that is entertaining, that is fun to read.

He recalled reading something that illustrated his first definition of news:

News is information that helps people solve their problems intelligently.

But what about the second category of news, entertainment? Well, as his grandfather used to say, man does not live by bread alone—he has to have an occasional delicacy.

The courthouse reporter's guidelines are helpful in figuring out what makes news. Another way to determine what makes news is to examine newspapers and the transcripts of newscasts. If we were to do this, we would find that news falls into three general categories.

Three Basic Determinants of News

Most news stories are about events that (1) have an **impact** on many people, (2) describe **unusual** or exceptional situations or events, or (3) are about widely-known or **prominent** people. The length of a news story is usually determined by the number of people affected by the event and/or the number of people interested in the event.

Impact

By impact, we mean importance or significance. One way to judge impact is to figure out what the results or consequences of a news story about the event might be. If many people will be affected, then the reporter knows that the event is important enough for a news story.

Impact. The battleship USS *Arizona* burns furiously after being struck by Japanese bombers on Dec. 7, 1941. The surprise attack caught the U.S. fleet at its base in Pearl Harbor, and 1,100 men were entombed in the *Arizona*. Their bodies remain in the hulk.
U.S. Navy Photograph

Unusual. Events that make us stop and stare or shake our heads in wonder are newsworthy.
Joel Librizzi, *The Berkshire Eagle*

One of the oldest definitions of news says that when a dog bites a man, it isn't news, but when a man bites a dog, it's news. The interruption in the expected, the different, makes news. If something makes a reporter stop and stare, wonder, exclaim, then the reporter knows that what he or she is looking at is newsworthy.

The Unusual

Prominence

People who are widely-known or who have positions of authority are said to be prominent. These are the newsmakers of our community and country. They may be politicians or car dealers, priests or labor leaders, entertainers or cabinet members. If you recognize the name and think your readers will, chances are that the person is prominent. What prominent people do, even if unimportant, is often newsworthy. Names make news.

Prominence is an important determinant that can be added to the courthouse reporter's list. She talked about the impact an event might have and its exceptional or unusual nature. But if she had been asked, there's no doubt she would have added prominence because in one of her stories the previous week she had written about the failure of the owner of the city's largest industry to pay his personal property taxes. The courthouse records list hundreds of people who are in arrears in their tax payments, but few become the subject of news stories. The reporter had singled out this individual for only one reason—the prominence of the businessman.

For several years, many newspapers and newsmagazines carried stories about the spats of the rock singer Mick Jagger and his wife, Bianca. When they were finally divorced, it was news in a number of publications. The personal life of the Jaggers is hardly significant in the scheme of things, and marital problems and divorces are hardly unusual.

Peter Gay, a Yale University historian, says that the "fundamental building blocks of the human experience" are "love, aggression and conflict."

But people like to read about those in the spotlight, whatever they might do. When the president has a cold, the governor spends a week in Wyoming fishing, a television talk show host has an argument in a night club—all this becomes news. We are inquisitive people, and we enjoy reading about the personal lives of the famous.

Four Additional Determinants of News

Conflict is one of four additional news determinants that we need to examine. Before we do so, it is important to point out that these four factors alone do not make an event newsworthy. Impact, the unusual and prominence are the three basic news determinants. The presence of one or more of the four additional determinants will heighten the news value of an event. The four are: **conflict, proximity, timeliness and currency.**

Conflict

Conflict underlies our lives. There are internal conflicts we are all familiar with. The student must master a list of Spanish verbs for a test the following day, but his friends are leaving for a movie. Conflict. The car owner notices that his car is slow to start. The battery is running down. A new battery will cost about $50. He has the money, but he had planned to use it for a special set of tools he saw advertised. Conflict.

Almost every meeting of the city council, state legislature or congress involves conflicts between advocates of different points of view. The U.S. Constitution purposely sets governmental powers in conflict so that no one branch of government may dominate the others.

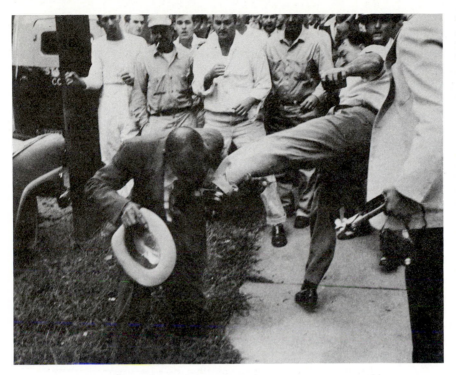

Conflict. Conflict exists at all levels of life. People wrangle over ideas, values and their ways of life. After the U.S. Supreme Court ruled school segregation is unconstitutional, a lengthy struggle began, and in some cities in the South violence erupted. When black youngsters tried to enter Little Rock Central High School, whites attacked the friends and relatives who accompanied them. Wilmer Counts photographed this confrontation outside the high school (top). Man also battles nature, as shown in this famous photograph by Arthur Rothstein of a farm family in Cimarron County, Okla., during the 1930s when drought ravaged farmland and created the Dust Bowl.

Top, Wilmer Counts, *The Arkansas Democrat; bottom,* Arthur Rothstein, Courtesy of the Library of Congress

Men and women are always struggling with something or someone—employers and employees; fathers and sons; husbands and wives; clerks and customers; teenagers with their consciences; adults with their responsibilities. Probably because we are so familiar with strife we overlook its drama except for the most obvious battles and violence. Overt conflict is newsworthy.

Less evident conflicts are the struggles of individuals against adversity—the woman trying to hold a family together on $100 a week, the historian with a view of Thomas Jefferson that conflicts with the established perception, the handicapped youngster trying to play baseball. Some of the best stories a reporter can dig up are the attempts by groups, organizations or individuals to counter prevailing attitudes. When women first banded together to protest what they called a sexist society, few reporters paid attention. In fact, the women were ridiculed as "bra burners."

The few reporters who recognized the movement became acquainted at the outset with what was to become a massive and effective drive for sexual equality.

Proximity

"Anything that is close to my readers or listeners is more important than something remote." This is how one reporter defines proximity. When sociology students at the local college stage mock marriages for a class project, that's news in a local newspaper. It's of no interest to newspaper readers in a neighboring state, unless one of the couples decides to elope there.

Proximity usually means something physically or geographically close. The fatal accident that the police reporter was covering in the first chapter was at an intersection near town. The accident would be of no interest to a newspaper or station 100 miles away.

Proximity can also refer to matters that are close in another way. People feel attached to those like themselves and to those with whom they share common interests. Catholics want to read about the activities of the pope, and many Jews are interested in events in Israel. Stockholders want to know what the board of General Motors has decided about the annual dividend. When a plane crashes in Cyprus, people in the United States wonder whether any Americans were aboard. They have an attachment to fellow citizens, even though the event was thousands of miles away. In carrying the event, newspapers and broadcast stations will tell readers and listeners whether any Americans were aboard. The fewer the number of Americans, the less important the story will be in the United States, regardless of the total number killed.

Proximity. We feel close to people and events with which we are familiar. The first warm day that brings out the surfers is big news to young people on the West Coast, and the day that the bluefish start running close to shore is news for surf fishermen. *Top*, Joseph Noble, *The Stuart News; bottom,* Pepperdine University

Prominence and Proximity—Willie Nelson and Distant Death

The United Press International ran these two stories on its major news wire on the same day.

> LOUISVILLE, KY. (UPI)--COUNTRY MUSIC SINGER WILLIE NELSON CANCELED HIS SCHEDULED APPEARANCE SATURDAY NIGHT AT THE KENTUCKY STATE FAIR'S CLOSING CONCERT BECAUSE HE IS HOSPITALIZED WITH A LUNG AILMENT.
> JULIE SHAW, MANAGER OF THE 10-DAY FAIR, SAID SUNDAY THAT NELSON--THE TOP DRAWING CARD AT LAST YEAR'S FAIR--HAD BEEN HOSPITALIZED IN ANOTHER STATE FOR A SERIOUS RESPIRATORY AILMENT.
> MRS. SHAW SAID SHE HOPED TO ANNOUNCE TODAY A REPLACEMENT FOR NELSON.
>
> 10:21 AED

The story above is not important, but Nelson's **prominence** led the UPI to give it this much space.

The following story is certainly more important than the illness of a country music singer, but its impact is diminished by its lack of **proximity** to readers in the United States.

> NEW DELHI, INDIA (UPI)--A BUS FELL INTO A CANAL TODAY IN THE NORTHERN STATE OF KASHMIR KILLING 22 PEOPLE, THE PRESS TRUST OF INDIA REPORTED.
> THE ACCIDENT OCCURRED NEAR PAHALGAON, ABOUT 400 MILES NORTHWEST OF NEW DELHI.

Timeliness

For some reason, we always want to know the latest, what's happening now. We march to the minute hand on the clock. Our all-news radio stations, our newspapers and our television stations rattle out a drumfire of news for us. We awake to the morning news, and we eat lunch to news and music. Driving to and from school or work, the news is with us in our cars. At home, we read the evening newspaper and turn to the network and local newscasts on television for news of the election returns or the high school football game.

News has a short life span in this barrage. Reporters recognize that what occurs today has greater impact than an event that occurred a week ago, even if that event was not reported at the time. This is why newspaper leads usually include the word *today*. News writers want to impress their readers with the timeliness of the story.

People will read about past events if they are highly significant or extraordinary. Some stories are always timely. Berkley Hudson's story (in chapter 1) of a man held years too long in confinement attracted readers. Investigative reporters are always digging into the past to unearth stories.

Important stories will always attract readers. So will a story about a situation that has been around a long time but never written about in detail. This takes us to the last of our news determinants.

Currency

Since the end of World War II, public schools have been educating large numbers of young people who in previous years would not have finished high school or attended college. At the same time, some educators and parents worried that one of the consequences was a dilution of the quality of education.

This concern has erupted in every decade since the 1940s. In the 1980s, the worry has led to the "back to basics" movement, the substitution of required courses for electives in college and an emphasis on reading and mathematics in the grade schools. These are hardly new ideas. Yet the movement is newsworthy because of the concern over the declining test scores of high school students.

What people talk about makes news. Reporters who are good listeners and who frequent the places where people gather are likely to discover news that fits into the category of currency. A reporter for a California newspaper who was taking a break from a political convention sat in the hotel lobby and overheard delegates chatting. They were not talking about any of the items on the agenda; nor were they exchanging political gossip. What concerned them was the rising property tax.

The reporter put the discussion in the back of his mind and the following week when he had time he looked into it. He was able to gather information from a number of cities and wrote a series that predicted what later became known as the taxpayers' revolt in California.

We have now sketched out the seven determinants of news: impact, the unusual, prominence, conflict, proximity, timeliness and currency. As we have pointed out, the first three are the most important. The other four extend or diminish the news value of an event by their presence or absence.

The Guide: Importance

The single most important guide to whether something is worth a news story is its importance. Another way of looking at news values is to put the event to this test: Does it meet the "primary purpose" of journalism? This purpose is described by the American Society of Newspaper Editors in "A Statement of Principles" this way:

> The primary purpose of gathering and distributing news and opinion is to serve the general welfare by informing the people and enabling them to make judgments on the issues of the time.

Obviously, not everything in newspapers or on newscasts is about a major issue. Newspapers, radio and television stations and newsmagazines try to reach a large audience of different needs and tastes. Still, if a study were to be made of the newspapers, stations and magazines we consider the best, we would find most of their articles to be about important issues.

A bit of advice at this point: Learning to differentiate the important from the inconsequential, the unusual from the ordinary, and the prominent from the little-known comes with experience. Reporters learn from reading newspapers, listening to newscasts and seeing how the professionals handle news. Every reporter sooner or later develops what is called news sense. Without news sense, a journalist cannot function.

Putting the Determinants to Work

We can apply the seven news determinants to the work of the reporters we observed in chapter 1.

The police reporter decided to devote most of his time to the fatal accident. He knew this would have greater **impact** on his readers than the reports of petty thefts, lost dogs and brush fires that he had picked up at the police station. Obviously, **timeliness** and **proximity** were also involved as determinants.

The city hall reporter chose to write about the zoning appeal by the department store because of the **prominence** of the store and the **impact** of the proposal on the community. The original request had been important enough for a news story, but the appeal had the added ingredient of **conflict** to make it even more newsworthy. Readers were interested in the opposition of people living in the residential area near the proposed building site.

The editor's decision to use the Phoenix plane crash involved the element of **prominence.** Although the event was far away, the victim was so well known locally that the story had to be carried. Another distant event made the newspaper that day, the Florida hurricane. Even though the storm was more than a thousand miles away and storms in this season are not unusual in Florida, the story described this as a "killer storm." This makes the storm **exceptional,** unlike the usual storms that batter the state this time of year.

Lindy Washburn knew she had a big story when she learned that more than 20 people had been killed in a New Jersey fire. Disasters make news. Had one or two people been killed, the story would not have been carried on the Associated Press wires. But 23 deaths has considerable **impact.**

In Hong Kong, Neal Robbins was interested in the flight of hundreds of Chinese from the mainland because he knew such a large exodus was **unusual.** Usually, the Chinese came individually or in twos or threes. Their arrival in colorful junks made the story even more unusual.

The lead story on the "CBS Evening News" was a major tax story, which obviously had great **impact** on the public. Although most of the stories on the newscast were significant to large numbers of people, the program also included a feature on a midwestern family with three brilliant children who were being taught at home by their parents—an **exceptional** family educating their children in an **unusual** way.

We are now ready to use these news determinants, or news values, to write news stories.

The first step the news writer takes before writing a news story is to determine its focus or main point. **What's this event about?** the writer asks himself or herself. At least nine times out of ten, the answer to the reporter's question is that the story is about either:

Finding the Focus

1. A **person** who has said or done something important or interesting or a person who has had something important or interesting happen to him or her.
2. An **event** of importance or interest to many people.

If we look carefully at the first paragraphs of news stories in today's newspaper we can verify this. The beginning of the news story, or **lead,** usually summarizes the main theme of the story. Look at a batch of news stories. Almost all of them will begin with a lead that answers one of these two questions:

1. **Who** said or did what? What was it that happened to the **person**?
2. **What** happened?

This takes us to the heart of news writing. When a reporter sits down to write, there are almost always two choices:

1. If a person is central to the event, the writer answers the question: **What did the person say or do; what happened to the person?**
2. When the event, occurrence or happening is important or unusual, the writer answers the question: **What happened of significance or was exceptional or unusual?**

Look back at the three sets of numbered items. They are parallel. All the items numbered 1 are related, as are items numbered 2. They are presented in detail because they are the starting point for news writing.

You might ask at this point what happened to the news determinants. Look closely at the numbered items and you will see that they embody the three key determinants—impact or significance; the unusual, exceptional or interesting; and prominence.

Focusing on the Person

When the event involves an individual saying or doing something, or when the individual has something happen to him or her, the writer first must decide whether the person is prominent. Will readers and listeners recognize the name?

Is the singer Mick Jagger or Ralph Martin? If it is Jagger, most people will recognize the name, and "Jagger" will go into the lead. If it is Martin, few will know that name, and some kind of **identifying label** will have to be used: "A 26-year-old rock singer," for example.

Here are some leads using the **name** of the person involved in the news event:

Who? (name) **said what?**

WASHINGTON—*Sen. Daniel Moynihan* said today that *terrorism is a common instrument of the foreign policies of a number of non-democratic governments.*

Who? (name) **did what?**

MALDEN, Mass. (AP)—*Malden Police Commissioner William A. Davidson* yesterday *ordered two police officers fired* after they arrested him for drunk driving.

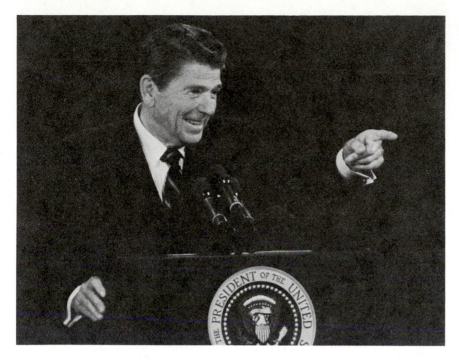

Who? (name) **said what?**

SPRINGFIELD—*Chancellor William E. Barnes told* entering freshmen today *the way to academic success is through "unstinting effort."*

If the person central to the event is not well-known to the news writer's audience, a label must be used that allows the reader or listener to quickly visualize the person. Sometimes, the label is **age** and **address** or **home town:**

Who? (label) **had something happen to him?**

A 39-year-old Kansas City, Kansas, man was charged Monday in Wyandotte County District Court *with the fatal shooting* early Saturday *of a patron* at a tavern in that city.

—*Kansas City Times*

The label can also be the **occupation** of the person:

Who? (label) **had something happen to him?**

A Kentucky State Police detective was *shot to death* yesterday afternoon while searching for marijuana in a field in rural Edmonson County.

—*Lexington* (Ky.) *Herald*

A person's **title** may be used as the identifying label. This is frequently done on radio and television news:

Who? (label) **did what?**

> *A federal judge* in Brooklyn today *imposed prison terms* on four former congressmen and two other codefendants convicted in the FBI's Abscam sting operation.
>
> —CBS "Evening News"

When the person's **connection to the event** identifies him or her, that relationship can be used as the identifying label:

Who? (label) **had something happen to him?**

> HOUSTON (UPI)—*A Rolling Stones fan was stabbed to death* during the British rock group's near-sellout show at the Astrodome, police said Thursday.

Focusing on the Event

When **the event** is the most important aspect of the story, the writer uses the lead to describe what occurred in the briefest way possible:

What happened?

> WASHINGTON—*Congress* yesterday *appropriated $3.5 million to fulfill the government's part of the out-of-court settlement of the Narragansett Indian land claim.*
> —*The Providence Bulletin*

What happened?

> THROOP, Pa. (AP)—*Eight teenage party-goers were crushed to death* when their car swerved into a guard rail, plunged some 190 feet through the air and crashed on its roof, officials said Friday.

What happened?

> CHICAGO (AP)—*DePaul University's student newspaper was shut down* Friday after printing a story about a rape on campus, in defiance of orders from the director of student publications, the editor said.

Focus on Event. When the news event concerns something that has happened, the event or occurrence is emphasized. Horse race, flood, or fire, the story answers the question: What happened?
Top, Susan Plageman, *The Berkshire Eagle; middle,* Jess Andresen, *The Daily News Tribune; bottom,* Stewart Bowman, *The Courier-Journal and Louisville Times Co.*

Direct and Delayed Leads

Look back over these 10 leads for a minute. Use the courthouse reporter's two guidelines to determine what kind of events the leads describe: important or unusual.

Clearly, each of the 10 is important or significant. This is why the leads are written in a straightforward, direct manner. But suppose the event you are writing about has no great importance or significance.

In this case, an indirect, leisurely beginning can be used as a lead. The courthouse reporter used this kind of lead when she wrote the story about the woman who sued a department store whose Santa Claus had, she said, slapped her son. Her story began this way:

Santa Claus is a child's best friend.

The kindly old gent pats little boys on the head and little girls on the cheek.

But two weeks ago, says Mrs. Carolyn Elliott, a Zale's Department store Santa whacked her six-year-old son, Dennis.

When the event is important or significant, the story stresses the main point at once. The lead is **direct.** When the story is about an unusual, odd or strange event, the story does not need to describe what happened or what was said at once. The lead, or main point, can be **delayed** a bit.

We can use these guidelines:

Direct leads are used on important news stories.
Delayed leads are used on feature stories.

A Delayed Lead News writers have to decide how important an event is before writing. When David Stacks was sent to cover an arm-wrestling tournament, he had a good idea that his story for *The Anniston Star* probably would not be the most important in the newspaper the next day. He was fairly sure that he would be writing a feature story, which meant he would need to watch for a good incident to begin his story:

Sweat beaded on Bruce Jernigan's forehead. His biceps swelled as blood rushed through his strong chest and into his right arm. His face grimaced with exertion.

Bruce's opponent, Claude Bradford, smiled in seeming defiance as the two boys' fists—locked in an arm-wrestler's grip, teetered slowly back and forth over the tabletop.

Then, with a burst of energy, 14-year-old Claude overcame his opponent's balanced show of strength.

Both boys fell from near exhaustion as the referee declared the match concluded.

Theirs was a test of strength, endurance and will. In the end, Claude managed to wear down his friend and adversary Bruce, 14, in the Anniston Park and Recreation Department's first arm-wrestling tournament Saturday morning at Carver Community Center on West 14th Street.

"It's all in the way you move," Claude said afterwards.

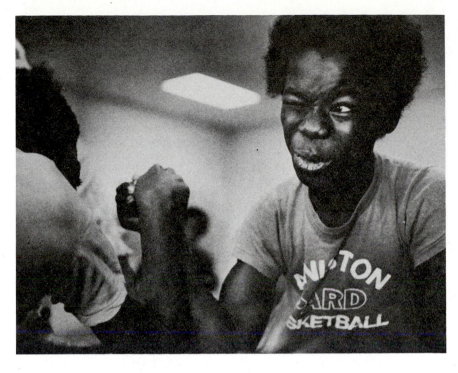

Gotcha. An arm-wrestling tournament was made into a feature story with a delayed lead.
Ken Elkins, *The Anniston Star*

Arm-wrestling is an ancient contest of power in which two opponents grasp each other's hands with their elbows resting on a flat surface. The one who forces the other's arm down to the surface wins.

Ancient people of the world regarded arm-wrestling as a non-violent test of strength where one adversary could defeat the other.

The contest Saturday was staged for a different reason, said Zebedee Murphy, the city recreation leader who coordinated the event and acted as referee.

"We're trying to get them (the boys) interested in something new," he said. Murphy said he used to arm-wrestle with other kids on the block when he was growing up, but this was the first time the city had ever sponsored such a tournament.

"We'll probably do it again next year," Murphy said.

About 20 boys from the Carver area of Anniston participated in the contest Saturday. Officials divided them into three age groups and pitted contestants against each other arbitrarily, Murphy said. . . .

For a minute, suppose that Stacks had decided on a direct lead. It might have been written this way:

```
Claude Bradford, 14, was one of three winners in the
first arm-wrestling tournament held by the Anniston Park
and Recreation Department on Saturday.
    Bradford defeated. . . .
```

"Big deal," a reader might say and pass on to real news. But with the delayed lead Stacks put on his story, the reader settles back and says, "Let's have some fun with this story." The reader knows at once that he or she will be reading a feature story.

Feature Story

The courthouse reporter who came across the document involving Santa Claus knew at once that she would write a short feature story. Her problem was how to write an entertaining lead. Before she sat down to write the story, she had a few ideas. The best one, she thought, was that although Santa Claus is considered a kindly old man, here he was accused of a cruel act. She decided to put this idea of contrasts into her lead:

    Santa Claus, that paragon of kindness, is being sued
    for cruelty to a child.

As with most first efforts, this wasn't exactly right. The idea was sound, she still felt, but not the way she had put it. Writers should use simple language, but here she was using the word "paragon," which some people might not understand. Although the lead was short, she preferred to have as little punctuation as possible in it. She tried again:

    Kindly Santa Claus is being sued for being cruel to a
    youngster.

She was more satisfied with this. But perhaps she should localize it, put the local department store's name in the lead. No, readers would know it was a local story because there would be no dateline.

The lead was still too flat, too close to a straight news lead. She knew that the lead is the most important part of the story, that it either attracts the reader at once or turns the reader away. "Hook him at once, or he's gone," an editor had once told her. This lead wouldn't even tempt the reader, she decided.

The tone was wrong. The beginning of a feature should be relaxed. It should beckon the reader and say to him or her: slow down a minute—I've got something funny I want to tell you.

Suddenly she realized there was a more serious problem than her choice of words, punctuation and tone. In her effort to be entertaining, she had neglected to be scrupulously careful about the facts. Her lead mistakenly identified the party the suit was brought against, the defendant.

It was not Santa Claus, as both drafts of her lead had stated. It was the department store. Some feature writers, she knew, are known for shading the facts in the interest of a well-written story. She did not want to give herself that kind of reputation. She had heard about their motto: "Never let the facts get in the way of a good story."

She knew that she did not have much space, so she could not spin out the tale for more than five or six paragraphs. After her leisurely beginning, she would have to get to the facts—name and address of mother, description of the incident, damages sought. She wrote:

Santa Claus is a child's best friend.

The kindly old gent pats little boys on the head and little girls on the cheek.

But two weeks ago, says Mrs. Carolyn Elliott, a Zale's Department Store Santa whacked her six-year-old son, Dennis.

Mrs. Elliott, of 49 East End Ave., wants $10,000 for her "humiliation and embarrassment" and her son's "nervous reaction." She filed suit against the store in the Grant County District Court yesterday.

The department store had no comment.

Straight News Story

Now let's look at the straight news story. In chapter 1, we watched a reporter begin to write the obituary of Rose Harriet Allen, former school teacher and principal. The event contains two news determinants, prominence and impact. Allen was well-known, and her death and the fund drive will have an impact on the readers.

This means the story will be written in a straightforward manner, as most obituaries are, and that it will be given a direct lead.

Just what the lead will say is not so obvious. We have two answers worthy of the lead when we ask the two questions that will give us the story focus:

1. What was it that happened to the person?
    Rose Harriet Allen died.
2. What happened?
    A scholarship fund is being set up.

Which should be the lead? One or the other, or both? Let's listen in on the writer's thinking:

"Everyone in town knows Allen, so I'll start with that and immediately go to the fund drive. The lead will include both elements."

    Rose Harriet Allen, 71, of 33 Fulton Ave., who taught
    school here for 30 years and was a school principal for 13
    years before her retirement, died yesterday in the
    Community Hospital. A fund drive will be. . . .

"No, that won't do. The first paragraph will be a blockbuster, much too long. Maybe the better lead is the fund drive since that has lasting significance. Obviously, with that as a beginning Allen's name will be worked into the story since the drive is in her memory."

> A college scholarship fund is being set up in memory of Rose Harriet Allen, 71, who died yesterday after a career of 43 years in the local public schools.

"That's better. It's shorter and it combines the two elements."

She continues to write, and in the middle of the fourth paragraph she suddenly stops and slowly reads what she has written.

"This is becoming a story about a fund drive, not the death of a well-known teacher who probably has thousands of friends in town. The impact, the real significance, is not the fund drive but her death. Allen's death will affect many of our readers.

"The lead should concentrate on Allen's death and the fund drive should go lower in the story."

> Rose Hariett Allen, whose teaching and administrative career spanned 43 years in local public schools, died here yesterday at the age of 71.
> Allen died in the Community Hospital where she had been since suffering a heart attack last week in her home at 33 Fulton Ave.
> For 30 years, Allen taught in several of the city's elementary schools. For the next 13 years of her education career, she was the principal of the Lincoln School. She retired six years ago.
> She is remembered as a friendly, outgoing teacher. As a principal, she delighted in taking a class for a teacher who was ill.
> "She was strict," recalled Albert Green, a local lawyer. "If you didn't do your homework, she wanted to see your parents in school the next day."
> Green and some of Allen's other former students said they are planning to establish a college scholarship fund in her memory.
> "Miss Allen came from a poor farm family," Green said. "She used to tell us how hard it was for her to stay in school at State Teachers College, how she worked for a family for her room and board and did chores six hours a day, went to class, and studied.". . . .

This version satisfied her. She was able to balance both important elements of the story, Allen's death and the fund drive. She had good quotes that told something of Allen's personality. The personal details about Allen helped the reader to visualize the kind of person she was.

Walter Lippmann, a newspaper columnist and the author of many books, said that "in our world the facts are infinitely many." He added, "We have to select some facts rather than others, and in doing that we are using not only our legs but our selective judgment of what is interesting or important or both."

Selection and Judgment

The news story is a keyhole view of the event. It does not pretend to tell all. However, it should give the "interesting or important" aspects of the event. It will, if the journalist has the ability to select the essentials of the event and the judgment to weigh their relative merits.

Selection and judgment come into play in reporting as well as in writing. No news story, no matter how well written, can be any better than the facts that go into it. In chapter 4 we'll look at reporting, which is another word for fact or information gathering. But before we do, a cautionary remark.

In chapter 1, we saw how the police reporter and the obituary writer decided to emphasize one story (the fatal accident and the death of Rose Harriet Allen) and to ignore or quickly pass over others. When Neal Robbins returned to the bureau he thought he had a big story. But because of more important news on the wires (the assassination attempt on the president and stirrings in Poland), the story had to be cut down to a length shorter than anticipated.

News Values Are Not Absolute

The news story that is worth 500 words on a slow news day may be shortened to 250 words on a busy news day. A story newsworthy on a day the newspaper is fat with advertising, thus allowing considerable space for news, might not be printed on a Saturday, when the paper is thin and news must be carefully chosen for the little available space.

Because readers, listeners and viewers are accustomed to a wide variety of news in their newspapers and newscasts, no story can run too long, no matter what its importance may be. Room must be made for features, business news, local news, obituaries, personal items, weather, sports and so on.

The nature of the audience influences news selection. An announcement from the Vatican will be given space in *The Bridgeport Post* because of the large Catholic readership in the industrial community. But it may not be carried in *The Advocate* in nearby Stamford, which has fewer Catholics.

The Audience

News from Washington about crop support payments is of little or no importance to New York readers but has considerable impact in the Midwest. Although a story about a meeting of the board of Eastman Kodak will not be carried in many newspapers, *The Wall Street Journal* will run it for its readers, whose average net worth exceeds $400,000 and who invest in stocks and bonds.

The New York Post is loaded with gossip about television and movie stars and has large headlines about sex crimes. *The New York Times* emphasizes international news, carries little local news on page one and has a reporter who writes about wine.

The journalist who goes to work for the *Post,* the *Times,* or any newspaper or broadcast station quickly learns to tailor news decisions to fit the

Figure 3.1 Readers Determine News. In this agricultural area of Minnesota, a wind and hail storm is big news because of the damage to crops, outbuildings and homes. *The Free Press* in Mankato devoted its entire front page to news of the storm.

THE FREE PRESS

Vol. 95   No. 73   28 pages   2 sections plus supplements
June 24, 1981   Mankato-North Mankato, Minn. 56001   25¢

Wednesday

A wet ending to a wild afternoon

While traffic creeps along flooded Carney Avenue in West Mankato Tuesday afternoon, Tom Browne, 934 Charles Ave., plants one foot and his hoe along a boulevard for security and fishes for a debris-clogged storm sewer grate. Portions of several city streets were closed temporarily.

Mother Nature does it again

By Staff Writers

A storm 40 miles wide, carrying hail and high winds, ravaged trees and crops and created openings for water damage in Blue Earth County Tuesday.

The brunt of the storm, with gusts of nearly 80 miles per hour, apparently passed directly over Mankato-North Mankato, causing flooding of streets and basements. At least half of

See related articles, photos on Pages 4 and 15

the Greater Mankato area was left without electrical power. West Mankato, where numerous large trees were uprooted, appeared hardest hit. The storm also struck the Lake Crystal and St. Clair areas.

TOTAL DAMAGE in the county, including the destruction of about 50 buildings, was estimated at $1.5 million by Blue Earth County Sheriff LaRoy Wiebold.

"As far as I'm concerned, Blue Earth County is a disaster area," he said.

Two Mankato area people were admitted to Immanuel-St. Joseph's Hospital, one with a back injury and one with an injury to the left eye, as a result of the Tuesday afternoon storm.

A hospital spokeswoman said seven residents were treated in the hospital emergency room for minor cuts and bruises following the storm, and released.

No tornadoes were spotted, although some people witnessed funnel clouds over Mankato.

MANY PEOPLE in Mankato watched the storm's approach. Ample warning was given, with sirens sounding long before the first rain drops fell. As the storm neared from the northwest, a wide band of white appeared, announcing the arrival

Strong winds, hail strip crops from fields

By MICHAEL FLAHERTY
Free Press Staff Writer

In some parts of Blue Earth County, it looks as though farmers never planted a crop. The fields, which only Tuesday nurtured promising young plants, lay black — completely stripped of foliage.

The storm that struck Tuesday will be billed as one of the worst disasters ever to strike Blue Earth County farmers.

Large hail whipped by high winds slashed fields and pasted young soybean and corn plants to the ground throughout the county. Observers estimate between 70 and 95 percent of the county's crops have been damaged, but the number of acres destroyed will not be known until farmers have had time to see how much of their corn crop recovers.

MOST OF the county's soybeans are gone. Soybeans even bruised by hailstorm usually have to be replanted. And Tuesday's hail smashed most of Blue Earth County's crop. Agronomists say farmers still have about a week to plant a new crop of soybeans.

Corn plants are usually more

resilient. In order to be killed, corn plants have to be severely damaged below the plant's growing point, which Tuesday was 3 to 6 inches from the ground.

But even parts of the corn crop have been wiped out. Elevator operators throughout the county say that many of their customers have given up hope that the shredded corn crop will recover.

Some farmers are going to try to replant the corn using an early maturing variety of seed, but many feel it is too late

that corn planted now would only have a ghost of a chance of producing a crop.

"But we'll just have to wait and see how much of the corn was hurt," said Byron Kunkel, county extension agent. "Corn will usually come back, and I don't want to get into a guessing game on how much was destroyed until we wait a few days."

Kunkel said the storm was the worst he'd seen in this area.

See CROPS
(Please turn to Page 8)

See STORM
(Please turn to Page 8)

Knee-high by the Fourth of July may be a tall order for some of Blue Earth County's corn crop battered Tuesday by strong winds and hail.

Why us? Meteorologist says to blame the terrain

The Minnesota River Valley's rough terrain magnified Tuesday's storm by about 30 percent, National Weather Service meteorologist John Graf said today.

Actually, Graf said, several storm systems struck southwestern Minnesota Tuesday, but the storm along the 100-mile long river valley from Montevideo to Mankato was particularly severe because of the valley's rolling terrain.

"Changes in the height and contour of the valley magnify a storm," Graf said. "The initial inflection point of the storm began in the upper sections of the valley, and 'lifting mechanisms' in the atmosphere were magnified by the rough terrain.

The Minnesota River Valley is an "ideal storm producer," Graf said, particularly when a storm flows in a northwest-southeast direction as it did Tuesday.

"The valley makes a storm generate more energy than it would normally, and once a storm gets under way, it perpetuates itself," Graf said.

The meteorologist said a storm system "pulsates; it elongates and contracts, like a living mechanism, something you might see in the sea."

Graf also said that Tuesday's storm was unusually long-lived, with severe weather lasting up to 40 minutes at some points along the storm path.

A helping hand

Need help with storm cleanup?

Hundreds of people in The Free Press circulation area need assistance to restore their homes and yards. Many students, 12 years and older, need summer jobs.

In an effort to help everybody, The Free Press is offering any student a free seven-day want ad between June 25 and July 1.

Details in the classified section.

The Inside Story

Mud Hens flying high

Although the major leaguers are striking, baseball still lives in cities like Toledo, Ohio, the top farm club of the Minnesota Twins. And in Toledo, the club makes it fun to come to the ballpark. Find out more about the legendary Mud Hens in Sports, Page 21.

Dancing to 90

When anyone approaches the century mark, everyone else wants to know his secret of long life. For Julius Peterson, it's dancing, and that's how he'll celebrate his 90th birthday on Friday. Mr. Peterson tells how he started dancing, in a story on Page 5.

Index

Accent	5,6,7	Markets	17
Business	16	Opinion	12
Comics	20	Outdoors	23
Deaths	19	Public Notices	24
Dear Abby	6	Records	18
Dr. Donohue	20	Sports	21-23
Horoscope	20	World	3
In the Nation	2		

Less dramatic

Clear to partly cloudy tonight and Thursday. Lows in the middle to upper 50s and highs in the lower to middle 80s. Wind northwest 5 to 15 mph tonight. Extended outlook: Partly cloudy Friday and Saturday. Chance of thunderstorms Sunday. Highs in the 70s north and 80s south. Lows mid 40s to mid 50s Friday and in the 50s Saturday and Sunday.

interests of the audience. A story that would be played up with explicit language in the *Post* might not be used in Huntington, W. Va., and if it were, the four-letter words and the sexual references probably would be eliminated.

Editors and publishers make decisions about what their audiences want to read and hear. When Rupert Murdoch, owner of *The New York Post,* bought the *Chicago Sun-Times* his editors decided to turn the newspaper into a zippy, zesty and sexy tabloid with brief, punchy headlines that would catch the attention of people going by street boxes:

Zinc Zaps Colds

Men Bear Children?

Coverage of crime increased. A study by three Northwestern University graduate students showed that the amount of space given to stories about rape increased 95 percent in the first month of Murdoch's ownership compared to the last month under the previous owners, the Fields. In that time, the number of reported rapes had actually dropped.

Other factors influence decisions on what appears on news programs and in newspapers. The newspaper with a correspondent in the state capital will have more coverage of political and state government news than a newspaper that lacks a statehouse bureau. Radio stations with few reporters rely on the wire services for news and may slight the day-to-day coverage of local events.

Advertisers exert pressure, too. Usually, newspapers and stations are adamant about resisting overt financial pressures. For years, the associate editor of *The Des Moines Register* said, "we have had very little chemical advertising." The cause, said Drake Mabry, was the newspaper's running excerpts from Rachel Carson's book exposing the dangerous effects of pesticides and insecticides, *Silent Spring*. "We did the right thing," Mabry said.

Next, let's see what happens to the news story when the reporter has finished writing it.

Moving the Story

Broadcast Copy

Broadcast news stories move from the writer to the news editor or to the person who will be reading the copy. The copy is edited to see that it can be read aloud without difficulty. Factual errors are corrected, and the copy is checked for broadcast style. Numerals are written out. The number 20 becomes twenty; 500,000 becomes 500 thousand.

Correspondents in the field write their own copy and read it on the air. Sometimes, they "wing it," meaning they speak without written copy.

In smaller stations with no news staff, announcers take wire copy directly from the AP or UPI Teletype machines and read it with little advance checking. This is called "rip and read," and it is the cause of many of the bloopers that are collected on records and sold as entertainment.

Figure 3.2 Local TV News Operation. This system is used by CBS-owned stations for their local news coverage and is in use elsewhere as well. The metropolitan editor runs the reporting staff and camera crews. The executive producer is in charge of the news program, overseeing the actual broadcast. At stations where there are several major newscasts, there may be separate executive producers and producers for each newscast.

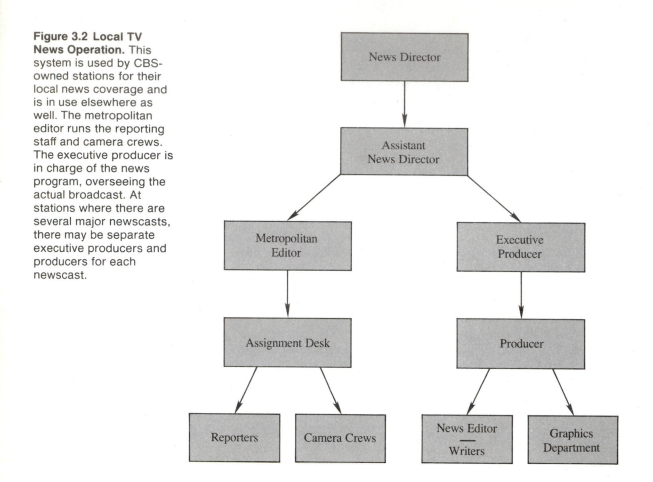

Newspaper Copy

The routing of copy for a newspaper is considerably more complex. After a story has been written, it is turned in to the city desk. If it has been written on a video display terminal, the city desk calls it up for examination on the screen at the city desk.

The city editor or assistant city editor reads through the copy to see that it is satisfactory, that the lead contains the main news point and all questions the reader may have are answered. If the story is inadequate, it is sent back to the news writer for further work. If acceptable, the story moves on to the next stage, the copy desk.

At the copy desk, the story is given a thorough reading. Grammar, punctuation and spelling are checked. The writing is made to conform to the newspaper's style—Street may be abbreviated to St., fourteen changed to 14. (A newspaper stylebook is included in Appendix B.)

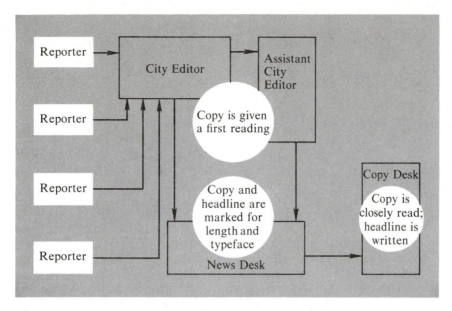

Figure 3.3 How a Story Moves. The reporter's story goes through several hands before it appears in the newspaper. The city editor or assistant city editor examines it, a news editor reads through it at the news desk and then a copy editor reads it closely and writes a headline for the story.

If the paper is tight that day, the copy editor trims the story, usually from the bottom. Unnecessary adjectives and adverbs are removed, even when the paper is open—meaning there is plenty of room for news. Redundancies (true facts, circulated around, 7 a.m. in the morning) are corrected. Sentences in the passive voice are changed to the active: "The burglar was seen by one of the children" becomes "One of the children saw the burglar."

A copy editor may spot something the city editor missed. If the problem is minor, the copy desk will solve it, but if it is major the story is sent back to the writer. If the education reporter used too much jargon—the specialized language of educators—the copy editor replaces the technical wording with everyday words and phrases.

When the editing is completed, the copy editor writes a headline for the story. The size of the headline is determined by the city editor if the story is local, by the news editor or managing editor if it is national or international.

Non-local stories are usually taken from the wire service machines, AP, UPI or others. If the newspaper subscribes to more than one wire service and the news editor wants to combine the dispatches of two or more of them into a single story, the news editor may ask the managing editor to assign the job to a news writer.

On large newspapers, such as the one diagrammed in figure 3.3, a regional editor goes over news from correspondents in nearby communities, the business editor handles news from the business staff and from the wires that the news editor or wire editor has turned over to the business desk, and the sports editor handles sports copy.

Each of these specialized departments has a copy desk of its own. On smaller newspapers, all copy is channeled to a single copy desk.

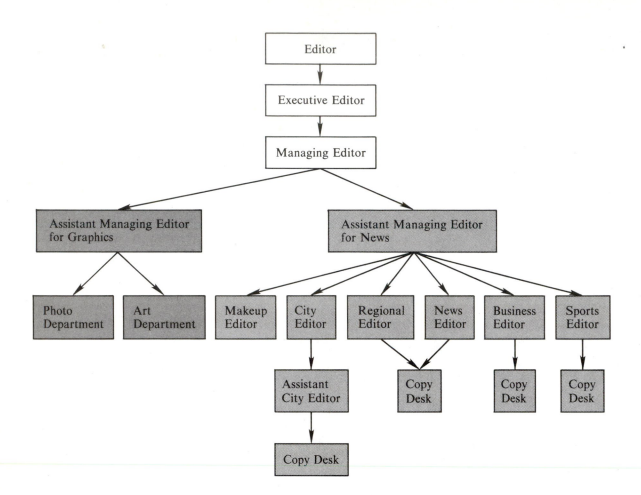

Figure 3.4 Newsroom Organization. Newspaper newsrooms are organized along these lines of authority, the editor at the top and various departmental editors and their copy desks under the editor. This diagram shows the organization of a large newspaper. Smaller newspapers may have just one copy desk—called a universal desk—that handles all copy but sports and social news.

As the news day develops, the makeup editor decides how to lay out the newspaper—where to put the stories. Material for the inside pages is laid out first: columns, editorials, comic strips and secondary stories.

On large newspapers, the decision about where to put, or **play,** stories is made at a story, or news, conference. There, the editors of the various sections present the best of their stories to the managing editor. The city editor discusses last night's city council meeting, the national news editor mentions a story from Washington about the federal budget. On some newspapers, a foreign editor is also present.

The managing editor decides what stories will go on page one and which will be given top play. The number one story is usually placed in the upper-right-hand side of the page.

On smaller newspapers, the decisions on play are less formal. The managing editor and the city editor chat with each other during the day and then instruct the makeup editor about their decisions.

In both cases, the photo editor, or assistant managing editor for graphics, informs the managing editor or another editor about the local and wire photos that are available to accompany the major stories.

Once the decisions have been made about play, it is up to the makeup editor to produce a pleasing display of the news for page one and for other section pages—those pages that begin different sections of the newspaper.

Increasingly, newspapers are being edited and made up on video screens. Just as the terminal keyboard has replaced the typewriter, the terminal is replacing the copy editor's pencil and the layout sheets, called **dummies,** of the makeup staff.

When the newsroom work is completed, the stories laid out are placed on plates, which are usually made up by photocomposition, and then are sent to the pressroom.

Reporting

In this chapter, we have discussed the way news stories are written. We have presumed that the facts of the stories have already been gathered. Before we go into more detail about news writing, we should look at the business of fact gathering. Chapters 4 and 5 will discuss what it is that reporters look for so they can make their stories interesting, complete and relevant to the needs of readers and listeners. We will see how reporting and writing are part of one overall process. This is an important point that can never be repeated often enough: News writers write reporting.

Reporting

Finding Information and Gathering Facts

News is developed from the journalist's observation of events, from interviews with the people involved and by research in records, files and reference material. To report an event properly, the journalist must know how things work—how city government functions, how the school system operates, how the local criminal justice system is structured. This knowledge is part of the general background the journalist applies to his or her reporting and writing. To obtain this knowledge, the journalist seeks a wide range of experiences, reads widely and knows how to use a variety of reference materials.

Looking Ahead

The news story stands on facts, and the facts that carry the most weight are those that the reporter gathers by direct observation.

A Firsthand Look

Penny Lernoux, who covers Latin America for a number of newspapers and magazines, was doing a story on tin miners in Bolivia who work under difficult conditions high in the Andes. Lernoux was determined to see the miners herself, although she had heard that the miners sometimes threw dynamite at visitors and were especially suspicious of women, whom they believed brought them bad luck.

She disguised herself as a man and went along with an engineer who had volunteered to show her the inside of a mine.

She was deep inside the Siglo Veinte mine, she recalled, "when a miner approached, a smile on his face and a stick of dynamite in his hand."

"Don't panic," the engineer shouted. "Just run."

Fortunately, there was a sharp bend in the corridor, which they scrambled around just as the dynamite exploded. Lernoux survived, and she had her story.

In Philadelphia, newspapers carried stories of crime, delays, fires and accidents in the city's subways. One story reported the case of a widely known Philadelphia lawyer who was beaten, raped and left for dead in the darkened track area. She was discovered 18 hours after the attack.

Terror Underground

Mike Mallowe of *Philadelphia* magazine decided to look into the subway system. He interviewed crime victims, patrolled with the police, worked with the subway motormen and rode the subway for months as a commuter. His piece, "Tunnel of Terror," included his findings:

> . . . . a trunk line to hell . . . 40 miles of dark, deadly terror . . . 40 miles of drunks collapsed in their own vomit; of howling teenage punks pissing in public; of hulking panhandlers, not asking, but demanding money; it's 40 miles of old people too terrified to look around them; of women alone, too scared to speak. . . .

Only direct observation could generate the tension and terror in these lines.

A Fish Story

On a skyway over Tampa Bay, a couple of fishermen are trying their luck. Jeff Klinkenberg, an outdoors reporter for *The St. Petersburg Times,* and another reporter are "catching nothing," as Klinkenberg puts it, when a fisherman walks by with what seems to be about 60 pounds of equipment.

He looks at Klinkenberg and his companion and laughs. "You'll never catch anything with that," he says to them, pointing to their equipment.

Then he begins talking about a shark he is determined to catch, name of "Old Hitler." Klinkenberg manages to get in a few questions before the fisherman goes his way. The reporters resume fishing, but Klinkenberg is distracted. He is thinking, this guy is worth a story.

Two weeks later, Klinkenberg called the shark fisherman and made arrangements to meet him on the skyway.

"I went back out there with him. We went to the bridge about 6 p.m. and stayed until 2 a.m., fooling around with sharks and ladyfish," Klinkenberg says.

Klinkenberg returned to the newspaper and typed up three pages of single-spaced notes for his story. Then he wrote. Here is how the story began:

> Ron Swint moaned in the dark about the shark called Old Hitler, the largest shark in Tampa Bay, as traffic roared by on the Skyway Bridge. Somebody in a car shouted and Swint automatically winced. He has been hit by beer cans thrown from passing cars. A huge truck rumbled by so fast the bridge shook. Diesel fumes hung in the air.
>
> The first shark to come along was not Old Hitler, but it was a big one, a shark Swint later estimated at 500 pounds, a shark that swallowed a three-pound live ladyfish bait and swam toward the lights of Tampa. The shark almost killed Swint.

The complete story is in Appendix C.

Again, we see that the reporter who has observed the event is able to make the story come alive for readers.

It is not always possible to see the event. A bank is robbed, a truck slams into a car, a flash flood rips out a bridge. These happen so quickly, only sheer luck would have the reporter there at the moment the news breaks. In these situations, the reporter turns to sources for information—eyewitnesses and authorities.

When Bonnie Van Gilder was assigned to do a story about street gangs for her journalism class, she hoped to observe a gang on the prowl. She was unable to do so, and so she had to settle for other sources.

The Crazy Bishops

For her story, Van Gilder could have used the police alone for information. She did interview police officers. She also examined police documents, along with news clippings. But she wanted more direct contact with a gang. She managed to locate a Times Square gang, the Crazy Bishops, and she was able to interview some members.

Here is her story:

NEW YORK—"China," a female member of a Times Square teen gang called the Crazy Bishops, narrowed her black eyes and declared, "If you want to be a Bishop, you got to mug people and beat them up and take whatever you can."

Like most of the other Crazy Bishops, China, 15, comes from a broken home, is a runaway and has an extensive arrest record. Police have identified 60 Bishops, but suspect as many as 200 Hispanic boys and girls, ranging in age from 14 to 19, are associated with the gang.

Detective John McNamee knew where to find China. When the 42nd Street policemen change shifts at 7:30 a.m., the Bishops come out of a nearby park where they sleep. They go to a local coffee shop or sit on the stoops of pornography and peep show businesses that line 42nd Street.

At night they work the streets and vast network of area subway tunnels. The gang has rampaged through the theater district, looting stores, mugging tourists and harassing transients.

"When you're a Bishop, you don't have no pity for people," China said, "You got to hustle to survive."

Area merchants complain about the gang. But police say they can arrest the Bishops only for disorderly conduct unless they are caught committing a more serious crime.

Louis Corbo, head of the Youth Gang Information Unit of the New York City Police, said, "We think this gang grew out of the film 'The Warriors.' It may just be coincidence, but there was never a gang around Times Square before."

Corbo said the Crazy Bishops are unlike any other youth gang he has investigated. Usually gangs are made up of neighborhood kids, living within the same 10-block residential area. But the Crazy Bishops operate in a commercial district and recruit members from gangs in the Bronx, Brooklyn or New Jersey. Also they recruit runaways at the New York Port Authority and outside "Under 21"—a church-operated organization that houses and feeds runaways.

To become a member of the Crazy Bishops, a boy must hand over $50 from robberies and allow a high-ranking gang officer to cut a one-inch gash in his arm. The initiation is different for the girls. To become a full-fledged Queen Bishop, a girl must sleep with several gang members.

"You got to prove you're hard," one gang member said, "They put you to the test when the godfather—the top man—cuts you."

The gang has an elaborate hierarchy. "Dice," 19, is the "pres," or top man, because he is older and shrewd. "Sinbad" is the war chancellor in charge of rip-offs and fights, and is said to be one of the most violent gang members. The group also has a vice president and an intelligence officer, who keeps track of treaties with rival gangs and arrest records for the Crazy Bishops.

"They aren't angels," said McNamee. "They usually don't carry guns. But they have makeshift weapons—sticks, belts with sharpened buckles or homemade blackjacks."

China admitted the gang carries chains and knives, but "stashes them" when the "heat is on." She said female gang members usually carry the weapons because they can't be searched by police officers.

"We do most of our stuff at night," China said. "We put a knife to a white boy's side and tell him to walk. When you get him to the park, you slice him up or beat the— out of him."

The Crazy Bishops are what the police call a horizontal gang because there are other divisions in other boroughs. Members of the Times Square Bishops—the third division—wear a rabbit's foot around their necks or a bandana around their legs for identification. There are no rumbles between Bishop divisions, but sometimes there are turf wars with rival gangs.

"When gang members 'fly their colors' (wear jackets with the gang's name emblazened on the back), that usually means a turf war," Corbo said.

Recently the Crazy Homicides—a Coney Island deaf-mute gang—flew their colors in Bishop territory. About 60 Bishops and Homicides fought with chains in 42nd Street subway tunnels. The police, however, were tipped off in advance. They stopped the fighting and arrested nine Bishops.

Van Gilder's vivid story stands out because she went beyond official sources to those directly involved in the event, the gang members themselves.

Talk to Participants

The reporter covering a flood will try to reach those on the scene, someone who saw the water's surge carry off the bridge. If he or she cannot find an eyewitness, the reporter will settle for quotes from someone who can attest to the storm's fury.

The reporter covering a fatal accident will try to talk to a passenger or the driver, if the accident is worth a detailed story. If this is not possible, the reporter will try to reconstruct the event from the investigating officers' written report.

A bank robbery story will be given the detail and color necessary through interviews with bank employees and customers who were in the bank at the time. The teller who was held up will be interviewed in detail.

Getting the Story.
Reporters have three basic sources for their stories: direct observation; interviews; and checking news clippings, files, reference works and documents. These provide the facts that make up the news or feature story.
Top, Perry Werner, *The Hays Daily News; lower left,* Bob Thayer, *The Providence Journal-Bulletin*

We have sketched out the three basic sources of information for news stories:

1. Direct observation.
2. Human sources. People who have witnessed the event; authorities and experts who know about the subject, and people who are involved in the event.
3. Reports, documents, reference material. This includes newspaper clippings; film and tape from broadcast station libraries; minutes of meetings; tape recordings; court, police and legislative records; budgets; tax records.

Three Basic Sources of Information

Know It All. Biking and ballet . . . Shakespeare and surfing . . . politics and pottery. . . . The journalist is expected to know something about everything. The journalist may be sent out to cover a political rally one day and to interview a famous ballerina the next. Wide-ranging reading and a variety of experience help the journalist to build the knowledge and information necessary to write accurate and informative stories.
Above, Jeff Widener, *The Evansville Press; opposite, top left,* Jeff Luper, Pepperdine University; *opposite, top right*, Jeff Luper, Pepperdine University

Most stories combine all three types of sources. Lernoux used her observations from her trip into the bowels of the Bolivian mine. She collected detailed material about the production of these mines, the salaries of miners, the profits of the mining companies from records and documents. And she gathered information from interviews with engineers, mining officials and others connected with the mines.

Mallowe rode the subways, talked to passengers, motormen, transit officials, and read all the newspaper clips he could dig up about the subway system.

Background Is Essential

We should add a fourth source of material. It is not precisely a means of gathering news, but it is essential to the content of the news story. This is the reporter's background knowledge, the information he or she has about the subject.

As an outdoors reporter, Klinkenberg knows fishing. He was able to add material to his story of the shark fisherman from his wide knowledge. He was also able to ask questions more intelligently, to understand some of the points Swint was making about the difficulties in landing a 500-pound shark from a bridge far above the water.

When a reporter is sent out on an unfamiliar story, he or she has to take a quick course in the nature of the event. The reporter assigned to interview a country music singer will do some fast reading if all the reporter knows is rock or jazz. When the singer says he is true to the tradition of Jimmie Rodgers and that other singers are cashing in on the bland commercial sound introduced by the Nashville record producers, the reporter should know what the singer is talking about.

Rewriting Publicity and Press Releases

Press releases and publicity handouts, additional sources of news, flood the newsroom. Some basic reporting steps are taken before they are rewritten for the newspaper or station.

One of the first discoveries new journalists make is their sudden popularity. They are sought out and courted. Most of these new-found friends, it turns out, have something they want to see in print or hear on the 7 o'clock news. The friends call and write, and the organized ones among them have material sent by press agents and public relations firms.

Some of this material makes good news stories. These sources account for as much as half the news in some newspapers. They supply information about the fund drive that is soliciting money to send needy youngsters to summer camp, and they tell the press when the governor will be in town to speak.

The proud mother calls in to tell the social news or lifestyle reporter about her daughter's engagement, and the bank's information officer announces the hiring of an executive assistant to the president. The local college sends out a press release about an award given to a professor of chemistry.

Whatever the source, however perfect the material may seem, the reporter always checks before writing a news story. Nothing is accepted at face value. The first check is with the newspaper files. The governor might be making his first visit locally since elected; the press release did not mention that. The professor of chemistry may have recently been denied tenure; the college press office neglected to mention that. And the mother may have forgotten to tell the newspaper her daughter is a former Rhodes Scholar.

Taking Notes

No reporter has total memory. All rely on their notes and some use tape recorders as well as their recollections of the event.

Some reporters prefer notes to the tape recorder in certain situations. Obviously, on a breaking story, the tape recorder is impossible to set up. It works well in a long interview where reporter and source are seated and in situations in which the source is accustomed to being interviewed. In some cases, the tape recorder may freeze a source. There is something ominous about speaking into a machine that is recording every word. The reporter has to be sure the source is open and calm in the tape recorder's presence before using it.

Taking notes requires on-the-scene selection. Since events are often confused and since sources speak rapidly, it is impossible for anyone but the reporter who knows shorthand to put everything down. The reporter tries to establish early the direction of the story. Notes are taken on the major ideas, and the extraneous is ignored.

Here is a little trick to help organize the story: When you have a theme, put a mark of some kind next to it in a circle—a check, an X, a diagonal line. When there is another theme or idea mentioned, use a different mark to identify it. During the interview the source may return to the first theme, or in covering an event a situation may develop that relates to the first theme. In this case, the first mark will be used to set off that quote or situation. Similar observations or comments are similarly marked.

The series of marks are used to organize the piece. By grouping similarly marked notes in writing the piece, the reporter gives the story coherence and logic.

The short item in the *Boston Herald American* read:

Avoiding Errors

> The Civic Symphony Orchestra of Boston, Max Hobart, conductor, will present the Beethoven Piano Concerto No. 4 with Stephanie Brown, soloist, in Jordan Hall, tomorrow night at 8:30. There'll also be an exhibition of pictures by Mussorgsky.

To many readers of the newspaper, the item was hilarious. Those who knew classical music realized that the reporter did not. Mussorgsky is a Russian composer who wrote a piece called "Pictures at an Exhibition." It was to be played along with the piano concerto.

The mistakes an editor of *The New York Times* had been seeing in the newspaper were far from funny. "Inexcusable," he wrote in a staff memo that also pointed out:

```
   National Organization of Women. (It's not "of" but
"for.")
   Proctor & Gamble. (It is Procter.)
   Roosevelt Hotel at 45th Street and Park Avenue.
   (The hotel is at 45th Street and Madison Avenue.)
   The state's four largest cities--New York, Rochester,
Syracuse and Buffalo. (Yonkers replaced Syracuse years
ago.)
```

A news writer whose wide range of knowledge included all kinds of music would not have made the error committed by the writer for the *Boston Herald American*. No one is expected to know every detail of every subject. But editors do expect their writers and copy editors to consult the appropriate references. The errors in the *Herald American* and the *Times* were unnecessary because a quick check of reference works would have caught them.

A good dictionary usually includes a list of biographical names, and Mussorgsky's is among them. News clippings would have shown the *Times* news writers their mistakes before their copy saw print. The facts, said the *Times* editor, were "readily available."

Before we examine in detail the reference works with which every journalist should be familiar, let's see what reporters are expected to know.

A Reporter's Range of Knowledge

Know the Beat

A reporter should know **how things work on his or her beat.** The police reporter knows the chain of command in the police department, why police officers sometimes throw the book at offenders and how juveniles are used by drug pushers to avoid felony arrests. The courthouse reporter knows the wheelers and dealers among the courthouse lawyers, the process from arraignment to trial, what plea bargaining is and why damage suits are settled out of court so often.

The Education Beat Let's look at what an education reporter needs to know to cover his or her beat properly. The reporter must know how a school system is organized and how it is financed, how the board sets the property tax. The reporter understands the politics of setting the property tax. Property owners want good schools for their children, but they resist increasing taxes. The educators usually want smaller classes, more teaching aids, athletic programs, a school band, a bigger library. All of this costs money, which is raised through taxes.

The board is usually caught in the middle. It is responsive to property owners since many board members are property owners themselves and often represent interests in the community with a concern for lower taxes. At the same time the board is also responsive to the educators.

In addition to knowing the system, the reporter keeps up with current affairs through visits to the classroom and by constant reading. The education reporter knows that public education is being attacked for failing to educate large numbers of youngsters. Through her reading, the reporter has established several guidelines for judging schools. She has them listed in a notebook:

Strong principal

Disciplined atmosphere

High expectations for students

Homework

Individual attention to students

Emphasis on basic skills

Systematic evaluation of pupil and teacher performance

Knowledge of the beat, says an editor at *Newsday,* guides the reporter in asking questions. The answers to these questions make it possible to write a complete story. The education reporter on her visits to schools bases her questions on the guidelines.

City Boy on the Farm Beat Editors want a reporter who can go out on a beat and take hold quickly. They do not have time to wait while the reporter learns at his or her pace. A veteran reporter recalls the problem he had the first time he was given a particular beat. A city boy, he was assigned by his newspaper in the southwest to cover agriculture. His first days on the job coincided with the county fair. The editor told him to do a story on the agricultural exhibits and the judging.

The reporter took careful notes of his editor's instructions and drove out to the fairgrounds. He located the exhibit area and looked at his instructions. He deciphered his handwriting carefully, but the best he could make out of one key word was "barrows." He had no idea what that meant. Must be wheelbarrows, he thought, some new kind of mechanical device for the farm.

His search for wheelbarrows got him nowhere. He asked a farm equipment salesman what kind of machinery a "barrow" is.

"Must mean harrows," the salesman replied. So the reporter took copious notes about harrows, but he had no idea how he would work that into the story since the salesman said that there hadn't been any new developments with the cultivator in a few years.

The reporter drifted over to the barns to get the results of the livestock judging. An official handed him several slips of paper with the results. At the top of the first slip was a single word, *Barrows.*

The reporter tossed away all the notes he had taken about harrows and made a beeline for the youngster whose barrows had taken the blue ribbon. (A barrow, for the information of city folks, is a castrated hog.)

The reporter should also know **how things work in the community.** The reporter should know about:

Know the
Community

The political process—how the mayor and city council are elected; who appoints the police chief; whether the mayor or the council is the source of power; how the judicial system works.

The social setting—who the influential people in town are; how people get along with each other; the racial, religious and ethnic makeup of the community.

The economics of the city—how people make a living; the major employers; who the power brokers are; the relationship of business and politics.

Press Law and History

Journalists also need to know press law, the history of the press and the special needs of their newspapers and stations. An understanding of the laws of libel and privacy helps reporters avoid troublesome legal suits and encourages them to be venturesome. (The law of the press is examined in Part 6.)

Understanding the history of the press opens the past to the journalist. Knowledge of those who helped to make the press a bastion of democracy gives the journalist courage when attacked, stamina when the routine approaches drudgery and inspiration when journalism is belittled. All these have been endured and overcome, the past tells us. Journalism has emerged as indispensable to a free society.

When Dan Rather was covering President Nixon for CBS television, the White House chief of staff accused him of inaccurate and biased reporting and tried to have him removed from the beat. Rather's tough coverage of the president antagonized Nixon and his aides. Rather's home in Washington was broken into. The only material taken was his files. Many people were convinced the theft was engineered by the same "White House plumbers" who broke into Democratic headquarters in Watergate and eventually proved the undoing of the Nixon administration.

Rather did not buckle. He knew what a journalist is supposed to do, and he persevered in his job.

Rather was described by one television critic as "the only person whom the network news system of journalism has produced since Edward R. Murrow who can conceivably supply the conscience missing from television news."

Murrow's name is prominent in any broadcast journalist's hall of fame. As a radio and television reporter, he took broadcast journalism from the routine reporting of official activities to the task of digging behind the pronouncements. His tradition remains powerful in broadcast journalism.

The Perpetual Student

The reporter never stops learning. He or she is always replenishing the storehouse of knowledge essential to the journalist.

"A good reporter is a student all his or her life," says Joseph Galloway Jr., a veteran foreign correspondent for the UPI. "Each new assignment demands a crash course in the theory and practice of yet another profession or system.

"From station house to courthouse, you have to find out what the official sitting in the chair knows, and you cannot recognize the truth from a position of blind ignorance."

Trying to accumulate knowledge of all kinds may seem to spread a person so thin he or she cannot learn much about a single subject, the subject that is the basis of the reporter's beat. It doesn't work that way. Information has a way of spreading, like ink on cloth. As the journalist finds out, often to his or her amazement, knowledge comes together.

There is a practical side to the matter. The journalist never knows when he or she will be called on to handle a story far off the beat. Most news staffs are shorthanded. The police reporter often has to cover an arraignment in court, and the courthouse reporter may double as an education reporter now and then. This is the rule on small newspapers. In radio and television, only the networks have beat reporters. Most broadcast reporters cover fires, arrests, political speeches and city council meetings.

The journalist also knows what is happening in the community, state, nation and the world.

Current Events

Technology has brought the far corners of the world closer together. The people of the world now live in one neighborhood, and the journalist who knows what goes on next door is better able to serve those in his or her home. Reporters keep up by moving among all kinds of people and seeking out diverse experiences. But experience is not enough. Journalists read—they read everything from novels, which are great teachers of writing, to geography and history, which help the reporter to understand the relationships of people, place and time.

"To be a good reporter, you must read," says Galloway, who worked his way up from a small daily in Texas to serve as the UPI's bureau manager in Moscow after combat correspondence in Vietnam.

"If in this electronic era you are not accustomed to it, then you must train yourself to gulp down the printed word with the same thirst of someone who has covered the last 15 miles of Death Valley on his belly.

"Read for your life.

"Read every newspaper that comes under your eye for style, for content, for ideas, for pleasure. And the books, my God, the books. The world of modern publishing has a 500-year headstart on you and is pulling further ahead every year.

"Never mind your transcript or your resume. Let me see your bookshelves at home and your library card."

Newspapers and Magazines Reporters keep current by reading newspapers and magazines. They read their own newspaper every day, watch the network news regularly and try to scan the regional newspapers and national newspapers, such as *The Christian Science Monitor, The Wall Street Journal* and *The New York Times.*

Ideas and information valuable to journalists can also be found in magazines. A reporter for a New Mexico newspaper wrote a prize-winning series of articles about drunk driving after reading an article in *The New Republic* about the cost of alcoholism in this country. Another reporter obtained a major local story after reading a magazine article about mining the ocean floor. His reporting revealed that a large local mining industry would be affected if international agreements were worked out to permit large-scale underwater mining.

Keeping up also involves learning what the tangled events of the nation and the world mean. This requires the journalist to seek out interpretative columns in newspapers and in magazines of opinion. Among the magazines journalists read are *The Atlantic, Commentary, Harper's, The Nation, National Review, The New Republic* and *The New Yorker.*

Favorite Authors

Books are helpful in two ways. Non-fiction books can aid the reporter in the accumulation of background information. Fiction has been an inspiration to many news writers, teaching style and the use of dialogue and description.

Some journalists find Ernest Hemingway a good model for their writing. As a young man, Hemingway was a reporter in Kansas City and the journalistic style can be seen in his fiction. The prose in his novels and short stories is cut to the bone. Hemingway was an avid reader. "Thank God for books," he wrote a friend. He most admired Mark Twain. Hemingway wrote:

"All modern American literature comes from one book by Mark Twain called Huckleberry Finn. . . . It's the best book we've had. All American writing comes from that. There was nothing before. There has been nothing as good since."

All writers have favorite authors. John McPhee of *The New Yorker* says he always reads Shakespeare with awe. There is nothing Shakespeare cannot do, he says. Dickens is a favorite of others who admire his feeling for the poor and defenseless, his powerful writing and his amazing output. Words tumbled from his pen.

A modern essayist many journalists respect is E. B. White, for years a writer for *The New Yorker.* Other American writers that journalists like and learn from are: Eugene O'Neill, the playwright; John Steinbeck, William Faulkner and F. Scott Fitzgerald, novelists; and John O'Hara, short story writer and novelist. Among the current generation of writers, journalists have learned from Gay Talese, Tom Wolfe, Hunter S. Thompson and the fiction writers John Updike, Norman Mailer, J. D. Salinger and Saul Bellow.

Some news writers have learned how to pace their stories from the mysteries of Raymond Chandler and Dashiell Hammett.

Know How to Use

City directory
Bartlett's Familiar Quotations
Reader's Guide to Periodical Literature
New York Times Index
Who's Who in America
Dictionary of American Biography
Current Biography

Journalists may go through their lives without reading Hemingway, Twain, **Reference Works**
The Wall Street Journal or *Harper's,* but they will be helpless without a mastery of basic references.

These references begin with the telephone directory and the dictionary. In cities where there is a city directory, this should be added to the list of essentials. The telephone directory is the authoritative reference for the spelling of names and for addresses and telephone numbers.

A number of good dictionaries are available, and some reporters carry a pocket size dictionary when they go on assignment out of town or have to send copy from outside the office. The dictionary is the authoritative source for correct spelling.

Editors may excuse a buried lead or a story that is disorganized. Even the best writers have their bad days. Editors accept this. But they snarl at misspellings. There is no excuse for an incorrectly spelled word. Worse, editors consider the reporter who consistently misspells to be indolent, too lazy to check the dictionary. The reporter who hasn't the energy to turn the pages of a dictionary doesn't belong on the news staff, editors have told poor spellers.

The city directory (fig. 4.1) is invaluable in checking information about individuals and businesses.

Every reporter should own the following:

Dictionary
World almanac
Grammar book
Atlas and road maps

The reporter also should have a copy of the newspaper or station stylebook, a guide to consistent usage in spelling, punctuation and grammar. (A stylebook is included in Appendix B. Use it.)

ALPHABETICAL DIRECTORY
WHITE PAGES

ⓗ **HEAD OF HOUSE**   ⓡ **RESIDENT (ROOMER)**

correct full name	Landon Edw G (Charlotte D) servmn B F Goodrich h1215 Oak Dr
occupation and employer	Landon Fred M (Mary E) supvr Reliance Elec h609 Norman Av
complete street address including apartment number	Landon Kenneth A (Carol L) clk First Natl Bk h1400 E Main St Apt 14
	Landon Kenneth A Jr studt r1400 E Main St Apt 14
student 18 years of age or older	Landon Virginia E (Wid Walter J) r1641 W 4th St
cross reference of surnames	Lane See Also Layne
	Lane Allen M (Joan M) (Allen's Bakery) h1234 Grand Blvd
	Lane Avenue Restaurant (Ernest G Long) 2106 L Lane Av
out-of-town resident employed in area	Lane James M (Betty B) brkmn Penn Central r Rt 1 Jefferson O
armed force member and branch of service	Lane Marvin L USA r1234 Grand Blvd
	Lane Robt B (Margt E) retd h1402 N High St
	Lane Walter M r1234 Grand Blvd
	Layne See Also Lane
wife's name and initial	Layne Agnes E Mrs v-pres Layne Co r2325 Eureka Rd
	Layne Albert M (Minnie B) slsmn Hoover Co h1919 Bellows Av
corporation showing officers and nature of business	Layne Co Inc Thos E Layne Pres Mrs Agnes E Layne V-Pres Edw T Layne Sec-Treas bldg contrs 100 N High St
	Layne Edw T (Diane E) sec-treas Layne Co h1407 Oakwood Dr
	Layne Ralph P (Gladys M) formn Layne Co h1687 Maple Dr
suburban designation	Layne Thos E (Agnes E) pres Layne Co h2325 Eureka Rd
	Leach See Also Leech
retiree	Leach Wm E USMC r1209 Ravenscroft Rd (EF)
	Lee Alf M (Celia J) retd r2106 Oakwood Dr
business partnership showing partners in parenthesis	Lee Bros (Louis J And Harry M Lee) plmbs 1513 Abbott St
	Lee Harry M (Karen L) (Lee Bros) h2023 Stone Rd
husband and wife employed	Lee Louis J (Martha B) (Lee Bros) h1616 Fulton St
	Lee Martha B Mrs ofc sec Lee Bros r1616 Fulton St
"r" resident (roomer)	Lee Minnie M Mrs h87 Eastview Dr
	Lee Muriel E (Wid Fred M) r810 LaForge St
"h" head of household	Lee Sterling T (Nadine S) mtcemn Eastview Apts h2020 Wilson St Apt 1
	Lee Thos W (Effie M) (Tom's Men's Wear) r Rt 2
owner of business showing name of business in parenthesis	**LEE'S PHARMACY (Lee A Shaw) Prescriptions Carefully Compounded, Complete Line Of Toiletries And Cosmetics, Fountain Service, Greeting Cards, 1705 N High St (21505) Tel 245-3312**
bold type denotes paid listing	
business firm showing name of owner in parenthesis	Leech See Also Leach
	Leech Doris E (Wid Donald L) tchr North High Sch h1323 W McLean St
widow indicating deceased husband's name	Leech Joseph B (Lucy V) slsmn Metropolitan Dept Store h824 Wilson St
	Leech Joseph B Jr studt r824 Wilson St
	Leech Marcia M clk Community Hosp r1323 W McLean St
unmarried and unemployed resident	Lewis Anne M Mrs clk County Hwy Dept r914 Wilson Av
	Lewis Ernest W studt r914 Wilson Av
more than one adult in household	Lewis Harold G (Anne M) mgr Cooper Paint Store h914 Wilson Av
	Lewis Robt B lab County Hwy Dept r1410 Union Hwy Rt 2
church showing name of pastor	Lewistown Methodist Church Rev John R Allen Pastor 515 Maple Valley Rd

Stories often require more detailed information than newspaper clips can provide. The reporter who wrote the series on drunk driving wanted to check what other work had been done on the subject.

First, he looked at *The New York Times Index,* a guide to all stories that have appeared in the *Times*. The index contains a brief description of the story and the date, which is used to consult the microfilms of the daily and Sunday editions of the newspaper. Many newspapers subscribe to the index and have the microfilms. This reporter's newspaper did not, so he used the material at the public library.

He also wanted to know whether any magazines had carried articles about the subject. He consulted the *Reader's Guide to Periodical Literature*. It contains summaries of articles from all the major magazines. Knowing the date the article appeared, the reporter can usually obtain the original article from the library. Some newspapers have access to data bases that contain stories from major newspapers and magazines.

Avoiding Bloopers   Some of the most embarrassing boners have been produced by writers who thought they were quoting a famous author correctly. For a front page picture about the return of spring weather to Chicago, a newspaper ran some lines of poetry. It attributed the lines to Shakespeare. They were actually from a poem by Elizabeth Barrett Browning. The writer would have avoided ever-lasting humiliation had he or she consulted *Bartlett's Familiar Quotations*.

For background on living Americans, *Who's Who in America* or *Current Biography* are indispensable. The *Dictionary of American Biography* contains biographical sketches of people of prominence who have died.

When All Else Fails

Sometimes an assignment is so complex or so unfamiliar to a reporter that he or she hardly knows where to begin. The clips on the subject prove to be too sketchy, and the references presume some knowledge of the subject. The reporter needs a crash course in the topic, but the assignment is due and there is no time for in-depth research.

This is what happened to Jan Wong on her second day as the marine news reporter for *The Gazette* in Montreal. She had been told to do the piece quickly because she would have another assignment the next day. She was adrift.

Wong did what reporters do in such circumstances. She turned to people who know what is going on, authoritative sources.

"I must have called 20 people," she says. "I called everyone I could find in the marine directory. People were very helpful, but I felt I was drowning."

The people she called were patient. Gradually, she learned enough from the sources to make sense of the clippings and to take advantage of other resource material in the newspaper library.

"I learned an awful lot in that one day about sources, phone books, the library and clippings," she says.

"I worked at the story until I was sure I had it right, and when I submitted it to the editor, he looked it over and approved it with minor changes."

"The very next day, I had to write a story about the acquisition of Canada's largest shipyard by Canada's largest petroleum company. That was just as hard as the previous day's story. I had no idea what was involved.

"But again, a million calls and reading the clips saved me. The story made the front page of the business section."

Wong has become more confident since her learning period, which all new reporters go through. She is a bit embarrassed by the questions she had to ask in her first days on the job though.

"I'm sure my sources thought I was asking dumb questions," she says.

For a reporter gathering information and background for a story, there are no dumb questions, and sources who have an interest in seeing that the stories about themselves and their concerns are reported accurately know this. They do, however, expect the reporter to learn the beat after a while.

Journalism is writing with a purpose. The news writer tells the reader, listener or viewer something definite, something specific.

Purposeful Writing

Every story that has been reprinted in this text was written with a specific news point in mind:

A fire killed 23 people.

Chester Jefferds should be released.

Many Chinese are fleeing a possible earthquake.

President Reagan signed a tax bill.

Obviously, each news writer had a particular news point in mind as he or she wrote the story. How did the writer get the idea? Did it suddenly occur to the writer in a burst of inspiration at the event, or did it come after thinking about the story at the typewriter or terminal?

The answer may be surprising. It is the key to good news writing. We will watch some reporters at work to find the answer.

How Reporters Work

Reporters develop an idea or framework for their stories before they do the reporting. This idea or framework guides their observations and determines the questions they ask their sources.

Looking Ahead

If a reporter's observations or the statements of sources point in a different direction, the reporter adopts a new idea for the story. Reporters follow the facts.

When the idea or framework is supported by facts, it becomes the lead of the story and the supporting facts become the body of the story.

Fred Zimmerman knew that he had a good story for his college newspaper. A teacher at nearby Emporia State College had been summarily fired. The teacher was young, bearded and had unconventional political and social ideas.

Give Direction to Your Reporting

"I raced all over Emporia, interviewed everybody I could think of," Zimmerman recalls. "I filled two notebooks.

"Then I sat down at a typewriter—where I found I didn't have the foggiest notion of what I wanted my story to look like."

Early in his newspaper career, Zimmerman learned about the reporting process that underlies news writing. He discovered that reporters begin to visualize their stories as soon as they are given an assignment, even before they begin their reporting. They are able to develop ideas for their stories from the nature of their assignments, from knowledge of their beats and from their general fund of information about current and past events. By the time a reporter sits down to write, he or she usually has a lead and most of the important themes for the story firmly in mind.

After his experience at the University of Kansas, Zimmerman went on to an extensive reporting career with *The Wall Street Journal,* which included covering the White House.

As a reporter, Zimmerman always had an idea or two in mind when he went out on a story. These initial ideas would give Zimmerman a framework from which to make his observations and to ask questions of his sources. If his observations or the answers to his questions indicated he was on the wrong track, he would ditch his original idea for one that better suited his findings.

The reporter who is assigned to interview a local banker about the steep rise in interest rates may banter with the banker about the weather for a few minutes. But the reporter knows exactly what he is there to find out: How has this increase affected local home building? Can people afford to build when they have to borrow at record-high interest rates?

The reporter who has been told to find out the reaction of university officials to a bare-bones budget just adopted by the state legislature knows what the focus of his story will be: What cuts will have to be made by the university? Will courses or programs have to be eliminated?

The reporting process is much like any other investigative process, whether it is conducted by a detective, a nuclear physicist or an astronomer. First, the investigator develops a theory. The investigator's observations will then either support or refute the theory. If it is not supported by the facts, the investigator develops a new theory.

In his story, *The Hound of the Baskervilles,* Arthur Conan Doyle described Sherlock Holmes sitting in seclusion in his Baker Street residence after learning of the murder of Sir Charles Baskerville. Holmes "weighed every particle of evidence, constructed alternative theories, balanced one against the other, and made up his mind as to which points were essential and which immaterial." Holmes needed a starting point for his inquiry, long before he visited the scene of the murder.

Unlike the master detective, the reporter cannot spend hours in seclusion mulling over particles of evidence. The reporter usually has only minutes to prepare. Remarkable as it may seem, reporters develop the ability to generate useful ideas under pressure.

The Sheriff Was a Criminal

Linda Kramer had done a number of spot news stories for the AP about Sheriff Richard Hongisto, who had an unusual approach to law enforcement. Now, she wanted to do a profile of the man who had once gone to jail on a contempt of court charge and was now in charge of the county jail in San Francisco.

Kramer said she first took time to "read years of clips on his doings and to interview people about him." She began to develop an idea for her story that crystallized when she spent a day walking around the county jail with him.

"His rapport with inmates and his pride in jail improvements showed the man in his element," she says. On her tour of the jail, she picked up quotations from the inmates and she made observations that buttressed the idea she had developed for her story of a new-style sheriff who was friendly with inmates and non-traditional in his approach to his work.

When she was ready to write, she knew how she wanted to begin her piece. She chose an illustration from her tour of the county jail that disclosed his easygoing relationship with the men behind bars:

SAN FRANCISCO (AP)—At a desk, he checks the .38-caliber revolver he wears in a holster at the waist of his dapper, pin-striped suit and enters the county prison for an inspection tour.

"Hey, sheriff," an inmate sings out, "we hear you was in jail."

"Yeah," sheriff Richard Hongisto replies, "you mind being seen with a criminal?"

Laughing, he saunters past. The inmate looks after him, admiringly. "He's different than most sheriffs," he says. "Sometimes I doubt if he's a sheriff at all."

Others have been similarly bemused since Hongisto, a former city cop, took office in 1971 and began shaking up traditional notions of how sheriffs should act.

Look again at how Berkley Hudson handled his story. When Chester Jefferds told Hudson about his lengthy confinement, Hudson developed an idea for the article: Jefferds was held without reason.

Hudson's early reporting was directed at seeing whether this theme was accurate. His reporting substantiated his original idea and it became the backbone of his piece.

When Bob Rose of *The Blade* of Toledo, Ohio, was told to interview the former president of the American Cancer Society, he had a framework in mind. He would ask about the major kinds of cancer and their causes. When he arrived at the hotel at which the doctor was staying, he happened to pick up a copy of the day's events at the hotel desk.

On the schedule was a room number for the R. J. Reynolds Tobacco Co. The company was using a suite to instruct workers involved in a local advertising campaign. Rose quickly changed his plans. He decided to focus on lung cancer and cigarettes. The story that emerged from his interviews is on the following page.

Rose sums up the process: "You know what you want to write and how you want to write it while you are doing the reporting." But whenever there is a hitch, be prepared to change plans.

Establishing the Framework

2 Men Worlds Apart On Smoking

Both In Toledo
To Promote Cause

By BOB ROSE
Blade Staff Writer

Two men who have a deep interest in whether Americans smoke cigarettes were in downtown Toledo Tuesday morning.

They were a floor apart in the Commodore Perry Motor Inn, but they were a world apart in what they said.

One was the immediate past president of the American Cancer Society. The other was a representative of the R.J. Reynolds Tobacco Co.

In an interview on the second floor, Dr. Lasalle Leffall, Jr. talked about what a killer lung cancer is.

In a talk to 14 temporary workers one floor above Dr. Leffall, the R.J. Reynolds man talked about handing out free samples of his firm's products.

Dr. Leffall, who until last week was president of the American Cancer Society, was eager to talk, to warn people about the more than 100 types of cancer.

The Reynolds man was not so eager. "The media is an entity that we do not deal with," he told his group in the smoke-filled room.

Dr. Leffall told about what he does when he meets a smoker. "If someone asks me if I mind if they smoke, I say, 'Yes, I do.' In doing that, I emphasize

— Blade Photo
DR. LASALLE LEFFALL
Eager to warn of cancer

that they are doing something dangerous to my health and dangerous to their health."

The Reynolds man recommended a different routine in handing out cigarettes:

"Are you a smoker or a nonsmoker? Regular or menthol? Full flavor or lights? Longs or regular length?"

Dr. Leffall would not like the euphemism, "full flavor." He'd say "High tar and nicotine."

And he would recommend neither high nor low tar. "The American Cancer Society believes that there is no safe cigarette, but that if you must smoke, the lower tar cigarettes cause fewer changes in your system that lead to lung cancer."

Dr. Leffall said he hopes smokers will kick the habit at least on Thursday, the date of the society's annual "great American smokeout."

Not willing to fight such an effort, the R.J. Reynolds man told his people to take the day off.

Dr. Leffall, who is chairman of the surgery department at Howard University's college of medicine in Washington, D.C., said the biggest opposition to the anti-smoking drive is the person who continues to smoke in spite of all the evidence that it can be deadly.

"We're not winning the battle," he said. "We're making progress, but we're not winning the battle."

The R.J. Reynolds man, who declined to give his name, said he has no quarrel with the American Cancer Society.

"They have their job to do," he said. "And we have our job to do."

The County Fair

When the Hamilton County Fair opened in Carthage, Ann Marie Laskiewicz of *The Cincinnati Post* had an idea for a story about the company that furnished the amusement rides. She had heard that the firm had been sued by people who claimed they were injured on the rides.

"I wanted to do a piece on how unsafe amusement rides are," she said. Then she started her reporting. She called a state agency that regulates portable amusement rides.

"I found out this company was one of the most safety-conscious in the state and that it had never been cited for an infraction of the state's safety regulations." Her whole approach changed.

"The evidence suggested another view. Instead of the original story, I wrote a story that detailed the difficulties for owners in keeping rides safe and the regulations that make Ohio one of the strictest states in the eyes of owners of portable amusement rides."

Back in Hong Kong

When Neal Robbins was told that a large group of Chinese had arrived near Hong Kong by boat, his immediate reaction was that they, like thousands before them, had fled China for political reasons. This was his tentative theme. When he arrived at the cove and found someone he could interview in Mandarin, his first question was an attempt to corroborate his idea:

"Did you leave China for political reasons?"

The answer was no, not for politics but from fear of an impending earthquake.

Because Robbins' original theme was not substantiated, he discarded it and worked on the theme that the source had given him. His questions were directed at gathering information about the departure of the Chinese because of their fear of an earthquake. He knew that this would be the lead.

By now, an important point should be clear. After it is substantiated, the idea or framework becomes the lead of the story, and the supporting evidence—the observations, quotations and research—makes up the body of the story. This is the reason we are spending so much time on this concept. An understanding of the process of news reporting makes writing the news story easier. All the professionals know this.

Remember: The idea or framework is always tentative or experimental. It is used to get the reporting moving. It is never used in the story unless the facts obtained in the reporting support the idea. The framework is only as strong as the beams and joints supplied by the reporting.

Working on Spot News Stories

Breaking news stories might seem an exception to this approach. After all, the reporter never knows what to expect on such a story. The fact is that most spot news stories do fit a pattern, and if the reporter knows the pattern, it is much easier to report and write the story. You could call this pattern the necessities or essentials of the story.

Look back at Lindy Washburn covering a fire for the AP. As soon as she heard that the fire in Bradley Beach was a big one, ideas came to mind and a framework developed. Her first question to the fire department dispatcher in Asbury Park was, "Any deaths?"

Washburn knew that an essential element of a fire story is the number of dead and injured. There are other necessities or essentials of a fire story, and if we look at Washburn's questions we can see what these essentials are. She asked the dispatcher for the address of the building, what it was being used for, when the first alarm had been received. She wanted to know the cause of the fire and what the building looked like. The answers to these questions would shape her story, Washburn knew.

The obituary writer also had a series of questions to ask because she also knew that the answers would be essential to her story: The name and identification of the deceased. Accomplishments. Survivors. Funeral plans.

These essentials can be established for various types of stories. Part 4 lists the basic ingredients or necessities for more than 20 types of stories.

No one can predict what turns and twists a news event will take. When the obituary writer learned that a memorial scholarship fund would be set up for Rose Harriett Allen, that was an unexpected element and it became an important part of her story. The standard questions she asked did start her on the way, and the answers provided considerable material for her story.

Be Prepared for Surprises

At a city council meeting with six items on the agenda, the reporter checks off those he or she thinks will be the most important. Our friend the city hall reporter in the first chapter was prepared for the zoning board appeal by the department store and had looked at the clips and taken notes. Since he knew that this would be an important item, he interviewed people for background before the meeting began.

The reporter was also prepared for surprises. He was alert to the possible introduction of some unexpected item, some sudden development that would make the department store material secondary.

The reporters and photographers accompanying President Reagan as he left the Hilton Hotel one afternoon were thrust suddenly into a totally unpredictable situation—an attempt on the president's life. In fact, one of the wire service photographers later said that he had the wrong lens on his camera for the kind of situation he unexpectedly faced.

Though surprised, the White House reporters did have a framework for such an event. Just as Lindy Washburn knew that for a fire story she had to include in her story certain essentials—number of dead and injured, location of fire and so on—the White House correspondents with President Reagan knew that the story of an assassination attempt had to be structured around two central facts: Was the president struck by any of the shots and if so, how badly was he injured?

In fact, in their haste to answer these questions, they were at first misled into presuming the president was unhurt. Although three others were hit and sent sprawling into the street, the president continued into his car. The reporters jumped to the conclusion that the shots had missed him. The truth was quickly put on the news wires when reporters learned that the president had been taken to a hospital emergency ward.

Trouble on the Playing Field

The reporter began to plan when he was told by his editor that he would have to cover an announcement by the president of the local college about the school's athletic program later that day. He checked the newspaper library for clippings about the college, and he learned that the school had been trying to improve its intercollegiate athletic program. It had recently hired a basketball coach from a Big Ten team. Another clipping described the activities of a booster club that was trying to raise money for the football team.

The reporter covered the college as a beat, but he was not acquainted with the athletic program since the newspaper's sports department handled that. He knew he had to amass a lot of information in a short time, so he called people on the campus whom he considered good sources.

A psychology professor who had once served on the college athletic board told him that there had been talk among the players of special favors and even of under-the-table payments. Perhaps the president was going to comment on these rumors. The reporter called the college public relations office and asked the head of the office, an old friend, about his theory. He hit his friend with the key question at once.

"Tom, is the president going to talk about the rumors of payoffs to players today?"

Tom was too old a hand to become flustered, and he laughed.

"I won't confirm that," he replied. A pause. "But I won't deny it either."

This last comment indicated to the reporter that he was on the right track. At the news conference later, he was not surprised to see the college athletic director and two coaches with the president. Nor was he surprised to hear the president deny the allegations about under-the-table payments. He had expected that.

No wonder that when the reporter returned to the office, he was able to write quickly and to have a comprehensive story ready for the early edition. He had been prepared with background information, and he had a concept of what the event might be—the denial of wrongdoing.

One of his most difficult tasks was selecting what to use. The president had spoken, and so had the college athletic director and two coaches. The reporters asked questions. Thousands of words and at least a dozen ideas had swirled through the room, but the reporter was told to hold his story to about 350 to 400 words. The reporter used his judgment to select material that was relevant to his central theme of the denial of illegal activities.

Selective Judgment

Walter Lippmann, one of the great figures in American journalism, once observed that there are too many facts for the reporter to gather and that even if a reporter could gather them all, nobody would want to read all of them. The nature of journalism, he said, is selective judgment.

News stories are capsulated reality. They can hold just so much—one, two, perhaps three major themes. The job of the journalist is to select the theme or themes that best describe and summarize the event. Since events are often disorganized and time is always short, the reporter seeks to get a jump, to have a headstart on fact gathering by developing an idea of the story as quickly as possible after receiving the assignment.

Then the task is to make the observations, ask the questions and do the background research that provides the details that make up the supporting or buttressing material that is placed in the body of the story.

Details Make the Difference

The word *framework* has been used to describe the ideas reporters have when they begin their reporting. The word is appropriate because these preconceptions are the possible scaffolding from which news writers hang the story's details. It is the details that make all stories unique. No two fires are the same, and no two basketball games are alike. The details make them different. Only solid reporting will dig up the details that make stories unique.

The following story came into the office of *Newsday* from one of its bureaus:

```
    PLAINVIEW--A 12-YEAR-OLD NEWSBOY DIED
WEDNESDAY AFTER HE WAS STRUCK BY A CAR WHILE
DELIVERING PAPERS BY BICYCLE, POLICE REPORTED.
    PHILIP GOLDSTEIN, OF 6 RAMSEY RD., LEFT HIS
HOME AT 5:48 AM AND RODE HIS BIKE TO OLD COUNTRY
ROAD, WHERE POLICE SAID HE CROSSED THE PATH OF A CAR
DRIVEN BY JOSEPH HAVRANCK, 53, OF 7 TIMON CT.,
HUNTINGTON. HAVRANCK, WHO WAS UNHURT AND WAS NOT
CHARGED IN THE INCIDENT, TOLD POLICE HIS CAR
SKIDDED ON WET PAVEMENT WHEN HE ATTEMPTED TO STOP.
    THE GOLDSTEIN BOY WAS TAKEN TO CENTRAL GENERAL
HOSPITAL, IN PLAINVIEW, AND WAS LATER TRANSFERRED
TO NASSAU COUNTY MEDICAL CENTER, EAST MEADOW, FOR
SURGERY. HE WAS PRONOUNCED DEAD AT 2:40 PM.
```

An editor at the newspaper sensed there was more to the story, and he asked a reporter to dig further. Here is the new story written by Jeff Sommer:

PLAINVIEW—By 9 AM Tuesday, doctors at Nassau County Medical Center told Gerald and Barbara Goldstein there was little chance that their 12½-year-old-son, Philip, injured in an auto accident, would live.

The Goldsteins thought of Philip's bar mitzvah—his ceremonial coming of age as a Jew—which was scheduled for tomorrow. And they thought of a close friend of Philip's who was to attend the bar mitzvah. The friend was confined to a Manhattan hospital, where he recently received a kidney transplant from his father.

"We decided immediately to donate his [Philip's] kidneys for transplants," Gerald Goldstein said yesterday, sitting in the sunlit yard of the family's Plainview home. "Philip was a very sensitive, compassionate boy. He was very concerned about his friend. We're sure he would've wanted it this way."

The seventh-grader, who hoped one day to attend Harvard Medical School and become a doctor, died Wednesday. And yesterday at Stony Brook University Hospital two young Suffolk residents who Philip never knew received his kidneys. Philip's parents say their son lives on, symbolically.

"I hope some day my wife and I will be able to break bread with these people," Goldstein, a Manhattan lawyer, said. "We have been told that they share our grief and we hope to be able to share their joy in this gift from our son."

The kidney recipients—Kathy Kuhl, 22, of 16 Reynolds St., Huntington Station, and Robert Tagliaferro, 23, of 15 Longacre Court, Port Jefferson—were in stable condition last night at the hospital, resting after their operations performed by a team of 30 medical personnel, headed by Dr. Felix Rapaport.

The recipients, who had been undergoing dialysis treatments because their own kidneys had failed, were chosen from among 60 people for whom the hospital is seeking kidneys, according to Winnie Mack, the hospital's transplant coordinator.

The tissues of Philip and of the recipients are so well-matched that the chance the operations will be successful is more than 75 percent—"as good as a parent-to-child transplant," Rapaport said at 4 PM yesterday, nearly 16 hours after the operations began.

Eva Kuhl, Kathy's mother, said last night she hoped the transplant would allow her daughter "to be independent . . . She's been through hell . . . If it doesn't take, she won't be any further back than when she started." Kathy has been a diabetic since age 12. She is legally blind but she "is a fighter," Mrs. Kuhl said.

The Goldsteins said they are not bitter about the accident, which occurred on Old Country Road while Philip was delivering newspapers on his bicycle. No charges were brought in the accident. "He was such a good, bright boy," Goldstein said. "But now all we can do is hope something good comes of it."

Rabbi Louis Stein had expected to see Philip bar mitzvahed tomorrow at Temple Beth Elohim in Old Bethpage. Instead, the rabbi was to officiate at the boy's funeral at 10:30 this morning at Gutterman's Funeral Home, Westbury. Burial was to be private.

"He was sure a fine, all-around boy," Stein said last night. "He was active in our congregation, in his school band, in the local soccer league. He had friends throughout the community . . . His parents have made a very thoughtful gesture—by extending life for others while their child has lost his own."

Good Reporting = Good Writing

Why is the second account so much better than the first? Only one reason— better reporting. This is an important lesson that journalists learn and relearn. It is what editors mean when they tell their reporters: You don't write writing; you write reporting.

No matter how proficient a news writer may become at manipulating words, there is only so much even the most gifted news writer can do unless he or she has the material to work with.

Listen to the latest songs; watch the television talk shows; recall the last movie you saw. When the material is ordinary and run-of-the-mill, not even the most gifted performer can make it come alive. Not every piece The Rolling Stones records becomes a gold record, and Bruce Springsteen cannot turn a so-so tune into a hit. Some of Michael Jackson's performances are flat. All of Johnny Carson's nimble wit cannot bring a dull guest to life. Even Burt Reynolds and Jane Fonda have appeared in some lemons they and their fans prefer to forget.

But given good material, the rock group, singer, talk show host, talented actor or actress can make you sit up and exclaim, "That's something." So can the news writer who makes perceptive observations and uses interesting quotations and relevant background.

Covering the Beat. Beat reporters do most of the reporting on newspapers. The police reporter handles motor vehicle accidents, usually from the police station, but will go to the scene of a serious accident. The political reporter usually has a specific beat—the statehouse, Congress, the White House. Other beats include education, cultural affairs, sports, the courts.
Bill Fitz-Patrick, The White House

On the Beat

The heart of news gathering for the newspaper is the beat. Reporters are placed at strategic locations where news usually develops, and these locations are designated as beats—the police station, the county courthouse, city hall, the federal courthouse. The reporters assigned to these locations are called beat reporters.

Some reporters have topical rather than geographical beats. While the police and the city hall reporters spend most of their time at one location (a geographical beat), the education reporter moves over a wide territory and examines a variety of topics to cover this beat (a topical beat). The education reporter visits grade schools, looks in on community colleges, attends school board sessions and even goes to the state capital to cover legislative sessions that deal with educational matters.

Other topical beats include medicine, science, labor, agriculture, politics and the performing arts. Sports is usually considered a topical beat since the sports reporter usually handles a variety of sports events.

Because radio and television stations have fewer reporters, almost all stations make general assignment reporters of their staffers. Only the networks and the largest stations have beat reporters.

Beat reporters are expected to have a thorough knowledge of the subject matter of their beats. This enables them to work quickly and accurately, whatever the deadline pressure. Their knowledge of how things work on their beats also enables reporters to do **enterprise** stories. These are the stories that are dug up by the reporter on his or her initiative. The coverage of a crime is a spot news story; the enterprising reporter delves into statistics to find that most crimes are committed between 9 p.m. and 2 a.m. by males in their teens and early twenties.

Persistence and good sources are essential. Persistence is necessary because news often has to be pried from reluctant sources. Good sources are essential because all news is not laid out for the taking like the goods at a flea market. Sources provide tips and ideas.

Authorities have a way of shrugging off reporters, and those who accept the turndowns often miss good stories. When Jan Wong of *The Gazette* heard that Mariners House, a residence for seamen, had been secretly sold, she wanted to do a story. There were two sides to the story, but she was able to obtain only the official version.

She needed to know the whole story to explain why the sale was made in such secrecy that even some members of the board of directors had no idea what was happening. Not even those who were living there had been told, not until the sale had been completed.

"I got yelled at and thrown out of the building when I tried to interview the manager," Wong says. "I was getting discouraged until that point, but that got me mad, and I regained my enthusiasm for the story.

"Every time someone tries to cover up something to keep it from me, I am even more determined to find it out, and I do.

"If you keep poking long enough, you'll find somebody willing to talk."

Good sources are indispensable to a reporter covering a beat. A reporter cannot be everywhere on the beat. In the courthouse, where hundreds of transactions occur daily, the reporter who has good sources will be called by a lawyer who is about to file a request for an injunction. Or the court clerk will leave a call for the reporter to check with her about the injunction.

In city hall, when a developer files a plan with the planning office for a large housing project, a secretary may spot the reporter in the hall and beckon him into the office to show him the plans.

A school principal will call the education reporter to invite the reporter to spend some time looking over a new reading program he intends to use in the fourth grade.

Sources are essential on every beat. When Dan Rather covered the White House for CBS News, he said he survived the highly competitive race for news by relying on his personal sources.

"They didn't pass me notes in invisible ink, but I made it my business to know them—secretaries, chauffeurs, elevator operators and waiters," Rather says. "They see a lot of papers and overhear conversations.

Know the Subject Matter

Persistence Pays Off

Develop Good Sources

Five Keys to Covering the News Beat

Know how things work. Know the laws that guide those in charge, the regulations and rules and the processes that underlie the daily activities of the agency, department or unit.

Cultivate sources. Good sources are not always those in charge. Secretaries, elevator operators, clerks, deputies, telephone operators can provide valuable information.

Keep abreast. Know what is happening in the field you are covering by reading good newspapers and specialized journals.

Be persistent. Dig beneath the handout and the press release. Do not take "no comment" for an answer from public officials.

Anticipate developments. Follow developments on the beat closely so that you have a sense of what logically must follow the present situation.

"I take them to dinner and keep them in cigars or whatever turns them on."

Courtesy, a cheerful word or two and personal interest often are enough to make friends of potential sources. People on the fringes like to be thought to be close to those in power and to feel they are a part of important activities. They do this by feeding information to journalists.

Sources are also essential for background stories. Every reporter has friends who can be counted on to explain the complexities of certain stories. When Marcia Chambers covered the criminal courts for *The New York Times,* she knew a few judges who could explain to her the fine points of the law, and when she moved on to cover education she developed sources on the school board who helped her penetrate the wall of silence of the bureaucracy.

Chambers knew that although her readers were well informed, they needed guidance, and she often wrote background stories explaining why plea bargaining is essential to the judicial system and how administrative hiring policies caused severe strains within the educational system. For these and some of her spot news stories, she had the help of knowledgeable sources.

Beat reporters face two dangers in dealing with sources: writing for them and getting too close to them. Sometimes, a reporter will become too technical in writing on a specific topic. The sources will understand, but the average reader will be lost. Since reporters are in frequent touch with their sources and can only visualize their readers and listeners, the tendency often is to write for the sources.

A more insidious danger is becoming too close to sources, so close that the reporter may be soft on his or her friends. A reporter may not want to risk losing a good source by writing a tough story. A certain distance must always be maintained between the reporter and a source.

Once a reporter has shown that he or she understands the way organizations, agencies and branches of government work in the community, the reporter may be given the go-ahead to do investigative reporting.

Investigative Reporting

Investigative reporters seek to uncover material that people want to hide. Some of the activities are illegal, and some are legal but abusive. By abusive, we mean that the practices in some way hurt people or deny them their rights.

In recent years, investigative reporters have turned their attention to the affairs of private industry and organizations. *The Charlotte Observer* won a Pulitzer Prize for meritorious public service for a series on the effects of unsafe and unsanitary conditions in southern textile mills. The series was titled "Brown Lung—a Case of Deadly Neglect." The Gannett News Service was awarded the prize for exposing the activities of a charity run by a Catholic order, the Pauline Fathers.

Investigative reporting is based on digging, the scrutiny of records, documents and files. To do this, these reporters have to know their way through the mazes of officialdom. They also rely on sources for tips and inside information. Good sources enabled two young reporters, Bob Woodward and Carl Bernstein, to expose the cover-up of Watergate for *The Washington Post*. These sources provided the reporters with enough information for them to reveal the fact that the so-called Watergate burglary was part of a plan by the Nixon administration to win re-election.

Although some reporters are assigned investigative reporting as a special beat, all reporters are expected to dig out information on their beats. The reporter who is content to accept handouts and press releases and who relies on the assertions of authorities without checking them fails to inform readers and listeners of the full dimension of his or her beat. Such a reporter can never hope to do investigative reporting.

Editors not only want reporters who can dig out the truth beneath a layer of public relations releases, they want reporters who can do interpretative reporting and writing.

Interpretative Stories

The reporter who knows his or her beat, who has good sources and who can put current events in context is often asked to write interpretative pieces. These articles, sometimes in the form of columns, sometimes called news analyses, give the **causes** and **consequences** of events.

For instance, a writer might try to show how a city ordinance came into existence—the groups that pushed for it, the organizations that opposed it and lost and the reasons for their positions. The writer will also describe the effect of the new ordinance.

The term **interpretative reporting** means that the writer seeks to find the meaning of the event. This is not editorial writing. Editorial writers tell readers or listeners that something is good or bad. That is, they make value judgments. The interpretative news writer puts the event in its context.

By putting an event in context, we mean that the interpretative writer's job is to place the news event in the stream of cause and effect. An event that is isolated for a news story is plucked from a larger cycle or stream of related events. The interpretative story puts the news event into this cycle or stream.

A city council decision to allow a developer to build homes on a small tract near the city limits may affect traffic, school population and utility services in the area. The action can be shown to be the consequence of population pressure, people in the inner city wanting to move out of older homes into newer houses.

Aids and Impediments to Reporting

In our discussion of reporting, we have stressed the logical, thoughtful approach to reporting. We have talked about reporters adopting tentative ideas, then going out on the story to find supporting material. If the material is not there, the reporter adopts another idea. This approach is useful for reporters because it helps them function despite the huge array of facts they must contend with in a limited time.

All of this makes the reporter seem cool and detached, dispassionately jotting down data from his or her observations, a scientist tracking electrons. Most journalists don't work that way. Like everyone else, they have feelings, attitudes and personal values. No one is exempt from these emotions, prejudices and biases. Some are positive and can reinforce good journalism.

Moral Indignation

The persistent underlying sentiment of many investigative reporters is a sense of moral indignation. They want to make the world a better place in which to live, and they cannot abide the misuse and abuse of wealth and power that makes life painful and arduous for so many. Not content with official statements, versions or excuses, reporters blessed—or afflicted—with moral indignation get things done. Look at what radio station WIND in Chicago did.

Accidents in big cities are frequent, so frequent they are not given much attention by the media. But this accident bothered the staff of the radio station. It involved a woman and her two children.

Their car had stalled on the Dan Ryan Expressway. The three waited almost two hours as thousands of cars passed, including several police cars. No one offered to help.

Finally, the mother and her 12-year-old son went to seek assistance. They left the other son, a paraplegic, behind in the car. But they never found help. As the older son watched from the car, his mother and brother were struck by an oncoming car and were killed.

The deaths angered a staff member of WIND. The stories and editorials the station carried revealed the need for a communications system on the 125 miles of expressway around Chicago. During the campaign, people called in with horror stories of their own. One man said his son had been driving on the Eisenhower Expressway when his windshield was shot out by a passing motorist.

"The car swerved, banged into the median and threw the boy out of the car," the station quoted the father as saying. "He lay by the side of the damaged car for nearly an hour before help came."

The campaign by WIND won a Sigma Delta Chi Award for public service by a radio station.

Although emotional involvement can lead to good stories, some feelings and attitudes can distort observations and can blind the reporter to some kinds of stories.

As we have seen, news reporting and writing is the art of selection. Reporters choose what they want to observe, and then they select from those observations the elements they want to put into their stories. The reporter who believes that the poor bring about their own misery would not have recognized the story that Mary Ann Giordano saw in the plight of a family living in a tenement without heat or water.

Personal Biases

The reporter who grew up in a home with liberal political views may be convinced that Republicans are well-to-do people whose philosophy is built on keeping taxes low so they can have more. The reporter may see all Republican candidates in this mold.

The reporter who was convinced as a college freshman that conservative values are the only valid political concepts may conclude that liberals—especially the kind found in the big cities—believe in a tax-and-spend theory of government that will bankrupt the nation.

If these reporters were assigned to cover politics, their stereotyped beliefs would produce slanted stories.

Unquestionably, many reporters do have strong political views, but they hold them in check. They realize that the complexities of life cannot be reduced to the simplistic absolutes of our young liberal and conservative.

Some reporters are unaware of their biases, of the distorted pictures they carry around with them. We all grew up with images of things and people we like and dislike, of ideas we find compatible and those we consider repulsive. Our parents, our church or synagogue, our friends, our schools, our favorite television programs—all these and more influence us to see the world in certain ways. Journalists have these pictures, too, and sometimes they can distort a journalist's perceptions.

Useless Baggage

The aspiring journalist should remember that no one, not even those whose credo calls for an open mind, compassion and a commitment to democratic values, is exempt from the prejudices of time and place.

Developing an open mind requires jettisoning some customs, beliefs and ideas that may go back to childhood: A parent's prejudice against Jews and Italians, a teacher's indifference to the slow learner, friends' hostility to blacks and Puerto Ricans, a church's intolerance of freethinkers.

One of the most difficult tasks young journalists face in freeing themselves from the weight of the past is establishing a proper attitude toward authority. The youngster is taught to respect and abide by authority—parents, teachers, experts. As children, we grew up doing what others told us to do.

Then there was the period of rebellion. If father is so smart, why can't he meet his bills? If the politicians are so wise, why did they get us involved in the disaster in Vietnam? As for teachers, every high school and college student has a favorite tale that proves teachers are hopeless cases. As someone said, "Those who can, do. Those who can't, teach."

There is a middle road. The journalist must be skeptical of authority. An assertion is not necessarily true simply because someone in power or an expert said so. The journalist's task is to check statements, claims and declarations, no matter how authoritative the source.

Skepticism is not cynicism. It makes no sense to turn away from someone in authority merely because the person is an expert or has a title. An open mind, a broad outlook, association with all kinds of people and the realization that although people have much in common they are different—these are useful to counter the pictures in our heads that can distort reality.

Some Realities

Of course, one of the realities of journalism is that it is a commercial enterprise and that some editors and publishers are more concerned with the bottom line on a ledger sheet than with complete coverage of the news. Some reporters, too, have priorities that are more self-serving than public spirited.

The young journalist preparing for a career should understand this and more: Much of the journalism of conscience is unrewarded by positive change. People often ignore what to the journalist is an obvious wrong. They will return incompetents, sometimes even a criminal, to office. They will tolerate an educational or a criminal justice system that the journalist has shown to be a failure.

An awareness of some of the realities of journalism, veteran journalists say, will prevent disillusionment. But newsroom politics, publisher greed and the indifference of the public have never kept the persevering journalist from fulfilling what he or she considers an obligation to seek out and to tell truths.

We are now ready for the next step, the arrangement of the reporter's notes into an accurate and interesting written account.

Writing

Planning the Story

Planning precedes writing. The news writer decides before writing whether the story will be a straight news article or a feature, how long it will be, the kind of lead that will be used and the structure of the story.

Looking Ahead

The lead for the news story and the feature story contains the most important aspect of the event, and the body includes supporting facts. These supporting or buttressing facts are quotations, anecdotes, incidents and significant details. The lead is usually placed in the first paragraph of the straight news story. For the feature story a delayed lead usually is used. The lead can be placed in any of the first four paragraphs of the story.

The basic sentence structure for all news stories is S-V-O: the subject, followed closely by the verb and then the object of the verb.

The city editor of a California newspaper who was known for his nasty temper and quick judgments would stride through the newsroom like the captain of a man-of-war. Although he did not whip the poor devils under his command, he had a steely eye and a rasping voice that made his victims squirm.

George was the last, or one of the last, of the old-fashioned city editors who believed that might made right.

One day during a midafternoon stroll after the final edition had been put to bed, he spotted a new reporter sitting at his desk and staring at the ceiling. The reporter had a piece of blank copy paper in his typewriter.

"What do you think you're doing?" George snarled at the reporter.

"Thinking, George," the reporter answered.

"You're paid to write, not think," the city editor shot back.

"George, you can't write if you can't think," said the reporter, and he resumed his communion with the newsroom ceiling.

For the first time in the memory of the oldest reporter on the staff, George had no reply. His mouth opened, shut, and he walked back to his desk without a word. He sat down and stared out a window. George had come across something so true, so profound—for him—that he ceased his newsroom wanderings thereafter.

First Steps

The reporter knew what he was talking about. Clear thinking underlies clear news writing. The reporter must have a plan before he or she starts to write. To begin with, the reporter has to decide:

Is this a feature or a straight news story?

If a feature, what anecdote or illustration will best begin the story?

If a straight news story, what is the major fact I must put into the lead, and what are the secondary or less important facts?

How entertaining or important is the event? How long should the story be?

How do I structure the story? What goes where?

Some stories require considerable planning, while others seem to write themselves. With experience, the planning period becomes shorter. But for the beginner, it takes time to plan every story.

Feature or News Story?

A story takes its form from its purpose. If the purpose is to tell people quickly about an important event, then the reporter writes a spot news story. If the purpose is to entertain, the reporter writes a feature story. Each type of story has a different kind of lead and structure.

The news story wastes no time in getting to the point. The main element—the most important item—is in the lead. The feature story may begin leisurely and get to the point of the story after three or four paragraphs.

Let's imagine that you have been told about a fire that damaged a student hangout, the Pork Parlor, located near the campus. You are to write a story for class. You gather information from the fire department and the owner. Here is the story you write:

```
    A favorite student dining spot, the Pork Parlor, at 150
College Lane, was damaged today by a fire that started in
the kitchen.
    The fire destroyed the kitchen and caused some damage
in the dining area. Fire department officials said fat in
a frying pan caught fire at around 6:30 a.m.
    The fire was under control in about 15 minutes, an
official said. No one was hurt.
    Damage was estimated at $25,000. The owner, Steve
Poulton, said insurance covered the loss. He said he
plans to re-open in three weeks.
```

This is a straightforward news story. But suppose you also heard that one of the part-time employees, a college student, lost something valuable in the fire. A fire department official says he recalls her looking through some charred equipment in the kitchen. He thinks he heard her ask about a manuscript she had left there. You call Poulton and learn her name, Karen Yount.

You manage to reach her and she says that she had just finished a term paper for her English class and had put it with her books in a cabinet in a corner of the kitchen when she went to work. The paper was to be the basis of her grade in the course. She is an English major and needs the course credit to graduate. But now. . . . Her voice trails off.

Now what do you do? Do you still write a straight news story and add Karen's loss to the piece with this paragraph at the end:

> But Karen Yount, a college senior, has no insurance for her loss. Her term paper for an English class was destroyed by the fire. She had put it in the kitchen when she went to work this morning at the Pork Parlor.

That's not a bad ending to the story. But would it have made a better beginning? Should Karen's misfortune have been put into the lead of a straight news story? No, that would have been overplaying her loss, which obviously has less impact on the community than the damage to the restaurant.

On the other hand, the fire was not serious. No one was hurt and $25,000 in damage is not large. As fires go, it is routine. What makes it different from other fires is Yount's loss.

All this reasoning could lead you to conclude that the fire might make a better news-feature story than a straight news account. You call Yount and obtain more information, and you write:

> For three months, Karen Yount spent most of her evenings in the library and over a typewriter.
>
> A college senior, she was writing a term paper on the novelist George Eliot. It was to be the basis of her grade in the class and, she hoped, strong enough to impress the admissions committee at the University of Michigan, where she hopes to do graduate work.
>
> But her paper, and perhaps her grade and her hopes, went up in flames this morning.
>
> A fire at the Pork Parlor at 150 College Lane, where Yount works, destroyed the kitchen. Yount had put her term paper and books in a corner of the kitchen. She had not made a copy of her paper.
>
> The fire broke out at. . . .

Washing Up. A student organization has collected $450 for a Toys for Tots fund drive in a one-day car-washing operation on campus.
Pepperdine University

Feature or Straight News Story?

Exhibition. A photography show of small-town America will be mounted next month in the local art museum. Some of the nation's prominent photographers will be represented in the exhibition with pictures taken in the past and present, a press release states. This photograph, taken in March 1942, is of Judith Gap, Mont. The photographer is John Vachon of the Farm Security Administration staff of photographers.
John Vachon, Courtesy of the Library of Congress

Burnout. Two people were injured and their hiking gear and personal belongings were destroyed in this fire on the freeway after their car was struck from behind.
Alex Robertson, Pepperdine University

Coming Event. Gordon Lightfoot's press agent gives you a photograph and information about the performer's local appearance next month.

Trailer Park. A real estate developer announces that his firm has started construction of a large trailer park outside town. Water lines are being laid. The developer says he bought the range land for $100,000 and plans "a large-scale park."
Mike McClure

Most editors would prefer this account, a feature version of the story, to the straight news account.

Leads to news stories need not be dull. When the city of Miami was unable to find enough lifeguards to guard its pools, it announced that pools would close at 5 p.m. instead of at 8 o'clock for the summer. What kind of lead do you prefer for the story?

Straight News Lead

City officials said today Miami's public pools will close at 5 p.m. this summer instead of at 8 p.m. because of a shortage of lifeguards.

News Feature Lead

Miamians seeking cool, wet relief on hot summer evenings won't find it this year at the city's public pools. For the first time in years, they are closing at 5 p.m.

It isn't a tight budget that is forcing the pools, traditionally open until 8 p.m., to close early in this summer of high inner-city unemployment. It's precisely the opposite.

The city can't hire enough certified lifeguards to staff them, said Brian Finnicum. . . .

The second lead was used by *The Miami Herald*.

Deciding whether the story should be a news or feature story is an exercise in judgment. The question for the reporter to decide is whether the event is significant or unusual. This takes us back to the news determinants we discussed in chapter 3. In the case of the Pork Parlor fire, there was little impact on large numbers of people, and Yount's story was unusual. So on balance, the event is given a feature treatment. Had someone been hurt or killed in the fire or had it destroyed the restaurant, the story would be too serious to make into a feature.

Length

Before a story can be written, the writer has to know how long it will be. Just as a tailor cuts a suit or a coat to measure, so a news writer writes to measurements. On large newspapers, the city editor instructs the reporter on length after hearing the reporter's summary of the story. On smaller newspapers, the reporter usually is expected to use his or her judgment.

Length is determined by importance and reader interest. An important story merits more space than a less important story. Obviously. Sometimes, however, a story that interests readers but has little importance is given plenty of space.

The marine news section of *The Gazette* is directed at commercial and business interests and its front page usually emphasizes straight news. But Jan Wong's feature story about an old salt who builds miniature ships in bottles was so interesting it was given the full page.

Here is how Wong began her story:

George McKee adjusts his spectacles and carefully eases a miniature clipper ship through the neck of an empty Dewar's whisky bottle.

"It takes a strong gale to push it in," he says with a wink and a trace of his native Irish brogue.

At 79, McKee is a retired seaman with 51 years of sailing under his belt. From "old salts" in the days of steampower when he was a youth on the "Australian run," McKee learned how to fill empty bottles with ships.

"When we got to Australia, we used to sell them for a bottle of beer," he says with a chuckle.

McKee still has the ruddy skin of a sailor—and the deep blue tattoos on his arms to prove it. Although he needs a hearing aid for each ear, his hands are steady. He holds them out for a visitor's scrutiny. "Not bad for an old man," he says proudly.

Nowadays, McKee spends long hours in his immaculate basement workshop, redolent with glue and paint fumes that exacerbate his emphysema.

Standards Vary   There are no absolute guidelines for the length of a story. Some newspapers have a policy of keeping everything short in an attempt to have as many different items as possible, much like the half-hour newscast that includes as many as 20 news stories. A reporter on such a newspaper is conscious of brevity and generally will write short, crisp stories. Some editors oppose such rules.

"I'm damned tired of journalism seminars that say you can tell the second coming of Christ in 700 words," says Eugene L. Roberts, the executive editor of *The Philadelphia Inquirer*. "Our task as editors is to make our newspapers more meaningful and relevant and readable for our readers, and sometimes the best way to do that is short, and sometimes it is long.

"Sometimes it is simple, and sometimes it is complex. Just like American society. Just like the cities and counties we live in. Just like life itself which, after all, is what we are supposed to be covering."

Roberts says that when the *Inquirer* ran 25,000 words over 10 pages on an accident at a nearby nuclear reactor, the readers were pleased. "And it was probably as well read as anything we've ever printed," Roberts said.

After the reporter determines whether the story will be a feature or a straight news story and estimates the length of the story, the reporter can then plan the lead and the story structure.

Old Salt. George McKee painstakingly constructs ship miniatures in bottles.
Jean Pierre Rivest, *The Gazette*

Lead and Structure

If the story is to be a feature, the news writer can use a delayed lead, the kind of lead used in the second version of the Pork Parlor fire story. A delayed lead means that the writer holds off, or delays, telling the reader the theme. The theme in the featurized version of the fire—the actual lead to the story—is in the third and the fourth paragraphs of the feature version.

If the story is a straight news piece, as the first version was, then a direct lead is put on the piece. It moves directly to the point of the event in the first paragraph.

We will examine delayed and direct leads in greater detail in chapter 8. These are the only two types of leads you need to know.

The story's intent or purpose also determines the structure of the piece. The feature story can move in a relaxed manner, allowing the reader or listener to savor the situation or the fun the writer is having with the subject.

The straight news story is tightly structured. Beginning with the direct lead, it moves methodically from point to point. If the news story has one major element, the lead contains that element and the body of the story is devoted to explaining, buttressing, elaborating that single element.

If the news story has one major element and some secondary material, the secondary material is put into the body as soon as the reporter has finished elaborating the major element:

Lead: Theme A
Body: More on theme A
Secondary material

We will read more about the structure of the story in chapter 7.

These essentials of the news writer's trade may seem rigid or mechanical. But every trade or profession has forms, outlines and directions that the craftsman or practitioner follows. A carpenter could not lay the floor, the roofer put on the shingles or the electrician lay out the wiring of a new house without strict attention to right angles, slope, voltage and the other essentials that underlie all construction. There are rudiments all craftsmen follow.

It is what is done with these rudiments, how they are used, that makes an A-frame house so different from a ranch house, the paintings of Vermeer differ from those of Rembrandt, and the music of the Stones unlike that of The Police.

Sometimes, a new form comes along that becomes the basis of a new line of creative expression. Bach, Beethoven and Wagner revolutionized classical music in their time, as the Impressionists and Picasso revolutionized painting. Jazz, be-bop, rhythm and blues and rock were new forms of popular music. The delayed lead was this type of innovation for journalism.

The delayed lead was born of the need to tell unusual stories in an interesting manner. The direct lead seemed to take the fun out of storytelling and reading. The delayed lead had to do battle against one of the oldest writing forms in journalism, the inverted pyramid.

For generations, beginners in journalism were told to structure all news stories in the form of an inverted pyramid. This means that all the important material is placed high up in the story, preferably in the lead, and the less important material is inserted as the story moves on. This type of story can be diagrammed as shown in figure 6.1.

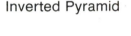

Inverted Pyramid

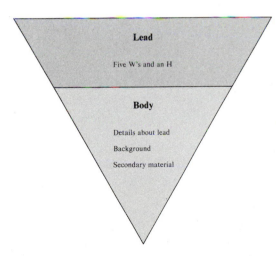

Figure 6.1 The inverted pyramid is an established and proven method, which can be used to organize nearly all news stories.

Five *W*'s and an *H*   To include as much information as possible in the lead, reporters were told to follow the rule of the "Five *W*'s and an *H*." All events—activities, speeches, interviews—could be reduced to this formula:

Who   Where
What   Why
When   How

The formula works well enough, as we can see in these leads:

Gov. Bernard Carberry will speak tomorrow at 7:30 p.m. in the Civic Auditorium on methods of reducing the number of violent crimes in the state, which increased 22 percent last year over the previous year.

John Whitticomb, 22, of Hampton, a college senior, was seriously injured last night when the motorcycle he was driving struck a tree after he lost control of the vehicle on a section of Highway 28 that had recently been damaged by a washout.

These leads hold so much information that they can just about stand alone as the entire story. For brief items, such as these, the principle of the Five *W*'s and an *H* works well. On longer or more complex stories, the length of the lead repels rather than attracts readers. Few news writers rely on the Five *W*'s and an *H* anymore as the basis of the lead, and no one in a newsroom talks about it. But the questions are helpful in directing the new writer to the key elements in a story.

Every news lead contains at least one of the Five W's and an H, and the story should contain answers to all of them, if possible. News writers who ignore them can look silly. *The Washington Post's* ombudsman, Sam Zagoria, called attention to some flagrant forgetfulness by *Post* reporters. A long article about a candidate's winning campaign had a lot of information but never identified her as a Republican. **Who** includes not only the person's name but some identifying characteristics.

Another piece ignored **Where:** A story about the construction of a University of Virginia hospital had plenty of detail but lacked the location. Another story described a home fire in great detail "but gave no information about who lived there," Zagoria wrote.

In analyzing a news event, you may want to list on a sheet of copy paper the six questions and then answer them with phrases or sentences taken from your notes. These answers should give you the important aspects of the story.

It's simpler, however, to remember our two basic news writing questions from chapter 3:

Who said or did what?
What happened?

The truth is that the Five *W*'s and an *H* and the inverted pyramid are survivors of a past necessity. When news stories that originated out of town were sent to the home office they were transmitted by telegraph, an expensive and sometimes undependable process. Reporters crammed as much information as possible into the first part of their stories, and that's often how the stories would appear in print.

In the newsroom, layout was at best a good guess. Stories were frequently too long for the space allocated, and extra type was removed by workers in the back shop. They were instructed to remove paragraphs from the bottom, where the less important material had been put. Hence, the inverted pyramid. Reporters put everything important high in their pieces, or they ran the risk of seeing the climax tossed into the lead pot.

Nowadays, the inverted pyramid survives for most straight news stories, since we know that not all readers read the whole story. But for features it is ignored. Many features have a punch line or climax at the end. Editors make sure that there is space for these stories.

Storytelling

Even some news stories ignore the inverted pyramid. Pieces that take a delayed lead—and increasingly newspapers are putting delayed leads on news stories—violate the principle of the inverted pyramid. Occasionally, the writer of a news story will deliberately save the climax for the ending, as storytellers do. The storytelling form is diagrammed in figure 6.2 on the next page.

Summing Up

We have discussed three ways to handle stories—writing a direct lead on a spot news story, writing a delayed lead on a feature story, and taking the storyteller's approach. Here are examples of each type of story:

The **spot news story,** which almost always takes a direct lead, includes the lead in the first paragraph:

A Bath County couple has filed a $200,000 suit in Rowan County Circuit Court against St. Claire Medical Center relating to the hospital's switching of their baby with a Morehead couple's son last year.

—*Morehead* (Ky.) *News*

When the situation lends itself to a more relaxed approach, we can use the **delayed lead.** The lead can be placed anywhere in the first four paragraphs:

> When Helen Alexander shipped her Nijinsky colt to the Fasig-Tipton sales last week, she thought he might bring $300,000.
>
> He was a good-looking colt with a pedigree, and capable of selling for that kind of price. But she cautioned herself not to get her hopes too high. "I've always had this feeling," she said, "that thinking too big can put the jinx on a horse."
>
> **Lead** But when the colt brought $1.3 million last night in the closing session of the two-day auction, Alexander couldn't believe her good fortune.
>
> "I'm in seventh heaven; I'm in another world," Alexander, the 29-year-old mistress of King Ranch, was saying after the colt shattered all yearling records for the Kentucky division of the sales company. . . .
>
> —*Lexington Herald-Leader*

This news story would interest many people in Kentucky. Yet it has a delayed lead. How does the writer know when to put the main theme in the first paragraph—making it a direct lead—and when to put the main idea in the third paragraph as Maryjean Wall did—making it a delayed lead? Judgment.

The news writer learns that a spot news story of considerable impact or consequence almost always takes a direct news lead. A feature story and a news story of less significance can take a delayed lead.

The **storytelling** approach was used by a *Wall Street Journal* reporter to describe the accuracy of the predictions of a market analyst whose forecasts were used by many people in determining whether to buy or sell their holdings. The reporter began his story by saying that the analyst had predicted the stock market would go down 16 points on Wednesday. Readers wonder what happened But the writer does not say—not until the 11th and last paragraph of the story. (See chapter 9, "Cloudy Crystal Ball," p. 208.)

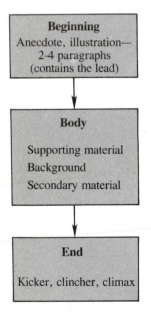

Beginning
Anecdote, illustration—
2-4 paragraphs
(contains the lead)

Body

Supporting material
Background
Secondary material

End

Kicker, clincher, climax

Figure 6.2 This structure follows the style of storytellers, saving the kicker or climax for the end of the story.

Facts, Facts, Facts

The news story and feature are only as convincing as the supporting material the reporter includes. One way of describing both news stories and features is to say that each consists of a statement (the lead) and the proof (the body of the story). A summary of the most important fact or facts goes into the lead, and the rest of the story includes the material that supports and buttresses the lead and secondary themes.

A reporter who has decided on the lead and is ready to write will flip through his or her note pad and circle or check all the facts that pertain to the lead element. These facts provide the main stem of the story. The reporter who sticks to this plan will prevent the story from becoming disorganized or losing focus.

This advice is important. Think about it. Ninety percent of the problems news writers have with their copy consist of either putting the wrong lead on stories or disorganization. By disorganization, we mean that the story does not move logically from fact to fact.

In looking through their notes for buttressing and supporting facts, news writers are on the prowl for quotations, anecdotes and illustrations or examples. They add zest to the story.

One of the best buttressing facts is the quote. It not only supports the lead with a statement by the main character or another involved in the event, but it puts the human element into the story.

Good Quotes Up High

Quotes help us to visualize the people involved. They add drama and excitement to a story. Look at this quotation from an auto worker recalling a sit-down strike during the period in the 1930s when labor was trying to win recognition for its unions:

> We were nervous and we didn't know we could do it. Those machines had kept going as long as we could remember. When we finally pulled the switch and there was some quiet, I finally remembered something . . . that I was a human being, that I could stop those machines, that I was *better* than those machines anytime.

After Jeff Klinkenberg had written his story about Old Hitler for *The St. Petersburg Times,* Roy Peter Clark of the Poynter Institute for Media Studies talked to him about the story.

"Is it a general method of yours to organize your story around quotations you've collected?" Clark asked.

Klinkenberg replied: "Yes. One of the things I've done when I've had the time: I'll type them out, and then I'll assign different values to different quotes. My best quotes I'll try to get up high in the story and then proceed in kind of descending order.

"I'll try to save a couple of good ones for the end. I think it's a good way to organize a story."

In an interview with Howell Raines, who went from *The St. Petersburg Times* to the Washington bureau of *The New York Times,* Clark asked about Raines's use of quotations.

Raines answered: "In political profiles, quotes serve two purposes, I think: one, they are the blocks of fact that you deal with. I want to have the actual words spoken by the man so there is no dispute about what he said or meant.

I don't paraphrase much. I try to use direct quotes or fragments of quotes rather than my own language. Because you cannot get around the authority of a quote.

"And, two, quotation establishes character. Quotes make a politician assume a personality in a story. One of the best political reporters I know is a good reporter in the sense of gathering information. But he writes without quotes, so his copy is dead."

When Klinkenberg was organizing his story, he did two things after he typed his notes.

He underlined his "best quotes," he said, and he broke up the story "into anecdotes." In addition to looking for good quotes, then, reporters search their notes and their memories for the anecdotes and illustrations that also support the lead. These, like the quotes, are used to add life to the body of the story.

Show, Don't Tell

The anecdotes and illustrations that the news writer selects for his or her story are used to **show** the reader what the person has done or was thinking. They introduce drama to the story.

The technique is borrowed from writers of fiction who use dramatic incidents and situations to give their readers deeper insights into their characters than mere **telling** allows.

If you look back at the beginning of Klinkenberg's story about the shark fisherman you can see how Klinkenberg **shows** us his fisherman on the bridge. The story begins this way:

Ron Swint moaned in the dark about the shark called Old Hitler, the largest shark in Tampa Bay, as traffic roared by on the Skyway Bridge. Somebody in a car shouted and Swint automatically winced. . . .

The reader is put on the bridge with Swint, in the dark, in the middle of traffic, hearing Swint moan, seeing the traffic roar past.

Telling this would have led to something like this:

```
Ron Swint is after the largest shark in Tampa Bay, Old
Hitler, and he fishes from the Skyway Bridge in the dark,
as traffic roars by.
```

That's not the worst lead that can be written, but it pales beside Klinkenberg's. **Showing** lets the reader see, feel, smell and even taste:

The food at political picnics in Vadonia County starts with chowder, large bowls of it with the clams so thick you can hardly see the broth. Then there are the vegetables—green beans, long and slender; zucchini, sliced lengthwise and chopped and—take your pick—fried or boiled; corn, heaped in bowls, a large gob of butter slowly melting into the kernels; beets, red and succulent, sweet as candy. . . .

Simply **telling** the reader takes away the joy of feeling, tasting, smelling:

```
    The food at political picnics in Vadonia County is
plentiful. There are various vegetables, clam chowder
and several kinds of meat to choose from.
```

Might as well write menus for the fried chicken outfit down the street with a touch like that.

The next step in planning the story is to decide on a writing approach.

Write the way you talk. This has become an axiom in the newsroom. It is obviously useful to broadcast news writers, and it has become increasingly important in the writing style of the newspaper news writer.

Writing Style

If you listen carefully to a conversation, a pattern of sentence structure will emerge. Most sentences begin with the name of a person or a thing, a noun:

Sam asked me to help him wash his car.
The **car** was a mess.
I wasn't going to get roped into that.
So **I** told him to forget it.
He found someone else.

You can detect something else in these spoken sentences: Often the verb closely follows the name of the person or thing that begins the sentence:

The Wildcats **lost** a close one.
Hooper **blew** it in the last two minutes.
He **called** the wrong play.
I **think** they ought to fire him.
If he **loses** another one, it's curtains for him.
We **need** a new coach.

The third point to notice is that the verb is closely followed by the object when a transitive (action) verb is used.

We have described the basic structure of the sentence pattern most of us use in dialogue: Subject-verb-object.

The S-V-O pattern of some of the sentences in the first group is:

S-V-O

S—Sam	S—I	S—He
V—asked	V—told	V—found
O—me	O—him	O—someone

Look at the second set of sentences, which contain many action verbs. The S-V-O pattern is:

S—Wildcats	S—He	S—he
V—lost	V—called	V—loses
O—one	O—play	O—one
S—Hooper	S—I	S—We
V—blew	V—think	V—need
O—it	O—they	O—coach

Notice the positioning of the subjects and verbs in these spoken sentences. They are snug, the subjects close to the verbs. This kind of positioning makes the sentences clear. When the verbs are as close as possible to the subjects, the listener knows who or what is losing, blowing games, calling plays, or thinking. Clarity—which is the goal of good writing—is achieved this way.

The S-V-O sentence arrangement probably should be the way three-fourths of your sentences are written. Because a barrage of S-V-O sentences would be boring, they should be varied with an occasional sentence that has a different structure, such as the use of a clause or phrase to begin a sentence—as this sentence begins.

Some editors are willing to accept exceptions to the S-V-O rule in the lead by placing the attribution at the end of the sentence:

> Tuition will increase 10 percent next year, President Robert Camuto told the Student Forum last night.

At times, the passive voice seems to be demanded by the news event:

> Mohandas K. Gandhi was assassinated today by a Hindu fanatic who objected to Gandhi's tolerance for Muslims.

The argument for this passive lead is that Gandhi's name is so important it must begin the sentence.

In writing the story, the journalist must be conscious of these three requirements:

Follow the S-V-O structure.

Use action verbs.

Keep the verb as close to the subject as possible.

Ranch Christmas. A writer describing Christmas preparations on this New Mexico ranch lets the reader feel the snap in the air, hear the soft thud of the horse's hooves and smell the resiny, new-cut sharpness of the fir tree that is being brought home. All writers understand that the nature of the event determines the style of the story.

Al Cabral, *Albuquerque Tribune*

In applying these requirements or principles of news writing, the news writer makes them fit the nature of the story. By this, writers mean that certain types of stories take certain writing styles. A presidential assassination attempt is a fast-breaking spot news story. It will take a short-sentence style, almost a rattle of short S-V-O sentences. An obituary of a longtime resident of the community will take a more solemn style, which means somewhat longer sentences.

Before writing, the journalist has to decide what kind of mood he or she wants to evoke in the reader or listener. If the mood is to be one of excitement, then the language, style and sentence structure should be consistent with that feeling. If the mood is to be thoughtful, reflective, then the sentences should be longer, the verbs will not be sharp or piercing.

Fit the Writing to the Story

The Active Voice

By staying with the S-V-O structure, the news writer will avoid a problem that seems to plague some writers. This is the use of the passive voice. By passive voice, we mean that the subject of the sentence is being acted upon. By active voice, we mean that the subject is the agent or cause of the action. Here are some examples:

Passive: Your letter was received and read by me.

Active: I received and read your letter.

Passive: The car was seen speeding toward the spectators.

Active: The spectators saw the car speeding toward them.

Look at the passive-voice sentences. They lack strength and emphasis. The words sit limply, passively. Active-voice sentences march across the page.

A more difficult habit to break—one that plagues beginners—is the tendency to put opinion into stories.

No Opinions, Please

How do these sentences differ?

1. The city council last night gave city workers an undeserved wage increase of 15 percent.
2. The city council last night gave city workers a wage increase of only 15 percent.
3. The city council last night gave city workers a 15 percent wage increase.

If your answer is that sentences 1 and 2 express opinions, you are right. Neither belongs in a news story, unless attributed to a source. The writer cannot make these statements.

The opinion in the first sentence is obvious. The use of the word *undeserved* reveals that the news writer believes the workers should not have been given such an increase. Opinions of this sort belong in the editorial section of the newspaper.

The second sentence implies that the workers deserve more than the 15 percent increase granted to them: They received an increase of *only* 15 percent. The third sentence is acceptable because it states the fact without opinion. The reader can draw whatever conclusion he or she wishes from the third sentence.

Opinion is the writer's injection of his or her feelings about the subject. Usually, it is an expression that indicates the writer's approval or disapproval. Sentence 1 implies the writer's disapproval, as does the second sentence. A lead like the following expresses approval, which is common in sports copy when the reporter becomes a fan instead of an unbiased observer.

The Spartans lost in overtime 58-53 last night to the LaGrange Wildcats, but the state champion visitors knew that they had met their match in the courageous Spartans.

At first glance, this may not seem to be opinion, and that's the trouble with opinions in copy. Nine times out of 10, the writer is unaware that they are there. Usually, opinions insinuate themselves into the story when the writer gets too close to the subject of the story. No question that the sports writer who wrote this lead was carried away by the home team's valiant effort. By putting in the adjective "courageous" the writer shows he or she approves of the team's effort. That's something the reader should be allowed to conclude from the facts the writer presents. Though sports writers do emphasize coverage of local teams, they should avoid being fans in print.

Good advice for writers: Keep cool. This is especially sound advice for sports writers. They have no business rooting for any team. Unlike radio and television sports announcers who are hired by local teams, the sports reporter should be as non-partisan as the political reporter.

Details, Details

"You have a hole in this story large enough for a truck to get through," the city editor says. The story states that a thief had knocked the night guard unconscious and had taken "several items from the construction site."

A pair of pliers, two lunch kits and a hammer? An air conditioning unit, a generator and three boxes of light fixtures?

No one will know because all the reporter has written is "several items." "Be specific," the editor tells the reporter. "Anticipate and answer all the reader's questions."

The news writer makes sure that all holes are plugged, all vague statements made concrete, estimates made specific if possible. When the story lacks specifics and concrete detail, the reader feels cheated:

The profile of a high school mile runner said he had been approached by a number of eastern colleges after running a fast mile in a state meet. But the story never gave the names of the colleges.

The reporter wrote that the jury had deliberated "half the night before retiring." But how many hours is that, and what time did the jury retire?

Most of these problems are avoided by seeking details while reporting. When President Reagan was hospitalized following an assassination attempt, Helen Thomas, the White House correspondent for the UPI, dug for details. She even asked what flavor Jell-O the president had been served for lunch.

"I was only trying to get the details into my story that would make readers feel as though they were here," she said.

This chapter has made one major point. To write a complete and accurate story, the reporter must be organized in reporting and writing. This means thinking through exactly what he or she wants to say. Next, we will look at the 10 rudiments of the news story.

Rudiments of the News Story

Just as the basketball player must abide by the rules of the game and the downtown merchant must conform to city regulations, so the news writer must adhere to a set of guidelines. These guidelines, also known as the rudiments of the news story, are: accuracy, attribution of statements, balance, brevity, clarity, human interest, proper identification of those named in the story, focus on the news point, objectivity and verification of information.

The news writer who follows these guidelines will write stories that are accurate, thorough, fair and readable.

For several days, the *Kansas City Times* had published a number of important stories on page one. Michael J. Davies, the editor, was pleased with his newspaper and the work of his staff. This is what first-class journalism is all about, he was thinking one day when he received a telephone call from the owner of a funeral home.

The caller said he wanted to talk about the accuracy of some of the obituaries appearing in the *Times*. He had some complaints to make.

"He wasn't shouting," Davies said. "He seemed resigned."

Davies' first reaction was irritation. Didn't this man appreciate the great job the newspaper had been doing? However, Davies agreed to examine the obituaries and get back to the caller.

"I was shocked by what I unearthed," Davies said. "We checked every obit in the *Times* the next day.

"There was an error of some kind—spelling, fact, you name it—in many obits.

"If we can't get obits right, how can we expect readers to believe our page one stories?" he said.

Davies took immediate action to guarantee greater accuracy.

The list of the rudiments for a news story begins with accuracy—words spelled correctly, the correct middle initial in names and the exact addresses of people in stories.

Accuracy

In their lectures on libel law, journalism instructors often reach into their bag of stories to find the one about the wrong initial. In one case, the courthouse reporter hastily wrote a *T* instead of an *F* when he was taking notes on a divorce action. In checking the telephone book later for the address of the divorcing couple, naturally he looked up the name under the initial *T*.

A couple of days after the story ran, the newspaper received notice from a lawyer for the non-divorcing couple. A libel suit was on the way.

The story brings forth the desired shudders among students, for a minute or two, and then they shrug it off as just another of those scare stories they have been hearing all semester.

Shrug away. These stories are based on fact. Most libel suits begin with a little mistake, a foolish error, a lapse in accuracy. Some could have been avoided with a check of references and sources. Not this kind of error, though. After all, if the reporter has John T. Smith in his notes, why should he think it's wrong? We do verify many details, but everyone, including the reporter, presumes reporters can copy material accurately.

Thus, accuracy begins with the reporter's painstaking attention to every detail when gathering facts and information. Names, ages, addresses—check. The precise number of fire trucks that answered the alarm. The exact words of the speaker. Check and double check.

When there is the slightest doubt, the reporter checks with the source or a reference. If in doubt about the spelling of a word, the reporter uses the dictionary. A misspelled word is a gross inaccuracy. If the reporter is not sure about the source of the idiom, "Out of the frying pan into the fire," *Bartlett's Familiar Quotations* can provide it. The exact number of deaths this year to date at the junction of highway 495 and interstate 95 can be found in the newspaper clips.

Should there be an error, the reporter writes a correction. No reporter likes to do this, but it is essential. For a long time, newspapers would not admit they made mistakes; they refused to run corrections. Now, almost every newspaper has a permanent place for corrections or will place them in the section or on the page where the error occurred.

Next time you are too rushed to double-check an initial or name or are too lazy to look up something in a reference work, remember this correction and the embarrassment it caused all concerned:

> Mai Thai Finn is one of the students in the program and was in the center of the photo. We incorrectly listed her as one of the items on the menu.

Mercifully, no mention will be made of the publication that committed this blunder.

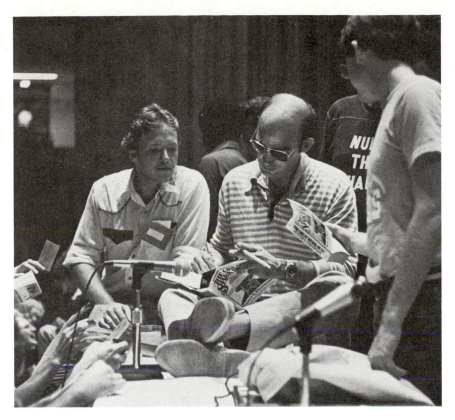

Attribution

All information and statements, except the most obvious, must be attributed to the source of the material:

> The police reported two people were killed when. . . .
>
> Mayor Sam Walker today urged. . . .
>
> Childhood diseases are declining, the agency said. . . .
>
> "College grades are meaningless," Professor Alvin Goodman told. . . .

However, no attribution is necessary for assertions that are obvious:

> July 4th falls on Tuesday.
>
> Lincoln was loved and hated in his day.
>
> The cost of living has steadily increased.

By the "obvious" we mean any statement, idea or situation that is commonly accepted as true. When the reporter is persuaded of the truth of an assertion or situation but there is no absolute proof or common acceptance, there must be attribution.

Notice the use of attribution in the following lead:

> Police said today they expect major roads out of the city to be heavily traveled beginning Friday at midafternoon. The holiday weekend will run from Saturday through Monday.

The first statement is attributed to a source. The second is stated as fact because it is obvious.

Actions are attributed to the person or group committing or performing them:

> Mayor George Albritton ordered all city offices closed next Monday in memory of the city's first mayor, Richard Beatty, who died last week at 104 years of age.

> The state Republican Party yesterday took the first steps toward holding its November state convention. The party. . . .

Generally, when we speak of attribution, we refer to what is called "sourcing" a quote or statement. That is, reponsibility for the material is placed with the source. When there is no attribution, the reporter, newspaper or station is considered the source.

The reporter needs no attribution for events he or she has witnessed. In the unlikely case of a reporter being on the scene at a bank robbery, he or she need not attribute to the police what he or she has seen.

Attribution to a source does not guarantee to the reader or viewer the truth of the statement. But it does place responsibility for the assertion. When reporters doubt the accuracy or truth of a statement, they try to verify it.

In his interview with Jeff Klinkenberg, who wrote about the shark fisherman, Roy Peter Clark wondered about some of the angler's statements.

"I notice at various points in the story you are careful to attribute statements he had made about what he can do with the sharks once he has caught them. Fishermen are notorious BS artists. . . . Do you often encounter problems of credibility in the people you interview?"

Klinkenberg replied, "No, but in this instance, some of the stuff he was telling me was so remarkable I had to protect myself a little bit. Many of the things he told me I double-checked and found to be true. Things I couldn't check I went with an attribution. And there are quite a few in this story."

Attribution. When the reporter is sent to watch divers pull a woman from her submerged car, the reporter can describe what he or she sees without attribution. The reporter who was not present when a slaying took place must reconstruct the event from investigators and their reports and from neighbors and then attribute the account of the event to these sources.
Top, Joseph Noble, *The Stuart News; bottom,* Marc Ascher, *The Home News*

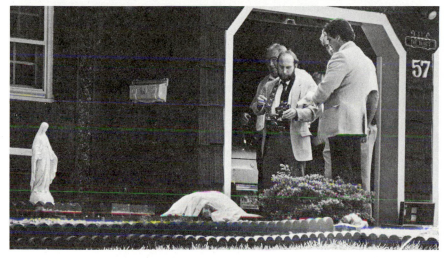

    With the name and the title or occupation of the source given in the story, the reader or listener can place responsibility. After a while, the public learns just how trustworthy the source is. This is important in writing about those in public life. They must be held accountable for their actions and their statements. A reporter who spots a distortion or a lie in a statement may well run it and alongside the inaccuracy give the accurate or truthful account. That way the source is on record, as is the truth.

    Attribution should be repeated throughout the story if the source is not clear. Once the source is evident, it need not be repeated for every assertion. However, the source should not be given only in the lead and then dropped. Repeat the source when necessary to avoid confusing the reader. Quotes should always be attributed so that the reader knows who is speaking.

Placing the Attribution in the Sentence

In his work as a broadcast news writer, Mervin Block uses this guideline: Attribution precedes assertion.

Placing the source of the information up front is essential for radio and television writing.

Newspaper writers also will often begin their leads with the attribution. Write the way you talk is becoming the guide for all news writers.

Placement within the Story   Some news writers say that attribution in the lead sometimes makes it too long or spoils the intended effect. They prefer to cite the source in the second or third paragraph.

This works, but only if the material is from an official record or document or is not controversial. No source is necessary in this lead because the event is obviously on record with the police:

> Three dead men were found afloat—in two Dade canals and a lake—at midday Sunday by a fisherman, golfers and a scavenger in search of scrap metal.

However, attribution is essential in any lead that contains accusations and charges:

> G. Arthur Levy today charged the state liquor authority with "capricious decisions" in denying liquor licenses to two of his clients.

Now and then a reporter will try to make the lead to a story like this more exciting by writing:

> The state liquor authority today stands accused of "capricious decisions" in denying two liquor licenses.

This kind of lead is unfair to the reader, who may conclude that the charge has been made in the courts or by some official body. When the source is finally revealed, the reader may feel cheated.

Anonymous Sources   Sources sometimes seek anonymity. They will offer information only if their identity is not disclosed. Newspapers are reluctant to run this kind of material since it absolves the source of responsibility for his or her statements.

When anonymity is promised to a source, the reporter may not use the name under any circumstances. Some editors demand to be told the source of such material, and if this is the case, the source must be informed that his or her name will be given to the editor. As a guideline, here is a memo from the UPI to its 200 bureaus around the world on unattributed information:

> The United Press International discourages the use of anonymous sources in all its stories. We prefer to list people by name and title. Where this is not possible, we seek to give the reader or listener the best possible clue as to the source's credibility, such as a Defense Department spokesman, a White House official, a Democratic party representative, and so forth.

When officials request anonymity, the reporter is in a difficult spot. The reporter who is told that without anonymity there will be no statement also knows that some officials like to float trial balloons. That is, an official will make a suggestion without attaching his or her name, watch the public response, and then walk away from the statement if the response is negative. Reporters do not like to be used that way. *The Washington Post* has accepted such material but has published pictures of the source with the source's official title, but not his or her name, under the picture. The message is obvious: We are going to let our readers know your identity. They are entitled to know.

Balance and Fairness

Most of the criticism directed at the press concerns its lack of balance and fairness. Much of the criticism has been deserved. In the past, it was not unusual for newspaper publishers and editors to use their newspapers to attack ideas, groups, individuals and officials. These attacks were made in news columns, which were supposedly free of opinion.

If an editor or publisher disagreed with or disapproved of an individual or group, the newspaper simply ignored them in its coverage. Not only did newspapers tend to ignore people with controversial views, they sometimes even refused to cover major political parties and their candidates.

In his book *The Powers That Be* (New York: Alfred A. Knopf, 1979), David Halberstam describes a visit a *New York Times* reporter made to California in 1934 to cover the campaign for governor. Upton Sinclair, the author of many books and a supporter of social and political change, was running against Frank Merriam, the Republican candidate. The campaign had attracted national attention because of its intensity. Sinclair was considered a wild-eyed socialist by his opponents.

On his arrival in Los Angeles, the New York reporter picked up a copy of the *Los Angeles Times* to look for news about the campaign, especially to learn something about Sinclair, who was a national figure. The only story he could find about Sinclair was one saying that he was un-Christian.

That night, the reporter went to dinner with the chief political correspondent of the *Los Angeles Times*. The reporter asked where Sinclair would be speaking so that he could cover some of his rallies.

As *The New York Times* reporter recalls, he was told, "Forget it. We don't go in for that kind of crap you have back in New York of being obliged to print both sides. We're going to beat this son of a bitch Sinclair any way we can. We're going to kill him." And Halberstam adds: "Which they did."

A quarter of a century later, in 1958, another New York reporter went to California to cover the turbulent political scene. The same Los Angeles correspondent was directing political coverage. He helped his eastern colleague with background about the Republicans. What about the Democrats? asked his visitor. "Oh, we don't bother with them," was the answer.

Those days of outrageous favoritism in the news are gone, except in some isolated instances. Today, the *Los Angeles Times* is listed among the best newspapers in the country. Although newspapers have recognized their responsibility to be fair, unfairness and imbalance do creep into stories now and then, usually because of carelessness.

By balance we mean that both sides in a controversy are given their say. In a political campaign, all candidates should be given enough space and time to present their major points. In debates, each speaker is entitled to reach the reader.

By fairness, we mean that all parties involved in the news are treated without favoritism. If someone makes a charge against another person and the newspaper or station carries a story that includes this allegation, it is obliged to obtain the other side and to put it in the story that contains the charge. Fairness requires that the reporter put the charge and the answer as close together as possible.

The reporter is not a Ping-Pong ball, bouncing from charge to rebuttal as the sources volley away. The reporter must check the truth or accuracy of a charge when he or she believes misstatements are being made. During the Democratic presidential primary in 1984, Bernard Weinraub of *The New York Times* examined Walter F. Mondale's charges that Gary Hart's record on civil rights and feminist issues was weak. Weinraub checked with the National Association for the Advancement of Colored People and the National Organization for Women and was told that the two organizations rated both candidates highly.

Let's go back to the lawyer who said his clients had been mistreated by the state liquor authority. The reporter sought the response of the authority and put it high in the story so that it would read this way:

G. Arthur Levy today charged the state liquor authority with "capricious decisions" in denying liquor licenses to two of his clients.

Levy, a local attorney, said the authority had no reason to turn down Fred P. Schmidt and Alice Long, both of whom sought licenses for outlets in shopping centers north of the city.

The executive director of the authority, Theodore Landau, denied that the state agency had acted without reason. He said the applicants had failed to satisfy the authority about their backgrounds. . . .

Balance. The reporter always gives both sides of an argument or controversy in a news story. When a charge is made against a person, the accused is sought out and his or her response is included in the story as close as possible to the charge. If the target of a charge or accusation cannot be located, the news writer says so in the story.
Rafael Trias, *The San Juan Star*

Fairness means completeness and relevance, giving the reader all pertinent information so that he or she can see the event in all its dimensions and reach a conclusion.

Fairness also involves the honest use of words. Look at these statements:

Jones admitted he had seen the documents.

Jones said he had seen the documents.

What's the difference? To most readers, the first sentence implies that Jones is under attack for having done something wrong, whereas the second sentence is neutral. There are appropriate occasions when admit, refuse, complain and other words that imply an attitude or a behavior pattern can be used. But these are loaded words. They signal caution. The writer must be fair in the use of language.

Cool Cal—A Man of Few Words

After Calvin Coolidge returned from a church service, a friend asked the president what the sermon had been about.

"Sin," replied Coolidge.

The friend asked what the clergyman had said. Coolidge replied: "He said he was against it."

Brevity

News writing, we have seen, is the art of knowing what to leave out and condensing the rest. Donald M. Murray, a University of New Hampshire professor and newspaper writing coach, says the most effective stories say one dominant thing.

Still, news writers run on and on if they drop their guard. They are born storytellers and tend to be long-winded. Actually, the news writer can include more facts than he or she thinks and still be brief. There are some tricks of the trade.

One way to make a little go a long way is to make one word do the work of three. You already have a method of doing just this—writing sentences with the S-V-O structure.

The S-V-O structure helps to cut sentences to the bone. By choosing a concrete noun, a noun that refers to an actual person, place or thing, the news writer can avoid adjectives. By using action verbs that whisper, sing and shout, the news writer can avoid adverbs. Good writers try to make their nouns and verbs work for them. They consider the overuse of adjectives and adverbs as an admission of weak writing.

When George Eliot, the English novelist, was writing *Daniel Deronda,* she wrote this sentence: "She began to sob hysterically." Eliot's manuscript shows that she crossed off the adverb *hysterically*, realizing that the verb *sob* was strong enough to carry the meaning she intended.

Look at these sentences. The weak ones are the wordy sentences. The strong sentences make their points succinctly.

> **Weak:** He was hardly able to walk.
> **Strong:** He staggered. (He stumbled. He faltered.)
> **Weak:** He left the room as quickly as possible.
> **Strong:** He ran out. (He rushed out. He dashed out.)

Action verbs do not need to be propped up by adverbs.

Concrete nouns are words that stand for something we can point to as real: table, desk, chalk, crayon, basket, Ted Kennedy, Prince Charles.

Abstract nouns have no physical reference: patriotism, perception, motherhood, freedom, values, hope. These words have different meanings to

people. The news writer should avoid using abstract nouns, except in direct quotes. When that happens, the reporter should ask the source how the word is being used.

Another cause of unwanted length is the piling on of irrelevant themes and details. As we have stressed, the average news story has one, two or sometimes three themes. It's up to the reporter to pick the most important. Some reporters want to include everything that happened. The news story will sag out of shape with that overload, bulging like a fullback who has trained on beer.

After the theme(s) has been selected, the reporter must pick the best quotes, anecdotes and illustrations for the supporting detail. A few quotes and a single pertinent illustration are all that are necessary to prove the point.

If an event is loaded with interesting and relevant material, the writer can use a device to summarize the secondary material. The additional material is listed at the end of the story:

Relevance

> The city council also:
>
> 1. Approved an expenditure of $5,000 for paving Grant Street between Arrow and Baltic Avenues.
> 2. Appointed Frank C. Barnes of 103 Elm Ave. assistant to the sanitary engineer.
>
> 3. Put off until next month consideration of a proposal to adopt an anti-litter ordinance.

The reporter did not believe these items were worth any more than a brief mention. This technique also can be used in an interview:

Nelson ranged widely over the field of music in his remarks:

"Country western will be around as long as people are romantics."

"The mainstream singers give people what they think people want. They're wrong. People want authenticity."

"Travel is no way to make a living, but it's our only way. We are today's minstrels."

"Country music appeals to grandpa and his granddaughter."

Clarity

Ask editors or readers what they want most from the people who write the news and the response will be almost unanimous: clear stories.

Reporters also value the ability to write stories that are clear and interesting. The reason is simple enough. Life is becoming more complex. Information at the source is often dense and technical. Tax rates. Arms control. Budgets. Foreign assistance. Stadium financing. Trends in crime.

All this and more confronts the reporter and demands to be translated into everyday English.

Clear Thinking

There are several ways the reporter achieves clarity. The common starting point is clear thinking. Badly written stories often are the result of muddy thinking.

"There is only one trick to writing clearly," says a Chicago editor. "The writer must understand the event before writing." If the writer has the information under control, then he or she can put it into understandable language. Reporter Jan Wong often consults references and makes dozens of telephone calls before she writes a story. She needs to have all aspects of the event she is reporting under her control before she writes.

George Orwell, the author of *1984* and *Animal Farm,* is admired for his ability to express complicated ideas in simple language. His journalism and novels are marked by plain, uncluttered colloquial prose.

Orwell said that the key to clear writing is clear thinking. If the thinking is uncertain and confused, so is the writing. He criticized writers who hide their ignorance of the subject with "purple passages, sentences without meaning, decorative adjectives and humbug generally."

Clear thinking extends to the writing as well as to the subject matter. That is, the reporter has to find the lead that will best summarize the event, and arrange all the supporting material in a logical and organized fashion.

When the lead is buried or the piece lacks focus, the reader is confused. News writers see themselves as guides leading the reader through the thicket of events. Inept guides lead their followers in circles or into a swamp of confusion.

Figures are hard to digest. Barry Kramer of *The Wall Street Journal* begins a data story without frightening his readers with statistics:

Health experts have begun an investigation of statistics that show a startling increase in the cancer death rate this year.

They are at a loss so far to explain figures released by the National Center for Health Statistics that show that more than 216,000 Americans died of cancer in the first seven months of this year, or a rate of 176.3 deaths per 100,000 population.

Court documents often are complicated. Look at how Mary Voboril of *The Miami Herald* tries to engage the reader by beginning her piece like a storyteller:

Ethiopian Zion Coptic Church members told a teenage cancer victim he would live to be 700 years old if he gave up chemotherapy and embraced their way of life, which includes smoking marijuana, the boy's mother says.

Tony Baron believed them. Then 17, he refused conventional cancer treatment, joined the Coptics, smoked their marijuana—and died less than a year later, says Rosario Baron.

She sued the Coptics and their leader, Brother Louv, in a wrongful death suit Wednesday in Dade Circuit Court. Filed by Miami attorney Ellis Rubin, the suit was in the form of a second amended complaint. Two other complaints have been found faulty by a Dade Circuit judge.

The lead is long. Voboril knew that. So the first sentence of her second paragraph is short, four words. The second sentence of this paragraph is dramatic. The dash and what follows are intended as a slap of cold water on the reader. The third paragraph describes the details of the suit.

Here is another court story that is made clear by the writer's obvious knowledge of the subject and by his ability to translate legal jargon into everyday language. This is how Neil Skene of *The St. Petersburg Times* began a story about a complicated legal question:

Do you know where your curtilage is?

No, it's not in your leg. That's cartilage. Do you know where your curtilage is?

The Supreme Court is trying to find out.

"Curtilage" is lawyer talk for the area immediately surrounding a house. Generally speaking, your house is your castle and your yard is your curtilage. But what if you have a fenced-in, five-acre tract with a house in the middle? Justice Ben Overton asks. Is all of that curtilage? Or is some of it open field?

Skene is trying to make clear to the reader an issue the Florida Supreme Court was trying to resolve. He knows that most readers do not understand the specialized language of the law, and he knows that readers cannot quickly digest a barrage of facts. So he eases the reader into the story. He paces the story at a walk rather than a run, the usual gait of most news stories.

To sum up, clarity in writing begins with the reporter's full understanding of the event. It also depends on the proper lead and the organized structure of the story. By this we mean that the story should march logically from start to finish, with no detours or side trips into irrelevant material. Finally, clarity is enhanced by the writing style: clear S-V-O sentences, short average sentence length, storytelling in an informal style when appropriate.

Explain, Explain

A news writer whose stories are invariably clear and interesting says he has only one guideline: "I write as though I'm talking to someone who is intelligent enough to know what I'm getting at if I make it clear enough." To make technical matters understandable, he sometimes inserts explanatory material in his copy:

Gold was sentenced to three to five years in the state penitentiary for his part in the confidence game.

One of the prosecutors said that with time off for good behavior, Gold would be out of prison in a little more than two years. "We need determinate sentences in this state," Assistant District Attorney Oliver Payne said.

Explanatory material

A determinate sentence means that the person sentenced must serve that period and cannot be released by a parole board before that time has been served. Many states have adopted the determinate sentence in response to criticism of lenient sentencing.

The third paragraph is entirely the reporter's. He is the source for this background. Without it, the reader may have no idea what the prosecutor is talking about. With it, a public issue of importance is explained.

Human Interest

The campus correspondent for a newspaper showed the city editor a story he had written for his college newspaper. He wanted to know whether it would interest the editor. The story began this way:

College students face problems ranging from alcohol abuse to loneliness, but the difficulties can be handled with a little friendly assistance, say members of the Campus Ministerial Association.

The organization's members, composed of ministers representing six denominations, say that students here are like other young people.

"Students are not that different from anyone else," the Rev. . . .

Human Interest. The news writer goes beyond the final score and the statistics to describe the exhaustion and despair of the players on the bench as they watch their team fall further behind at the state finals.
Robert Burke, *The Sunday Courier and Press*

The city editor looked up after reading the story. The piece has possibilities, he told the student. "You've done a lot of work. You quote the director of the Wesley Foundation, the director of the Baptist Student Center, a Catholic priest and an Episcopal vicar.

"They have interesting things to say about students experimenting with drugs, sex and alcohol and then feeling guilty or lost.

"But the story is missing a key element. It's about the problems of students, but there are no students in it. You haven't talked to any students. You don't have any case studies.

"It lacks human interest. It moves all around the subject but never shows us the people directly involved."

He suggested the student reporter return to his sources and ask for some typical cases. The reporter could promise not to use names. Some of the sources might even know students who would allow the reporter to interview them, the editor said. Whatever he did, he would have to include the human element.

Almost every news story involves people, and reporters are being told these days that readers and listeners want to see, hear and read about the way people are affected by events. Reporters are instructed to include people— their reactions, their expectations, their concerns—in their news stories. Since the human element catches the reader's interest, it should be put high in the story. Tell the story in human terms. This is essential.

Beyond the Statistics

We all want to get behind the walls and fences people construct around themselves, and we want to pierce the anonymity of the city. We want to know what went on inside a room down the hall last night when someone screamed. Or whose 10-speed bike was left chained to a post and stripped of every part but the frame. Or what happened to the family whose home burned last night. Who took them in? Have they any clothing?

We want to know what people do under stress, what they think about when they have problems. We wonder why the striking postal worker cannot make it on his salary, what people do when their homes are flooded. What, we ask ourselves, does the unemployed teenager want—a job or a handout? The church page has the usual sermons, but nothing about what the seven-year-old child or the old woman in the black shawl are praying for. The newlyweds are honeymooning at the Lake of the Ozarks, but the wedding story says nothing about why they chose this particular place.

Good stories answer our questions. They give us the information we need and want.

After high waters flooded three Kentucky counties, R. G. Dunlop of *The Courier-Journal* talked to some of the people in the area. He began his account with a human interest detail.

SALYERSVILLE, KY.—For the second time in less than three years, Anita Frazier will be shopping for new carpet.

The old rugs in her home on East Maple Street didn't wear out—they were soaked useless by flood waters.

December 1978 was the first time the water had ever crept into the house where Mrs. Frazier has lived since 1920.

Monday morning was the second time.

Residents in Magoffin, Morgan and Bath counties continued to clean up yesterday in the wake of flooding that damaged many roads and bridges and an estimated 300 homes, and that laid waste to countless acres of tobacco, corn and family gardens.

Magoffin Judge-Executive Calloway Montgomery estimated yesterday that 60 percent of the county's gardens and corn and tobacco crops were destroyed.

In Salyersville, Mrs. Frazier's home was fairly typical of the ef-

forts to bounce back from nature's blows.

Volunteers swept puddles outside and washed grimy floors and baseboards.

A box of quilts, salvaged from a flooded pantry, rested on a bed, and furniture was stacked up in the dining room.

Water continued to seep through the tiles on the kitchen floor, almost as fast as Mrs. Frazier mopped it up.

The remains of her carpet and its padding lay in a soggy heap on the front porch. Out back, the propane gas tank that had nearly floated away was strapped to a post.

"This was the quickest and the dirtiest flood I've ever seen," Mrs. Frazier said. "I'm getting tired of replacing this carpet. I hope it's the last time."

So does city Fire Chief Harry Puckett, who watched 4 feet of water creep into the fire station and. . . .

When postal workers went on strike, Marcia Chambers, then with *The News Tribune* in Perth Amboy, N.J., dug beneath the union and government statements to look into the life of a striking worker. Here is how her story began:

Spaghetti and Stew

This March Joe Capik will have worked as a mail carrier in Perth Amboy for 20 years. He takes care of his wife and four children on $110 a week.

Mostly he and his four children, who live at 56 Maplewood Ave. in a Cape Cod bungalow in Keasbey, eat dinners of stews and soups and spaghetti. Things were bad enough last year, he said, that he applied for food stamps. But the county turned him down.

As a mail carrier, he cannot afford much more than stews and spaghetti.

Last week Joe Capik went out on strike for the first time in his life. He joined 49 letter carriers who were on strike for the first time in the 195-year history of the postal system.

"I don't feel right about striking. I really don't," he said outside the deserted post office in Perth Amboy.

"But it's a question of desperation. The situation has been forced upon us," he said.

He was still in uniform, a pleasant, smiling man of 49 whose maroon tie was perfectly knotted. He wore his hat with the number 16, which has been his number for 20 years.

"I feel chagrined," he said, as he smiled to an occasional customer who walked into the post office. "I am disappointed in an employer of this scope who makes it necessary because of inaction and gross unconcern—for us to strike."

Capik was referring to a pay raise of 5.4 percent the postal carriers were supposed to get last October, but which has been held up in congressional committee.

"How come it is so easy for Congress to vote itself raises and their raises never get bottled up in committee?" Capik asked, not really expecting an answer.

Human interest takes the reader to the heart of the event. A strike involves people seeking to change their circumstances. Joe Capik represents that human desire.

Another dimension of a strike was seen by Marilyn Greenwald of the *Citizen-Journal* of Columbus, Ohio, in her story about a strike and its consequences for those touched by its ripples. She singled out a family with school children to show what happened when non-teaching employees struck in Columbus. Here is her story:

Life in a Buick

Human interest introduction in the first 10 paragraphs

A few weeks before school started this fall, Barbara Eberts had visions of staying home alone during the day and relaxing for the first time in 15 years.

The youngest of her four sons would enter first grade, and she thought she would have time to take some classes at Ohio State University.

Unfortunately, Mrs. Eberts made those plans before the start of a strike by bus drivers and other non-teaching employees of the Columbus schools; since the strike, she has become a full-time chauffeur and transportation planner for her four children, all of whom attend different schools.

"This was going to be free time," she said Thursday afternoon.

Instead, Mrs. Eberts has found she spends most of her time sitting in her Buick Skylark.

She gets up at 6:30 a.m. each day to help sons Howard, 15, Matthew, 6, Joseph, 11, and Michael, 14, get ready for school. About 7:30 a.m. she begins a trek to either Fairwood Elementary School or St. Charles, or sometimes both, depending on her car-pool schedule that day.

About five hours after returning to her home at 5159 Holbrook Drive, Mrs. Eberts begins the journey back to St. Charles, Yorktown Middle School, Fairwood or any combination thereof.

During the day, she refuels and helps arrange schedules among the nine parents who participate in the three car pools of which she is a member.

Parents in her neighborhood are already accustomed to driving large groups of children to school and have even identified "favorite" routes, she said.

When she learned earlier in the week that state officials will reimburse parents about 55 cents a day for driving their children to school, "I laughed," Mrs. Eberts said. "That won't even start your car."

General news—final six paragraphs

Columbus school officials said Thursday that more students continue to enroll in the district despite the strike by members of the Ohio Association of Public School Employees that entered its sixth day.

About 90 percent of the 73,000 expected in class enrolled by Thursday, Superintendent Joseph L. Davis said.

Although 14 bus drivers reported to work, most of the 439 drivers are still on strike, school officials said. Eight bus drivers worked Wednesday.

About 42 percent of the district's 2,600 non-teaching employees were on the job Thursday. About a third worked Sept. 4, the first day of school and the strike.

Assistant Superintendent Frank Maraffa said private trash haulers who serve some schools will not cross the picket lines, causing an accumulation of trash.

School officials are continuing to advise parents to send children to school with packed lunches, although lunchroom operations were running in 58 schools Thursday.

Sharp Observations

As the dean listened to students presenting a student council study of dormitory regulations, he drummed his fingers on the desk in front of him. He frequently looked at the clock on the wall above the door, and now and then he stared out the window for half a minute or more.

What do you think the dean thought of the student presentation? Whatever he might have said about the study, his actions seem to speak eloquently of his impatience and boredom. A story that includes these observations would capture the full dimension, the human dimension, of the event.

We can tell the reader or listener a great deal by including these human interest details. The house whose lawn is littered with beer cans says as much about the people living there as any direct quotations from the residents themselves.

At the Job Market

Let's say you are sent to cover the annual convention of college and university teachers of English and foreign languages. The convention, which draws thousands of instructors from over the country, is devoted mainly to the exchange of scholarly papers, seminars and discussions. It also attracts hundreds of graduate students who hope to buttonhole the heads of departments for jobs. Thus, the convention is also a job market.

You have written a story about the general meeting that opens the convention and you decide to look into the job market aspect. You learn immediately that there is a tight market for the young men and women seeking employment. You could begin your story this way:

```
The hundreds of graduate students seeking jobs at the
annual convention of the Modern Language Association are
having poor luck.
```

```
"This is not a good year for them," said Professor
Calder W. Nolan, head of a committee that makes
arrangements for job interviews.
    "We have about four applicants for every job opening,"
he estimated.
```

There is nothing wrong with this beginning. But many editors would want this redone. Remember the advice of the editor who was shown the story about the problems of college students at the start of this section on human interest? He told the college journalist to go directly to the students themselves instead of quoting people who help them and to make the students the center of the piece. Here, too, the focus is off-center.

The story would be more interesting, and more valid, if it centered on the job-seeking students. You return to the convention and interview a number of students about their experiences. Then you focus on a particular student and begin your story this way:

```
Patrick Mead and several hundred other graduate
students were learning a lesson here today not covered in
their postgraduate studies: The academic job market is
extremely tight in the humanities.
```

The reader is at once engaged and wants to know about Mead's problems and the problems of students in general who seek work. You go on:

```
    The annual convention of the Modern Language
Association has as its main business the exchange of
scholarly material. But for Mead and his fellow students
it serves as a job market.
    They are not having much luck. Mead sent scores of
resumes to colleges and universities saying he would be :
at the convention. He asked for appointments for
interviews. He received four positive replies.
    But these difficulties have not dampened Mead's
enthusiasm. He has spent four years studying 18th century
British literature at Rice University in Houston. He
knows how to be patient.
```

Other students and Professor Nolan can then be quoted on the general employment situation, and the story can end with some of Mead's experiences at the convention.

The Wall Street Journal pioneered the technique of beginning a news story with the human element. The idea was to make complicated stories easier to understand by showing the effect on people of the situation being reported. The device works for many types of stories, but discretion has to be used. It cannot always be used on spot news stories.

Human interest can also be put into a story by the use of personal pronouns and concrete nouns:

1. Johnson put **his** pencil down and closed **his** book.
2. Johnson put the pencil down and closed the book.
3. For a textbook, he thought, it was as lively as one of **Professor Albrecht's** good lectures.
4. For a textbook, he thought, it was as lively as a good lecture.

Sentences 1 and 3 have human interest: 1 contains a personal pronoun, and 3 has the name of a teacher, a concrete noun. Compare the following sentences and indicate which have human interest:

5. It had a bad odor.
6. It smelled like burned rubber.
7. His back ached.
8. His back felt like the football team had practiced on it.

Sentences 6 and 8 introduce the human senses. Reporters should always try to do this by asking their sources what it smelled like, just how bad it felt, what the noise reminded them of, and so on.

The historian G. M. Young wrote, "The real, central theme of history is not what happened, but what people felt about it when it was happening; in Philip Sidney's phrase, 'the affects, the whisperings, the motions of the people.'" For journalists—historians of the moment—this is good advice.

Writers identify the people they are writing about so that readers and listeners can visualize, locate and identify these people. The standard identifying material is **name, age, address** and **occupation.** These are often included in general news stories and always in obituaries.

> Vincent Trevino, 74, of 540 Newton Ave., died last night at Harbor General Hospital after suffering a stroke earlier in the day. He was a retired electrician.

Another kind of identification is essential in stories that quote a source as an authority. In this situation, the source must be identified by title or background to give the person the credibility to speak on the subject on which he or she is being quoted:

> "Freedom of the press is guaranteed only to those who own one," A. J. Liebling wrote. Liebling, a reporter who turned to magazine and book writing, was a staunch critic of the press. For years he wrote a column called "Wayward Press" for *The New Yorker* magazine.

Identification is the journalist's way of drawing a quick portrait of the people about whom he or she writes.

Name The best source for the proper spelling of a person's name is the individual. The telephone book and city directory are usually accurate. If a person uses a middle initial, include that in the story. Nicknames are rarely used except in sports stories or features.

Age A person's age should be used only when it bears directly on the story. It is always used in obituaries and in stories about the victims of accidents and fires. It is also used when it helps to make the point of the story:

> A 14-year-old girl was released from General Hospital yesterday after a year-long fight against near-fatal burns.

When Ronald Reagan was seeking the Republican nomination for president and later the presidency, his age became an issue.

The older that people become in this youth-conscious culture, the more reticent they are about their age. When it is relevant, the reporter is obligated to put it in. This can be done with taste:

> She was graduated from high school in 1932.

> He was 30 when the United States entered World War II, and he immediately volunteered.

Address Where a person lives can tell the reader a great deal. An address in a high-income neighborhood sends one kind of message, an address in a poor neighborhood another. The address also helps the reader to put the person in a setting—large lawns and single residence homes or low-income city projects. The address can indicate a life-style.

Occupation Work defines many people. That is, the jobs that people hold often describe their character and personality. Think of the images that you build from the following job titles: hotel maid, film producer, grocer, commercial fisherman, teacher, actor. Obviously, those pictures are general and we cannot push them too far or we will stereotype individuals. But occupation does say something about the person.

These four identifying characteristics—name, age, address and occupation—give us the broad picture of the person. To fill in the detail, to provide the fine brush strokes, we need to visualize the individual.

Height, weight, hair color, distinguishing physical characteristics. How a person speaks, his or her posture and mannerisms. All these help us see a person. They are used in profiles and feature stories when the writer is trying to draw a full portrait of the subject.

Race, religion and national origin are sometimes essential to a story but too often they are injected when they have no bearing on the story.

The New York Times Manual of Style and Usage cautions writers:

> Race should be specified only if it is truly pertinent. The same stricture applies to ethnic and religious identifications.

In its in-house publication, *Winners & Sinners,* the *Times* cites a violation of this warning:

> **Race out of place—again.** "All eight men, slashed while they were either asleep or intoxicated, were listed in stable condition yesterday. . . . Four victims were white, three were black and one was a Hispanic man." . . . Our stylebook says we specify the race of a person in the news only if it is truly pertinent . . . the writer must *show* the pertinence.

When the Roman Catholic Church appointed an archbishop in France, news stories pointed out that he was born a Jew. To keep him from death in the Nazi concentration camps, his parents turned him over to a Catholic family, which reared him in the Catholic faith. His parents died in the Holocaust. Obviously, religion was pertinent in this story.

News Point

Every story must have a point, and this point must be made high in the story. Usually, in spot news stories, it is in the lead in the first paragraph. For features, as we indicated in chapter 3, the point may come lower in the story. Few editors will permit the point to be delayed beyond the fourth or fifth paragraph.

The news point is also the main theme of the story. It provides the spine of the story.

The news point is consciously decided upon by the reporter, usually at the scene of the event being covered or while the person is being interviewed. It is done at this time so that the reporter can gather as much supporting and buttressing material as possible for the story. No reporter should begin to write without knowing what the news point is.

Objectivity

The great strength of American journalism is its objectivity. Unlike the journalism of many countries, objective journalism attempts to present a complete report that is not colored by the opinion of the reporter or the demands of the prevailing government.

An objective story includes facts that can be shown to correspond to objects, things the reporter can point to. These objects may be physical items: a burned building, a gun, a damaged vehicle. They can also be the documents that record events: the fire and police reports, the tape of a speech, the minutes of a legislative meeting, a bill submitted to congress, a proposed budget.

Objectivity also—in the words of James Boylan, who teaches journalism at the University of Massachusetts at Amherst—"has gradually come to be understood not only as an impersonal 'balanced' style of newswriting (which is the commonplace, or newsroom, sense of the word) but also as representing the broader claim of journalism for its position in society—that of an impartial third party, the one that speaks for the general interest."

Boylan says that objectivity's chief philosopher was Walter Lippmann, who "depicted journalism as an institution apart, charged with supplying society with reliable, impartial information."

It's no coincidence that objectivity in journalism was developed by U.S. journalists. The idea that through experience, the amassing of facts, a person may find truth reflects the American style of life. Journalists came naturally to adopt the objective approach of American empiricists and pragmatists.

Objectivity has been criticized because it limits journalists. Facts alone are sometimes insufficient; they must be given meaning through analysis and interpretation. Journalism recognizes this.

If we look back at our discussion of the five W's and an H, we see that two of these elements can involve interpretation—why and how. To tell the reader or listener why or how something happened often takes the writer away from a strictly objective account of events. Properly labeled as such, interpretative stories are used by many newspapers. However, before a reporter is trusted with interpretative reporting, the newcomer must prove he or she can copy the correct middle initial in a lawsuit, add up a column of figures in a budget without a mistake and accurately quote from an interview with the survivor of a fire. Then the reporter will be given wider latitude.

Verification

When a reporter checks his or her information against some kind of objective source, we say that the material has been verified. Forty years ago, the password in newspapering was: Go with what you've got. This was recognition of the need for speed. Today, the motto is: Verify what you've got, and then go with it. This is recognition of the need for truth.

Jackie and the Press

A reporter for a Fort Lauderdale newspaper was walking into a night club when the owner stopped him.

"You just missed Jackie Kennedy," he told the reporter. The club owner said that the Secret Service men assigned to follow the president's wife had looked over the club and issued orders against any pictures or publicity.

Jackie Kennedy's comings and goings were news during her husband's presidency, and although this story may not seem like much, the doings of attractive, young Jackie were chronicled by an eager press. The AP picked up the story and ran it over its wires.

Two hours later, the AP added an editor's note:

CHECKS THUS FAR FAIL TO CONFIRM THE STORY.

The truth, it turned out, was that a woman who resembled the president's wife was in the club. The Fort Lauderdale paper made a check before going to press and killed the story.

The New York Times has a rule: "Don't trust anybody on anything that is checkable." This rule applies even to the most trustworthy sources. They can make mistakes, such as the press release from an artists' representative who reported a show at a gallery on East 66th Street. The reporter given the release made a routine check in the phone book. The gallery was on East 61st Street.

Don't trust something simply because it is in print. *The New York Times,* probably the most carefully edited newspaper in the country, once carried a story about a trip one of its writers took on the "Superchief Express." No such train. It was the Super Chief. He said he stopped at Raton, Colorado. Raton is in New Mexico. He also described the train as it rolled past Cairo, Illinois, on its way east. The tracks do not go near Cairo.

The story was entertaining all right—but loaded with errors. This leads us to a second rule: "Don't sacrifice accuracy and truth for effect."

Dealing with Hoaxes

For Chicago Bears and Dallas Cowboys football fans, the story Paul Harvey told was a big one: The two teams had traded quarterbacks. Harvey is heard by 5 million people on 774 radio stations over the country. The story had originated with radio station WLS in Chicago, which reported that a vice president for the Bears had called the station with the news.

The caller was an imposter.

Some hoaxsters are ghouls. They delight in calling in death notices for the obituary page. Every veteran reporter can tell at least one story about such an attempt. Most fail because reporters are trained—or learn the hard way—to verify information telephoned in by sources they do not know. The simplest tactic is to hang up and phone the number on record for the supposed source—CBS headquarters, the Chicago Bears information office, a hospital, a funeral home, the police, a coroner.

Never ask the source to call back. You, the reporter, make the call.

At 9:45 p.m., the phone rang in the newsroom of WRC-TV, the NBC affiliate in Washington, D.C.

"The mayor has been shot," the caller said. He identified himself as James Taylor, an aide to Mayor Marion Barry. Taylor said Barry was in serious condition with wounds he suffered when he was shot on the front lawn of his home. Barry was in the hospital at Andrews Air Force Base. Two suspects were in custody.

Taylor gave the television station a number to call for confirmation.

Minutes later, the station was on the air with a news bulletin. Soon, three other Washington television stations had the story. At 10:06 p.m. the UPI put the story on its national news wire. CBS and NBC put the news on their 10 p.m. radio newscasts.

One of those watching television at the time of the bulletin was the mayor himself. He was visiting the home of his legal advisor.

After broadcasting the bulletin, the news staff at WRC-TV tried to obtain additional details.

"The cops knew nothing. The hospital knew nothing. All of a sudden, things started to fall apart," an official at the station said. At 11 p.m., a station anchorman confessed to viewers, "We've been had, folks."

The station had gone wrong by using for verification purposes the telephone number that the caller had supplied. What had happened was simple: The imposter had given his own number so that when the station called back for confirmation he verified the false information.

Although reporters often are warned about shooting from the hip, about going with what they've got before verification, even the most sophisticated are taken in now and then. One day, a messenger showed up in the New York UPI newsroom with a death announcement from a law firm. The obituary was on the firm's letterhead, and the packet included a biographical sketch of the deceased and a photograph. The dead man was L. Dennis Plunkett, aged 31, editor-in-chief of *National Lampoon,* according to the statement. Plunkett died, the note said, after addressing about 300 students at Cornell University the previous evening. Cause of death was undetermined.

The UPI desk moved the obituary on the wires, and within a short time the UPI's Chicago bureau called New York and said the obituary sounded fishy. New York killed the story and checked with the magazine, which informed the UPI it had no one named Plunkett on its staff and no such title as editor-in-chief. At the New York AP bureau, the staff was trying to verify the obituary when it was called by the UPI to warn the agency about the hoax.

UPI tightened its procedures to require verification of all obituaries.

The Goal Is Truth

The point of verifying or confirming material is to try to guarantee its truth for the reader or listener. Accuracy is important, but it is not enough.

"The fact without the truth is futile; indeed, the fact without the truth is false." The source is G. K. Chesterton, an English writer who lanced shams and charlatans. This same idea was taken up in the 1950s by Elmer Davis, a radio journalist who was one of the few journalists who sought to determine the truth of the charges of treason and subversion being made by Sen. Joe McCarthy of Wisconsin.

While it was a fact that McCarthy said many people prominent in government were members or sympathizers of the Communist Party, which the press dutifully reported, Davis asked: Is it true? He asked further: Does the press have an obligation to tell people the truth of the fact?

Attribution does take the responsibility of assertions, charges and declarations from the shoulders of the press. But in serious matters, shouldn't the press try to dig out the truth on its own?

Davis said yes, and the press through the years has come to agree with him. Reporters have made independent verification of charges, statements, accusations, even of convictions in court.

Paul Henderson of *The Seattle Times* took seriously the protestations of innocence of a man convicted of first-degree rape, which in Washington carries a penalty of three years to life. Henderson dug into the story and five days before the man was to be sentenced, he uncovered new evidence that set the innocent man free.

Reagan on Immigration

During his first campaign for the presidency, Ronald Reagan was quoted as saying to an audience in Texas that he favored giving visas to illegal Mexican immigrants for as long as they wished to stay in the United States. Reporters carried this in their stories.

Next day, he denied saying that. He had said, he stated, that they should be given temporary visas. Many reporters were content to include Reagan's denial in their stories. Certainly, this was accurate reporting. It was a fact that he denied having said they should be given permanent visas.

A reporter for *The New York Times* who was accompanying the Reagan campaign sought to find the truth. He was convinced he had quoted Reagan accurately the day before. He consulted tape recordings of the speech Reagan had given that day.

In his story of Reagan's denial he also included a sentence stating that the tapes "clearly show that Mr. Reagan said that he was for Mexican workers staying as long as they liked."

Keeping the Public's Trust

Readers and listeners rely on what they read and hear. They trust their newspapers, and radio and television stations to give them accurate, complete and interesting material in news stories.

To meet this trust, news writers are careful with the facts and painstaking with their writing. Writers realize that much of what people know comes from the news stories they read and hear—the information that reporters gather and write.

By adhering to the requirements of the news story, from accuracy through verification, the news writer—and consequently the public—can be confident that the story will be reliable and, when appropriate, entertaining.

Writing the Lead

The lead of a news story describes the most important element of the event. It is a brief statement of the fact or facts that make the event newsworthy.

Looking Ahead

To write a lead, the news writer asks himself or herself these questions:

1. What do I want to say? What is the theme of this story?
2. Will this be a straight news story or a feature story?
3. Should I use a direct or a delayed lead?
4. What facts should I put into the lead?

The first two questions usually are answered at the scene while covering the event. The other two are asked just before writing.

No one can resist reading a book that begins this way: "Mom and pop were just a couple of kids when they got married. He was eighteen, she was sixteen and I was three."

This is how jazz singer Billie Holiday starts her book of recollections. (It also happens to make a good beginning for a textbook chapter.)

People whose job it is to communicate information, ideas and feelings to others know that the beginning is the most important part of the work— whether it be a poem, play, novel, news story, song or symphony. Not only does an interesting beginning grab the attention of the reader, viewer or listener, it also helps the writer or composer to organize his or her material.

Robert Schumann, the composer, advised a fellow composer, Johannes Brahms, to study the "beginning of the Beethoven symphonies . . . to try to make something like them.

"The beginning is the main thing; if only one makes the beginning, then the end comes of itself."

Schumann could be speaking for the city editor here. If the news writer writes a good lead, the story falls into place. With a lead that is on target, the story almost organizes itself. The reason is that the lead points the writer as well as the reader or listener in a specific direction. Once the theme is expressed in the lead, the writer must run with it in the body of the story.

"With me, it's the first sentence that I wait for, and the rest follows," says Sven Birkerts, a young writer of articles and short stories.

Donald M. Murray, a University of New Hampshire professor of writing who coaches news writers for several newspapers, says the writer must engage the reader at once. "Three seconds and the reader decides to read or turn to the next story," he says.

When we see a lead like the following we want to know more about this con artist:

> A 73-year-old man was sentenced Tuesday to 10 years in prison for using the mails and telephone lines to cheat 30 people, including a Kansas City widow and a San Francisco physician, out of more than $500,000.

This crisp lead by Mary Voboril of *The Miami Herald* is inviting:

> A Dade Circuit Court jury Friday ordered General Motors to pay $1.5 million for a fiery Christmas Eve collision that left a Dade woman fatally burned and her husband badly scarred.

The reader is lured by the name of the company—many people drive GM vehicles—and by the size of the jury's award. This lead does more: It also tells the reader what the story is going to be about. This is the job of the lead—to lure the reader or listener into the story and to give him or her an idea of what's coming up.

Writing the lead is the most difficult job the writer faces in putting a story together. Let's analyze the lead-writing process to see if we can make the task easier.

Finding the Theme

News stories usually fall into two general categories: Someone has said or done something important or entertaining; or something significant or unusual has occurred. The first step in determining the theme is to decide whether the event focuses on a person or group or on an occurrence: Who or What.

If a person or group is central to the event, then the story will be based on the statements and actions of the individual or group. If an action, occurrence or idea is central, then the story is directed at one of these.

Looking back to some stories we have discussed in this book, we can see the differences. In chapter 7 we read about Joe Capik, a mail carrier on strike. This story is about an individual. In chapter 1, we saw how Lindy Washburn covered a fire, a story about an event. Jeff Klinkenberg's story was about Ron Swint, a shark fisherman, and Dan Rather's lead story in chapter 1 was about the signing of a tax bill, an occurrence.

Once we identify the focus of the story—person or occurrence—we can isolate the person's statement or action that best describes what was said or done, or we can isolate the action that best sums up what happened.

There are two practical ways to do this. The first is to jot down a skeleton summary by using the Subject-Verb-Object form:

Who said or did what

S—Joe Capik   S—Ron Swint
V—cannot afford   V—fishes for
O—much   O—Old Hitler

What happened

S—Fire   S—President
V—kills   V—signs
O—23 people   O—tax bill

The other approach to finding the theme uses the "Five Ws and an H." Writing the answers to these questions will help the writer to find the starting points or possible themes for a lead. Applying this technique to Neal Robbins' story from Hong Kong gives us these answers to our six questions:

Who—Hundreds of Chinese
What—arrived in Hong Kong
When—today
Where—in a cove
Why—fear of an earthquake
How—in their junks

It's all there, waiting to be rearranged in a lead. If this procedure works, use it. If the S-V-O skeleton does the job, use that.

Underlying our selection of the theme or themes of the story is one of the definitions of news from chapter 3, the practical definition: The stories that are published in newspapers and are used on newscasts almost always concern events that have **impact,** involve **prominent** people, or are **unusual** or **exceptional.**

A good idea for beginners is to write down the gist or main point of the event. This requires selective judgment. There is no formula for getting to the heart of a story. It takes practice.

News or Feature?

Once you've determined the theme, the second step is to decide whether the story is important or entertaining. If it is serious, a straight news story will be written. If entertaining, it will be a feature story. This decision is important because, as we saw in chapter 3, the lead and the structure differ for each type of story.

Look back at the four stories for which we constructed the S-V-O summaries. The fire and tax bill stories are important—news. Ron Swint may take himself seriously, but the story is entertaining—a feature. What about Joe

Capik, though? The postal strike developments are a likely topic for a news story. However, news stories usually have some immediacy. The Capik article has no immediacy, and yet it is not exactly entertaining.

For stories like Marcia Chambers' piece about the postman we have a third category, the news feature. Mary Ann Giordano's story about the poor family without heat or water is considered a news feature. So is Lew Moores' story about the muggers who prey on the poor.

For writing purposes, the news feature comes under the general heading of the feature.

Now that we know the criteria for determining the type of story to be written, we can determine the kind of lead to use.

Direct or Delayed Lead?

Although you might have heard differently, there are only two kinds of leads that reporters use. One is the direct lead, the lead that tells the reader at once what the story will be about. This is used for the straight news story. The major theme is in the first sentence of the first paragraph of the story.

The second type of lead is the delayed lead. That is, the major theme is not placed in the first paragraph but is given later in the story, sometimes at the very end of the piece where it is used as a kicker or climax. The point of using the delayed lead is to give the story drama, excitement, color, an entertaining twist.

Although the delayed lead is used most often for news feature and feature stories, it is sometimes effective for a straight news story. Look at this lead:

> Hiram Thompson was taking a midmorning bath in his Mattapan apartment yesterday when he heard intruders slamming around downstairs in Willie Hodo's flat.

No question that most readers would be tempted to read on. What happened downstairs? What did Thompson do? But suppose the story began this way:

```
Hiram Thompson, 48, shot and seriously wounded an
intruder in his building at 50 Meadowlands Ave.
yesterday.
```

The reader might go on, but if the reader were in Boston, where this incident occurred, he or she probably would not go further. Robberies are frequent and gunplay almost as common.

Joe Heaney and Bob Keeley of the *Boston Herald American* gave the story the drama it needed by using a delayed lead.

This approach should be taken with caution. Events that have great impact cannot be handled this way. A writer cannot begin the story of an attempted presidential assassination by describing the lunch menu or the chit-chat of the president as he left the hotel, and then get to the shooting in the fourth or fifth paragraph.

This delayed lead approach to news stories is frequently used by news magazines, and for good reason. When readers receive the weekly newsmagazines *Time* or *Newsweek*, they already know that the president was shot, the ambassador was sent packing by the Chinese, the revolution was put down. Newsmagazines use delayed leads to give stories a fresh slant.

Guideline If the event is important and if it requires the use of today, tomorrow, yesterday in the lead because of timeliness, the story is most likely a straight news story and should take a direct lead.

As we can see, once we determine whether the story is a news or feature piece, the type of lead selects itself. Here are 10 themes, slightly enlarged from the S-V-O summary. Jot down whether each is a news or feature story and the type of lead each requires. We will see what reporters have done with some of them:

Take 10

1. A Trans-American jetliner on a flight from Los Angeles to Miami runs out of fuel and must put down in Tampa.
2. Disturbances occur in Worcester, Mass., when it is revealed that the Cockroaches, a rock group giving a concert at a local night spot, are actually the Rolling Stones practicing for their first American tour in three years.
3. A group of women block the approach to a nuclear reactor in Diablo Canyon, Calif.
4. A company makes a wage offer to striking steel workers.
5. More city jobs will be eliminated Friday to balance the budget.
6. An 18-year-old high school student in Wisconsin devises a program to teach youngsters about the dangers of alcohol.
7. A New York City radio station switches music formats and becomes the most-listened-to station in the nation.
8. A new state law sends youngsters into the adult court system.
9. A figure skating champion is superstitious.
10. A blind man sails a 35-foot sailboat.

We will refer to this list in the next section as we examine how reporters have dealt with some of these themes in actual stories. Keep your notes about the type of story and lead handy.

We are now ready for the last and most important step.

Study each picture and the accompanying information. Decide whether the story (1) is about a person or event, (2) should be a straight news story or a feature story, and (3) should be given a direct or delayed lead.

Blaze. A fire does $175,000 damage to an oceanfront apartment building. One person is injured.
Mona Oxford, Pepperdine University

Official. A city official says she will run for mayor, the first woman to run for mayor in 40 years. She makes the announcement at a news conference outside city hall.
Leslie Jean-Bart

Shark. A shark-fishing contest began today, and one angler landed this 725-pound, 12½-foot-long tiger shark.
The St. Petersburg Times

Rock. The leader of a local rock group says most young rock musicians are "musically ignorant, cannot even read music and are probably tone- deaf." He suggests they take music lessons or "forget about trying to make it as musicians."
Kathy Strong, Pepperdine University

Spring. This is the first day of spring and the local weather was warm enough for a nap in the sun. The temperature reached 68 degrees. The forecast for the next three days calls for continued temperatures in the high sixties.
Terry Keys, *The Kentuckian*

Writing the Lead

The writer doing a straight news story knows he or she must get to the point at once. Major theme (or themes) in mind, the reporter sets to work. Since the lead will revolve about someone saying or doing something, or something happening, the writer begins with the person or the event—Who or What.

If the writer is working from the S-V-O summary, the **Subject** will begin the lead. If the Five W's and an H are being used, **Who** or **What** will start the lead.

The S-V-O of number 1 of our list is:

S—Jet
V—makes
O—emergency landing

The Five W's and an H give us a more complete set of facts to work from:

Who—Jetliner
What—made emergency landing
When—today
Where—in Tampa
Why—ran out of fuel
How—unknown

From either the S-V-O skeleton or the answers to the Five W's and an H, the lead is built. First, the Who or Subject of the sentence is written:

`A Trans-American jetliner on a flight from Los Angeles to Miami`

Notice that we say as much about the jetliner as possible to identify it, to separate this jetliner from the thousands that were flying on this day. We do the same thing when the **Who** or the **Subject** is a person. We don't say a man or a woman. We say a 29-year-old steel worker or Mrs. Mildred Sherman, 69, of 166 Chapel St.

Next, we move to the What or the Verb and the Object:

`made an emergency landing in Tampa today`

Notice that we added the Where and the When here. Place and time are usually placed near the verb or the object.

We could stop here, but the lead would leave people wondering about the cause of the emergency, the Why. So we add:

`when it ran out of fuel.`

Now we have:

```
A Trans-American jetliner on a flight from Los Angeles
to Miami made an emergency landing in Tampa today when it
ran out of fuel.
```

This is almost a word-for-word duplicate of the wire service leads on the story.

Our presumption in number 1 was that this was a news story that required a direct lead. But what about number 2?

Our first reaction is that this could be serious business—news story, direct lead. For those with some knowledge of the music scene, it was a disturbance at a Rolling Stones concert in Altamont, Calif., that led to the knifing death of a spectator. But the Cockroaches? There's something funny about that. Maybe a feature would be better. Hold on.

When in doubt, play it straight. That is, if the choice is not obvious, the best way to write the story is with a news approach and a direct lead. This is the safe way. To make light of a serious matter could be offensive.

Number 2 was played straight by most newspapers, though there were no serious injuries. Some damage was done, however, by people cruising through the streets.

Number 3: Straight news story. Direct lead.
Number 4: Straight news story. Direct lead.
Number 5: At first glance, this seems like a straight news story. But is it?

A tipoff to why number 5 is a delayed lead is the word *more*. This means the layoffs are part of a series of layoffs. Words like *again, still, continued* indicate there is not much new. Thus we lose the news determinant of immediacy.

Bob Rose of *The Blade* in Toledo made the event into a news feature with some enterprising reporting. In his story, he used a delayed lead. The theme does not come until the sixth paragraph:

Delayed lead: Use of incidents to begin the story

> One night this week, some Mabel Street residents went hunting for rats that had moved into their North Toledo neighborhood.
>
> "I called rodent control, and they're closed up," Tom Munger said. "I talked to the mayor's office and the woman who answered the phone said she didn't know what I could do about it. She said I should have voted."

Delayed lead (continued)

Mr. Munger, who admitted he did not cast a ballot on the payroll-income tax increase issue last month, said he and a neighbor took the problem into their own hands. "I think we got one," he said of the pests.

One night later, L. Michael Duckworth, assistant city manager, got a telephone call at home from someone asking when the city's swimming pools would open.

Transition to theme

City officials know it, but some citizens apparently do not: With 846 layoffs in the last two years, Toledo cannot control rats and it cannot open the pools. It cannot do a lot of things it used to do.

Theme: Newspoint

When 262 more city jobs are eliminated Friday, the city will have taken another step toward balancing its budget by bringing the work force down to 2,875. But the list of what it cannot do will grow longer.

Elaboration of theme

"It's hurting," Mayor Doug DeGood said of the city's inability to provide necessary services. "It's hurting."

When times get rough, city officials like to point to silver linings or better times ahead. But with an $11.5 million deficit to erase over the next 18 months, neither Mr. DeGood nor City Manager J. Michael Porter can find much cause for optimism.

The combination of the 262 lay-offs and not filling 67 police and fire division jobs is expected to save $10.2 million for the city's general fund. An additional $377,000 is being chopped off by deferring a 2 percent wage increase for city workers until Jan. 1.

The layoffs will be devastating.

"With no recreation program, bi-weekly refuse collection, a dwindling police force, and fewer firefighters, some basic services will not be provided at an adequate level," Mr. DeGood said. . . .

The writer has to make two decisions when using a delayed lead. First, he or she must decide just what the lead is. In this case, the S-V-O is: City will eliminate 262 more city jobs Friday. The writer must then find a fitting quote, incident, example that will take the reader right into the lead. Rose chose two examples of the consequences of the layoffs—eliminating the rodent control program and closing down the city's pools.

Rose shows rather than tells the reader what impact the cutbacks will have. Then in the sixth paragraph he explains the cuts the city must make. The next several paragraphs relate the details of the cutbacks. Rose completes the story by recounting the various cutbacks, parks and park buildings closed, golf courses shut down, recreation programs for the handicapped curtailed.

Number 6: This story obviously does not require a today in the lead. It is a news feature, so the AP put a delayed lead on it:

FOND DU LAC, WIS. (AP)--SOMETIMES THE BEST HELP A JUNIOR HIGH SCHOOL STUDENT CAN RECEIVE COMES NOT FROM A TEACHER OR PARENT BUT FROM A SENIOR HIGH SCHOOL STUDENT.

THAT THEORY, ''KIDS HELPING KIDS,'' IS THE IDEA BEHIND A NEW ALCOHOL AWARENESS PROGRAM DEVELOPED BY A ST. MARY'S SPRINGS HIGH SCHOOL STUDENT FOR ELEMENTARY AND JUNIOR HIGH SCHOOL STUDENTS.

THE PROGRAM WAS DEVELOPED BY JEFF WEINSHROTT, AN 18-YEAR-OLD SPRINGS SENIOR. . . .

The lead idea is: High school student develops program to combat alcoholism. The AP writer realized that the unique or unusual aspect of it was a student teaching students about the dangers of alcohol. The writer emphasized the unique aspect by using that general idea to begin the story. The lead follows quickly in the second and third paragraphs.

Number 7: What happened here? An FM station switched from mellow music to disco and its ratings jumped. Significant or entertaining? For a magazine devoted to reporting broadcast news, this is significant and a direct lead is in order. Something like this:

By switching to disco, New York radio station WKTU-FM has become the most-listened-to station in the country.

But for a general audience, the reaction to that lead may well be: So what. For Geoff Walden, a student who wrote this story on assignment for a journalism class, this was an entertaining story, and so he put a delayed lead on the piece. He dramatized the switch this way:

> NEW YORK—Last July 24th, at 5:59 p.m., WKTU-FM "Mellow 92," was playing Neil Young's soft-rock song, "It's Over."
>
> At 6 p.m., WKTU-FM, "The new Disco 92," was playing Donna Summer's "The Last Dance."
>
> For Donna Summer, the song went on to win this year's Oscar for the Best Original Song, for the movie "Thank God It's Friday." For the radio station, the song was the start of an all-disco format that has made WKTU the most-listened-to station in America, with an average of 275,000 people tuning in every quarter hour.

The direct lead tells readers: Here comes something important. Walden's beginning tells them: Relax, I'm going to entertain you. But notice that the theme or lead idea is exactly the same for both:

S—Format change
V—makes
O—station most-listened-to

Number 8: This story falls into the category editors call an update. This type of story brings the reader or listener up to date on something that has happened. An update usually is not a straight news story and does not require a direct lead. How should the story be approached?

Richard Higgins, another journalism student, reasoned that his story should describe youngsters in the adult courts. So he began his story by portraying young offenders in the new courtroom setting.

> NEW YORK—Rafael Torres and Hector Valdez sat at the brown wooden table, playing with Superman coloring books, combing their hair, waving and occasionally shouting to friends in the room.
>
> It could have been a scene out of the South Bronx junior high school where they are enrolled in the eighth grade. But it was the beginning of an arson and multiple murder trial in the Bronx Criminal Courthouse and the two skinny, squirming boys were not there to learn; they were the defendants.

In the next paragraph Higgins introduces the lead that tells the reader that these youngsters are in court because of a new law and that other youngsters are being tried in the adult courts. He makes a news feature out of his material.

Number 9: For this kind of feature story, Linda Kramer, an AP reporter, says she gathers "piles of material for a story." When she writes, she tries to "weed out the non-essential copy. I want to choose the anecdote that best reflects and highlights what I want to say."

This is a precise description of how the writer must use the anecdote or incident chosen to begin the feature or news feature story. The material must feed directly into the theme or lead.

"In writing about figure-skating champion Linda Fratianne, I led with a description of a lucky charm she pins to her costume during competition. To me, this little touch of superstitiousness illustrated the 17-year-old behind the star," Kramer says. This, then, was her theme—although Fratianne's magnificent presence on the ice makes her seem almost regal, the real Linda Fratianne is a youngster with a girl's feelings. Here is Kramer's first paragraph in her delayed lead:

> Tucked in a tiny blue pouch pinned to Linda Fratianne's sequinned skating costume are two four-leaf clovers, a piece of gold foil, and a snip of green yarn.

Number 10: The news writer takes the reader aboard the blind man's sailboat:

> Keeping a grip on the sheet, Albert Adams draws the maximum amount of speed from his 35-foot sailboat.
>
> The yellow-hulled boat responds to Adams' touch and picks up speed. Adams turns to his crew—his wife and two teen-age sons—and asks them to lend a hand.
>
> Adams has been blind since birth. The 33-year-old accountant sails regularly. He can tell from which direction the wind is coming by ear. . . .

Like the beginning of many features, this one **shows** the subject doing something.

Summing Up

Some of these leads, and others in the textbook, might seem beyond you at this stage of your writing development. Don't be concerned. Behind almost every one of the journalists whose work is represented here is an apprenticeship with a lot of trial and error. For every good lead that these writers have hammered out, they can tell a sad tale of one they botched.

The trick now is to master the process, to learn the way leads are written. No writer can dash off a lead without going through the basic steps outlined at the beginning of this chapter.

After these steps, the lead is ready to be written. Go back to the words you have jotted down as the theme. They may be in the form of the S-V-O skeleton summary, or you may have written a complete sentence. If the lead is a direct lead, make sure that you have the time element (when)—today, yesterday, tomorrow. Make sure that the person, group, or action (who or what) is adequately identified, which means that he, she, or it is named or given an identifying label. Be certain that the subject of the action is precise. It is not the council but the city council; not the court but Federal District Court or Grant County Court, and so on.

What to Do and What to Avoid

The journalistic boneyard is littered with the carcasses of young writers gone wrong because they thought clever writing was the beginning and the end of journalism. The largest section of this graveyard is reserved for those who wrote brilliant leads but could not deliver the facts in the body of the story to back up those glorious leads.

Everyone—editors, colleagues, readers and listeners—likes good writing. But the journalist must be honest with his or her words. The words must reflect reality, the actual event. By writing a bright lead a writer may well tease, cajole, or entice the reader or listener to tarry a while. But the story must deliver on that promise.

We've all been lured into carnival tents, movie houses and theaters or to dances, parties and blind dates only to find that the pitch or come-on was more exciting than the reality. Honesty may not mean much in the entertainment world, or, to be more generous, one person's "best ever" is another's mediocrity. In journalism, honesty is everything. If the writer regularly cheats the reader, the boneyard beckons.

Short and Sweet

Try to make the lead read well. The best test of this is to read it aloud before you hand it in. If it's smooth, fine. If it stutters, ditch it.

If it's too long, cut. There is no last word about the proper length of a lead, but most editors want short leads. That means under 40 words almost everywhere, under 35 most places, under 30 in some.

Reporters like to talk about leads when they get together—the most colorful, the most dramatic, the shortest. H. D. Quigg, a UPI reporter, and Homer Bigart, a veteran of New York City newspapers, once reminisced about the shortest leads they had read. Quigg's favorite went back to 1927, a dispatch in *The New York Times* about Charles Lindbergh's solo flight across the Atlantic Ocean:

PARIS—Lindbergh did it.

Bigart recalled a shorter one he wrote himself. The piece was from West Point, where cadets who were engaged in artillery practice were so far off target that some shells landed in a farmer's field. Bigart knew he had done the *Times* lead one better. His lead had two words. He was not sure whether it was "Oops, missed," or "Cease fire."

To write short leads, the writer needs to keep in mind the guide that the lead should, if at all possible, contain only one basic idea. Here is a lead that should be reworked because it does not conform to the guideline:

> THE BOARD OF REGENTS LAST NIGHT VOTED TO
> REQUIRE THAT COLLEGE ATHLETES HAVE AT LEAST A C—
> AVERAGE TO RETAIN ELIGIBILITY, AND IT RECOMMENDED
> THAT THE COLLEGE-OWNED BOOK STORE BE SHUT DOWN TO
> AVOID ``FURTHER DEFICITS.''

Obviously, the writer is trying to put two ideas across. However, two sentences would allow the reader to grasp the ideas with greater ease. A simple solution is to put a period after the word *eligibility* and start a new sentence.

Not all long leads are difficult to understand. Good writing, drama, human interest and rhythm can make a long sentence read well. Some operas are tediously long. Mozart's "The Magic Flute" is hours long but few walk out on it, despite its length. The difference is quality. Bad stuff is boring. A Bruce Springsteen concert can never end for his fans, but the high school rock group makes noises that drive listeners to seek shelter elsewhere.

Look at this lead from the *San Francisco Chronicle* and decide whether it is too long:

> The tortured young drifter who paralyzed Market Street traffic with random rifle fire during much of the weekend, hanged himself in his jail cell yesterday, confident that the reincarnation he believed awaited him would free him from an existence he found intolerable.

It's long. But it has the ingredients of a tragic novel. This writer knew what he was doing, but most long leads are the result of thoughtlessness. They go on and on, like the songs of the inept high school rock group, the "Stopped-up Sink."

Imagine what the reporters on the old *Chicago Daily News* had to endure when the newspaper decided that no lead could run over 17 words. One of their star reporters, Edwin A. Lahey, was sent to Connecticut to cover a murder trial shortly after the rule went into effect. One of his leads read this way:

> BRIDGEPORT, CONN.—
> Witnesses paraded through the chair like customers in a 25-cent barber shop.

Red Smith, the dean of American sports writers, said his favorite lead was by John Lardner about a prize-fighter who was murdered in his prime:

> Stanley Ketchel was 24 years old when he was fatally shot in the back by the common-law husband of the lady who was cooking his breakfast.

This lead is a gem. It takes less than 30 words to say and suggest a lot. Lardner was working on a book about drinking in America at the time of his death. The first sentence in the manuscript was:

> Most of the early settlers of this country had never tasted water except for religious or medicinal purposes or unless they fell off a bridge.

Humor—Be Careful

Good leads, leads that are remembered, are hard to write, and the hardest of the hard are the humorous leads. Most journalistic humor has a short life—about the time it takes to cross the distance from the writer's typewriter to the copy desk.

One lead that has endured was written by John Polly of the *Rocky Mountain News*. In the 1930s, Denver was wide open. One night, a disgruntled customer set a house of prostitution afire. Polly wrote this lead:

> There hadn't been so much excitement at the Silver Dollar since the night a patron came in and asked for a room.

Howell Raines of *The New York Times* likes to write unusual leads, and he is not above a pun or a play on words. For a story he did about transplanted easterners who immediately buy boots and Stetsons on moving to the West, he began:

> You can tell by his outfit that he is a cowboy.

Raines wondered how this went over, and at a journalism writing conference he asked a group of 15 reporters if they got it. Two started humming at once, and one sang the words. The other dozen had no idea what was happening. Raines had borrowed his lead from the old western ballad, "Streets of Laredo."

For another piece, this one about Bruce A. Smathers, a public official in Florida whose father was a United States senator, friend of presidents and a big-time lawyer, Raines wrote this lead:

> Will the son also rise?

Raines was asked how he decided on the lead to the Smathers story, which is a takeoff on the title of a novel by Ernest Hemingway, *The Sun Also Rises*. Raines replied:

"This is one of the few times in my career that I used a pun lead. And it seemed so inevitable . . . in talking to Smathers about being his father's son and how he had planned his career . . . the phrase just kept running through my mind.

"I couldn't believe that no one had ever written it because it seemed so obvious. . . . The lead caused a lot of comment, generally favorable, as I recall. I consider that sort of lead a gamble. I was so taken with it, though, that I was prepared for it not to be well thought of. But it was inevitable that I use it."

Some puns and witty leads have become so irresistible that they keep coming back for repeat performances. When a music reviewer hears a school orchestra play off-key all night, his review may begin with this one:

> The Fairfield School Orchestra
> played Beethoven last night. Bee-
> thoven lost.

Of the actress whose emotional range was limited, another critic wrote:

> She ran the gamut of emotions
> from A to B.

This last one is credited to Dorothy Parker, who also is responsible for one of the most devastating put-downs a critic wrote:

> She was the toast of two conti-
> nents—Australia and Greenland.

Three great temptations that afflict beginners trying to write good leads are the "question," "quote" and "you" leads.

Forbidden Fruit

The Question Lead:

> Looking for something to do today? In Darien, try the
> Hindley Happening. In New Canaan, take in the Country
> School Clothesline Sale. . . .

The Quote Lead:

```
"The colleges of this country are in the hands of an
untouchable elite--tenured professors."
This was the charge made last night by. . . .
```

The You Lead:

```
You may not know it, but the land beneath you rises and
falls each day by as much as two feet, like the tides of
the ocean.
You don't notice it because, in the words of. . . .
```

Editors consider question, quote, and you leads the reporter's way of surrendering. They allow the writer to avoid stating a theme.

"This often means that the writer never comes to grips with the story," Lynn Ludlow of *The San Francisco Examiner* says. "As with the question lead, a quote lead frequently begins a disorganized narrative in the rambling manner of a memo.

"If a quote is irresistible, keep it short and snappy. Plainly state the theme in the next graph."

Ludlow offers an example of a short and snappy quote lead that worked:

"Celibacy is like ice skating,"
said Roman Catholic Bishop Robert
O'Mooney. "It gets easier with
practice."

Concrete Nouns, Action Verbs

Good writers know that sentences travel on their nouns and verbs. A noun that refers to a specific thing and a verb that flies, floats, or sizzles makes the sentence move.

Weak writers torture the language with labored similes and not-so-clever phrases. Here's an example from the statehouse bureau of a wire service:

```
ALBANY--SEVERAL OF THE TOP NOSES IN GOV. HUGH
CAREY'S ADMINISTRATION WERE OUT OF JOINT TODAY,
FOLLOWING CAREY'S CREATION OF A $48,000-A-YEAR
POSITION FOR A MAN THEY NEVER MET.
```

Why not say "Carey's associates were muttering" about the appointment. The verb *mutter* has just the ring for this situation.

There is always an exact noun and action verb for the situation the writer is describing. The English language is a writer's language. It has a treasure trove of words that convey different shades of meaning: mutter, shout, moan, whisper, croon, sing, coo, sigh. . . .

Down in the coal mines, a canary sings the songs of life. When the canary stops singing, the coal miners get out. They know that if a canary can't live with whatever is in the air, coal miners can't either.

A canary, a kitten, and a puppy died last summer in a mobile home in Dallas. The pets' owner was a little girl who also became sick— with an enlarged liver and toxic hepatitis.

This is how Bonnie Britt of the *Houston Chronicle* began her story about the use of formaldehyde in the woodwork, paneling and walls of mobile homes. The prose flows naturally because of her use of concrete nouns and action verbs.

In Britt's lead we are made aware that something important is happening. Our concern focuses on the child's illness. The lead from Albany about the governor's appointment makes us notice the writer. Readers and listeners want to know about the subject of the piece. The writer should be invisible.

Summary

Most of the leads we have been discussing in this chapter are single-element leads. One element, or theme, was the subject of the story: jet airliner makes emergency landing, fire kills 23 people, president signs tax bill, student develops alcoholism program.

Good leads can be written with two, even three, themes; we have seen some of these. Generally, newspaper editors prefer one-theme leads, and single-theme leads are almost always used for broadcast news.

Structuring the single-theme story is fairly easy. The newswriter faces more complex problems writing two- and three-element stories. In chapter 9 we will examine the ways to structure news and feature stories for events of one, two and more themes.

Structuring the Story

The news story is structured according to the number of main elements or themes the writer decides to use in the lead.

Looking Ahead

The single-element lead is the most common. The body of the news story includes the facts, quotes and incidents that explain, buttress and support the element used in the lead. Less important elements and themes are included in the body of the story after the lead element has been adequately explained.

Some stories have two or three important elements. Leads for these stories include all the elements or a summary of the elements. The body of the story takes each element in order and supplies the reader with the supporting material, to buttress each element. After this, the writer includes any secondary material.

The news writer is a builder. From notes and knowledge he or she constructs a logical and complete structure. Like any builder, the news writer works from plans. Just as the builder has one set of plans for an office structure, another for an apartment building and a third for a three-bedroom home, so the news writer has different plans for different types of stories.

After the writer selects the main theme or themes and decides whether the event will require a news or feature story, the next decision is how many themes the story will include. The third decision is the type of lead to put on the story. From these decisions, plans are devised that will structure the story.

If one idea, action or occurrence clearly stands out as the most important or unusual aspect of what was said or done, then the writer has a single-theme story. All other ideas, actions and occurrences are secondary. A single-theme story requires a single-element lead.

When two or three aspects stand out, the writer has a two-element or three-element story. Again, the lead will reflect these elements. Once the writer selects the main theme or themes and decides what type of story the event requires, he or she begins to structure the story.

Single-Element Story. The score in this soccer game is the major element of the story and goes into the lead. The names of the players who scored, the key offensive and defensive plays, the changes in the standings and the home team's next game are additional facts that go into the body of the story.
Susan Plageman, *The Berkshire Eagle*

Organizing the Straight News Story

To begin our study of story structure, let's first examine the organization of the straight news story. The starting point is deciding how many major elements or themes the story will include.

When we talk about themes or elements we don't mean individual facts. A story may contain many facts but only one, two, or three major themes or elements. You might say that a theme or element of a story is the summary of a set of facts.

The city council votes 4–3 in favor of a major street paving program—that becomes the major element for the lead. The arguments for and against the program, the present condition of city streets, the city engineer's statement that twice the proposed amount is needed to fix the streets—all these are facts that go into the body of the story to support the major element in the lead.

The city council also considered other items that the news writer will include in the story. These additional items are: the hiring of a new director for the city recreation department, a preliminary discussion of a city-county garbage disposal plan and the suggestion that holidays be scheduled so that city employees can have three-day weekends.

These themes are secondary in importance to the street-paving program and are included in the story after the news writer has given ample attention to the street-paving program, which is the major theme.

If the city council had also voted to spend $500,000 on improving the sewage treatment plant, that would have been a major element. Both could be made into the lead and then amplified in the story. When these had been written up, the writer would go on to the secondary material.

Donald M. Murray, the news writing coach, says the lead can be thought of as the promise and the body then makes good on that promise. The lead says to the reader or listener: Hey, look at what I found out. The body says: Let me explain it to you.

No news story should promise so much that the reader or listener will turn away in confusion. This is why the news story must confine itself to only the most important or interesting aspects or elements of the event.

Single-Element News Story

A plane crash kills three people. A local clothing store is swept by fire. The president flies to Mexico for a conference. A former school principal dies. The Orioles beat the Red Sox.

These are spot news stories, and like most spot news stories, they make for single-element news stories. All single-element news stories take the basic structure shown in figure 9.1.

The first paragraph contains the lead. The second paragraph either elaborates on the lead or provides the necessary background. The story continues with additional supporting and buttressing information about the lead. When the writer has finished with all the relevant material to support the main element of the story, secondary themes are then added.

Forest Fire The following is an example of a spot news story with a single major theme, a one-element story.

Lead: Fire may spread

A fire in the Daniel Boone National Forest that has destroyed 500 acres of woodland is threatening to spread to private lands.

Explanation of the lead: High winds causing fire to spread

The Kentucky Division of Forestry reported today that high winds have made control of the blaze difficult. The winds are pushing the fire toward timberlands to the northeast, agency officials said.

Background: When started, cause, weather conditions

The fire broke out Thursday. The cause is undetermined. Forest fires are common during periods of dry, warm weather such as the area is now experiencing, an official said.

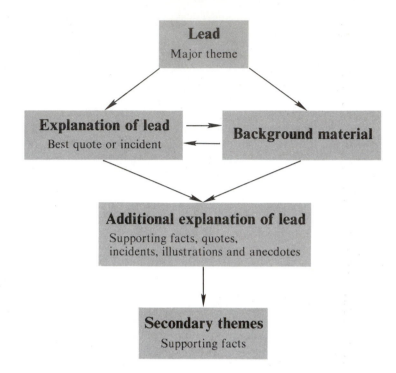

Figure 9.1 Single-element story structure.

Lead
Major theme

Explanation of lead
Best quote or incident

Background material

Additional explanation of lead
Supporting facts, quotes, incidents, illustrations and anecdotes

Secondary themes
Supporting facts

Additional explanation of the lead

The forestry division has sent 40 firefighters to the area to try to contain the fire. But they have been hampered by the lack of access roads.

More explanation of the lead

No inhabited areas are threatened by the fire, the official said. But there are valuable timberlands to the northeast owned by private growers.

Secondary Theme

The forestry division is trying a new form of forest-fire spray that was developed by the state's engineers. In addition to digging trenches and felling trees in the path of the fire, the firefighters are using a spray that temporarily causes leaves and needles to drop, thus making it more difficult for the fire to spread.

Two-Element News Story

The governor announces that because of financial problems he is ordering an immediate halt in the $25 million construction program on college and university campuses. He also says he will recommend to the state board of education that all salaries for public school teachers in the state be frozen for next year.

As a reporter on your college newspaper, you want to know whether construction will be halted on your campus. You discover that the order eliminates a plan for a $3 million dormitory to be built with state funds. This gives you a good single-element story. The freezing of salaries for public school teachers does not directly affect your readers, so it becomes secondary material.

Press association reporters and state capital bureau reporters from large daily newspapers realize that both announcements will interest their readers. Because the reporters consider the items of equal importance, they will construct their stories on a two-element lead.

There are three ways to structure the two-element story:

1. If the two elements conveniently fit into a single sentence, the writer can put them both in the first paragraph.
2. If combining both elements into a single sentence requires more than 35 or 40 words, the writer will have to give each element a sentence of its own. This option allows the writer to place both sentences in the first paragraph or to make each sentence into a separate paragraph.
3. If the two elements cannot be squeezed into a sentence (option one) and the writer does not want to write a two-sentence or two-paragraph lead (option two) because it would be too long and cumbersome, a third option is available—the summary lead. A summary lead is just what its name implies: It sums up the two elements by using an introductory statement. Here is an example of a summary lead:

The Springfield City Council last night took two major steps toward improving city services.

The council voted 4–3 in favor of a $1 million street paving program to be paid for by revenue bonds. It also voted, 6–1, to spend $500,000 to improve the sewage treatment plant, which a state study team declared to be "obsolete" last month.

The council was urged by Mayor Sam Myer to adopt both measures. "Unless we do so," he said, "we will fall behind in meeting the basic needs of our residents."

Despite his pleas, three of the council members were dubious about putting the city into debt for the paving program. . . .

Money Troubles Let's see what a news writer for a daily in the state capital does with the governor's announcement about financial cutbacks. He takes the options in order. He would prefer a lead that can handle both elements in less than 35 words (the first option). He writes:

```
Gov. Mark Acosta said today that financial problems
necessitate an immediate halt to a $25 million state
college construction program, and he also said he will
recommend a freeze in salaries for public school
teachers.
```

The lead just makes it by word count, but it has a jammed-up feel to it. He decides to try the second option, two sentences:

> Gov. Mark Acosta said today financial problems necessitate an immediate halt to a $25 million state college construction program. He also said he will recommend a freeze in salaries for public school teachers.

No. Still jammed-up. What's more, he suddenly sees he has the lead turned around. He should put the wage freeze first since there are obviously more teachers, parents, and pupils affected by the freeze than by the college construction program.

Even if he does reverse the elements, he still has a bulky lead. As for making each sentence into a paragraph, he does not like two-paragraph leads unless he is forced to use them.

Can he cut down on the number of words? Yes, he can put the reason for the governor's drastic actions in the second paragraph:

> Gov. Mark Acosta said today he will recommend a freeze in salaries for public school teachers next year, and he ordered an immediate halt to a $25 million state college construction program.
>
> The governor said financial problems necessitated his actions. He said that cutbacks in federal aid for education had not been anticipated when the construction program was adopted.

That's better, he thinks. He has also managed to insert background material into the second paragraph. But the city editor is a short-lead advocate. He likes leads under 25 words, so the reporter now must try a summary lead, the third option. In writing a summary lead, the trick is to find something common to both elements.

The reporter notes that the actions were described by the governor as "drastic" and so he decides to use that as the basis of his lead:

> Gov. Mark Acosta said today financial problems have forced him to take "drastic" action on teacher salaries and the state college construction program.
>
> The governor said he will recommend a freeze on the salaries of public school teachers. And he ordered an immediate halt to the $25 million college construction program.
>
> The governor said unforeseen federal cutbacks necessitated his actions. . . .

Two-Element Story. A story about a flood that takes several lives and causes considerable property damage has these two elements in the lead. Rescue efforts, loss of power and telephone service, the weather forecast for the rest of the week and closed highways are secondary facts that are placed lower in the story.
Stewart Bowman, *The Courier-Journal*

Trouble at the Dump Here is a two-paragraph lead (the second option) that a reporter wrote about a city countil meeting because he decided the two major elements could not be squeezed into a lead sentence:

> The city council last night voted to postpone a
> decision on the purchase of acreage north of the city for
> a garbage dump after angry residents in the area
> disrupted the council meeting.
> In another action, the council voted 4-3 to end
> financing of the city's summer educational programs
> despite protests from other groups.

Too much action for the reader to grasp, the writer thinks. He decides on a summary lead (the third option). He has to find a common idea that links the two elements. Obviously, one common idea is that the two actions were taken by the city council. But that's so broad it says next to nothing. Another idea is that the actions are important, but that's too broad also. There is another common idea, the protesting groups. He tries to make something of this:

```
One group of residents had their way with the city
council last night, but a second group of angry
protesters lost out.
```

Not too bad. Let's accept this, then see what comes next. The writer must immediately elaborate on the two actions in order with specific material:

```
The successful protest was aimed at the council's
consideration of the purchase of acreage north of the
city for a garbage dump. Residents from the area
disrupted the council meeting with their protest.
    The council postponed a decision.
    In the other important action, the council voted 4-3 to
end financing of the city's summer educational programs
despite the protests of various groups.
```

Although the summary lead takes a while to get the reader to the heart of the story, it is preferred by many newspapers and is the way broadcast leads for complex stories are written. It does not overwhelm the reader or listener. The summary lead beckons the reader to come into the story.

So much for the lead. Let's consider the body of the two-element story.

Organize Supporting Material   We saw in the single-element story that the body of the piece consists of background information and the explanation or elaboration of the lead. Additional or secondary material is included deep in the story. The two-element story follows the same general outline with one major difference.

The important principle to remember in writing multiple-element stories is not to jump around. The writer should not write a paragraph with material that supports lead element A and then jump to a paragraph of supporting material for lead element B, and then back to A, and so forth. The result would be a confused reader or listener.

The guideline is to put similar material together. Put all the supporting material about lead element A together before you begin to elaborate on element B. In the city council meeting story, the body includes material about the garbage dump first since that was the first element mentioned in the lead. After the key supporting material about the dump is used in the body, the reporter writes a transition or swing paragraph introducing the summer program, and then the buttressing material for the vote on the summer program is used.

To jump from lead element A to lead element B would be too abrupt. We need a transition from one element to the other. By this we mean a paragraph, a sentence, one or two words that will swing the reader from one topic to another. The move must be made in a graceful sweep.

Here is a possible transition in the council meeting story after the explanation of element A (successful protest against the garbage dump) to element B (vote to end the city's summer programs):

```
While the garbage-dump protesters were pleased by the
council action, the parents hoping to retain the summer
programs were disappointed.
```

A good transition tells readers where they have been (action on dump) and then informs them where they are being taken (action on summer program).

Notice the word *while* in the sentence that serves as a transition. *While* is a conjunction, which is a word or phrase that serves as a connector. Connectors join the different elements in a story and make the piece have the structure of a linked chain. There are many conjunctions. Here are some of them:

and	next
but	before
however	after
on the other hand	in addition to
meanwhile	moreover
although	later
then	furthermore
now	nevertheless

You can see that these words are two-directional, taking the reader back and then projecting the reader forward. Notice their use in these transitional sentences:

The Hawks had no trouble with tonight's opponents, **but** tomorrow's game should be another story.

In addition to commenting on the high price of fuel she discussed the need for home insulation.

Next in his list of objections was the department's action on street repairs.

No reporter should be a slave to a formula. Sometimes, a news writer handling a two-element story will amplify A and B with a paragraph or two for each before moving into the fairly rigid compartmentalizing of the supporting material for each.

Three-Element Story. The writer covering this speech by gubernatorial candidate Charles Robb decided Robb's three major points were equally important and included all three in the lead.
Thomas L. Brossart, *Daily News*

Some news writers will bring up secondary material before they have finished with all the supporting material for the lead elements. They do this when they consider the secondary material to be important but not important enough for the lead.

For beginning news writers, the structures suggested here are good starting points. These structures make for stories that are more easily understood than new stories following any other structure.

We are now ready to turn to the three-element story. There are no surprises. Our basic approach is the same.

Three-Element News Story

Here is a three-element lead:

> JONESVILLE—Residents of Lee County turned out in force yesterday to hear gubernatorial candidate Charles "Chuck" Robb propose more jobs, more efficient use of coal and hope for the small farmer as the young Democrat brought his campaign here.
>
> —*Daily News* (Middlesboro, Ky.)

There were three major elements in Robb's speech: (1) promise of more jobs, (2) more efficient use of coal, and (3) hope for the small farmer. The writer, Cary B. Willis, chose to include all of them in the lead because the three elements were not complicated.

Still, the lead runs well over 30 words. This is the problem with trying to cram all three elements in the lead. However, this type of lead does immediately tell the reader just what has occurred or what someone has said or done. It also helps the writer with the story structure.

In the next few paragraphs of the story notice how Willis goes into each of the lead elements, A, B, and C, in order. Then, secondary material and the background are given:

A—jobs

He told a standing-room-only luncheon crowd of close to 200 that he plans to create jobs for 50,000 Virginians if elected to the state's top executive position Nov. 3. He said he had "the most comprehensive plan ever offered by a candidate for governor" to stimulate Virginia's economy.

B—coal

One of the major topics in Robb's brief speech to the audience at the newly-renovated Joyce's Antiques was what he called "Virginia's energy future."

"Coal has to be the cornerstone of Virginia's future," he said in a loud, clear politician's voice. He said the state needs to make better use of its coal reserves, reducing by 20 percent its dependence on outside energy sources within the next 10 years.

"We've got to use more of what we're generating here," he said, stressing the need for a balance between coal that is exported and that which is used locally.

C—farmers

He moved quickly on to agricultural matters, speaking with apparent optimism about this year's tobacco crop in southwest Virginia, as well as mentioning his disappointment with the off year cattle farmers are experiencing.

Secondary matter

He touched on topics common to any good politician's campaign, including education, financial difficulties, roads and care for the elderly.

Background

The 42-year-old Richmond resident, presently serving as lieutenant governor to the outgoing Gov. John Dalton, said Virginia's poor financial condition is one of the most serious challenges the state has faced. . . .

Coping with Crime   A reporter covering an address by the state prison warden to the state legislature decided to emphasize three of the warden's recommendations. In his first lead, the reporter combined the three major elements into a single-sentence lead:

```
State Prison Warden Ralph Newman told state
legislators today that the return of the death penalty, a
new state penitentiary and tougher laws for violent
crimes will halt the spiraling crime rate in the state.
```

The lead has exactly 35 words. This seems to do the job effectively, but some editors balk at including so many ideas in a single sentence. One idea to a sentence if possible, they tell their writers. The first option of putting all the elements in a one-sentence lead is infrequently used for the three-element story. The second option is used more often:

```
State Prison Warden Ralph Newman today called for the
return of the death penalty to help halt the spiraling
crime rate in the state.
    He also said that a new state penitentiary and tougher
laws for violent crimes would help to cut the rate.
```

Not bad. But many writers prefer the summary lead for any story with more than two major elements. The writer then tried a summary lead:

```
State Prison Warden Ralph Newman today gave state
legislators a plan he said would halt the state's
spiraling crime rate.
```

This is so short the writer decided to add the fact that Newman described it as a three-point plan. Here is the final version:

State Prison Warden Ralph Newman today gave state legislators a three-point plan that he said would halt the state's spiraling crime rate.

Newman recommended the return of the death penalty, the construction of a new state penitentiary and tougher laws for violent crime.

The warden testified at a house-senate committee hearing on crime. Last year's crime rate was up 22 percent over the previous year, with violent crime increasing 27 percent.

Newman said the death penalty would. . . .

After amplifying the warden's testimony on the death penalty (A), the reporter discussed the construction of the prison (B). Then he buttressed the element about tougher laws (C).

Teenagers and Dope   The city editor has just finished reading a story in the Sunday *New York Times* about youngsters and marijuana. He calls over a reporter and tells her, "Boil this down and give the *Times* full credit. We're going to have a series on the local drug scene among youngsters and I want to show our readers that we are not sensationalizing the local scene."

The reporter reads through the story and sees that there are three elements: Teenagers can find pot easily, don't feel guilty about using it and have no fear of using it.

The reporter takes three sheets of paper and puts one element at the top of each sheet. Under each element, she lists the supporting data. (Some professionals, like Saul Pett of AP Newsfeatures, make outlines for their features.)

On her first sheet, for example, under the heading "Find easily," she writes:

```
Buy from classmates.
Buy from street salesmen.
Even pushers at famous Public Library.
Cocaine and heroin also sold here.
```

She makes similar lists on the other two sheets. On a fourth sheet she lists the secondary material, such as the increase in drinking among teenagers.

She is now ready to write. She would like to put all three elements in the lead for emphasis, to show the scope of the situation:

```
New York teenagers who smoke marijuana can find it
easily, do not feel guilty about using it and have little
fear of being arrested.
    These are the findings of a survey of 1,000 high school
students as reported in "The New York Times"
Sunday. . . .
```

Now, all she need do is go to her first sheet and elaborate on the availability of pot. When that is finished, she will write a transition and go to the second sheet about lack of guilt, and so on until she has completed the secondary material.

The 1, 2, 3 Approach Reporters occasionally use a variation of the summary lead for a story with three elements. The 1, 2, 3 approach (the fourth option) looks something like this:

```
    The city council took three far-reaching actions at its
meeting last night.
    The council voted to:
    1. Open bids on the controversial community center
that had been stalled in court.
    2. Buy three parcels of land for a new downtown mass
transit center.
    3. Construct a pedestrian overpass over Highway 28
where the Arden Hills Shopping Center will be built.
```

The three items can also be listed right at the outset as Margaret Sullivan does in a story for the *Buffalo News* that begins this way:

• If a woman is really smart and aggressive in business, she's good at hiding the fact that she's smart and aggressive.

• The sexual thing just doesn't go away in business situations.

• Nightmares, depression and stress are the price women pay as they make their way through a male-dominated corporate superstructure.

Those statements—the words of a Buffalo businessman, a local woman accountant and a Stanford University study—just begin to tell the story about women in business, a story that doesn't show up on any company's balance sheet.

Suddenly, without warning, women have become a presence in Buffalo business, and not as glorified secretaries—not by a long shot.

There are a couple of partners in national accounting firms, a bank president and several vice presidents, some owners of mid-sized businesses and a big group of up-and-comers.

So far the sailing hasn't all been smooth, and as women head into the 1980s—a decade that should see them growing in numbers and prominence—they'll face problems most businessmen never even think about.

In the fourth paragraph, Sullivan summarizes her points by saying that the three items are part of the story on women in business. The fifth and sixth paragraphs give background.

Sullivan is then ready to tackle the supporting material to back up her major themes. She needs a transition to swing into the body, and she does it in the seventh paragraph.

Now to the supporting material. To buttress her first theme, she quotes the dean of the School of Management at the State University at Buffalo, Joseph Alutto:

"Businesswomen are often very aggressive and need to be, but it's a trait that people accept better in a man than in a woman."

She also quotes a woman shopowner in Buffalo:

"Women walk a thin line in deciding how forward to be."

To buttress her second theme, sexual relationships in business, she writes:

"The sexual issue does create problems," says Rand Capital Corp. president Donald Ross. "There are lots of liaisons, and they complicate and obscure the real issues."

Romantic involvements are nothing new, these business people note, but they add that it's different now that some women are men's equals on the job.

"No one cared when women were only secretaries and could be replaced like disposable parts," says Susan Jacoby.

"It's always a two-way street, but usually there's a poor, misguided female involved who thinks that's the way to get to the top," observes stockbroker Rosemary Ligotti.

To support her third theme, the price women pay for going into business, she begins with a quick transition and then goes into the subject:

The problems may lie deeper—taking a toll on a woman's emotional well-being.

"Women may not realize the kinds of sacrifices they have to make to forge a successful career," says Miss Ptak.

"They have to realize that it means taking things home, making business calls at night," she continues. "It's not 9-to-5. And it's stressful. They may have to sacrifice their social lives."

Women who try to do it all—manage a family as well as an executive position—are far more likely to become depressed, anxious, and suffer nightmares. They also are four times more likely than men to seek psychological help, according to a Stanford University study of business school graduates.

"These women are very hard on themselves. They feel they constantly have to be proving themselves," says co-author Harvey Weinstein.

The Chronological Approach

Now that we have outlined the basic structure of the straight news story, we will look at a technique that is often used for the dramatic news story.

Ever since humans sat around a fire in a prehistoric cave and listened to the storyteller, the tale has been popular. No matter how often it is told, people will listen. Even when they know the outcome, they will hear the speaker out.

This is the reasoning behind the chronological approach to the breaking news story. Essentially, the story is told twice.

The lead tells the reader what happens, and a few paragraphs of buttressing and supporting material amplify the lead. Then there is a transition and the writer turns back to give an account of how the situation occurred—the day the crime was committed, the excitement of two couples as they set out for a wedding party, the first play of the dramatic last two minutes of the game.

Here is how the story of a frightening ride on a school bus began in *The Advocate* in Stamford, Conn.:

Forty junior high school students on school bus 10 were terrified Friday afternoon.

Their normal 15-minute ride home from Cloonan Middle School to the Westover and Long Ridge sections took more than an hour. The students said they spent the hour watching the bus careen around curves and listening to drivers of oncoming cars honk warnings to slow down.

Some believed they were being kidnapped by their driver, but the school bus company said the man was merely lost.

"All the kids were screaming and some of the kids were crying," said Karen Seren, a seventh-grader, "We screamed to a policeman out the window, but he didn't believe us."

In their fear, eight students jumped out the rear door when the bus stopped at Rippowam High School, and they flagged down a police car for help. All the students eventually were returned home, late but safe.

Allen Graften, assistant superintendent of schools, said he will look into the incident and have some answers by Monday.

In these six paragraphs of this spot news story, Rita Jensen and Kevin Flynn have described the climax and the essentials of the event. The account could stop here. But there is so much local interest in an event of this kind, the writers knew, that they decided to go on. They wrote a transition paragraph and then picked up the chronological account that appeared this way:

From accounts of the parents and children who called "The Advocate" and from the manager of ARA bus operations here, the ride of terror and confusion began when. . . .

Notice the word *began*. This tells the reader to sit back while the writer spins out the tale of terror.

Inverted Pyramid—Again If you noticed, these stories do not end with a climax. The climax is at the beginning, in the lead. The writer gives the major material, then the secondary information. It's the ancient story structure, the inverted pyramid.

This is a perfectly good overall guide to the straight news story. For important events, readers and listeners want to know what happened—now.

However, its use does limit the storytelling abilities of the writer. The chronological approach is one way out, but this approach can be overused.

For a long time writers struggled with the bonds of the inverted pyramid. In fact, they made it the symbol of the limitations of journalistic writing. It became fashionable for gifted writers to scoff at the inverted pyramid.

Writers like Tom Wolfe wanted to tell stories, not live by forms and structures that they saw as chains binding them to a stake labeled "news writing style."

Their protests were valid—to a point. Actually, news writers who had mastered the basic style had for years been able to transcend the inverted pyramid and the traditional structures of the news story—when the occasion permitted it. The last clause bears repeating—when the occasion permitted it.

Long before the New Journalists burst onto the scene, A. J. Liebling was writing brilliant, non-traditional stories, as were other journalists. One former newspaperman recalls covering the appearance of Miss America in California with an approach that predated the New Journalists.

Enter: Miss America "I was sent out to a motel where Miss America was to hold a news conference," the former reporter-turned-journalism teacher recalls. "She had just been crowned and she was making a national tour. That was news in those days, the 1950s, in small and medium size towns."

The two print reporters and a television camera crew and reporter were sent to her suite, and they awaited her arrival in one of the rooms. In a corner was Miss America's mother, ironing a dress. They waited. After a five- or 10-minute delay, Miss America entered.

"She was holding a Pepsi, as I recall. Clutching it to her bosom, unopened. On one of the bureaus was a cardboard poster advertising another sponsor of the Miss America pageant," he said. "The whole business seemed arranged, staged."

At that point, he had the idea for his story about Miss America's visit. It would be in the form of a stage play.

He began his story with stage directions:

> Stage right: Mother ironing blue evening gown. Advertising poster on bureau to left. Opened luggage on low racks. Reporters and camera crew sitting, chatting quietly.
>
> Enter from rear of center stage: Miss America. She enters slowly, holding a soda bottle to her breast, unopened. There is a moment of silence. She speaks.
>
> Miss America: "Thank you for coming. I have something to say and then I will answer questions. . . .

The former reporter says that when he handed in his story, the city editor laughed, started to hand it back, then decided to run it. "It was a one-day stand. I never wrote another play, but not because the idea was bad. I never had the opportunity. But it fitted the occasion."

At that time, such editors were rare. Most stayed with formula writing: Five *W*'s and an *H*, even when the lead ran 50 or 60 words; inverted pyramid structure on most stories. These days, most editors want imagination and color in the writing, and when the event will allow it, they urge their reporters to use the techniques of the feature writer, even on straight news stories. Enter the news feature.

Before we examine the news feature in detail, let's look at the other parent that produced the hybrid we call the news feature—the feature.

Organizing the Feature Story

The feature is journalism's grab bag. It can be about anything under the sun—even the sun itself. The feature can be as light and fluffy as a cream puff, or as solid and substantial as a rib roast. It can make us cry or laugh. One difference between the straight news story and the feature is that while the news story informs us by involving our reason and logic, the feature informs or entertains us by engaging our feelings.

Another distinctive mark of the feature is its style. The straight news story is just that, a straightforward account of an event. The feature is . . . well, there is no telling what form the feature may take. And this may well be its trademark. Some are humorous, some somber. And some cannot be catalogued, like this one:

> Six-year-old Brian Waters spotted a fence down the street from school yesterday and made a detour from his usual way home.
>
> He stared at the iron fence: IIIIIII.
>
> Then he decided to look into the yard through the fence: IIIoIII. But when Brian had seen enough he couldn't pull his head back.
>
> A passerby called the fire department and a fireman approached the fence with a sledgehammer: /
>
> In short order, he had pried apart a couple of the bars: II(o)II. Brian wiped his tears and went on home.

Writing the Feature

Style: Relaxed, informal. Let the people in the story do things; let them talk. Underwrite. Keep the story moving with quotes and incidents. If possible, use dialogue. That is, have people talking to each other; have them interacting by watching them at work or play. Tom Wolfe, master of the profile, said "realistic dialogue" fascinates readers. Use verbs that make pictures for the reader. When possible, use the present tense to give the reader a sense of continuing action or of being present at the scene.

Lead: Delayed leads are preferred. An anecdote or incident can be used to begin. Stress human interest in the lead by using someone directly involved in the situation. Make sure the lead fits into the main theme of the feature.

Body: Avoid overwhelming the reader with detail. A few well-chosen quotes and incidents will tell the story. Selection is the essence of the feature. What is left out is as important as what is put into the piece. A Zen saying makes the point: "To make a vase, you need both clay and the absence of clay." You are not obligated to use everything a source has given you. Remember: One good quote, one telling incident is all the reader needs to put the paper down and say: "That's interesting. I never knew that."

The style of the feature is, as we can see, simple and relaxed. In a feature by Mike Stanton that moved over the AP wires, the story roams around almost as much as its subject—a college student who rode the rails to gather information for a term paper. Despite the rolling, informal style, Stanton gives us enough information by the end of the sixth paragraph that we have a solid picture of the person and what he did.

Here is the beginning of the story:

AMHERST, MASS. (AP)—Ted Conover's classroom was a rolling boxcar, his first big test a fight with a drunken hobo. He fell off a train, foraged through garbage cans for food and got lice in his hair.

The Amherst College student rode the rails for 3½ months, living the life of a railroad tramp, to research his senior thesis.

He found that it wasn't all bad.

"There's something about jumping on a freight train that just feels right," said Conover, a 23-year-old anthropology major from Denver.

"It's the feeling of the wind in your face and the train pulling you along. I think there's some truth to the saying that every red-blooded American boy should hop a train."

Conover rode the rails for 10,000 miles last fall, criss-crossing the American West to study what author John Steinbeck called "the last free men."

Conover said he didn't want to "suffer in the library" researching his thesis, so he spent a semester observing or interviewing 460 tramps. He estimates there are at least 10,000 hobos living in the United States today.

"They're invisible to most of us," he noted. "But there's a romance about tramps. They've found something valuable that the rest of us have missed."

But Conover also discovered some unpleasant realities about the life of a tramp.

"I went 2½ weeks without a shower once," he said. "My friends thought it sounded romantic to get really dirty. But when I got lice it took away a lot of the romance."

Focus on a Theme

Because the feature has a relaxed, leisurely approach and contains many quotes and several interesting incidents, beginners think all that is necessary to write one is to pile on quotes and anecdotes and then glue them together with a few transitions.

Tom Wolfe says that too many feature writers think "that somehow if you get in enough details, enough random fact—somehow this *trenchant portrait* is going to rise up off the pages."

Yes, he agrees, detail and dialogue are essential, but the good feature writer "piles it all up *very carefully,* building up toward a single point. . . ."

Wolfe's "single point" is the theme or point of the article. Every story must have a theme or point, and the writer must know it before writing.

When a news writer sits down to write a feature, some idea of the point of the piece must be clearly in mind. The writer cannot simply toss together detail, fact, quote. That's the potluck dinner approach: Toss a lot of ingredients into the pot and hope someone finds something worth eating. As Wolfe says, the writer must give the reader only those quotes, facts and anecdotes that illustrate and buttress the point the writer intends to make.

In this respect, a feature is no different from any news story. It must have a main theme, and this must be clear from the beginning, certainly by the fourth or fifth paragraph of the feature.

The main theme is always the spine of the story. Everything else branches from it. Most feature writers have a general idea of what they want to say even before they conduct their interviews. At least they have an idea that guides their questions.

If a better theme comes along, they pursue it. The reporter who interviews a rock singer who has just been released from a clinic for alcoholics and drug addicts has a good idea of the questions she needs answered for her feature. So does the sports writer who wants to do a piece about the 38-year-old pitcher who has been named Comeback Player of the Year.

Feature Ideas. The feature can be about any subject that the reporter thinks will interest or entertain readers. Standard features include the holiday piece—Independence Day, Memorial Day, Christmas, New Year's. Good reporters enterprise features. Recalling a community's past can lead to an interesting feature. Half a century ago the country suffered a severe economic depression and many people, like this farm family, headed west. You may find old-timers who recall these days. This photograph of a 20th century prairie schooner was made in Pennington County, S.D., in 1936 by Arthur Rothstein.
Arthur Rothstein, Courtesy of the Library of Congress

The rock singer may surprise the reporter and say, "I'm through with music. With music, I am going to be back on the habit. Without it, I'll be poor, but alive." The pitcher may be petulant and angry. Instead of being happy about his award, he may take off about his salary, fellow players, and the baseball commissioner. The unexpected material becomes the main theme of the story.

The Ending

Most features have a strong ending. Rather than end on a secondary piece of information, the feature may have what is called a kicker, a punch at the end. It can be an exciting quotation or a significant anecdote or incident. The ending usually drives home the theme of the feature.

In a story about a woman who visits prisoners in the Dade County Jail to help them with their problems, *Miami Herald* reporter Shula Beyer describes Georgia Jones Ayers as "53, an activist in the black community with a degree of access to the criminal justice system that is unique."

Ayers is shown to be sympathetic to prisoners she believes unjustly accused and imprisoned, but she is no bleeding heart. She does not tolerate crime. To make this point about Ayers, Beyer ends her story with this dramatic incident and quote:

> One of the stories people tell about Georgia Ayers is that she turned over a drug pusher to the police. He was sentenced to eight years. The pusher was her son, Cecil.
>
> "When my own children do wrong, I don't uphold them. The law is the law. He respects me for what I did. I couldn't afford to see him destroy himself.
>
> "I would rather see him behind bars than for someone to call me to identify his body in a morgue."

The News Feature

Early one cold Saturday morning, as Bob Rose was at home preparing to go to work at *The Blade* in Toledo, the telephone rang. It was the police reporter. A house a few blocks from Rose's apartment on Parkwood Avenue had caught fire. Could he get over there? Yes, he could.

Rose started out in minutes. He tried to drive, but the frost on his car window was unyielding. After a few blocks, he hopped out of the car and ran the rest of the way.

"I arrived in time to see the fireman carry a child out of the house," he said. He spent about an hour at the scene gathering information from fire department officials and from the people who had been driven out of their home.

At the office, he checked the hospital where the injured had been taken, and by early afternoon he had finished his story. But he was not happy with it.

"Somehow it didn't seem right," Rose recalled. He asked the assistant city editor what she thought of the story, and she told him she thought it lacked drama. He worked on it some more and left the office feeling somewhat satisfied.

Soon, he had another call. Ed Whipple, an assistant managing editor, had made a change. "He wanted to bring the reader right into the story. My lead ended up being the third graph, and the scene of a tearful firefighter with the dead girl went first," Rose said. The story was put on page one.

In the past, most editors would have wanted Rose's straight news lead. But Whipple wanted a news feature. Rose's story as it appeared in *The Blade* is on the next page.

The news feature takes its content and structure from the feature. In content, it emphasizes human interest and drama. It uses the dramatic quote and the telling incident to point up the major theme. In structure, it may use the delayed lead to lure the reader into the story, and then get to the point of the piece after several paragraphs, or it may put the lead theme in a kicker at the end.

Rose's story puts the reader on the scene at once. We visualize this large man in his dark cold-weather clothing holding tight to a small figure.

The second paragraph stuns the reader with that brief quote. The summary paragraph, which in a straight news account would be part of a first-paragraph lead, comes in the third paragraph. The way the story is told reflects the poignancy of the event more closely than would a straight news story with this direct lead:

A four-year-old child died and two other family members were hospitalized when their home at 2346 Lawrence Ave. was damaged by a fire this morning.

Girl, 4, Dies In Fire; 8 In House Rescued

By BOB ROSE
Blade Staff Writer

It was 7:50 a.m. Saturday when fireman Jack Rynn carried 4-year-old Quanous Russell out of a burning house at 2346 Lawrence Ave.

"She's gone," he said minutes later of the bundle in the blue baby blanket, his eyes welling with tears.

Fighting zero-degree weather and their own emotions, Toledo firemen — aided by alert neighbors — helped save eight other family members in the house.

Timmy Hicks, 2, was rescued by fireman Fred White, who, like Mr. Rynn, struggled through thick smoke and flames to take the child from an upstairs bedroom.

Timmy had stopped breathing, but paramedic Larry LaVigne revived him en route to St. Vincent Hospital, where he was in serious condition Saturday.

Neighbors Help

Before firemen arrived, neighbors had helped others from the home.

Paula Russell, 26, the mother of the dead girl, jumped from a second-floor window into the arms of Bruce Ethridge, who heard her screams from a block away. She was in fair condition at St. Vincent Saturday.

Johnny Hicks, 4, was found on steps in the house by Eron Villanveva, who lives next door. He had summoned firemen after hearing screams and breaking glass.

Others escaped through the front door or were pulled from the roof of the house by firemen who arrived at 7:33 a.m., two minutes after the alarm sounded.

Curtain Was Burning

Kevin Russell, 19, said he was the first to be wakened by the blaze. "Something told me to wake up," he said at a neighbor's house after other family members were taken to the hospital. "When I woke up, my curtain was burning down the side."

An electric space heater in his room had ignited the curtain. He struggled to put the fire out, first by stamping on the curtain and then by running for buckets of water, but the fire was winning.

"It happened so quick, I couldn't even get everybody woke," he said.

His father, Clinton Russell, 72, wearing a tattered coat zipped over his pajama top, shivered as he watched firemen work on the white frame house he has owned since the 1960s. He was the only family member sleeping on the first floor.

"I can't think," he finally said after trying to name other family members who had gone to sleep in the house the night before.

All But 2 Released

They were identified by hospital and fire officials as his daughter, Elizabeth Hicks, 23, who was visiting from Cincinnati with sons Timmy and Johnny. Others were Clinton's wife, Lois, 52, and son, Quincy, 16.

All but Timmy Hicks and Paula Russell were released after treatment.

Toledo Fire Chief William Winkle arrived soon after he was called at home by firemen. "Those guys did a hell of a job," he said of the men who were directed in the freezing weather by acting deputy chief Ron Sturgill.

Chief Sturgill, who estimated damage at $18,000, said the two closest fire hydrants were frozen and water from pumper trucks had to be used while another hydrant was hooked up.

"The first guys there ran into the house without masks (for air) and got to the top of the stairs," Chief Winkle said. "But they couldn't go farther. Guys with masks had to go in to get the kids."

Chief Winkle kicked a snow bank when he talked about the year's first fatal fire. "Damn," he said.

This straight lead is satisfactory, but the point of this fire is the tragedy of a child's death. A youngster's death is pathetic. Why not show the reader this and let the reader share the grief. The lead on the published story fits the event.

Many news features use the delayed lead in order to set a mood or establish a scene. Look back to Berkley Hudson's lead on his story about Chester Jefferds. The lead is delayed seven paragraphs, and finally, in the eighth, we are told: Jefferds is not sick; he does not belong in the state institution. For her news story about the visit of officials from a Vietnam Era Vet Center, Avice Meehan of the Dalton weekly newspaper used a delayed lead on her story. It began:

> For many Vietnam veterans the war has not ended.

After two paragraphs of quotes, she put the lead in the fourth paragraph: The officials of the center are in Dalton for a visit.

Not many readers will pass by a story that begins as Meehan's does. This is precisely the value of the news feature: It permits the writer a bit more license to entice the reader into the story.

Volunteers to the Dying The news feature is usually built around incidents, examples, anecdotes and quotes that involve people. Human interest is a major factor in the news feature.

Rick Sluder, a reporter for *The News and Observer* in Raleigh, N.C., built his story about a hospice around the people involved. A hospice is an organization that serves the needs of the dying and their families.

The story originated in a press release from the recently formed Hospice of Wake County. "My editor felt this was a worthwhile organization and that I should look into it," Sluder said. "Getting the lowdown on how the organization worked was the easy part. Volunteers and officials were eager to meet with me."

Sluder decided that this kind of information was only part of the story. He knew he needed the human element. The story should be about the people the hospice volunteers worked with, the dying. He wanted to **show** the hospice at work, not **tell** about it through the words of officials.

"This caused officials to rub their hands for a moment," he said. "Their concern was understandable. Relationships in situations like this are confidential." They did agree to reach some families to ask whether Sluder could talk to them.

"A day or two later, I got the names of the Silvers and the Voelkers. And that's when it became a bit sticky for me. I found myself phoning these people to ask if they would talk to me, a stranger, about the deaths of their loved ones."

Sluder learned what many young reporters find surprising. Despite the tragedies that afflict some people, they are willing to talk to reporters if they believe the reporters are sincere and want to perform a service by writing the story.

Notice how Sluder structures the beginning of his story. This is an example of the delayed lead that is used on news features and features:

Three-year-old Bethany Voelker was sick, and she didn't want any visitors. When Elizabeth Hernandez appeared, she said so.

"Would it be all right if I came to visit you?" Ms. Hernandez asked.

"No," Bethany said. "I'll throw you out."

"I'm going to come anyway."

"Well, I'll throw you out again."

Undaunted, Ms. Hernandez came—and she visited again and again. As days passed, Bethany's uneasiness gave way to tolerance. Friendship followed, and finally, surely, love.

One day the two were together and Bethany was feeling worse than usual. They talked little. As Ms. Hernandez bent to kiss her, Bethany whispered with childhood's sincerity: "I'll be your friend forever."

The bond was sealed. And though Bethany died of leukemia a few weeks ago, it remains strong. Loved ones are not forgotten.

Bethany's parents, Robert and Darlene Voelker of Raleigh, are certain the friendship brightened their daughter's last days of life, just as Ms. Hernandez says she is richer for having known Bethany.

It's a sentiment shared by most of the volunteers with Hospice of Wake County, an organization intended to minister to the needs—physical and emotional—of the dying and their families.

But it's hard to think of Hospice as an organization, with budgets and letterheads and articles of incorporation. Instead, Hospice is people, caring people, who celebrate each second of life by meeting moments of death, accepting death for what it is, refusing to turn away. It is, by any reckoning, in the major leagues of human interaction.

Hospice of Wake County began accepting clients in April. So far it is serving six families; deaths have occurred in five of them.

Its mission is simple, said Dr. William R. Berry, medical director. "We provide medical care for terminally ill patients in the home setting," he said. "We help them and their families any way we can to meet their needs."

In the first nine paragraphs, Sluder shows us how a hospice works, though he never uses that word. It is not until the 10th paragraph that he introduces the hospice, and this and the next three paragraphs provide the lead and background. No question that this is the more effective way to begin the story.

The ending of the news feature and feature must be carefully crafted as well. Unlike the straight news story, which stops when the writer runs out of secondary material, the endings of these two kinds of feature stories must leave the reader or listener with a reminder of the point of the piece. Sluder does this with a vivid combination of incidents and quotes about the two families in which deaths occurred, the families of Bethany Voelker and James Silver. Here is the end of his story:

Bethany turned 4 shortly before she died. She got a birthday party her little friends are still talking about. Uncle Paul from TV and Guppy the clown were there. So were many of the Hospice workers, who with some others helped arrange it.

James Silver had a birthday party, too, the Friday before his death on Monday. He had planned it and left instructions it was to be held even if he couldn't attend. "He wanted his friends, the ones who had done so much for him, to have a good time," Mrs. Silver said. The Hospice people were there.

They were there at the two funerals, too. And they're still there, the families said, calling, dropping by, sharing lunch and memories and hopes for the future.

"Sometimes you forget how wonderful people can be," Mrs. Silver said, "but I guess it's like James always said. It isn't how long you're on Earth, it's what you do while you're here."

Cloudy Crystal Ball   One way to end the news feature or feature is to put the climax, or kicker, at the end.

A writer for *The Wall Street Journal* decided to have a little fun with a market analyst whose predictions are taken seriously by many people—so seriously that when he told his clients to sell stock, the stock market industrial average fell 23.8 points. The *Journal* sent Alan Bayless to cover a talk by the analyst, and this is how his story began:

VANCOUVER—Market prophet Joseph Granville made news again Tuesday night, predicting a 16-point selloff of shares in the Dow Jones industrial average on Wednesday . . .

The story then describes some other predictions Granville made, including a Los Angeles earthquake, and then, in the 11th and final paragraph of the story, Bayless writes:

His prediction for Wednesday was, presumably, a minor matter. Instead of falling the 16 points or so that it was supposed to, the industrial average rose by more than eight points.

So much for the prophet. Notice that Bayless **shows** the reader that Granville failed. By giving Granville's forecast in the lead and then noting the actual market performance at the end, Bayless leaves his readers with the facts to make their own decisions. The kicker has a wallop no reader can miss.

A less experienced writer might have started the story this way:

```
Market prophet Joseph Granville flopped miserably in
his prediction of a large drop in the stock market
Wednesday.
```

That's telling, not showing. It also gives the story a seriousness that Bayless decided the event did not merit.

The feature and news feature are built around the examples, anecdotes and quotations that the writer uses to illustrate the story. The writer is trying to unfold a tale, and the structure depends on whether the writer chooses to get to the point immediately or to hold the reader in suspense. Sometimes the lead will be up high, in the first paragraph or two. This is the first option for the news feature and feature. Often, the lead comes after an introductory section, as in Sluder's piece about the hospice (second option), or it may be placed at the end, as Bayless did with the market prophet (third option).

These alternatives are diagrammed in figure 9.2.

Look carefully at the material in these columns. Notice that the writer is directed to be selective in using incidents and quotes. Some writers think that they can select any exciting incident, any interesting anecdote or startling quotation and use this as the human interest material at the top of the story. It does not work that way. The most common error made in writing features is the sloppy selection of anecdotes, illustrations, incidents and quotations for the beginning.

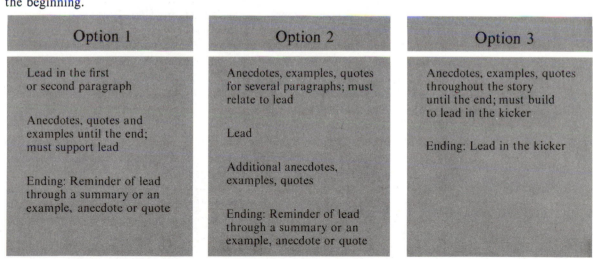

Option 1	Option 2	Option 3
Lead in the first or second paragraph	Anecdotes, examples, quotes for several paragraphs; must relate to lead	Anecdotes, examples, quotes throughout the story until the end; must build to lead in the kicker
Anecdotes, quotes and examples until the end; must support lead	Lead	Ending: Lead in the kicker
Ending: Reminder of lead through a summary or an example, anecdote or quote	Additional anecdotes, examples, quotes	
	Ending: Reminder of lead through a summary or an example, anecdote or quote	

Figure 9.2 Alternate story structures for feature and news feature stories.

The material selected for the beginning must lead directly to the major theme. Look at how this *Wall Street Journal* story begins:

> It was 1940 when Elmer Novak walked out of his sophomore year in high school and into the coal mines, just as his brothers had before him and his father before them.

Immediately, the reader has a picture of the treadmill life of this family. The reporter follows this beginning with such pieces of information as, "Novak has a mortgage, 10 kids, and black lung." From the present, the reporter looks back: "He quit the mine once, in 1947, after his brother was crushed to death by a coal car, but in a few months he was back, for the money."

The article was part of a series on jobs that are physically draining and mentally numbing. For this piece on coal mining, the incidents and quotes used were selected to make this point.

Summary

All the diagrams and all the advice and examples presented in this chapter are useless unless the writer has the ability to identify the major theme or themes of the event. No amount of careful structuring can make a story work if the writer picks an unimportant or irrelevant fact as a theme.

Once the theme or themes have been decided, the battle to whip the event into shape is half won.

By listing the themes—mentally or on paper—the writer has them clearly before him or her. If the story is to be a news story, certain options are open. Generally, the theme or themes will be placed in the first paragraph or two. If the story is a feature, other options are open.

With thought and planning, even the novice writer will soon write stories like those written by professional journalists.

Making Words Work

The news writer chooses words that accurately reflect the person or event being described in the news or feature story.

The writer adheres to the rules of grammar and avoids clichés, redundancies and journalese. These words and phrases lead to stories that are flat, tired and uninteresting.

Looking Ahead

Misspellings, incorrect punctuation, poor grammar and mispronunciation surround us. The sign on the canopy over the pumps at an Exxon service station in Batavia, N.Y., reads:

CLEARENCE   12′ 9″

A sign at the entrance to the Publix Supermarket in Homestead, Fla., warns customers:

According to our license, alcoholic beverages may not be drank in this store or on the parking lot.

A poster in Roosevelt Hospital in New York City invites patients and visitors to a nutrition clinic with this sign:

Want to loose weight?

The AAA Tour Book for Georgia, North Carolina and South Carolina contains an advertisement for the Swamp Fox Motor Inn in Myrtle Beach, S.C., that boasts of a "**seperate** meeting room."

A sign on U.S. 90 invites travelers to visit a "**Tradeing** Post" in Uvalde, Tex.

An article describing the Copper Queen Hotel, built around the turn of the century when Bisbee, Ariz., was the largest copper mining town in the world, says that the town "remains architecturally as it stood in **it's** heyday."

The wrap in the freezer unit of the Safeway market in McKinleyville, Calif., indicates that the packages contain **"sordfish."**

A radio commercial for a resort hotel in Pennsylvania suggests to listeners:

Why not get out this weekend and lay under a tree?

The people whose job it is to write or to broadcast the news do little better.

The story in *The Miami Herald* about the death of actor William Holden said that after a drinking bout, he fell, gashed his head and "went to **lay** on his bed."

The network sports announcer commented that Notre Dame was completing many passes because the pass defenders "**have overran** the receivers."

The headline in *The San Francisco Examiner* read:

Climber peaks inside volcano

The Washington Post, The New York Times, The Boston Globe, The Milwaukee Journal and other usually well-edited newspapers have also contributed to the pollution of the written language:

The *Post* described attempts to keep Northern Virginia's **principle** reservoir from drying up. It mentioned a company that **has became** the first to put a new machine in use.

The *Times* contained this quote: "But I have **alot** of respect for the people. . . ." The *Times* described a character in a movie "struggling to wrap a skimpy towel around his **waste.**"

The *Globe* referred to a man who had been arraigned on a charge of **"negligible homicide."**

The *Journal* ran a story about tourists who "**pour** over English lessons."

The Des Moines Register ran a headline, "Insurance agent **please** guilty of theft."

The wire services contribute their share to the mess:

A UPI story from Peking begins—"China's official media **is.** . . ." It describes an attack by nationalists on a United States air base that **"totally destroyed"** eight airplanes.

The AP wrote of the **"first annual** International Congress." From Jackson, Miss., it reported FBI agents "are **pouring** over thousands of pictures. . . ."

The *Surfside News,* a magazine for visitors to the Outer Banks off the coast of North Carolina, reports that a college student "plans to **persue**" his study of geology.

James Reston, the respected columnist for *The New York Times,* told his readers of a **"serious crisis"** abroad.

If a carpenter treated his tools the way some journalists treat the language, the carpenter's walls would sag and his floors would slope. He would be on the unemployment line before long.

Granted, language does change. What is considered unacceptable usage one day is acceptable the next. Language grows. Journalists used to be warned to make a distinction between "people" and "persons." People was used for large or uncounted groups of individuals, and persons referred to smaller groups. Now, people is replacing persons for all references to more than one person. But some things never change.

Periods will always be used to end sentences, and the verb will always have to agree with the subject. The spelling of *grammar* will always have *ar* at the end, not *er,* and *sophomore* will undoubtedly always be spelled that way and never *sophmore.*

David Shaw, the media writer for *The Los Angeles Times,* interviewed editors around the country about the problems they were facing.

"Bad grammar. Misspellings. Incorrect punctuations. Poorly constructed sentences. Misused words. Mixed metaphors. Non sequiturs. Clichés. Redundancies. Circumlocutions. Imprecision. Jargon."

This was Shaw's list of deficiencies gathered from his interviews. We will be looking at these errors and those that others have pointed out.

First, an important point needs to be made about why these mistakes occur. Much of the time they are the result of poor thinking, or no thinking at all.

Muddy Thinking = Mistakes

Every person who works with tools knows just what each tool can do. The auto mechanic would not think of using an air pressure gauge to measure the gap of a spark plug. It makes no sense. Writers sometimes fling words around with that kind of abandon. They reach into their word kit and haul out something that looks or sounds as though it can do the job.

```
    TWO SOVIET COSMONAUTS SUCCESSFULLY DOCKED
THEIR SOYUZ 35 SPACE CAPSULE. . . .

    GOSSIPOL WAS FIRST DISCOVERED IN 1971 AFTER
PEASANTS IN. . . .

    ARMED GUNMEN SUNDAY KIDNAPPED THE OWNER AND
EDITOR OF THE WORLD'S LARGEST CIRCULATION. . . .
```

These are from wire service stories.

The fact that the capsule was docked indicates it was a successful venture. The modifier *successfully* is a wasted word.

The second excerpt has another unnecessary modifying word, *first*. When something is discovered, it is obviously for the first time. It's as though we were to write: Columbus first discovered America in 1492, and then discovered it again a few years later on another voyage.

As for the third sentence, ask your friends if they have ever heard of an *unarmed* gunman.

These three sentences are examples of redundancies, needlessly repetitive words. We'll look into this error in detail later in the chapter.

Another common error is the misused word: *effect* for *affect, imply* for *infer, disinterested* for *uninterested*.

"Recent reports have said a number of graduates cannot even read or **right,**" said an editorial in a college newspaper in Kentucky. The editorial writer could not have been thinking when that was written.

"Albert Henry, the **disposed** former premier of the Cook Islands, has died. . . ." This is from a UPI story. How could the writer confuse disposed with deposed? Obviously, he was not thinking as he wrote.

Word Usage

Writers can sometimes profit from their mistakes and the mistakes of others. Mervin Block, who writes news for network television, watched the news wires for the most frequent errors, bloopers and blunders. In a few days he came up with a two-inch pile of redundancies, poor grammar and improper use of words.

What was remarkable about the errors he collected was not that the mistakes were made by professionals but that the same errors occurred time and time again.

Here is some of the material Block found:

A pair of small earthquakes about an hour apart. . . .

A trio of bandits held up a. . . .

Some might argue that technically these sentences are acceptable. But not to the journalist, who uses common sense along with the dictionary. To the journalist, shoes come in pairs and trios form singing groups. Be careful when choosing unusual words in place of commonplace words, such as two and three. When writers push too hard they distort language, as in this lead:

A Frankie Valli and the Four Seasons concert—part of Philadelphia's Fourth of July Freedom Festival—ended in tragedy Saturday night when high winds sent 40 spotlights crashing onto a bandstand.

Tragedy is a strong word. Familiar with accounts of people being trampled at rock concerts, the reader expects the worst. What actually happened: A pianist suffered a broken hand and others had cuts and bruises.

When thieves tunneled into a bank vault in Massachusetts and made off with the contents of 700 safety deposit boxes, the AP described the theft as a robbery. Robbery involves taking by force and is a crime of violence. Burglary is theft of property, which was the case here.

The most frequent misuse of language in Block's collection was the cliché.

If at first you don't succeed, try, try again. Hit the nail on the head. Cool as a cucumber. Out of the frying pan into the fire. Sadder but wiser. Make hay while the sun shines. Love makes the world go 'round.

Clichés

At one time these were original and picturesque expressions. But their novelty was their undoing. Writers picked them up and used them, and overused them. They have been ground down to the humdrum and dull, so that today phrases like these are known as clichés. No writer who is proud of his or her writing will resort to using these stale and tired expressions.

Because these sentences and phrases are heard everywhere, all the time, writers have them imprinted in their memory banks, and in the struggle to find an apt expression they pop out. Shove them back in again.

George Orwell advised writers to be wary of using any phrase they are accustomed to seeing in print.

Here is a list of clichés Block put together from the wires of the press services. Block says these are a small portion of those he gathered in a few days:

```
     CHICAGO--THIS IS THE UNKINDEST CUT OF
ALL. . . .
     KHARTOUM, SUDAN--THE SOVIET MILITARY
INTERVENTION IN AFGHANISTAN AND THE IRANIAN CRISIS
RANG BELLS OF ALARM. . . .
     NEW YORK--THE FIGHT FOR THE NOMINATIONS SEEMS
TO BE ALL OVER SAVE THE SHOUTING.
     NEW YORK--ALEX KARRAS CONTINUES TO BE THE
EXCEPTION THAT PROVES THE RULE. . . .
     FORT WAYNE, IND.--MARTHA COLEMAN . . . MET
WITH FEDERAL AGENTS BEHIND CLOSED DOORS. . . .
     NEW YORK--ABC AND NBC BELIEVE COMEDY IS THE
WAY TO KEEP LAUGHING ALL THE WAY TO THE BANK.
     HOLLYWOOD--PAUL LYNDE WILL RETURN TO THE
SAGGING ``HOLLYWOOD SQUARES'' GAME SHOW NEXT
SEASON A SADDER BUT WISER COMEDIAN.
     UNIONDALE, L.I.--THE NEW YORK ISLANDERS
COMPLETE A RAGS-TO-RICHES CLIMB TO. . . .
```

Block says the most breathtaking set of clichés he heard came from the typewriter of a radio news writer describing the entry of a reluctant candidate into a race: "Jones dropped the other shoe, threw his hat in the ring and now it's a whole new ball game."

Redundancies

In the early part of this chapter we quoted wire service stories that described planes that were "totally destroyed" and a meeting that was the "first annual" Congress. When something is destroyed, that's it. It's gone, a pile of scrap. It cannot be partially destroyed. If a meeting is the first of its kind, it cannot be annual, which means something that has happened yearly. It may be "the first of what its sponsors plan to make an annual. . . ."

David Shaw says that the redundancy "seems to be an occupational hazard for journalists—as witness 'planning ahead' (*Boston Globe*), 'apparent heir apparent' (*UPI*), and 'ominous portent' (*Los Angeles Times*)." A moment's thought and the absurdity of some of these pairings would be obvious. One way to avoid redundancies and other mistakes is to train yourself to be wary of adjectives and adverbs:

totally destroyed—adverb
first annual—adjective
serious crisis—adjective
successfully docked—adverb

Nouns and verbs do the work in journalistic writing, and all good writing for that matter. Look at this sentence:

```
The workers trudged slowly past the factory in the
rain.
```

The verb *trudged* was picked precisely because it means to walk wearily. It does not need any propping up with the adverb *slowly*.

Some of us learn the hard way. I learned about redundancies when I wrote about a man whose hobby was building "one-wheel unicycles." My city editor pointed out that a unicycle only has one wheel and that what I had written was the equivalent of saying a round circle.

The student who wrote of a professor who "carefully scrutinized" all student papers learned the hard way, too. "Have you ever heard of anyone carelessly scrutinizing papers?" the student was asked in a marginal comment. Puzzled, the student went to the dictionary and looked up the word *scrutinize*. He learned it meant to examine closely, minutely, critically, in detail—all of which certainly implied that the papers were carefully read. His word *carefully* was a waste.

Beware these Redundancies

Here is a list of the most common redundancies seen in newspaper copy. It was compiled by the Minnesota Newspaper Association. You may want to add some of your own.

absolutely necessary	enclosed you will find	reasonable and fair
advance planning	exactly identical	redo again
ask the question	fair and just	refer back
assemble together	fall down	refuse and decline
at a later day	first and foremost	revert back
attached hereto	friend of mine	right and proper
at the present time	gathered together	rise up
canceled out	honest truth	rules and regulations
city of Chicago	important essentials	send in
close proximity	necessary requirements	small in size
consensus of opinion	open up	still remain
carbon copy	other alternative	temporarily suspended
continue on	patently obvious	totally unnecessary
cooperate together	plain and simple	true facts
each and every	postpone until later	various and sundry

Journalese

The dictionary defines journalese as the language style characteristic of newspaper writing. That's the sanitized version. Among journalists, journalese is known as the combination of clichés, hack writing, overwriting, exhausted phrases, and supercharged prose that are the signs of the hopeful beginner or the tired veteran.

In journalese, costs and the crime rate are always "skyrocketing," and officials who worry about speedy solutions to problems often "raise the red flag."

When a group meets for any period longer than an hour, the meeting is said to last "long hours." The facts raised in meetings are "cold facts," sometimes "hard facts."

Close elections are always "cliff-hangers," and when someone is elected he or she may "kick off" the term with an inaugural speech. An official who does something unusual is said to have "written a page in the political history books."

When someone is pleased by something, the person often "hails" the action or statement.

The AP once polled its correspondents to determine the most overworked word or phrase in reporting. They chose the verb *to hail*. Or, as journalese would have it, "to hail took the honors."

Watch Out—Trouble Here

Coke This word, like Kleenex, Stetson, Styrofoam and others, is a trademark. Such words are registered by the manufacturer and protected by law to keep others from using the words. These words must be capitalized.

finalize, prioritize Watch out for invented words, especially those that arise from the unintelligible jargon of government agencies.

irregardless No such word. The word is *regardless*.

minorities Do not use when you mean members of minority groups:
Wrong: "When women and minorities are selected to open. . . ."
Right: "When women and members of minority groups are selected to open. . . .

The same caution applies to faculty, as in: "Five faculty served with the president." It should be: "Five faculty members served with the president."

miracle Much overused, as in, "Jones miraculously escaped death when. . . ." Leave miracles to the spiritual world.

most unique Delete *most*. Unique means one of a kind. Same for very unique, and quite unique.

presently The word means soon. It does not mean now, although usage may alter the meaning some day.

**Said—
The Scare Word**

Another strong entry was the variety of synonyms for the word *said*. For some reason, writers are leery of this four-letter word. They prefer declared, stated, asserted; whispered, shouted, declaimed; repeated, recalled, remembered; inquired, asked; pronounced, related and announced.

The reluctance to use the word *said* has at least two causes. One is a fear of using the same word twice in a news story. If a news writer is doing a piece about Expo '86, it's perfectly all right to use synonyms—exposition, event, exhibition, display, presentation. But *said* catches no one's attention, no matter how often it is used, and substitutes for it usually exaggerate the nature of the statement or mislead the reader.

The other cause is the inherent desire of the writer to strut his or her stuff. Anyone can use the verb *said*. "Look at how many words I can think of to dazzle you," says the writer. In its extreme state, this self-intoxication leads to the refusal to use simple words. A person does not repeat something he or she has heard. He "echoes" it. A project is not completed but "finalized." An event is not set or scheduled to begin but "slated." Future events are "upcoming."

Journalese is contagious. A word or phrase that is unusual is quickly picked up. President Nixon was mocked for using "at this point in time" for *now* and "at that point in time" for *then*. Nevertheless, these cumbersome phrases began to work their way into speech and then into news copy.

"She was credited with the murder of her son." This sentence is from a wire service story. The phrase "credited with" makes the sentence grotesque. Even so, some reporters use it to express causation. A similar phrase is "thanks to," as in this one from a southern newspaper: "Thanks to the recent storm, 600 people were left homeless in the delta area." Soon we may expect to see sports writers writing: "Thanks to Johnson's tackle, Simms suffered three broken ribs and a fractured nose." The political reporter will write: "Thanks to the voters, Mayor C. Cal Evans was overwhelmed yesterday at the polls in his try for re-election."

Mental Images

Some bloopers come about because writers do not visualize the images created by their words. Here is a paragraph from a UPI story:

```
    WHITE SOUTH AFRICANS STILL BELIEVE IN FRONTIER
JUSTICE WITH A GUN IN ONE HAND, A HANGMAN'S NOOSE IN
THE OTHER AND A BIBLE--INTERPRETED TO JUSTIFY WHITE
SUPREMACY--CLUTCHED BETWEEN THEIR TEETH.
```

This is a grim picture indeed, until you visualize the image. Then it becomes ludicrous.

A wire service reporter in Knoxville described an exposition as being "centered around energy." Let's see that again. You center **on** something. But to center around something? Impossible.

It's a good idea to make a mental image of new and unusual combinations of words.

One reporter described the feminist movement as a "slumbering giant newly awakened." Another described a baseball player who broke out of a batting slump as suddenly having "his battery charged."

These words are not only silly but dishonest. They inject the situation with a form of verbal adrenalin. Being honest with language means finding the words that describe the situation accurately and truthfully.

Next, some brief remarks about everyone's favorite subjects—grammar, spelling, and punctuation. If the writer's task is to make the gathered information clear to the reader or listener, then every obstacle in the way of complete understanding must be cleared away. Among the impediments to clear communication are errors in grammar, spelling and punctuation.

Grammar

Grammar seems to have disappeared from the syllabus of the English department. As a consequence, journalism instructors and editors find it necessary to teach the subject. Here are some of the basic problems student journalists encounter, according to their instructors.

Agreement

A verb must agree in number with its subject. Writers encounter trouble when they are unsure of the subject or when they can't decide whether the subject is singular or plural.

Uncertainty often arises when there are words between the subject and the verb:

> **Wrong:** John, as well as several others in the class, were unhappy with the instructor.
> **Right:** John, as well as several others in the class, was unhappy with the instructor.
> The subject is *John,* singular.

> **Wrong:** The barrage of traffic noises, telephone calls and similar interruptions make it difficult to study.
> **Right:** The barrage of traffic noises, telephone calls and similar interruptions makes it difficult to study.
> The subject is *barrage,* singular.

A collective noun takes a singular verb when the group is considered as a unit and a plural verb when the individuals are thought of separately:

> **Right:** The committee usually votes unanimously.
> **Right:** The family lives around the corner.
> **Right:** The family were gathered around the fire, some reading, some napping.

The pronouns *anybody, anyone, each, either, everyone, everybody, neither, no one, nobody, someone* and *somebody* take the singular verb.

A pronoun must agree in number with its antecedent:

> **Wrong:** The team has added two players to their squad.
> **Right:** The team has added two players to its squad.
> **Wrong:** Everyone does their best.
> **Right:** Everyone does his or her best.
> **Wrong:** Each of the companies reported their profits had declined.
> **Right:** Each of the companies reported its profits had declined.

Dangling Modifier

A word or phrase or clause dangles when it floats in a sentence without clearly referring to some other word. Some dangling modifiers:

> Hunting in the winter, the air was cold.
> Being an A student, the teacher thought he would succeed.
> While in school, my father took sick and died.

These sentences can be corrected by inserting the word the modifier refers to or by rearranging the sentence:

While hunting in the winter, I felt cold.
His teacher thought Jim would succeed because he was an A student.
While I was in school, my father took sick and died.

Misplaced Words

Related parts of the sentence should not be separated. When they are, the sentence loses clarity.

Adverbs such as *almost, even, hardly, just, merely, scarcely, ever* and *nearly* should be placed immediately before the words they modify:

Vague: He only wanted three keys.
Clear: He wanted only three keys.
Vague: She nearly ate the whole meal.
Clear: She ate nearly the whole meal.

Avoid splitting the subject and verb:

Awkward: She, to make her point, shouted at the bartender.
Better: To make her point, she shouted at the bartender.

Do not separate parts of verb phrases:

Awkward: The governor said he had last year seen the document.
Better: The governor said he had seen the document last year.

Avoid split infinitives:

Awkward: She offered to personally give him the note.
Better: She offered to give him the note personally.

Note: Watch long sentences. Misplaced clauses and phrases can muddy the intended meaning. Read the sentence aloud if you are unsure about the placement of certain words. Generally, the problem can be solved by placing the subject and verb of the main clause together.

Parallel Construction

The parts of a sentence that express parallel thoughts should be balanced in grammatical form:

Unbalanced: The people started to shove and crowding each other.
Balanced: The people started to shove and crowd each other.
Unbalanced: The typewriter can be used for writing and to do finger exercises.
Balanced: The typewriter can be used for writing and for doing finger exercises.

Sentence Fragments

A phrase or a subordinate clause should not be used as a complete sentence:

Fragment: The book was long. And dull.
Correct: The book was long and dull.
Fragment: The score was tied. With only a minute left to play.
Correct: The score was tied with only a minute left to play.
Fragment: He worked all night on the story. And then collapsed in a heap.
Correct: He worked all night on the story and then collapsed in a heap.

Note: Sometimes writers use a sentence fragment for a specific writing purpose, usually for emphasis: When in doubt, always use the dictionary. Always.

Sequence of Tenses

Maintain a logical order of tenses. Keep an eye on the verb in the principal clause as a guide:

Wrong: We wrote him when we had heard of his unhappiness.
Right: We wrote him when we heard of his unhappiness.
Wrong: They enjoyed their lunch after they played all morning.
Right: They enjoyed their lunch after they had played all morning.

Meaning and Punctuation

The story is told of the reporter who was unable to use punctuation properly. His motto was, When in doubt, leave it out. Rather than work on his problem, he left the task up to the copy desk. "I'm the writer," he told one copy editor after the editor had asked him about some punctuation in a story. "You're the copy editor. I write. You supply the commas and periods and that other stuff."

The copy editor was a patient man and waited for his opportunity.

A few weeks after this conversation, the reporter had a story about a youngster who had been ill for some weeks and had to be fed intravenously. The boy's parents and his grandmother were at the hospital one day, and they fought back their tears as they looked at the child. Benny was pale and had lost much weight. He had not eaten for days.

"Suddenly, Benny looked up," the reporter wrote. "The color seemed to return to his cheeks. He turned to his visitors.

" 'I'm hungry,' he said to them."

And then came the opportunity the copy editor had waited for. He gloated as he left the reporter's climactic sentence stand as it was written in the story:

" 'Let's eat Grandma.' "

Appendix B contains a stylebook, which includes a section on the 13 punctuation marks. Refer to it often.

Spelling

The rarest find of all is not the flawless diamond or the white whale but the perfect speller. Everyone has to use the dictionary from time to time. Some use it infrequently, to check unfamiliar words. Others have mental blocks when it comes to spelling certain words and have to refer to the dictionary every time they use words such as *arctic, consensus, embarrass, analyze, separate.*

Good spellers use the dictionary. Poor spellers do not.

Every editor knows that some writers cannot spell well. Editors accept this, but they do not accept excuses for misspelled words. They expect all their reporters to use the dictionary.

The first step in improving spelling is to diagnose the particular spelling problem. One frequent cause of misspellings is mispronunciation. We usually spell as we pronounce, and if we pronounce goverment, sophmore, Febuary, athalete and hinderance, this is how we will spell these words—incorrectly.

One way to overcome a spelling problem is to keep a list of words you often misspell. Poor spellers usually assume they are spelling correctly, which is one reason poor spellers give for not using the dictionary. To start your list, here is a compilation of 50 commonly misspelled words. Look them over. If any surprise you, jot them down.

a lot	environment	occurrence
accommodate	exaggerate	parallel
already	exhilarate	possess
altogether	exorbitant	precede
athlete	February	prejudice
arctic	finally	privilege
calendar	forty	restaurant
career	governor	separate
cemetery	grammar	sophomore
commitment	harass	strictly
competent	hindrance	tragedy
consensus	immediately	truly
dependent	indispensable	undoubtedly
descendant	lightning	vacuum
ecstasy	mathematics	villain
eighth	nickel	weird
embarrass	nuclear	

Don't despair if your list is long, and don't worry if you find you are adding to your list and consulting the dictionary often. That's a lot less embarrassing than the humiliation suffered by a major publishing house that had just published a journalism textbook. The publisher produced a brochure that was to be mailed to teachers all over the country. It was a handsome and costly effort. One of the sentences read: "There are exercises in spelling, punctuation and grammer." Several thousand brochures had to be burned.

Stylebook

Stylebooks are used by newspapers and broadcast stations to make the use of abbreviations, capitalization and spelling consistent. Is it 145 Meredith St. or Street? Should it be 10 a.m. or 10 A.M.? The federal power commission or Federal Power Commission? The stylebook tells the news writer how to handle each of these.

Symbol	Instruction	Original Text with Copy Editing Symbols	Corrected Copy
⬭	*Spell out*	The ⟨MTA⟩ today decided to increase	Metropolitan Transit Authority
⬭	*Use numeral*	the bus fare ⟨eighty-five⟩ cents a ride.	85 cents a ride.
⌐	*Begin new paragraph*	⌐The new fare will go into	The new fare
^ /	*Insert correction/ lowercase*	ᵉ/Affect Thursday at 6 P. M.	effect/ a.m.
⌒	*Run in; no paragraph*	More than 100,000 people	6 a.m. More than
= ^	*Delete word/ insert new word*	a day use̶ the city's buses. (ride)	a day ride the
⬭	*Abbreviate*	The ⟨Metropolitan Transit Authority⟩	MTA
^	*Insert new word*	voted 6-2 for the ^fare. Only (new)	the new fare
=	*Capital letter*	albert Franling and Sue Barker	Albert Franling
^ ⊙	*Insert new word and period/ close up*	voted in̶ ̶t̶h̶e̶ ̶n̶e̶g̶a̶t̶i̶v̶e̶. Barker (no)	voted no. Barker
⌃	*Insert comma*	said "The state should help	said, "The state
|	*Separate*	support|our fare. There is	support our fare.
∽	*Transpose letters*	enoûgh in the state treasury	enough in
⊙	*Insert period*	to lower the fare"	the fare."
⬭	*Spell out*	The ⑥ in favor agreed that	The six in favor
⌄	*Insert apostrophe*	the citys funds alone would have	the city's funds
⊃	*Close up*	to be used.	to be used.

Figure 10.1 Copy editing symbols.

Most newspapers do not use the postal system's abbreviations for states. It is MA for mail, but Mass. for newspapers. The stylebook lists the abbreviations for states.

The stylebook is useful in editing copy, which writers always do before turning in their stories. In addition to checking the content and structure of their stories, reporters make changes in spelling, punctuation, grammar, abbreviations and similar technical matters.

When editing their typewritten copy, reporters use the copy editing marks that are shown in figure 10.1.

Here are some examples of how copy editing marks are used. Story A is the news writer's original version. The numbers refer to the errors that the reporter caught before handing the story to the copy editor.

Story B is the way the story was edited by the reporter. It contains changes the reporter thought were necessary in the original copy. Story C is the way the story appeared.

Drunk driver

A

1.
A man who spend through Brockton with his car hood up
2.
was arrested Sunday morning after losing control of his
3.
car and crashing into the front lawn of a North Brockton
4.
home, Brockton police said today.
5.   *6.*
Arrested was Josehp Small, 45, of Rockville. He was

charged with drunk driving. His car came to rest on the
7.   *8.*
law of the home of Peter Ronney, 16 Eastern Avenue. There

was no damage to the Ronney home, police said.

B

1.
A man who sped through Brockton with his car hood up
2. he had lost
was arrested Sunday morning after ~~losing~~ control of his
3. (landed on)
car and ~~crashing into~~ the front lawn of a North Brockton
4.
home, ~~Brockton~~ police said today.
5.   6.   *(was arrested and*
~~Arrested was~~ Josehp Small, 45, of Rockville, ~~He was~~

charged with drunk driving. His car came to rest on the
7. n   *8.*
law of the home of Peter Ronney, 16 Eastern (Avenue.) There

was no damage to the Ronney home, police said.

Explanation of Editing Marks

1. The word is sped. Black out the *n* and close up the word.

2. I would rather have "lost" than "losing." It goes better with the past tense of the main verb of the sentence.

3. How can you crash into a lawn? Makes no sense. "Landed on" may not make strict sense; after all, he wasn't flying a car. But it's graphic.

4. Don't need Brockton. After all, he was driving in Brockton. No other police could make the arrest. Wasted word.

5. "Arrested was. . . ." is what they call *Time*-ese because *Time* magazine reverses subject and verb. Too cute. Stick with S-V-O. I'll start a new paragraph with the man's name and make one sentence out of two here.

6. Transpose the letters in his first name.

7. That's *lawn*. Insert *n*.

8. Make that *Ave.* The stylebook abbreviates avenue and street in addresses.

C

A man who sped through Brockton with his car hood up was arrested Sunday morning after he lost control of his car and landed on the front lawn of a North Brockton home, police said today.

Joseph Small, 45, of Rockville, was arrested and charged with drunk driving. His car came to rest on the lawn of the home of Peter Ronney, 16 Eastern Ave. There was no damage to the Ronney home, police said.

Stabbing

A

A Brockton man died from stab wounds Monday night after

a dispute with his former girlfriend, Barbara Garth, 39, *1.*

25 Elm St., had turned violent.

Lee Sam Bensley, 42, died at Bayfront Medical Center
2. *3.*
Monday evening after the fight, and his former girl-

friend was later arrested and booked for investigation
4. *5.*
into the murder. The incident occurred in Bensley's

apartment at 423 W. 120 St.
6.
Police said the two had been seeing each other but split

up two months ago when Miss Garth learned he was married.

B

A Brockton man died from stab wounds Monday night after

a dispute with his former girlfriend, ~~Barbara Garth, 39,~~ *1.*

~~25 Elm St.,~~ had turned violent.

Lee Sam Bensley, 42, died at Bayfront Medical Center

2.   3. The woman, Barbara Garth,

~~Monday evening after the fight, and his former girl~~

39, 25 Elm St., was

~~friend was later~~ arrested and booked for investigation

4. death.   5. Bensley was fatally

into the ~~murder.~~ ~~The incident occurred in Bensley's~~

stabbed in his

apartment at 423 W. 120 St.

6.

Police said the two had been seeing each other but split

up two months ago when ~~Miss~~ Garth learned he was married.

2. This phrase is a repetition of material in the lead. Tighten up.

3. This is a run-on sentence. Begin a new sentence here and put in her name.

4. Oops. Murder is the finding of a jury after a trial, or a charge. She's only been booked. Call it a "death" and that is safe.

5. Hard to call what seems to be a killing an "incident." I can't say "death" because I've used that. Major surgery necessary.

6. Do I really need this on what may have been a drunken brawl? Might as well let the desk decide. Our newspaper does not use courtesy titles on second reference. So *Miss* is deleted.

C

A Brockton man died from stab wounds Monday night after a dispute with his former girlfriend had turned violent.

Lee Sam Bensley, 42, died at Bayfront Medical Center. The woman, Barbara Garth, 39, 25 Elm St., was arrested and booked for investigation into the death. Bensley was fatally stabbed in his apartment at 423 W. 120 St.

Police said the two had been seeing each other but split up two months ago when Garth learned he was married.

Boots

A

1.

For 5 weeks they have been walking, despite the summer

heat, the mosquitoes and their aching, blistered feet.

2.   3. 4.

Up over hills. Down sharp rocky hillsides. And along

5.   6.

narrow ledges. From 6 a.m. in the morning until 4 or 5 P.M.

7.   8.

in the evening they walk. The fifteen soldiers have hiked

15 miles a day, even more. They are on the road to . . .

9.

Nowhere!

The soldiers have been walking in circles, since the

middle of July they have been walking over a test course.

12.

They are testing a newlydesigned combat boot. By the time

13.

they have completed their rounds the men will have walked

14. 15.   16.

nearly 750 miles. "Its wild, wild", said one of the

soliders.

The tests are being conducted on the Aberdeen Proving

Ground in Maryland. The new boot is made of a brown suede.

17.

"No more boot polishing, that's the only thing that makes

18.

this worthwhile," said another.

Explanation of Editing Marks

1. Spell out numbers from one through nine. Stylebook rule.

2. Insert a comma between adjectives.

3. *And* does not work. It spoils the parallel structure and rhythm set by the previous two sentences.

4. Capitalize the letter *a*.

5. Redundancy; a.m. means before noon.

6. Lower case P.M.

7. Redundancy; p.m. means after noon.

8. Use the numeral for numbers 10 and above.

9. Delete the exclamation point. Let the reader supply it, the stylebook says.

10. There are two sentences here. Use a period instead of a comma.

11. Capital letter for beginning of sentence.

12. Separate.

13. I want the reader to pause here. There may or may not be a grammatical reason for this, but commas can be used to stop the reader for an instant.

B

1.

For ⑤ weeks they have been walking, despite the summer

heat, the mosquitoes and their aching, blistered feet.

2.   *3. 4.*

Up over hills. Down sharp rocky hillsides. ~~And~~ along

5.   *6.*

narrow ledges. From 6 a.m. ~~in the morning~~ until 4 or 5 P.M.

7.   *8.*

~~in the evening~~ they walk. The ⟨fifteen⟩ soldiers have hiked

15 miles a day, even more. They are on the road to ...

9.

Nowhere ⟨X⟩

10. 11.

The soldiers have been walking in circles, since the

middle of July they have been walking over a test course.

12.

They are testing a newly designed combat boot. By the time

13.
```
they have completed their rounds,the men will have walked
        14. 15.                       16.
nearly 750 miles. "It's wild, wild", said one of the

soldiers.

   The tests are being conducted on the Aberdeen Proving

Ground in Maryland. The new boot is made of brown suede.
                  17.
"No more boot polishing that's the only thing that makes
                                      18.
this worthwhile," said another  soldier
```

14. New paragraph. The quotation introduces a new idea.

15. Troublesome word. Here I need the contraction for *it is*. Insert apostrophe.

16. Transpose. When ending quotations, the punctuation goes inside the quote mark.

17. Delete the comma, put in a period and close up.

18. Another what? The prior reference to a soldier is too far away.

C

For five weeks they have been walking, despite the summer heat, the mosquitoes and their aching, blistered feet.

Up over hills. Down sharp, rocky hillsides. Along narrow ledges. From 6 a.m. until 4 or 5 p.m. they walk. The 15 soldiers have hiked 15 miles a day, even more. They are on the road to . . .

Nowhere.

The soldiers have been walking in circles. Since the middle of July they have been walking over a test course. They are testing a newly designed combat boot. By the time they have completed their rounds, the men will have walked nearly 750 miles.

"It's wild, wild," said one of the soldiers.

The tests are being conducted on the Aberdeen Proving Ground in Maryland. The new boot is made of brown suede. "No more boot polishing. That's the only thing that makes this worthwhile," said another soldier.

The Right Word

So far we have been concerned with avoiding mistakes. Let's move on to a more pleasant subject—making your writing a pleasure to read.

This involves finding the words that match the situation you are trying to describe. They are out there. The trick is to make your reach long enough. The English language has an enormous number of words, so many that the writer can always find the exact word he or she is looking for.

If a child is crying quietly about a neighbor's dog that has been struck by a car, we would not say she is *wailing*. We might say she is *sobbing*. A student who stacks up a heap of library books on his table and then sits there staring at them could be said to be *contemplating* the books and his assignment. If his contemplation lasts a long time, we might say he is *avoiding* his assignment.

Next, let's turn to some journalists for advice about good writing.

Writing

The Right Word. Examine the pictures on these two pages and try to find the one word or two that will best describe the scene or emotion that each picture projects. If you want to write a lead around the word or words you select, go ahead.

Opposite, top left, Joe Luper, Pepperdine University; *opposite, right,* Joseph Noble, *The Stuart News; this page, top,* Matthew Brady, Courtesy of the Library of Congress; *this page, bottom,* Arthur Rothstein, Courtesy of the Library of Congress

Fine Tuning
the Story

News stories are written so people can understand them quickly and effortlessly. The news writer uses everyday words in short sentences and paragraphs, structures the story so that it moves logically from beginning to end and includes quotations, incidents and specific details that make the story interesting and convincing.

News writers select a style for each story that reflects the nature of the event. A story about a game decided in the last minute may contain unusually short sentences to give a sense of the quick movement of the game, whereas a story about a teacher retiring after many years will have longer sentences and a relaxed pace.

When he was a young reporter struggling to make a name for himself during the rough-and-tumble days of New York tabloid journalism, Jim Bishop was taken aside by a famous columnist and given some advice.

"If you want to write," Mark Hellinger told him, "you are going to have to learn to pound out terse sentences composed of small words."

Bishop took the advice and applied it to all he wrote. He became a successful reporter, then a syndicated columnist and the author of such books as *The Day Lincoln Died, A Day in the Life of President Kennedy* and *The Day Christ Died*. In his stories, columns and books, Bishop wrote short sentences and he used words that we use every day.

The result of Bishop's commitment to short sentences and ordinary words is clarity, one of the most important ingredients of the news story. The news story must be understandable. If it is not, it is nothing.

The good news story has two other ingredients. It is convincing, and it is natural. By this, we mean that the story can be believed and that the style matches the nature of the event. We will examine the ways to achieve these goals in this chapter.

Easy to Understand

Clarity is achieved through language and structure. The language is ordinary language. The words are familiar to everyone. Sentences are short and follow the S-V-O pattern.

The story is structured with the reader in mind. From beginning to end, the story moves in a logical progression. A theme is stated in the lead and immediately developed. If there is more than one theme, the themes are developed in the order stated in the lead. When a delayed lead is used, the incidents and quotes used in the first few paragraphs move directly to the theme.

William J. Storm uses a two-paragraph delayed lead to move the reader into his story. Notice how many short sentences Storm uses in this excerpt:

Delayed lead

OLD FORGE, PA.—Until Wednesday night, no one in this Scranton suburb complained much about Joseph Aulisio.

The teen-ager rode a noisy motorcycle up and down the street, one neighbor said. He overturned garbage cans, another claimed—"mostly kid stuff."

Lead

But now Aulisio, 15, is accused of the shotgun slaying of two neighborhood children, Cheryl Ziemba, 8, and her brother Christopher, 4. The neighbors were shocked.

Aulisio, son of a former Old Forge school board member, is being held without bail in Lackawanna County Jail, charged with criminal homicide, kidnapping, hindering an investigation and arrest.

"We never expected anything like this," said Joan Lilli, the mother of a 4½-year-old girl.

"We're all really worried around here," Ms. Lilli said. "We just don't know what's going to happen."

"I was never afraid in my life," said Ceil McGarry, 62, who lives next door to the Ziemba family. "We never had to be afraid in this area, and now I'm numb."

About 500 searchers, including Aulisio and his brother and father, began hunting for Cheryl and Christopher shortly after they were reported missing early Sunday evening. They were last seen in the 18-unit trailer park where Aulisio lives.

Early Monday morning, three bloody sandals and two pieces of rug containing human bone fragments and brain tissue were found at the top of an overgrown, 100-foot-long abandoned strip mine where a neighbor said Aulisio used to ride his motorcycle.

The bodies were discovered shortly after noon Tuesday in a nearby abandoned strip mine pit.

Investigators are checking the possibility that the children were slain in a nearly finished house that Aulisio's father, Robert G. Sr., was building next to the mobile home he shared with Joseph and another son, Robert Jr.

The house is about 500 yards from the children's home on Drakes Lane.

Not every sentence in this story is short. A parade of 10-and 12-word sentences would be tedious. The trick is to set a rhythm of a few long sentences with several short, concise sentences. (Also, notice the frequent use of quotes.)

Frederick C. Othman, a master reporter for the UPI, was asked to give advice to colleagues about the art of writing. He said: "I shall not repeat any warnings about the need for keeping sentences simple, but I do urge you count words. If you've got a long sentence, make the next one short. Like this.

"The idea is to produce variety, but if your average is more than 25 words per sentence, your reader will desert you. That's been proven scientifically."

Later, we will look at this proof. Now, you can use the work of good writers as proof. Look at the first three sentences in this story from *The Washington Post:*

They came in darkness before the dawn of Dec. 11, 1978. There were six or seven of them, with ski masks over their heads and guns in their hands, and they knew what was supposed to be in the Lufthansa cargo terminal that morning. Millions.

The sentence lengths are 11, 33, 1. That's 45 words in three sentences, average length 15 words. Just as important, there is rhythm—short, long, very short.

Sentences are given their surge and power by their verbs. Action verbs propel the sentences. They move the subject to the object.

Verbs Provide Action

Stanley Walker, a legendary city editor in New York, advised young reporters "to avoid adjectives and to swear by the little verbs that bounce and leap and swim and cut."

Carl Sandburg, the poet, said at age 75, "I'm still studying verbs and the mystery of how they connect nouns. I am more suspicious of adjectives than at any time in all my born days."

Beginners try to reach their readers by injecting their stories with adjectives and adverbs—and failing in the task. Shoving the adjectives *dramatic, spectacular, terrifying, exciting* and others like these into stories is not writing. Nor is the use of adverbs to prop up verbs: *walked quickly, ran awkwardly, collided noisily.* This is hitting the reader over the head with words. It's also lazy writing.

The good writer does not call attention to his or her writing with these high-school antics. The task of the journalist is to communicate information directly, quickly and clearly. Well-chosen verbs help the writer to do just that.

Less Is More

As a rewriteman, Robert Peck's job was to take stories whose meaning was cloudy and make them shine clearly. One of the major problems was the long sentence, which was the result, he said, of writers trying to include too much information in the sentence. Peck, acknowledged to have been one of the finest rewritemen ever to work in New York, said he would cut the sentences "to little more than subject, verb, and object."

The result, he said, was a story that gained "grace and speed."

There, in those few words, is the essence of the good story. It is well told, and it moves quickly and gracefully from beginning to end.

Not only would Peck pare down sentences; he also removed extraneous material from the story. Writers gather large amounts of information in their reporting, and they are reluctant to discard any of it, even though some of it may not bear on the major theme or themes.

If the story is about a speaker discussing the need to return to science and mathematics as requirements for college graduation, then his remarks about the beauty of the campus and the bracing spring weather are irrelevant, no matter how clever.

Know Your Audience

Simplicity and clarity are important because of the different kinds of people who read and listen to news. Most journalists are aware that the public is diverse, and that they must direct their writing at a wide range of readers and listeners.

At one end are those with minimal reading ability. A study of 23,000 recruits at the San Diego Naval Base showed that 37 percent of them could not read at the 10th grade level. At the Walter Reed Army Hospital in Washington, signs were rewritten to the third-grade level because many enlisted men had found them difficult to understand.

At the other end are college graduates and others who would resent being written down to.

Some journalists have a specific type in mind. Martin Nolan, veteran reporter for the *Boston Globe,* has "a sort of image of the guy who works with his hands but retains a lively interest in what's going on and doesn't need to be given clichés and comfortable slogans in the copy."

Dan Rather of CBS News thinks back to his youth in Texas.

"I know people who work with their back and hands in Texas. A number of them are in my family. And I ask myself, will they understand this story? They're the people I know best . . . good, decent, intelligent people."

Readability

Studies have been made of written material to determine what is easiest and what is most difficult to read. The studies emphasize sentence length. Some also conclude that paragraph length and word length are factors. This table is given to wire service reporters:

Average Sentence Length	Readability
8 words or less	Very easy to read
11 words	Easy to read
14 words	Fairly easy to read
17 words	Standard
21 words	Fairly difficult to read
25 words	Difficult to read
29 words or more	Very difficult to read

If the sentences are long, one way out of the trouble is to remember the advice of the English author George Orwell, "If it is possible to cut a word out, always cut it out." A good place to start cutting is with adjectives and adverbs. A sentence that repeats a previous idea should be cut. An old rule for journalists helps to cut sentence length: one idea to a sentence. Watch for the words *and* and *but.* These words sometimes introduce a second idea. Try putting a period before the *and* or *but.*

Paragraphs should not be long. A long paragraph can discourage a reader. By dividing the number of words in the article by the number of paragraphs, an average paragraph length is obtained. Some editors say they prefer no more than 50 to 70 words to a paragraph. A faster way to check paragraph length is to limit paragraphs to no more than three or four sentences.

Big words, by which we mean words with three or more syllables, are difficult for readers to understand. The fewer big words, the better. One long word in 10 at most. Orwell put it simply: "Never use a long word where a short one will do."

Muddy writing can be made clearer with these techniques. But no one can learn to write by using a formula. The formula is a thermometer to measure potential trouble. If you write simply, clearly and directly, if you use quotes and anecdotes and illustrations, and if you write with a firm idea of what you want to say, then your writing will meet these guidelines.

Three Tests One way to test the readability of a story is to look at: 1. *Sentence pattern*— Average number of words per sentence. An average of 20+ means the story is hard to read. 2. *Fog index*—Abstract or complex words per sentence. Simple words are understood easily. Replace "rendezvous" with "meeting," "compelled" with "forced," and so on. 3. *Human interest*—People are interested in people. Name people; show them talking and acting.

Most troublesome for news writers is the inability to say something simply. "There are some common defects that we know contribute to bad writing. And, by far, the worst is failure to say it simply," says the AP in a study of readability. The AP says that the heart of all the formulas that have been used to check readability is this: "Say it simply and say it in short, easy-to-understand sentences."

Not only does the reporter have to write each story simply and clearly, but he or she must also prove the case, must convince the reader that the story is true.

Convincing

A reporter, on assignment in a Central American country that had been ruled by three generations of dictators, beginning with the grandfather of the present head of state, wanted to learn what the people thought of the grandson. The grandfather had been ruthless. One of his favorite methods of torturing opponents was to dip them head down in a well.

The grandson was supposedly enlightened. The reporter went into the countryside to find out what the peasants thought of the three presidents. In one of his interviews, he asked an elderly farmer whether there was any difference among them.

"Un arbol no puede dar tres clases de frutas," the peasant replied, and the reporter wrote this in his story, along with the English translation, "One tree cannot give three kinds of fruits."

Those who read the story understood. Despite the president's elaborate and expensive public relations apparatus in the United States, directed at painting him as democratic, the reporter's story had the ring of truth. The homespun saying of the peasant carried more weight than the press releases of paid propagandists.

The combination of on-the-scene reporting and good writing carries conviction. By convincing writing we mean stories that illustrate with examples (show, don't tell), that quote people involved in the event and that contain specific details.

Showing Carries Conviction

When Jeff Klinkenberg interviewed A. J. McClane, a world-famous fisherman, he wanted his readers to draw some conclusions about McClane. He could have said that McClane is world-famous. Instead, he **shows** the reader this with the following incident:

> Inside ritzy Capriccio's Restaurant where luncheon guests include ITT's board chairman, waiters hover about A. J. McClane like pilotfish around a shark. A waiter lights his cigarette while another pours his drink. The maître d'—and then the owner—stop and ask him if his meal is satisfactory.

We might have taken Klinkenberg's word for it if he had told us McClane was famous. Or we might not have. But after reading this incident, we know. We are convinced.

Klinkenberg wants to make a point about the democracy of fishing. On a stream, in a river, at the ocean, all are equal. Klinkenberg uses McClane's voice to provide the incident to make this point. Here is McClane speaking:

> I went fishing once with King Zahir of Afghanistan, but do you know what I remember most about the day? I remember him reaching deep into his wallet and producing a little snapshot of him holding a five-pound trout. Here was this king, and all he wanted was to show me a fish he was proud of. Remarkable! The point is this: Fishing is a universal thing. When people are fishing, it does not matter who they are. They're all the same.

Klinkenberg spent five hours with McClane, read some of his writings and interviewed several people who knew him. The result was a notebook filled with material that showed McClane's abilities as an angler. From these notes, he wrote for nine hours. He revised the story 17 times.

"I would have done better if I hadn't had the flu," Klinkenberg said of his effort.

Flu or no, the reader put down Klinkenberg's story with the feeling he or she knew McClane.

Sometimes, the showing can be done quickly. The reader can see a great deal with one shaft of light. When Red Smith, the great sports writer, wanted to tell his readers about the power of the owner of the Los Angeles Dodgers baseball team, he did not say that the owner, Walter O'Malley, was more powerful than Bowie Kuhn, the commissioner of baseball. Smith showed the reader by writing:

> When O'Malley sends out for coffee, Kuhn asks, "One lump or two?"

Red Smith wrote a column and columnists are given plenty of freedom. However, the point is still valid: Show the reader or listener and conviction follows.

Quotes carry conviction. Mervin Block, a former newspaper reporter who writes television news, was assigned to do a magazine piece about the newspaper war between the *Daily News* and *The New York Post*.

He quotes the *Post's* metropolitan editor:

Quotes Convince

> "What competition?" snaps the Post's metropolitan editor, Steve Dunleavy scornfully. "If it's war, it's a massacre—by the Post. We're gaining two to every one they lose . . . we're so confident we walk around the trenches with our helmets off."

Ten Keys to Good Writing

Begin to write only after you know what you want to say.
Write the way you talk.
Use the S-V-O sentence structure for most sentences.
Use action verbs.
Avoid adjectives and adverbs.
Keep sentences short.
Show, don't tell.
Good quotes up high.
Use words you're familiar with.
Never turn in a story you think you can improve.

We can visualize the colorful, confident, if not cocky, editor as he talks.

Studs Terkel interviewed a telephone solicitor for a Chicago newspaper. The woman, Enid Du Bois, would call people to ask them to subscribe. She worked with about 30 others, mostly women. She talks to Terkel:

At first I liked the idea of talking to people. But pretty soon, knowing the area I was calling—they couldn't afford to eat, let alone buy a newspaper—my job was getting me down. They'd say, "Lady, I have nine to feed or I would help you." What can you say? One woman I had called early in the morning, she had just gotten out of the hospital. She had to get up and answer the phone.

They would tell me their problems. Some of them couldn't read, honest to God. They weren't educated enough to read a newspaper. Know what I would say? "If you don't read anything but the comic strips . . ." "If you got kids, they have to learn how to read the paper." I'm so ashamed thinking of it.

In the middle-class area, the people were busy and they couldn't talk. But in the poor area, the people really wanted to help the charity I talked about. They said I sounded so nice, they would take it anyway. A lot of them were so happy that someone actually called. They could talk all day long to me. They told me all their problems and I'd listen.

They were so elated to hear someone nice, someone just to listen a few minutes to something that had happened to them. Somehow to show concern about them. I didn't care if there was no order. So I'd listen. I heard a lot of their life stories on the phone. I didn't care if the supervisor clicked in.

In these quotes, so much is revealed: the compassion of Du Bois, her disgust with her job, the generosity of the poor, the terrible solitude and loneliness of people. All of this in just four paragraphs.

Terkel is a master interviewer. Many of his taped interviews have been collected in books. His interviews with working people are included in *Working: People Talk About What They Do All Day and What They Think of While They Do It* (New York: Pantheon Books, 1972). *The Good War, An Oral History of World War II* (New York: Pantheon Books, 1984) relates stories told by the fighting men.

Quotes convince us because we can visualize the people and the circumstances. Quotes are memorable. An international economist recalls being seated in a restaurant next to a family of three, father, mother, and a boy of eight or ten. The waitress brought the menus and waited.

The boy decided. "I want liver and bacon," he said. The mother said she wanted a steak. Father turned to the waitress. "Three steaks," he said. The waitress nodded and replied as she wrote, "Two steaks, one liver and bacon."

The boy turned to his mother. "Mommy," he said, "she thinks I'm real."

No wonder the economist remembered this story. The boy's excited statement sums up the refusal of some parents to take their children seriously.

Reporters always listen for the quote and watch for the incident that sum up the situation. Not only will the quote be good reading; it will convince the reader.

Be Specific

Finally, conviction is achieved through specifics. The writer who writes, "There were about a dozen people in the courtroom" is not taken as seriously as the writer who writes, "There were 11 people in the courtroom."

We know that the writer who wrote "11" was there.

If the book stolen from the library was 4 inches by 6 inches, don't say it was a "small book." Say, "The book was 4 inches by 6 inches, small enough to fit into a coat pocket."

Readers love details, specific details. Readers can visualize the event if they are told that the suspect was five-foot-four, thin, wore blue jogging shoes, a close-cropped haircut and used a small handgun that fitted in the palm of his hand.

The reporter notes sizes, weights, numbers of things, colors, smells. Was it as large as a baseball or a basketball, as heavy as a letter or a book? Did it smell like onions, garlic or newly cut grass? Was it a deep blue, almost black, or the light blue of a sky after a rainstorm? Did it sound like the snap of a firecracker or the bang of a backfire?

Notice that in these questions, the specifics have been linked to particular things that can be seen, touched, smelled, heard. Writers use images that appeal to the senses to make their specifics spring to life and to give them the exactitude of reality.

Words as well as observations can be abstract. Just as we avoid saying "around a dozen" or "small," we do not use abstractions, such as patriotism, equality, affection, unless they are tied directly to a specific event or situation or we are quoting someone.

Abstractions have no agreed-upon meaning. What is obscenity? As a federal judge observed, "One man's lyric is another man's obscenity."

Words must be anchored to real things in nature. Should the source talk of love, freedom, happiness, fear and anxiety, the reporter is immediately alert. The reporter knows that these words mean all things to all people. Their meanings are elusive. The reporter has to grab the slippery subject and tie it down.

The reporter will ask the source, "Can you give me an example of what you mean by happiness?" As one reporter put it, "I always ask anyone who speaks in generalities for a for-instance."

By using quotations, by citing specific situations and sources, by showing readers and listeners through anecdotes and illustrations and quotes, journalists may regain the confidence of their public. The Gallup Poll has shown a consistently low level of public confidence in journalists. About a third of those polled say they consider journalists honest and competent.

Natural Style

Our third component of the well-written story is an appropriate writing style. By this, we mean that the style of the story fits the subject. Words, sentence patterns, even the paragraph lengths are chosen to be consistent with the subject matter.

The profile of a young woman who has just won a beauty contest will not be written with the same somber style as the obituary of a well-known local resident. The profile will be breezy, even brash:

Evelyn Marie Welton woke up yesterday morning with a headache.

Last night she went to bed with a head full of dreams.

The 19-year-old Mason City college sophomore was crowned Miss Douglas County at the Civic Auditorium last night. Next month, she goes to the state finals.

"I felt terrible, just terrible all day," Welton said after her victory. "But as soon as I walked into the auditorium, something happened. Like, you know, it snapped."

The lights, the excitement of competition, the possibility of going all the way to the top had its effect.

"I just knew I could do it," she said. . . .

On the other hand the obituary will be somber and reserved:

Albert Funnel, 78, of 45 East Alpine Ave., who served as city clerk for 46 years before retiring, died yesterday after a long illness.

Funnel had been hospitalized a week ago with lung cancer.

The former city worker was known throughout the state for his innovations in the office of city clerk. He instituted a new system of. . . .

A Grim Story

Mitch Mendelson had a tragic story to cover, a house fire in which five people died. His style is simple and direct. He lets the facts show the tragedy. He gives them no adornment. Here is the beginning of his understated story, which appeared in the *Birmingham Post-Herald:*

The use of a delayed lead puts reader on the scene.

A coroner stood in the rain yesterday afternoon and poked through the smoldering rubble of what had been a house. She was looking for the bodies of four young children and their great-grandmother.

A helper standing nearby shivered.

One by one, the tiny, charred figures were carefully zipped into black vinyl body bags and carried away.

A chilling quote sums up the tragic event.

As the coroner, Dale Cunningham, was leaving, a passerby asked if there were any bodies left in the ruins. "Five is all," she said. "Five is too many."

The essential facts of the story

> Reginald, 4, Stephanie, 2, Roderick, 2, and Amanda Gardner, 6 months, and Fannie Harvell, 88, were killed by a fire that destroyed their Dolomite home yesterday morning.
>
> The children's mother, Sandra Gardner, 23, was reportedly visiting neighbors when the fire started. Her 19-year-old brother escaped the house. Ms. Gardner was treated for shock at Lloyd Nolan Hospital in Fairfield.
>
> All four of the children were in the same room. One body was found in a corner, another under a bed.
>
> Mrs. Harvell died near the back door.

Mendelson says that he wanted to get behind the tragedy "to find reasons and aggravating circumstances." Once they have been discovered, he says, "the task is to weave the reasons and the message into the dramatic fabric, supporting the themes with facts and vivid descriptions."

In covering the fire, Mendelson learned that there were three possible reasons for the deaths. The burglar bars on the windows may have hampered escape. The community of Dolomite has no firehouse. And, third, the area has no fire hydrants.

Here is the rest of the story. Watch how Mendelson weaves these three possible causes for the tragedy into the account:

Burglar bars

> Preston Countryman, a fire medic from the Hueytown Fire Department, stood in the front yard and picked up one of the steel "burglar bars" that had been on a front window. "Death traps," he said. Every window on the house had burglar bars. "They're good for keeping people out . . . plus keeping people in," he said.

No fire protection

> And Dolomite, an unincorporated area of Jefferson County sandwiched between Hueytown, Pleasant Grove and Midfield, has no fire protection. By the time Hueytown firefighters arrived on the scene about 9:40 a.m., the one-story, wood-frame house at 669 Washington Ave. was, according to firemen, "heavily involved."

No hydrants

> Add a third chilling fact: The area, which is heavily residential with many one-family homes, has no hydrants. Fire companies from Hueytown and Brighton had to shuttle water to the scene.

Elaboration of possible causes of the deaths

> "The county should furnish protection, but they don't," said Hueytown firefighter Dale Roberts yesterday afternoon as the men cleaned up in the firehouse. "And one thing that hampers firefighting is having to shuttle water. One question that should be asked is, "Why is the Center Point area furnished with fire protection but other unincorporated areas aren't?"

Possible dangers for the future (Mendelson's "message")

> The Hueytown men made it clear they are not required to answer calls outside the city. "We go provided we can get our auxiliary (volunteers) in. We can't send everyone outside of the city," said Roberts.
>
> "It's an awkward situation."
>
> Added volunteer firefighter Luther Brown: "I'm glad that we had enough help that we could go out. It might not happen the next time."
>
> While the two companies had the blaze under control in about 30 minutes, Brown pointed out there was valuable time lost in finding teams to respond. "Five minutes makes a lot of difference," he said.

Description of the scene

> The rain poured down on the charred ruins yesterday afternoon, and steam rose from the rooms that had been torn apart by the blaze and the men who came on a mission of mercy to fight it. The rain made pools in the front yard where Countryman stood and talked about the burglar bars. It turned to thick mud the yards around the house and the garden in the back.
>
> At the house next door, family, neighbors and friends gathered to console the living and mourn the dead.

Vonnegut on Style—Respect for the Reader

Kurt Vonnegut, the author of *Slaughterhouse Five, Cat's Cradle* and other novels, says that when an author works on his or her writing style it is "a mark of respect" to the reader.

"If you scribble your thoughts any which way," he says, "your readers will surely feel that you care nothing about them. They will mark you down as an egomaniac or a chowderhead—or worse, they will stop reading you."

Vonnegut says that writers must care about the subjects they write about. "It is this genuine caring, and not your games with language, which will be the most compelling and seductive element in your style."

He adds this advice:

Do not ramble.

Keep it simple. He points out that the Bible opens "with a sentence well within the writing skills of a lively fourteen-year-old: 'In the beginning God created the heaven and the earth.'"

Have the guts to cut. Every sentence, he says, has to "illuminate your subject."

Sound like yourself. Write the way you speak.

Say what you mean to say.

Description of the scene (continued)

The rain fell on the twisted pipes that had been a kitchen set and on a scorched refrigerator and on the children's toys in the front yard.

The neighbors stood on their porches and looked out at the dismal scene. A sheriff's officer splashed through the yard and said, "mess," and shook his head.

At the house next door, Shirley Williams, Ms. Gardner's sister, slumped next to a window and looked out at the place where her grandmother and four of her nieces and nephews had died.

Driving home the message

Steve Mahan, another Hueytown fire medic, said at the scene, "Half of our fire department is here and the city is unprotected. But it's hard to say 'No, we can't come.'"

A recent report by the National Fire Data Center said Alabama and other southeastern states have the highest fire death rate in the industrialized world. Birmingham ranks second to Newark, N.J., in fire death rates among large American cities.

20 Tips for Good Writing

This list was put together by the Gannett newspapers. Most of the tips were supplied by Jim Bishop.

1. Be fair. Presenting all sides of a story is not copping out.
2. Observe good taste.
3. Make the lead provocative, clear and simple.
4. Sentences should be short.
5. Quotes improve a story. Use them.
6. An important story need not be long.
7. Select adjectives carefully. Too many are dangerous.
8. Don't be impressed with an important assignment.
9. Go directly to the source on every story when possible.
10. Leave no reasonable question unanswered. Do not assume readers know the background. And don't be afraid to write a good story you think readers already know.
11. Be polite, but don't be servile.
12. Get details. If your congressman wears high-top shoes, scratches his ears and uses a spittoon, you've created a word picture.
13. Don't be afraid to try something that isn't in the book.
14. Even if you have mastered the language, use short, easy words.
15. Stories are improved by the injection of the time element.
16. After the lead, blend the story from paragraph to paragraph.
17. Don't insult a race, an ethnic group, a minority or other separate entity. Identify when it adds information. The distinction is thin at times.
18. Don't abuse your privileges or the weapons of your industry.
19. Admit errors quickly and fully.
20. Name the source of your story when possible. If it is an exposé from a confidential source, protect that source.

Some editors would move this paragraph higher since readers want to know the cause of the fire.

Driving home the message (continued)

Supplemental heaters, such as space heaters, are considered the biggest cause of fatal fires in the South, the report said.

The cause of yesterday's fire will be investigated by the state fire marshal's office, Roberts said.

As much as Mendelson wants to get his message across, he does not lecture or preach. The message is made by the people he interviews. He lets his sources do the talking.

The story won a writing award from the Scripps-Howard organization, of which the *Birmingham Post-Herald* is a member newspaper. The judges praised Mendelson for his "great sensitivity" and for "superbly organizing his facts so that readers when they had finished knew they had read something special."

Resistance to Journalistic Writing

The clear, simple writing in the fire story is typical of good journalistic writing. Despite the clarity of such writing, some teachers of high school and college English resist this kind of writing. Worse, they condemn it. Why? Why hasn't journalistic prose won many converts from the cloister of the English classroom?

A study by two professors may provide the answer. In a series of experiments, they found that some English teachers are more impressed by wordy, complicated language than by clear and concise writing. Rosemary L. Hake of Chicago State University and Joseph M. Williams of the University of Chicago asked English teachers to rate pairs of student essays that were the same in everything except style.

One of each pair was written in the clear and direct language journalists use. The other essay was devised so that the language was flowery, the sentences complex, the verbs passive.

The two professors discovered that some of the English teachers consistently preferred the muddy prose to the clear writing. Not only this, but the teachers saw more errors in the clearly written essays than in the complicated essays.

"The teachers tended to find errors of logic and meaning in the verbose papers and mechanical errors in the others—even though the papers were identical in the errors they contained," Dr. Hake said in a newspaper interview.

In other words, the teachers seemed to be impressed by purple prose and turned off by simple writing.

Clear Writing	Muddy Prose
Simple language	Flowery language
Active verbs	Passive verbs
Straightforward sentences	Complex sentences
Tight writing	Loose writing
Easily understood	Difficult to follow

The professors said their findings indicated that many teachers were "encouraging precisely the stylistic values we claim we reject and discouraging precisely the stylistic values we claim we support."

The study is described in the September 1981 issue of the journal *College English*.

Rewriting

Young writers should not be discouraged by the realization that writing requires work. Everyone who writes for a living—reporters, poets, novelists, magazine writers—knows the joy of making ideas come to life on paper. And the agony—especially the pain of rewriting.

"Good writing is rewriting," says Fred Zimmerman, an editor at *The Wall Street Journal*.

"Even on deadline, a good writer will take at least 20 or 30 seconds to glance over a piece of copy, not really editing it, but simply because it is the writer's habit to reflect on what he or she has written before letting go of it," Zimmerman says. The more time the writer has, the more attention he or she will give to the copy.

"Rewrite, rewrite and edit," says Zimmerman.

The original manuscript of the American classic *Walden* by Henry David Thoreau shows how hard Thoreau worked. He produced seven versions in the six years he worked on the book. Behind the beautiful and clear story of his two years alone by a Concord pond are years of toil.

Caskie Stinnett, an essayist and critic, says Thoreau "stopped and started, tinkered and rearranged, selected and discarded, chose and reconsidered, and fought with the English language until he forced it to come to terms with him."

Compressing six years into 60 minutes or six, the task for the news writer is the same one Thoreau faced.

Here are some checkpoints for the writer as he or she re-reads copy:

1. Is the lead on target or buried? A key to the answer: What is most of the body of the story about? If it is not about the theme selected as the lead, the lead is wrong.
2. If a delayed lead is used, does the quote or incident move directly into the main theme?

3. Is the story organized properly, or does it jump from one topic to another and back? Is secondary information put above primary material in the body?
4. Does the story move? Do the nouns and verbs carry it forward with an internal momentum? Do the facts that are chosen give movement to the piece?

A copy editor for a newspaper in New York was asked to list some of the most frequent problems he sees in the copy that moves past him.

1. **Not enough self-editing.** Reporters fight so hard to put their words on paper, they have a vested interest in them and are reluctant to change them. No story is perfect on first writing. Don't cherish every word you write. Always ask: Does this word, this sentence, this paragraph move the story forward?
2. **Wrong lead.** The writer has used a secondary theme for the main point of the story. The news writer has to keep asking: What made this event different from all others like it? The answer is the lead.
3. **Poor organization.** This is often the result of not locating the main theme and getting it high in the story. The reader should not be forced to go beyond the first four paragraphs to have a good idea of the thrust of the piece.
4. **Misuse of the delayed lead.** Too many hard news stories are given a soft news approach.
5. **Overwriting.** You don't have to use every quotation, every observation. In journalism, quantity does not count—the quality of the quote and the observation do.
6. **Dullness.** This can be the result of overwriting. It also stems from poorly selected verbs, long sentences, lack of quotes.
7. **Holes in the story.** Unanswered questions.

First the Formula, then Mastery

The news writer who masters the essentials outlined in these six chapters on writing is on the road to creating a personal writing style.

One of Elvis Presley's songwriters said that after five years of writing successful songs for Presley, he realized he was repeating himself. The songs were successful, but they were ground out to a formula, the writer said. There was no reason for Presley to change his style since it had proved to be a huge financial success.

However, the writer felt he was not being challenged, so he decided to move on to new forms of music.

Much of what has been said may seem as much a formula as the ingredients of Presley's hits. Granted. But there is nothing wrong with a formula if it guides the user to successful work. Once the formula is mastered, the writer can move on, like Presley's songwriter.

Broadcast Writing

Stories written for radio and television are written in conversational style, clearly and simply. The listener or viewer must be able to understand the story at once.

Complicated news stories are simplified by emphasizing only one or two themes. Leads are short and the present tense is used whenever possible. Attribution is always placed first in the sentence so that the listener or viewer knows at once the source of the information.

Monica Kaufman anchors the 6 p.m. and 11 p.m. newscasts on WSB-TV in Atlanta. Her news day begins at 2:30 p.m. and ends at 11:45 that night. But that's deceptive. She is always working.

"My day starts with reading the morning paper," she says, "and listening to the all-news radio station. If I have time, I tune in the cable news station on television."

By the time she shows up at the station early in the afternoon, Kaufman has a good idea of the day's news.

"My first stop at the station at 2:30 is the assignment desk to see what stories we're covering." These stories will be used on the 6 o'clock newscast.

"My second stop is the producer's desk to see what copy I have to write to fit between stories that reporters have turned in."

Her third stop is the wire machines where the news services click off reams of copy. She tears off the stories that she wants to use.

"Then it's writing time." Kaufman may rewrite the lead-ins that local reporters have written. These are the brief introductions to the reporters' stories. She will change them to conform to her speaking style.

If she is working on a special story of her own, she leaves the station to conduct interviews and to do her research.

"About 5 p.m., we begin to firm up the show. I write a 30-second promo, which is a tease to interest people in the 6 p.m. newscast. I do the promo live at 5:28:11.

News Check. Monica Kaufman and assignment editor Morris Pyle of WSB-TV in Atlanta go over the wire news before preparing the 6 p.m. news program.
Karen Clark

"When I come back up to the studio, it's time to look at the scripts that the reporters have written. They have been torn apart. White goes to the tele-synch operator. Blue to the show director. Green to the anchor who reads the piece. Goldenrod goes to the anchor who is listening. Pink to the show producer. Yellow to the editor."

Kaufman is on the set at 5:50 when she does a final read-through of the script.

After the show, she has hardly time to relax before preparing for the 11 p.m. news program. Usually, she goes out on a story for the late evening show.

"I try to make the 11 o'clock program different with new material. We update the 6 o'clock news whenever we can."

At 11:30 p.m., she takes a breather, and by midnight she is on her way home.

"At home, I try to read some magazines to keep up with what is going on in the world."

Life for Kaufman is not always rush and more rush. Now and then she slows down to take on a major project that requires in-depth reporting and thoughtful writing. Often, these stories turn out to be series, one segment being presented each day.

Clarity the Goal

Much of what we have been discussing in this textbook applies to newspaper copy, which is writing for the eye alone. Although we are discussing writing for the ear and the eye in this chapter, the principles of broadcast writing are no different from those of print journalism—clarity, accuracy, honesty of expression. There are, however, some differences in the application of these principles.

The first rule of broadcast news is that the story must be clear at once. Unlike the newspaper reader, the listener has no second chance to go over the material. Radio and television news is as fleeting as the wind—here for the instant, then gone.

There are several ways the broadcast news writer makes his or her copy clear.

Language Broadcast news writers **use everyday words,** the language of conversation. Colloquialisms and contractions are acceptable. The style is informal. Look at some brief news items broadcast on the CBS television news program "Newsbreak":

Mail carriers are still making their rounds, while postal unions and management are still going round and round. There was tentative agreement on a new contract early today, but later the deal fell through. Now negotiations have resumed, and the unions say they have no plans for a strike.

Nato foreign ministers, meeting in Rome, today said nyet to Moscow—rejecting the Soviet demand for a moratorium on deployment of nuclear arms in Europe.

A Singapore Airlines jumbo jet left Southeast Asia today with a new way to help passengers pass the time. The plane, bound for San Francisco, is fitted out with six slot machines—for high fliers.

Ideas Broadcast news writers **simplify the complex.** The story written for a newspaper plunges right into the heart of the event. The broadcast story often has a brief introduction before the theme is stated. Each of the three "Newsbreak" stories above has an introductory clause or sentence.

When the mayor and the city council disagreed over a proposal to increase the city sales tax from 3 to 4 percent—a week after another disagreement over taxes—the radio copy of a local station began this way:

The mayor and the city council are feuding again. This time, the issue is the city's sales tax.

The writer used this as a brief introduction to the heart of the story. The writer then went into the details:

The city council last night turned down a proposal to increase the city sales tax from 3 to 4 percent. Mayor George Grogan said the city faces trouble unless it takes in more revenue.

And the only way the mayor can see to add to revenue is to raise the sales tax.

But the council voted six to one against the increase.

Count the number of sentences in the story. Then count the number of words in each sentence. There are six sentences, and they contain the following number of words: 9, 9, 20, 14, 18, 10. Clearly, most of the sentences are short, much shorter than the sentences would be in the same story written for a newspaper. The average number of words per sentence in this radio news copy is 13 or 14.

This leads us to the next point.

Brevity **Sentences are short** for broadcast stories. Long sentences cannot be read easily by the announcer, and the listener has a hard time following them. Here, side-by-side, are the UPI news wire and broadcast accounts of a major story from Atlanta:

News Wire

ATLANTA (UPI)--Wayne B. Williams, flanked by his defense team and surrounded by sheriff's deputies in a packed courtroom, pleaded innocent today to charges that he murdered two of 28 young blacks whose slayings kept Atlanta on edge for almost two years.

Williams, wearing a dark suit and a shirt open at the collar, appeared before Fulton County Superior Court Judge Clarence Cooper under extremely tight security.

Movements into and out of the courtroom were tightly controlled, with deputies using electronic metal detectors to search each of the about 300 reporters and spectators who jammed the small room.

During the 10-minute session, the charges were read to Williams. . . .

Broadcast Wire

The man charged in two of the Atlanta slayings has pleaded innocent. Wayne Williams appeared in a packed courtroom today to answer to the charges that he killed two of 28 young blacks. The courtroom was under extremely tight security that included a search of everyone who entered. The judge tentatively scheduled the trial to begin October 5th. The 23-year-old Williams remains the only person charged in any of the 28 slayings that terrorized Atlanta for almost two years.

The news story continues for 20 more paragraphs. The first four sentences of the news wire story contain 106 words. The average sentence length is around 26 words. The five sentences of the broadcast story total 81 words. That averages to a bit more than 16 words per sentence.

We know the way to write short sentences. Follow the S-V-O style. Look at the broadcast version. Every sentence begins with a subject, and the verb usually follows the subject immediately.

Broadcast news has been described as a headline service. It is intended to give the listener or viewer only an outline of the event. A half-hour newscast may have as many as 20 news items crammed into the 22 to 23 minutes allotted to news. The 68 seconds that the CBS "Newsbreak" program has for news will have four to six items. One day there were seven. That's a bit less than 10 seconds for each story, one or two sentences a story. Altogether, the news script for a Newsbreak program contains about 170 words, which is the equivalent of a three-to-four-inch story in a newspaper.

In other words, there are more words in a routine traffic accident story in a newspaper than there are in the entire Newsbreak program, and on the longer television news programs most stories have fewer words than a newspaper story about a non-controversial appointment by the governor.

All the news on a half-hour newscast would not fill the front page of a newspaper. The news on an hour program would run slightly more than one page.

Brevity—writing tightly—is the result of clear thinking. In order to write broadcast copy, the writer must be able to reduce news stories to their essence. The broadcast writer always asks himself or herself: **What happened here? Who said or did this?**

The answer, in simple S-V-O form, is the basis of the story.

The thinking process is the same, whether the news is gathered by a local reporter or is rewritten from the press association wires.

When stories are rewritten from the AP and UPI wires for television newscasts, these stories are described as **tell** stories or **readers.** That is, the anchor tells the listener about them, instead of showing film or tape. Tell stories do not excite viewers, broadcast people believe. So the tell story must be as brief as possible. Few tell stories run more than 20 or 30 seconds, which limits them to 50 to 75 words, the equivalent of one or two newspaper paragraphs.

In the CBS "Evening News" program we examined in chapter 1, there were eight tell stories. Not one ran more than 30 seconds. Even the stories with videotape were short. The lead story—the signing of a tax bill—ran two-and-a-half minutes, 365 words. The same story in *The New York Times* had 1,000 words. *The Washington Post* story of the event contained 1,200 words.

Tense Use the **present tense** whenever possible. Broadcast writers frequently use the present tense in their leads. Newspaper stories almost always contain the past tense throughout. The broadcast version of the Atlanta murders story used the verb *has pleaded,* which is the present perfect tense. The news wire story said that Williams *pleaded* innocent. This is the past tense.

The reason for using the present tense is simple. Broadcast news is supposed to give the listener or viewer the sense of immediacy, of events being covered as they happen. Sometimes, the present tense would sound silly, so the writer uses the past tense. Evening news programs use the past tense in looking back on events that occurred during the day.

If the mayor announced at a noon news conference that he will not seek re-election, the radio news account begins this way:

> Mayor George Grogan **says** he will not seek re-election. The mayor **made** his intention clear at noon today in a news conference. He **said** he wants to go back to running the family business.

Notice the present tense in the first sentence. The tense then switches to the past in the next two sentences when it describes the actual news conference statement. The logic behind using the present tense in the lead sentence is that his statement still holds true at the time of broadcast. The present tense does not violate the truth.

In its seventh "World in Brief" newscast of the day, the UPI's broadcast news staff wrote these leads on some of the news items:

Present tense   Portuguese air traffic controllers **are** engaged in a two-day boycott of U.S. flights in sympathy with the walkout by American controllers.

Present tense   A survey done by the University of Michigan **says** American consumers feel much better about the economy than they did a year ago.

Present tense   Country music star Willie Nelson reportedly **is** ill.

Present perfect tense   Elvis Presley's manager, Colonel Tom Parker, **has** vehemently **denied** allegations he defrauded Presley.

Several items did begin with the past tense. The writer had no alternative for these:

Five hundred people **attended** a memorial service honoring Elvis Presley at Memphis State University yesterday.

A youth evangelist and one hundred members of the First Assembly of God Church in Guthrie, Oklahoma, **made** a bonfire of rock music albums yesterday.

Incidentally, notice how short these leads are. They contain 22, 23, 8, 13, 15 and 25 words. Most newspaper leads run 30 to 35 words.

Not only are the leads and most sentences in the broadcast news story short, the stories are short. Brevity is the key that unlocks the door to broadcast news writing proficiency.

Rewriting the Wires

Although radio and television stations have staff members who write and broadcast the news they gather, much broadcast news originates from outside the station. Except for the networks, which have correspondents scattered over the world and in major U.S. cities, most stations rely on the AP and UPI for their national and foreign news and for much state and regional news.

This news is rewritten by broadcast news writers and put into broadcast form. Smaller stations usually subscribe to one broadcast wire and use the material just as it comes in. Large stations usually subscribe to both the AP and UPI news wires and the writers rewrite these stories for broadcast.

One reason bigger stations rewrite the news wires is that news directors prefer that their writers see the original story, before it has been filtered by a broadcast rewrite person at the wire service. The wire service rewrite may neglect an aspect of special interest to local listeners, or it may be routinely written.

Clash over the Mediterranean

Shortly after 9 o'clock one morning in August, the press association news wires began to move a story they marked "urgent." Two Navy jets had shot down two Libyan jet planes in a dogfight over the Mediterranean Sea. The U.S. Defense Department stated that the Soviet-made Libyan planes had attacked the F-14 fighter planes, which had fired back.

In the CBS newsroom in New York, Mervin Block was preparing the "Newsbreak" television newscast, which goes on at 11:57 a.m. As he watched the wires move the story, he knew that it could not be told in the 10 or 15 seconds each item on Newsbreak is usually allotted. By 10 a.m., the AP had moved three leads on the story, and by 10:30, the UPI was transmitting its fourth lead.

This was a big story. Did it mean Libya was planning to attack a neighboring country and wanted no U.S. surveillance? Was Libya's president anxious to demonstrate his nation's defiance of the United States, which he had described as the most dangerous country on earth?

Block had to monitor the wires for developments. Because the story was going to take more than a couple of sentences to tell, he could not wait long before sitting down with the thousands of words of AP and UPI copy to draft his broadcast story.

The people involved with the program—producer, editor, anchorperson and writer—agreed that the story would be given 40 or 45 seconds, which is long for a tell story. This meant Block had to boil down the wire stories to about 135 words.

Figure 12.1 Mervin Block explains how he chose the few words allowed him to convey the pertinent facts of the news story within the 45-second time limit.

BLOCK'S COMMENTS

This headline--admittedly a fragmentary sentence--gives the viewer a quick preview. The wire services said "off the coast of North Africa," but I jettisoned "the coast of" as needless. Near the top, I cite the source of the story. In broadcasting, attribution precedes assertion. Again, I took pains to name the source for the second assertion. My producer, however, might have thought the second sourcing was redundant, and he deleted it. Or he thought I was running long. Apparently, no reporter saw the dogfight, so we must make clear who told us. The wires quoted the Department of Defense, but I condensed it to "Pentagon," which has more punch. The wires also quoted the State Department; I reduced that to "Washington." We're constantly struggling for tighter scripts, even on two-hour newscasts. Although a viewer can't see quotation marks, I use them so the anchor can change his delivery. I use direct quotations seldom, and I say "quote" or "unquote" rarely.

After I gave the gist of the accusation, I reported the other side's response. And I tacked on a bit of background about the territorial claim. I couldn't take time to elaborate on the claim or to report on U.S.-Libyan relations. Nor did I waste time with name-dropping or name-calling. Until now, I hadn't identified the type of U-S jet. At 11:57 a.m., most of our viewers are probably housewives, and, chances are, few, if any, know an F-14 from an F-4 or even a 4-F. The wires said the Nimitz is nuclear-powered, but I saw no need to waste words about its propulsion. The AP said the encounter was "60 nautical miles" off Libya. I know that a nautical mile is about a mile and a seventh, which would make it nearly 70 miles. I wrote "almost"; years ago, my editor on the CBS Evening News told me an anchor can get a better grasp

SCRIPT

A jet battle off North Africa: The Pentagon says two Libyan jets fighters attacked two U-S Navy F-14 jets over the Mediterranean today. and the ~~Pentagon says the~~ Navy jets shot down both Libyan craft. Washington says the attack against the U-S jets was ``unprovoked'' and that it took place in ``international air space over international waters.'' Libya says the U-S jets violated air space over its waters, but Washington does not recognize Libya's territorial claim. The U-S jets, Ef-fourteen Tomcats from the carrier Nimitz, were taking part in Sixth fleet exercises. The Navy says its jets were almost seventy miles off Libya when the Soviet-made Libyan jets fired at them.

(MORE)

on "almost." That editor also told me,
repeatedly, that viewers are only half-
listening. So I strive for simplicity.
My maxim: Make it minimal. That's one
reason that in the first sentence I
didn't mention "F-14." But the
director dug up a photo of an F-14, so
he prevailed upon the producer to
insert "F-14" high up. He obliged, and
I was shot down.

The Navy says neither
of its planes was
hit. The State
Department has
protested, and it
warned Libya against
any new attack.

After taking one last look at the wire and ripping off the latest leads, he went to the typewriter and began to write. He had half an hour, but he had been thinking about the story since he saw the first "urgent." He knew that he had to tell CBS television viewers the essential facts—that U.S. planes had downed two Libyan jets.

"There are some things I would change now," Block says. "Maybe I would use plane instead of craft on the first page of copy.

"But in broadcasting there are no second chances. I was reading a book the other day with the title *Done in a Day,* about newspapers. It describes the work that has to be done, all in a day, to produce a newspaper. But in broadcasting, it's done in minutes, sometimes seconds."

Block says that he always looks for the short word and that he tries to write short sentences that conform to the S-V-O sentence structure. For example, at one point in the script he used *taking part* instead of *participating.*

His script is shown in figure 12.1.

The broadcast news writer has to keep in mind that the story is to be read aloud by someone. This means that the copy should be prepared in a certain way. Stations differ in their rules for copy preparation but here are some suggestions.

Name or initials of writer in lower right-hand corner.
Slug of story in upper right-hand corner.
Time the story takes to run is placed above slug.
Date in lower left-hand corner.

Use wide margins in preparing radio copy. The margins are normally set for 45 to 50 units and the length of lines is kept as uniform as possible. Depending on the speed of the announcer, each line will take about three seconds to read. Knowing this, the announcer can estimate how long it will take to read the story.

Copy Preparation

Radio and television stations have different requirements for preparing copy for broadcast. These are suggested on the basis of their use by a number of stations and many schools of journalism.

Behind the Set. In the ABC control room, technicians check the monitors as the network news program "World News Tonight" begins.
ABC News

On Location. Monica Kaufman reports on a feature story.
Karen Clark

Writing

Television copy is prepared on two-thirds or half of the right-hand side of the page. The left-hand side is used for instructions, such as the name of the anchor or correspondent and whether the copy will be read over a film or tape (*VO* for voice over).

Each page is numbered and slugged at the top. At the bottom, an end mark is used when the story is completed—#, 30, END. The word *more* is written and circled at the bottom of pages of stories that are continued.

Each page should end with a complete sentence. If the page ends in the middle of a sentence, the announcer will be forced to pause as he or she reaches for the next sheet of copy.

So much for the basics of preparing copy. Next, some rules about writing style.

Style Rules

These rules have been used by broadcast news writers for many years to avoid confusion for the announcer reading the copy and to help the listener quickly grasp what he or she hears:

> **Numbers** are spelled out.
> **Abbreviations** are not used.
> **Titles** are placed before names.
> **Initials** of agencies and organizations are not used unless they are widely known.
> **Quotes** must be clearly introduced as direct quotes. "As the senator put it. . . . In the words of the president. . . . To quote the prime minister. . . ."

Writing Guidelines

We have already seen that broadcast news is written in simple, conversational language. The sentences are short, and they are usually in the S-V-O form.

Every word is selected to do something; every word has a purpose. Broadcast news is timed to the word. Omitting unnecessary words is the key to success.

Avoid using lengthy phrases and clauses to begin sentences. Get right to the point. When a source is being used, put it at the beginning of the sentence. Use action verbs. Stay away from adjectives and adverbs unless they are essential.

Introductory phrase

> **Avoid:** Stressing the increased number of cars on campus, the Student Council has asked for more parking spaces near dormitories.
> **Improved:** The Student Council wants more parking spaces near student dormitories.

Attribution	**Avoid:** There are two cars for every parking space, says Student Council President Tom Jarrett.
	Improved: Student Council President Tom Jarrett says there are two cars for every parking space.
Action verb	**Avoid:** The Council was unanimous in its vote for the proposal.
	Improved: The Council voted unanimously for the proposal.
Adjective	**Avoid:** Dean Albert Levine reacted with strong criticism of the vote.
	Improved: Dean Albert Levine criticized the vote. (Or: Dean Albert Levine condemned the vote.)

Leads A listener should not be overwhelmed with a long lead to a story. Complicated stories can be introduced with a general statement, such as:

> The parking-space issue has heated up. Dean Albert Levine said this afternoon. . . .

> The Russians want no part in the U.S. plan for feeding the hungry of the world. Soviet leaders said. . . .

Do not begin a story with the name of an unknown person. If you must, precede the name with the person's title or some identifying label. You can begin with a name if the person has what Block calls "star quality." That means the president, the pope, the governor of your state, a senator or congressman, your mayor.

For a story about the death of Robert Moses, who built many of the major highways in and out of New York City and a number of its major buildings, Block realized only New Yorkers would be familiar with the name, and then not all of them, as Moses had been out of public life for many years. He was writing for a network news program. Here is how he began the obituary:

> The man credited with building even more than the Pharaohs of Egypt—Robert Moses—died in a New York City suburb today at the age of 92.

Here the identifying label is an arresting description. People will listen.

Do not start a story with a quotation. The listener cannot see or hear quotation marks and may think the words are those of the broadcaster. Some writers start with a quote and their next sentence is "Those were the words of. . . ." or "This advice, warning, challenge came from. . . ." Block says the technique does not work because it confuses listeners.

Storytelling Names make news in newspaper stories, but the fewer names in a broadcast story the better. Listeners are confused by lists of names and by a cast of characters in a story. The fewer people in a story, the clearer the story.

If Roger Grimstead, a spokesman for the governor, says something, simply write: The governor's office says. . . .

If the secretary of defense, Allen Weinstein, issues a comment in a story about the president's defense bill and there are already too many names, just write: The Pentagon commented that. . . .

A newspaper story may have a major theme and two, three, even four secondary themes. The broadcast story should have a major theme and perhaps one other theme.

What It Takes

For those considering a career in broadcast journalism, the ability to write well under pressure is essential. A study by Professor Stephen Lamoreux of Colorado State University found that broadcast editors want writers who can write simple sentences in a conversational style, men and women who can write lively, colorful copy and who have imagination.

Mastery of the writing craft is not enough, says Block. "The writer has to have a wide knowledge. He or she should know what is going on in the world. Also, the writer should understand how things work—government, the criminal justice process, zoning boards, state government.

"The data bank in the writer's mind has to have a jillion bits of information because the writer must be able to retrieve a lot of data, and do it almost subconsciously."

The easiest way for an inexperienced writer to enlarge his or her world is through reading.

Summary

Broadcast writers try to follow these guidelines:

- **Use everyday language.** Instead of *impact on,* the writer uses *affect.* Instead of *interface,* the writer uses *match.*

- **Simplify complex stories.** One way to do this is to begin a story with some background material: "Last month, the city council decided to revise the city's zoning regulations. Last night, it adopted a new master plan that will affect all new commercial and residential development in the city." Another technique is the headline to introduce a story: "Schools are open again." This could begin a story about the settlement of a long teachers' strike.

- **Use short sentences.** The listener cannot follow a long sentence. Any sentence over 25 words should be broken into two sentences. One way to cut down on the number of words in a sentence is to eliminate unnecessary words: "At this point in time" becomes *now,* "revenue enhancement" is changed to *taxes,* and such redundancies as "totally destroyed," "cold, hard facts" and "first annual" are corrected. Introductory phrases and clauses are dropped. Stick to the S-V-O sentence construction.

- **Favor the present tense.** Give the reader the sense of immediacy by using the present tense for leads when possible.

- **Keep items brief.** Find the major theme of the event and concentrate on it.

Story Essentials

The beginning reporter is supposed to be able to do it all. Well, maybe not everything, but a lot. Even though the city editor may assign the beginner a beat, the editor also expects the new hand to be able to write personal items, turn out a feature about the volunteer program at a local hospital, make readers smile with clever brights and help out with obituaries and weekend traffic accidents.

On the small- or medium-sized newspaper—where most beginners start their careers—there are few specialists. Everyone has to be able to handle the basic types of stories.

The next three chapters will show you how to handle some of these basic stories. Chapters 13–15 look at the essential ingredients of a dozen different kinds of stories.

Every story that a reporter writes can be fitted into a type or category. There are game stories that sports writers handle, fire and arrest stories police reporters write, meeting stories that a variety of beat and general assignment reporters cover and write. There are also interviews, news conferences, obituaries, accidents, robberies, weather and personals. Each of these types of stories has essential ingredients or elements that must be included.

Here is what we mean by the essential elements of the news story:

An obituary obviously must include the name of the person who died. Since the reader wants to know something about the person, every obituary must also include the person's address or home town and his or her occupation and accomplishments. There are other absolute necessities for the obituary, one of which was left out of the following wire service story. See if you can find out which essential is missing.

```
AM-HOBGOOD DIES, 180<
OLDEST WAR VETERAN DIES<
     ARKADELPHIA, ARK. (AP)-FUNERAL SERVICES
WILL BE HELD MONDAY FOR NORMAN HOBGOOD, THE MAN THE
GOVERNMENT CALLS THE NATION'S OLDEST WAR VETERAN.
     HOBGOOD, WHO DIED FRIDAY, ENLISTED IN THE ARMY
IN 1898, SERVING IN THE THIRD KENTUCKY VOLUNTEER
INFANTRY DURING THE SPANISH-AMERICAN WAR. THE
VETERAN'S ADMINISTRATION SAID HE WAS THE OLDEST OF
30 MILLION VETERANS LISTED IN ITS RECORDS.
     ONLY ABOUT 250 VETERANS OF THE SPANISH-
AMERICAN WAR ARE LIVING, ACCORDING TO THE VA.
     THE KENTUCKY NATIVE ALSO WAS ARKANSAS' OLDEST
STATE LEGISLATOR. HE WAS ELECTED TO THE STATE HOUSE
OF REPRESENTATIVES FOR TWO TERMS IN 1925 AND 1927.
```

HOBGOOD, WHO LIVED IN AN ARKADELPHIA NURSING
HOME, FREQUENTLY WAS INTERVIEWED ABOUT HIS STATUS
AS THE OLDEST VETERAN. HE ALSO WAS IN THE LIMELIGHT
IN THE ANNUAL VETERANS DAY CELEBRATIONS IN
ARKADELPHIA.
    LAST YEAR, HOBGOOD WAS AWARDED THE ARKANSAS
DISTINGUISHED SERVICE MEDAL IN A VETERANS DAY
CEREMONY AT HENDERSON STATE UNIVERSITY.
    HOBGOOD WAS A LAWYER, TEACHER AND FARMER. HE
FARMED UNTIL HE WAS 99 AND PREACHED THE SUNDAY
WORSHIP SERVICE AT HIS CHURCH ON HIS 100TH
BIRTHDAY.
    AP-NR-03-02 1413EST<

A few minutes after this story moved on the wires, an alert editor caught
the lapse and ordered a new story written with the essential information included. The new story was identical to the first except for this second paragraph:

HOBGOOD, WHO DIED FRIDAY AT THE AGE OF 108,
ENLISTED IN THE ARMY IN 1898, SERVING IN THE THIRD
KENTUCKY VOLUNTEER INFANTRY DURING THE SPANISH-
AMERICAN WAR. THE VETERAN'S ADMINISTRATION SAID HE
WAS THE OLDEST OF 30 MILLION VETERANS LISTED IN ITS
RECORDS.

(In case you did not catch the blooper, the news writer had forgotten to
include the man's age, an essential ingredient of all obituaries.)

Non-negotiable Essentials

Journalists like to say that there are no rules for journalism. Since no event
is quite like another event, there can be no rigid rules for writing stories, they
say. It is true that no two basketball games are exactly alike. One may be an
easy victory, another may be won in the last three seconds. Even the games
won at the final buzzer differ. One may be won on a foul shot, another on a
desperation-heave from midcourt. A third might be won by a guard playing
his first game. Another game was not so much won by one team as lost by
another when the defense made a few blunders. And so on.

Every event—game, speech, interview, obituary, arrest, accident—is different from others like it, and the good news writer handles each differently,
no matter how many games he has covered, how many speeches she has had
to sit through, how many interviews he has conducted.

Yes, all events are different. Each should be handled with an individual
touch, with full attention to its unique characteristics. However, every basketball game story must include the score, the names of the teams, the key
plays and the names of the players scoring the most points. Every speech story
must include the main point of the talk, the speaker's name and his or her

title or occupation, where the talk was given, the response of the audience. All accident stories tell the reader or listener the names of those injured, where the accident occurred, the names of the drivers involved and the cause.

To sum up, there are rules for every type of story and they cannot be broken. They are non-negotiable essentials. You can complain about being forced into a rigid style by these rules all you want. But break one of them and you will face the embarrassment of the wire service writer who neglected to put in the obituary the age of the Spanish-American War veteran.

These essentials can be placed anywhere in the story—in the lead, the middle, at the end. Placement is up to the news writer and his or her feel for the structure of the story. Regardless of placement, they must be included.

The most important element in one fire story we will examine in chapter 15 was that a man died because of his smoking, and that went into the lead—cause. Another fire story began with the damage done to a grain elevator—property damage. Cause and damages are essentials of the fire story. The writer has to determine which of the essential elements to put into the lead and which to place further down in the body of the story.

No list can predict the full dimensions of any story. The writer must be aware of the unique aspects of the event. Often, it is the unusual, the strange fact, that makes the story that is being written different from other fire, sports or speech stories. If the fact is unique and significant, the writer begins the story with it—the tears in the firefighter's eyes as he carries the body of the child from the smoking ruins, the mistake of the base runner in the ninth inning, the sparse attendance at a meeting of school board candidates.

Journalism is not mechanical. It cannot be carried out by the number, like a drill team automatically stepping out its patterns. Journalism is an art that requires its practitioners to look with a fresh eye at each event so that the unique aspects of the event can be captured in the story. But the eye must have a focus, a direction in which to begin looking.

The essentials in the next three chapters point the news writer in the proper directions for several types of stories.

To begin our examination of story types, we will look first at the interview. Editors say that the ability to conduct an interview is one of the most important competences they look for in a new staff member. We will then go to other types of stories involving the spoken word—meetings, news conferences and speeches. In chapter 15, we will look at how accident and fire stories, crime and court stories, obituaries, sports stories and personals are handled.

The Interview

There are two types of interviews. Spot news interviews are used to develop information that supplements the news story. Profiles and personality interviews focus on the person being interviewed.

To conduct a successful interview, the reporter should know something about the subject of the interview, ask simple and direct questions, listen and watch carefully. In writing the interview story, the reporter should use plenty of quotes, but only those that are directly related to the theme of the news story or feature.

The news story is the written version of what the reporter sees and hears. In this chapter and the next, we will be discussing what the reporter hears, though we won't ignore what he or she sees. Our main attention will be on what is said by sources in speeches and interviews and at meetings and news conferences.

The interview is at the heart of just about every news story. Bank robbery or fire. Municipal budget or college basketball game. Campus rock group concert or sociology instructor with a new theory about student relationships. In every one of these stories, a reporter has asked someone for information.

Since we know that the news story should reflect the nature of the event, we have a starting point for stories based on interviews: **Use quotes**—but not just any quotes. Use the quotes that capture the meaning of the event.

Of course, we want background material and description in these stories, too. But our stories will revolve around what we hear.

In some of these stories, the focus is on the event. The interviews for these stories are called **spot news interviews.** In others, the emphasis is on the person. These stories are called **profiles.**

Figure 13.1 Interviews Make News. Information for the two major stories on page 1 of *The Hays Daily News* came from spot news interviews. The city's fire chief, an employee of the grain elevator and the elevator owner were interviewed for the fire story. For the story about the wheat crop, an economics professor, a banker, a chamber of commerce official and others were interviewed. The three stories described across the top of the page refer to profiles on inside pages for which depth interviews were conducted.

The spot news interview is used to supplement the theme of the news story. The person being interviewed provides background material about the event. Properly interviewed—asked the right questions—the source can add information that makes the story complete and convincing.

Reporters interview police officers for information about crimes, fire marshals for possible causes of fires. Sports reporters talk to coaches and players for background material for game stories. In these spot news interviews, the reporter usually is looking for supplementary material—the facts and background that will illustrate or highlight the event being described.

This usually leads the news writer to play down the person being interviewed because the focus is on the event rather than on a personality. This does not mean that we ignore the source's direct quotes. Often, the quotes add drama and interest as well as meaning and conviction to the event.

In the following story, a state highway patrol officer was the source of information about a fatal traffic accident. Look where the writer put the officer's quote:

Three people were killed in a grinding collision between a truck and an automobile on Highway 10, 15 miles north of Morgantown, the state highway patrol reported.

Those fatally injured were in the automobile. They were Albert Foster, 22, of 237 Western Ave.; his brother, Michael, 18, of the same address, and the driver, Bert Pierce, 21, of Tampa, Fla. The truck driver, George Allen, 48, of New Orleans, suffered minor bruises.

A state highway patrol spokesman, Robert Jackson, said the automobile apparently tried to make a U-turn off the westbound lane and moved into the path of the truck as it sped eastward.

"The car was demolished," Jackson said. "There were parts all over the road for 100 yards." Traffic was delayed on the eastbound section for 90 minutes, he said. . . .

Notice that the lead contains the major news theme—the deaths—and attribution. The next paragraph gives the names and identifications of the victims. The third paragraph describes the accident, and the fourth contains a good quotation.

This is the standard approach to the spot news story. Since we have a dramatic quote, it is possible to use it high in the story:

```
    Three people were killed in a grinding collision
between a truck and an automobile on Highway 10, 15 miles
north of Morgantown.
    "The car was demolished," said Robert Jackson of the
State Highway Patrol. "There were parts all over the road
for 100 yards."
    Those fatally injured were. . . .
```

This version is an improvement because the direct quote captures the essence of the event—a horrible traffic accident.

The patrol officer's description was in response to the reporter's question asking him to describe the scene. Good questions not only lead to valuable information; they also can evoke responses that provide the color and excitement that give life to a story.

Information from sources for spot news stories usually is summarized or paraphrased. The reporter who listens attentively can sometimes find the quote that breathes life into the news story. A good direct quote is better than any paraphrase.

For a story about a refresher course offered by the School of Nursing at the University of North Carolina at Chapel Hill, a woman who had taken the course was interviewed. She had been a nurse, then married and had spent 20 years at home raising a family. She decided to return to nursing and took the nursing-update course. Here is a quote from the story in *The Coastline Times* of Manteo, N.C. It captures the story's theme:

"I would not have dared walk on a hospital floor without having gone back to school," she said. "There have been so many advances and so many changes."

Nothing earthshaking about the quote, but it does the job.

Generally, when an editor asks a reporter to interview someone, the editor has a personality sketch or profile in mind. Here, the individual is the center of the story. Before we turn to the profile, some points have to be made about the business of interviewing.

Interviewing Techniques

Whether the interview is for a spot news story or a profile, the key to a successful interview is knowing what you want to find out. The spot interview often is conducted by telephone with busy sources. The reporter has to get to the point quickly. Because the people interviewed for profiles usually set aside valuable time for the interview, the reporter cannot waste the subject's time fishing for information. Also, the reporter must appear to be knowledgeable. A firm grasp of the subject will usually make the person being interviewed more willing to open up.

Here are some guidelines for interviews:

- **Have a good idea of what you want to learn from the source or subject.**

- **Get to the point quickly.**

- **Ask if there is anything important you did not ask about.**

- **Ask the source if he or she can be called back should you need further information.** (Some sources will not take calls at home after they leave the office. Ask for the name of another person who can be called.)

We are all curious, maybe even nosey. We want to know why the brightest young woman in the class suddenly quit school, how the elderly couple around the corner can afford a new Cadillac every year, why the couple down the street suddenly separated. We wonder what kind of person Mick Jagger really is, how the new outfielder for the New York Yankees spends all of his $1.5 million salary.

Most of our questions will never be answered, but some will—by a reporter writing a profile or personality feature. The fact that people have always been curious about the lives of others has made the profile the most frequently written feature story. Sooner or later, every reporter writes a profile.

Sometimes, the profile can be a small snapshot in a long piece. In a series on Rhode Island's jewelry manufacturing business—the state's largest industry—Bruce Butterfield of *The Providence Journal-Bulletin* tells us about Mary, a high school student who does part-time work in a factory. Butterfield lets Mary talk:

> . . . . Like, what I'm doing now. I stand up the entire time. I go in there for three hours and 45 minutes a day.
>
> It's in a room and you have metal that's melted down. I think it's twelve hundred degrees.
>
> There's people who've been working in there 25 years and they're still making less than $4 an hour.
>
> And they deserve more 'cause they're such nice people that work in there. And they just can't do anything else. They either don't have a high school diploma or they just have a high school diploma and there aren't many jobs in our society today for these people. And they're over 40.
>
> They deserve more.

These quotes tell us something about the factory and a lot about Mary. She works hard at an arduous job and is concerned about the people she works with. She is a decent young woman, and a bit naive: They deserve more, she says, because they are such nice people. But she is realistic about her co-workers' lack of education. She knows there aren't many jobs for people without an education.

"They deserve more." Mary's words make the reader put down the newspaper to reflect a minute. Although we are told little about Mary, we feel we know her.

Our first requirement for the profile: It must capture the real person.

That may seem to be emphasizing the obvious. It isn't. Many profiles are written about people in public life—politicians, entertainers, athletes, television personalities, business leaders. These people cultivate a public personality. It is not easy to strip away the public relations image.

Here are four guidelines for successful interviews for the profile:

1. **Prepare carefully.** Know the subject matter and the person who is to be interviewed.
2. From these preparations, **devise a theme** or two as the basis of questions.
3. **Establish a relationship** with the subject that induces him or her to talk.
4. **Listen carefully and watch attentively.** Be alert to what is said and how it is said. Look around at the room or office for clues to the subject's interests, tastes, personal life.

Preparing for the Interview

Careful preparations begin with the newspaper or broadcast station library clippings about the subject matter and the person to be interviewed. The clippings provide background and suggest questions to ask at the interview. The next step is a quick look at references. The new college president may be listed in *Who's Who in America.* Although *Who's Who* is brought up-to-date frequently, biographical material should always be checked with the subject. The enrollment of the college she comes from can be found in the *World Almanac.*

If the new president is a specialist in a field, she might have written articles that are indexed in the *Reader's Guide to Periodical Literature.* Her comments about a subject in one of her articles could be the basis of the first question. Sources are flattered by a reporter's interest in them and their work.

When Mal Vincent of the *Virginian-Pilot* in Norfolk, Va., was preparing for an interview with actress Jacqueline Bisset, he went back to an interview he had with Bisset 10 years before.

Vincent had tried to interview Bisset on the set of a thriller in which she was co-starring with Alan Alda. In those days, Bisset had been cast in her movies as a sex object. She had done a nude scene in a surfing movie, "The Sweet Ride," and she had played a bedhopping jetsetter in "The Grasshopper."

At that time, Vincent had a definite personality in mind, the kind of young actress that moviegoers glance at in minor films and forget. But Bisset had surprised him then.

She had taken over the interview. "The name is Bisset," she had said at the outset. "It rhymes with *kiss it.*"

When Vincent had tried to ask her about her relationship with actor Michael Sarrazin, Bisset bristled. Although she had been widely publicized as living with Sarrazin, she refused to discuss the matter.

Vincent then tried women's liberation, a new phenomenon at that time.

"I have no intention of discussing women's rights with you," she had flared at him. "You wouldn't agree with me." She beckoned to her chauffeur and departed.

Bisset was a prickly subject for an interview, Vincent knew. In his preparations for his current interview he found that she was financing a movie in an attempt to convince critics she could act. As the co-producer, she had a stake in good publicity for the new film. Therefore, Vincent knew, she had to be patient with interviewers. He also knew she had a mind of her own—as she proved in the new interview.

"I don't want to be a pinup," she told Vincent curtly. "I want to be something more than just an attractive woman. The public makes a mistake in labeling people that way."

Still bristling Bisset—but she stayed through the interview this time. Vincent knew how to approach her because of his preparations.

Vincent's preparations for his interview with Bisset point out the importance of figuring out some lines of questioning by having a tentative theme or idea for the story before the interview.

Devising a Theme

Sometimes, the theme is the news peg, the reason the individual is newsworthy. For example: A local merchant is recognized by the city's United Way organization for his charity work. A profile of the businessman will focus on the activities that earned him the award. Often, though, the news peg is not the theme. In a profile of the new college president, the news peg was the appointment, but the theme of the profile was the appointee's ideas for reorganizing the college curriculum.

The news peg tells the reader: Here is a newsworthy person. The theme says: Here's something interesting you ought to know about this person.

The depth interview is a confrontation between reporter-with-theme and subject-with-idea. By this, we mean that both interviewer and interviewee have points of their own they want to make. In Vincent's second interview with Bisset, she was trying to tell readers and moviegoers, through Vincent, that she is a serious actress, that they should forget her roles as a sex object, which had been stamped on the minds of the public by her scene in the movie "The Deep" in which she appeared in a wet, clinging, transparent T-shirt.

Vincent's new theme was the change from young starlet in grade B films to mature woman of 37 making serious movies. The interview went well because both themes, Bisset's and Vincent's, were parallel and not on a collision course.

Sometimes collisions are unavoidable. The reporter sent to interview a gubernatorial candidate for a profile knows that the candidate is a political novice, a person who has never sought public office. The reporter's theme is: What makes this man think he can handle the complexities of state government with no political experience whatsoever?

The candidate's campaign theme is: A new broom sweeps clean.

The reporter is too experienced in politics to buy that cliché without lots of proof. So the reporter will be pressing and probing the candidate to prove that he has the ability to clean up the statehouse. Friction looms, unless the reporter can make the candidate relax and talk freely.

The reporter devises a theme from checking the background of the subject and from the reporter's knowledge of the situation in which the subject is involved.

The theme or themes are launching pads for the reporter's questions. If nothing comes of the questions, the reporter works up new themes.

A profile or personality sketch cannot be a shapeless biography. There is no room in a newspaper, or time on a news program, for an endless recounting of a life or a situation. Every story must focus on a theme that limits the story to a specific situation involving the subject.

The profile of the new college president may have as its theme the fact that the appointee has been hired to make massive changes in the curriculum. The profile will be written with that in mind. Or the new president may be temporary, while the board of trustees tries to figure out a new educational policy and then seek someone to match the policy. A transitional appointee may not want to discuss this theme. When the reporter is sure of the validity of the theme, it is up to the reporter to steer the source in the proper direction. This takes us to our third guideline for successful interviews.

Inducing the Subject to Talk

Reporters use many tactics to induce their subjects to talk freely and act naturally. Gene Miller of *The Miami Herald* says he tries to make himself as agreeable as possible during interviews.

"I nod a lot," he says, to appear to be agreeing with what the subject is saying and to encourage him or her to keep talking. "No tape recorder and no notetaking if I suspect I'll turn off my man. The unpleasant questions always come last, often apologetically."

Miller's technique is the opposite of the confrontation tactics used by some television interviewers. After a while, a reporter learns the technique best suited to him or her. Of course, the nature of the interview will often determine the technique used. An interview with a manufacturer whose factory has been polluting the city's air and a nearby river cannot be much else but a confrontation.

The story is told of how Truman Capote, on an assignment from *The New Yorker* magazine, induced Marlon Brando to talk about his mother's alcoholism.

Capote flew to Japan where Brando was on the set of "Sayonara." They got together in the evening.

In his story for the magazine, Capote quoted Brando as saying: "I didn't care any more. She was there. In a room. Holding on to me. And I let her fall. Because I couldn't take it any more . . . breaking apart, like a piece of porcelain. I stepped right over her. I walked right out. I was indifferent. Since then, I've been indifferent."

Later, Brando was asked why he had been so open with Capote about such a personal matter.

"Well," said Brando, "the little bastard spent half the night telling me about all his problems. I figured the least I could do was to tell him a few of mine."

Ralph Ellison, the author of *Invisible Man,* the classic about the lives of black Americans, interviewed many people during the 1930s for the Federal Writers Project. Those were the days of the Depression, and few had jobs. Writers had a particularly hard time, and the government hired some of them to obtain first-person accounts of Americans of all kinds.

Ellison's technique for making people talk was similar to Capote's.

"I would tell stories to get people going, and then I'd sit back and get it down as accurately as I could."

A gentle nudge is all some people need. For most, the reporter has to ask questions, a lot of questions.

Asking Questions

The first questions asked in an interview may be throw-away questions designed to put the subject at ease if the source is not accustomed to being interviewed. The first meaningful questions will reflect the theme that the reporter has in mind for the story.

"What I ask gives me my story," says Jane Brazes, a reporter for the *Cincinnati Post.* "What I don't ask I won't find out."

Answers to questions suggest additional themes. "When you think you have found an answer, you'll have found another question," Brazes says. The key to interviewing, she says, is to "find questions and never stop asking them."

Questions should be simple and direct. Larry King, whose radio talk program, "The Larry King Show," is carried by more than 200 stations around the country, is a skilled interviewer. He says that "if it takes you more than three sentences to ask a question, it's a bad question."

Complex questions should be avoided. King recalls an interview Sandy Koufax did with the winning pitcher of a baseball game. Koufax, one of the greatest pitchers in the history of the game, was an inexperienced interviewer. He asked:

"In the game tonight, I noticed that in the fourth inning you took a little off your fast ball—you still had it in reserve because you had a 4–0 lead. Then, in the seventh inning, you used your curve ball. And in the ninth inning you went back to your fast ball and you still had it left."

King recalled, "All that the pitcher could answer was, 'Right.' "

King says the best question for the interviewer is "Why?" The object of the interview is to make the subject talk, and questions like, "Why," "How," "Give me an example of what you mean" induce people to talk.

Sometimes, silence can lead a person to talk. David M. McCullough, who interviews authors for the *Book-of-the-Month Club News,* says, "I found that a little silence often gets a better response than a pointed question."

Some experienced interviewers remain silent after a source or subject has made an apparently untrue assertion. Except for a raised eyebrow, the reporter will not move. The interviewee has the feeling that the assertion isn't going down well, and usually he or she will feel obligated to fill the silence with an explanation that moves closer to the truth.

Generally, the tactics used and the questions asked in an interview vary with the source and the kind of information sought. A source may prefer to say little or remain silent. But a public official cannot be silent about public business, and reminding the source of this may be necessary to pry information from him or her.

The subject is not the only person a reporter should interview for a profile. Friends, relatives, employees, employers, teachers—the list of those who can provide interesting information is endless. Sometimes, these sources may have a perception of the subject that gives the reporter a fresh insight, material for a theme the reporter had not thought about.

Listening and Watching

By asking good questions and by listening carefully, the reporter usually can find the one quote that best sums up the person or the event. When Wayne King was sent by *The New York Times* to cover a coal mine disaster in Colorado, King interviewed the brother of one of the 15 miners who had died. The man looked toward the western slope of the Colorado Rockies where the Dutch Creek mine is located and said, "That big mountain ate my brother."

King put the quote high in his story. It symbolized the life and death of the miner.

Listening and watching may reveal more than words alone disclose. There is a language of gesture that says a great deal. The narrowing of a person's eyes as he or she speaks can underline a statement as emphatically as boldface type in a written sentence. And if the source turns away as he or she says something, this may signal that the person is uncomfortable about what he or she is saying.

When the interview is conducted in the subject's home or office, notes are made of the furnishings, pictures on the wall, magazines on the coffee table or desk. These sometimes reveal a person's interests, tastes and concerns.

A well-known journalism professor covered his office walls with pictures of himself with famous people. Noticing this during an interview, a reporter concluded that the man's ego was monumental, that he needed to parade his fame to visitors. More than this, the reporter concluded that the professor—as famous as he was—had a sense of inferiority. The reporter filed away his observations for later use. Reporters often do this. Some save observations, anecdotes and stories they hear for a year or more, until the right moment.

Howell Raines of *The New York Times* saved an anecdote a source gave him about a rising young politician. "I saved that quote because I knew that some day I would need it," Raines said. A year later he used it as the concluding anecdote in a profile of the young politician.

Many reporters use tape recorders for profiles, but a few prefer the note pad, finding it less obtrusive.

"I take notes a lot," Raines told Roy Peter Clark, who interviewed him about interview techniques. "If I'm working with a notebook, I bring it out early, and I take a pen out early. I do a lot of business with them. People then lose interest in your taking notes.

"If someone really gets cooking on something and I feel taking notes will be obtrusive, I won't take notes. Then, when the person is finished on that point—I've got a good memory—I'll take out my pad and write down what he said.

"But I try to be open about taking notes for two reasons. One, it establishes your authority. No one is going to come back to you and question a quote that he's seen you write down as it came out of his mouth. And two, these are people that are used to seeing reporters."

The reporter's job is to write stories. Off-the-record interviews may help the reporter obtain background, but they do not lead directly to stories. Most experienced reporters are reluctant to go off the record, and they almost never bring up the possibility with a source.

"I never suggest putting anything off the record," Raines says. Most of those he interviews are experienced sources. They know that what they say is going to be used.

"I never put anything off the record retroactively," Raines says. "If they say to me, 'What I just told you is off the record,' they can say that all they want to, but I'm not bound by it. I'll usually tell them that, but I don't feel compelled to tell them that."

Raines does accept off-the-record information. When he does, he scrupulously follows certain ground rules: Off-the-record material may be used only on the grounds the source stipulates. Here are some ground rules sources may set:

> Quotes are not to be attributed to the source but to "an official," or some such vague source.
> The statement is to be paraphrased and used without attribution.
> Material is to be used only if it is obtained from someone else and then not attributed to the original source.
> For background use only—not for publication in any circumstance.

We are now ready to look over the essential elements of the profile or personality sketch.

Profile Essentials

- Name and identification of the subject of the profile
- Theme of profile
- Reason for profile (This is called the **news peg.**)
- Background of person
- Incidents and anecdotes from the subject and from friends and associates of the subject
- Physical description
- Direct quotes from the subject and sources
- Observations of the subject at work, home or play: mannerisms, gestures
- Strong ending

Most profiles are feature stories, and as such they must move quickly. Story movement is accomplished through the use of quotes, description, anecdotes and incidents.

The news peg for Vincent's story about actress Bisset was her new film, "Rich and Famous":

Delayed lead for first two paragraphs	Hollywood—Don't call Jacqueline Bisset beautiful. Not if you want to get along with her.
	"I don't want to be a pinup," she says curtly, the famous gray-green eyes flashing. "I want to be something more than just an attractive woman. The public makes a mistake in labeling people that way."
News peg at the beginning of the third paragraph	Currently, Bisset is chairman of the board—even if she is the only person on the board—of Jacquet Productions. As such, she is coproducer of "Rich and Famous," the plush, expensively mounted new soap opera movie that stars her as a respected novelist who has affairs, sometimes casually, with younger men.
Theme at the end of the paragraph	The film, currently showing at the Lynnhaven and Circle 6 Theaters, gives Bisset what she calls "a chance to prove, once and for all, that I am capable of being a serious actress."

The last sentence of the third paragraph also serves as a transition or swing sentence. It takes the reader to a fuller explanation of the major theme of Vincent's piece—Bisset's attempts to prove she is more than a pinup. Notice that the news peg is not the theme of this profile. In his fourth paragraph,

Vincent picks up the theme mentioned at the end of the third paragraph, Bisset's desire to be a serious actress:

Although she thinks she has proved herself previously, she is aware that some critics haven't observed as much. "For some reason, critics like to take pot shots at me," she said. "In that way, my career has been similar to that of Candy Bergen, my costar. We've both had our knocks from the critics."

For a profile or personality sketch, the news peg need not be momentous. It may be as simple as the one used in the following profile by Timothy Weiner—Sonny Greer, a famous jazz drummer, is playing in New York City.

The story begins with a brief incident in Greer's life and shifts in the second paragraph to background. The third paragraph states the major theme—that Sonny Greer at 83 is still playing the drums and enjoying life. It continues with quotes from Greer and the pianist who plays with Greer.

Greer is described at the drums. We can see his "cannonball serve," the drumsticks doing a "tapdance on the high-hat cymbal."

The ending reinforces the theme with a good quote from Duke Ellington, with whom Greer played for 32 years.

All the elements of the profile are here. Notice that Weiner does not try to tell Greer's life story. No profile can be any more than a brief glimpse into a person's life. Here is Weiner's profile:

NEW YORK—When jazz great Sonny Greer was a kid, back in 1910, he had a single driving ambition: to be the world's greatest pool hustler.

Had Sonny not traded in his pool stick for drumsticks, he might never have teamed up with a young piano player named Duke Ellington in 1919. He couldn't have brought the Duke Ellington Orchestra to New York in the 1920s, where it gained fame as a worldwide paragon of jazz. And he might have spent most of his 83 years behind the eight-ball instead of behind his battery of drums and cymbals.

At an age when the rhythms of most people's lives have slowed to a crawl, Sonny Greer hasn't missed a beat.

Every Monday night at 8 o'clock, an impeccably dressed Greer sets up his drums onstage at the West End Cafe in New York City. Young admirers sit at the old gentleman's feet as he spins out stories of Harlem speakeasies and the halcyon days of jazz.

"My favorite place to play," Sonny said with a smile and a faraway gaze in his eyes, "was the old Kentucky Club. Fats Waller and me used to play duets there and sing risque songs. We'd play all night and come walking out of the club in the morning, the sun shining and all of us walking down Broadway laughing, feeling no pain. Those were good days, baby, oh yeah."

For 32 years' worth of good days, Sonny Greer's percussion was the beating heart of the Duke Ellington Orchestra. For thousands of nights he sat like a king on his throne, elevated above the rest of the band at center stage, surrounded by chimes, gourds, tympani, vibraphone and kettle drums, a great brass gong shining behind him like a halo.

In the 1930s and '40s, the Duke Ellington Orchestra was the closest thing to royalty the jazz world has ever known. But the band's fame didn't dampen the members' creative fires.

"While we were onstage," Sonny said, "as the evening progressed, we would experiment. If Duke liked it, he would keep it in. If he didn't, well, it cost nothing—throw it out, forget it.

"The guys in the band were amazing. They always had ideas, a million ideas. They were very creative. They created."

Sonny Greer is now the sole survivor of the original orchestra. He is probably the oldest jazzman active today. What keeps him going?

"Look, the drums are my life," he said, lighting a cigarette and cradling an Old-Fashioned glass of whisky. "I get a great pleasure out of playing and making the people happy."

Brooks Kerr, the 27-year-old blind pianist and Ellington scholar who plays with Sonny, said, "One thing that Sonny has that so few people of any age have is that desire to play. I think he lives to work and works to live."

At showtime, Sonny leads Brooks to the piano and seats himself at his drums. The drums, encrusted with tiny mirrors, sparkle in the spotlights. Brooks hits the first chords of "Take the 'A' Train" and shouts, "Sonny Greer, ladies and gentlemen!"

Sonny swats his snare drum with a flick of his wrist, the sound of a cannonball serve. His drumsticks tapdance on the high-hat cymbal. His bass drum pulses. Everyone in the audience is keeping time, their fingertips and feet following the drummer's beat, their bodies swaying slowly in unison.

Sonny's drums are talking. His drumming is musical syntax, giving structure to flowing musical language. And something more: echoes of Harlem, a conjuring of the past.

He's telling his life's story on the drums, distilling all those years of remembered rhythms into fluid syncopation. Listening to Sonny Greer is a trip back in time to the golden age of jazz. To hear him solo on the drums is to briefly recapture a classic style.

Sonny Greer's drum solo won't go on forever. But, as Duke Ellington once wrote, "Sonny Greer is an endless story."

Ending the Profile

A good idea in writing the profile is to use an incident or anecdote at the end of the piece that reinforces the major theme.

In his profile of Bruce A. Smathers, the son of a powerful political figure in Florida, Raines makes the point early in the story that Smathers' political future is dubious because he lacks the steely determination of his father, "who," Raines writes, "never hestitated to backstab a friend for political advantage."

Raines writes of young Smathers high in his piece:

. . . .With his fawn eyes and unlined face, he has more in common with Bambi than with the rapacious roebucks normally encountered in the political forests of Tallahassee.

Yes, Bruce Smathers says, smiling, he knows about those jokes that he is indecisive, that he would starve to death in a cafeteria line trying to choose between the Salisbury steak and the Spanish mackerel.

That rap, as Smathers tells it, is the price he must pay for having a trained mind and introspective nature.

"I have almost a repulsion of the easy answer," he says, and one hears in the scholarly tone echoes of Yale, where he won honors in economics. . . .

The picture Raines draws is clear. Young Smathers is an intelligent, decent person, perhaps unfit for the raw political infighting of southern politics. For his ending, Raines drives home his theme. The last two paragraphs read:

Perhaps Smathers' political gifts are that great, but many who know politics as it is played at the top question whether this young man loves it enough or is hard enough. Most people who make it as high as governor or U.S. senator have something—a hunger, a fire in the gut, a toughness—that one can sense. It is not necessarily a good thing to have, but it is essential to winning and surviving in office.

This is not the picture of Bruce Smathers that emerges from a story once leaked from his office—an intimate of Smathers was quoted as saying, "Somebody offered him some money for a vote and Smathers got up and went out of the room and threw up."

Bambi in the Jungle. Bruce Smathers, the subject of a searching profile by Howell Raines, and his wife at the time Smathers was a candidate for secretary of state. Raines showed that Smathers lacked the toughness and ruthlessness necessary to succeed in Florida politics.
The St. Petersburg Times

This is the anecdote Raines says he had heard a year before and saved for the time when he would need it.

Capturing the Spoken Word

Meeting stories are of two types. They either focus on the decision reached or on the discussion. The decision or vote is the lead for the first type of meeting story. The consensus reached or the most significant issue raised in the discussion is the lead for the second type.

For **panel discussions and symposia,** the writer first looks for an area of agreement or significant differences among the panelists to use as the lead. If there is no common ground, the writer may choose to single out important points made by one speaker.

News conferences can range over many subjects. The news writer selects the theme with the greatest impact on readers or listeners. Most news conferences are called for a specific purpose, and this is usually the lead.

Speeches have an even wider range of subject matter than the news conference. The speech story can concentrate on the speaker's main point, audience reaction or questions asked by reporters after the speech.

These stories must contain quotes that back up and buttress the theme the writer has selected for the lead of the story.

Much of the public's business is conducted in meetings. Important as they may be, few people attend them. It is the journalist's job to cover official meetings and to write clear, complete stories so that the people know what their appointed and elected officials are doing. Reporters are entitled to attend these meetings.

There are, of course, all kinds of meetings in addition to those of official bodies. The parent-teacher association holds monthly meetings. College political clubs meet every so often. Church, civic and professional organizations meet regularly. Reporters are invited to attend these meetings.

The meetings of groups that are not financed with tax funds can be closed to the public and the press. A political club can call a closed meeting if it wishes. The board of the Kiwanis Club is not obligated to allow reporters to enter.

Once admitted to a meeting, a reporter can report anything that is said, unless the reporter is allowed to attend a meeting of a private organization that sets limits on coverage. When meetings are closed, the reporter can use anything else he or she obtains by interviewing those who attended the meeting.

Two Types of Meetings

Meetings usually have a purpose, and often the matter at hand is resolved by agreement or vote. Sometimes, there is only general discussion. Each type of meeting is handled slightly differently.

The story of a meeting that results in an action emphasizes the action taken:

> A bill to change West Virginia's 10.5-cents-per-gallon liquor tax to a percentage of the wholesale price was soundly rejected by a joint House-Senate finance subcommittee yesterday by a vote of 9–2.

The meeting that does not result in any decisive action usually stresses the most significant part of the discussion:

> A student petition for more parking spaces on campus received sympathy but not much more from the trustees at yesterday's monthly meeting of the Board of Trustees.
>
> "We know it's a problem," said Alfred Breit, Board chairman. "But it is so complicated. . . ."

Meeting (Action Taken) Essentials

- Vote, decision, agreement
- Summary of the issue
- Reason(s) for action taken
- Arguments for and against issue
- Names of those for and against, if important issue
- Consequences of decision
- Discussion leading to vote or action
- Background of the issue
- Significant additional issues discussed
- Purpose, time and location of meeting
- Additional agenda items
- Makeup of audience and number attending
- Statements, comments from audience
- Significant departures from agenda
- Agenda for next meeting

Any one of these essentials can be the basis of the lead, and the story need not follow the order outlined in the list of essentials.

Here are some leads that are based on meetings in which a decision was reached. The leads stress the vote, agreement or decision.

Vote lead
The city commission voted unanimously last night to increase the property tax rate by $5 for each $1,000 in assessed value.

Agreement lead
The County Bar Association agreed yesterday to allow Grant County lawyers to advertise certain legal services.

Decision lead
Parents today warned the city school board they will fight the proposed closing of the Donald Vogt Elementary School "by every possible means."

Another type of lead can be used when an action is taken. Readers usually want to know the consequences of an action, or what it means. The reporter who wrote the agreement lead above asked lawyers what the action would mean and was told the advertised legal services, such as divorce actions and drawing up wills, would probably cost less. With this information in mind, the writer decided to rewrite the agreement lead:

Consequence lead
It may be cheaper to draw up a will or file for a divorce in Grant County soon.

When the Alabama Public Service Commission granted permission to a bus company to run bus lines from a suburb into Birmingham, the reporter had two choices, a decision lead or a consequence lead. Judge for yourself which is better:

Decision lead
The Public Service Commission yesterday granted B&B Transport and Limousine Co. permission to run bus service from Alabaster to Birmingham.

Consequence lead
People who don't want to fight commuter traffic between Shelby County and Birmingham may soon have a new way to get to work.

Let's examine a meeting story in which an action was taken:

Decision lead

> The Oldham County Planning and Zoning Commission yesterday recommended a denial of new zoning for a 68-unit townhouse and apartment complex in La Grange.

Next step

> The recommendation goes to the La Grange City Council, which will make the final decision.

Summary of the issue

> Terry and Donna Powell want a change from low-density residential to high-density residential zoning on 7.28 acres near Russell Avenue and Madison Street in a section of La Grange known as The Courts.

Audience, time of meeting; transition to discussion

> About 50 people attended a planning commission hearing on the request yesterday. Charles Brown, county zoning administrator, said the commission cited these factors in voting against the rezoning:

Reasons for vote

> ✔The area contains suitable land already zoned for apartments.
>
> ✔Two other apartment complexes have been approved in the past year in or near La Grange.
>
> ✔The property is not close to such services as shopping areas.
>
> ✔The proposal conflicts with La Grange's comprehensive land-use and zoning plan.

Argument against proposal

> Opponents from the neighborhood argued that the development would compound traffic problems. They also expressed concern that dynamite to be used during construction might damage their homes.

Argument for proposal

> James Williamson, attorney for the applicants, contended that the apartments are needed. Some of them would have been reserved for the elderly and handicapped. The developers proposed building five townhouses and six apartment buildings.

—Louisville Courier-Journal

Meeting (Discussion) Essentials

- Most important aspect of discussion: consensus (stated or implied); significant statement; strong disagreement
- Arguments for and against issue(s)
- Names and identifications of those for and against
- Background of major issue(s)
- Purpose, time and location of meeting
- Additional matters discussed
- Makeup of audience, number attending, comments
- Statements, comments from audience
- Significant departures from agenda
- Agenda for next meeting

When the meeting does not lead to a decision, vote or action, the writer's task is more difficult. In this situation, the writer may want to focus on what seems to be the consensus of the participants or on some important statement made during the meeting:

Consensus

City council members last night displayed impatience with local residents who protested a proposed increase in the property tax rate.

Significant statement

City Councilman Garth Maguire last night told a delegation protesting a proposed property tax rate hike their opposition was "too strident, too narrow and too late."

Sometimes, what emerges is a strong disagreement:

Strong disagreement

City council members last night failed to take action on the property tax rate increase City Manager Kelly Simmons proposed last week.

Look at the beginning of this story about a meeting of candidates for the school board. What do you think of the lead?

Burying the Lead

Mt. Pleasant's magnet schools, education for the handicapped, and the quality of schooling were the focus of debate Saturday as the six candidates for at-large seats on the school board answered questions posed by area black leaders.

The election for the three posts will be held May 15.

The candidates appeared before the Mt. Pleasant Black Civic Organization at a meeting at the First Methodist Church at 609 Claremont Ave. last night.

Among the charges by the black leaders were assertions
that magnet schools and special-education classes were
being used to defeat integration, that the quality of
education is poor, and that the system allows inferior
teachers to remain in the classroom.
Although they differed in their responses, in general
the board members, Beatrice A. Florentine, Kyle Smith and
Linda Stern, defended the school system. . . .

The story has an agenda lead. That is, it tells the reader the subjects
that were discussed. But it does not state what was said about these items, the
conclusions reached, the consensus. The reporter did not write a specific lead.
We could make a lead out of the fourth paragraph:

Black leaders told school board candidates last night
that local schools are failing to educate and that
special classes and magnet schools work against school
integration.

Or we could make the fifth paragraph the subject of a lead:

School Board members defended the school system last
night against charges by community black leaders that it
is not doing its job.

You may have even better leads than these two. Notice that the point of
the rewritten leads is to pull the reader right into the meeting where there
were charges and defending statements. Try your hand at writing four or five
paragraphs and see whether you can put life into this important story.

**Panel Discussions
and Symposia**

A panel or symposium is actually a meeting, but usually there is no intention
to reach a decision. A consensus may emerge, however. If so, that should be
the basis of the lead.

Most of the time panelists insist on going their own way, each person
giving his or her opinions or findings. This puts the writer in a bind. Three,
four or five people each merrily piping his or her own tune does not make for
a smoothly written story.

Sometimes, the presentation of one speaker is clearly more newsworthy
than that of the other speakers, and this becomes the lead, as in the story on
the opposite page by Ray Cohn from *The Lexington Herald.*

No other speaker but Welch is quoted until two-thirds down the story.
The third speaker isn't even mentioned until the end of the story. The writer
may have decided to give Welch top billing because of his experience as an
FBI agent and his authoritative position as the state's top official in the justice
system.

Justice Secretary Says System Losing War Against White Collar Criminals

By Ray Cohn
Of The Herald Staff

White collar crime costs the country about $200 billion a year and the criminal justice system is losing the war against it, state Justice Secretary Neil J. Welch told a University of Kentucky symposium on crime and punishment last night.

Welch, a top FBI official before he came to Kentucky last year, said there has been an overwhelming increase in this type of crime.

"Profit is the motive," he said.

To illustrate the magnitude of the problem, Welch said that tax officials estimate $16 billion a year in taxes should be collected on interest income, but that only $2 billion is actually collected.

"We have won some battles," Welch said, "but we are losing the war."

He said that a conference was held about two years ago at University of California — Los Angeles on how to fight organized crime.

"You would think in 1980 we would have a strategy against organized crime, but we don't," he said.

Welch is credited as one of the masterminds of the FBI's Abscam investigation. In that probe, FBI agents posed as representatives of Arab sheiks and accepted bribes from congressmen and other public officials. The scandal resulted in the conviction of several congressman and Sen. Harrison Williams of New Jersey.

Neil J. Welch

Since becoming head of the state Justice Department in 1980, Welch has placed a heavy emphasis on combating white collar crime — and has come under fire for it.

At last night's forum he said "new leadership" is need to combat crime effectively.

He said in the past the emphasis in the United States has been "too oriented toward the legal system." The criminal justice system must now draw "on the finest business brains" to help fight white collar crime, he said, and greater use must be made of modern technology.

But Welch's approach was

oppposed by another member of the symposium panel, Dr. Ernest Yanarella, UK associate professor of political science. He said law enforcement officials must avoid the "nice lure" of technology as instruments of social control.

There was sharp disagreement among some panelists on a proposal made by a task force for U.S. Attorney General William French Smith to modify the exclusionary rule. Under that rule, evidence that police obtain illegally may not be admitted in court.

The national panel wants to permit the intoduction of such evidence if the police officer can show he made good faith effort to obtain it legally.

Yanarella said the position of civil libertarians is "that one has to make a difficult choice." But he insisted it is better to permit some guilty people to go free than "to permit great excesses."

Welch, on the other hand, said it doesn't make sense to exclude evidence because the police "may make a slight error."

Dr. Robert Granacher, a Lexington forensic psychiatrist, illustrated how difficult the issue can be.

He said "the killings in Atlanta stopped when that man was incarcerated." Yet, Granacher said, the suspect, Wayne Williams, will probably have to be released if a court rules that the fiber evidence the police seized from his home was obtained illegally

When it is possible, an area of agreement should be used as the basis of the lead. It may be that the speakers' only agreement is to disagree. If so, the subject of their disagreement can be the basis of the lead.

It may not be easy to find a common theme, but the reporter should try. Editors know that singling out a single speaker for the lead is the easiest way to write a lead. They value the reporter who has the ability to put the statements and ideas of different speakers together, to pattern his or her observations. The ability to extract a meaningful theme from what appear to be separate ideas is a competence that every writer tries to cultivate.

Here is the beginning of a story for which the writer found a common theme:

High schools are not attracting the best teachers, panelists agreed last night in a discussion on the future of the public schools.

The panelists were not of one mind about most of the issues facing public education. But they did agree that a series of factors has made high school teaching unattractive.

The panel, which met in the Community College Auditorium, was sponsored by the college's department of education.

High school teaching has suffered from the following, the panelists said:

• Women are no longer forced to go into teaching because of limited opportunities in other fields.

"Whole areas of professional life and business have opened to women," said Professor Esther Josephs, associate professor of education at the College.

• The public has "little or no confidence in high schools, and morale is at the lowest point in years," said Raymond Peterson, principal of Lima High School. "No one wants to go into a profession in which the public lacks confidence."

• Salaries are lower for high school teachers on the average than for any other field but social work, said Harry Metzger, an official of the state office of the National Education Association. . . .

Sometimes what is said is secondary to an incident in the audience, or even what is not said, as when speakers tiptoe around a controversial issue.

In the following story by Karen Ellsworth of *The Providence Journal-Bulletin,* who did and did not show up for a political meeting became the basis of the lead. Had any of the candidates said anything of significance, that would have been the lead. But Ellsworth concluded that most of what was said was not new. Instead, she decided on what her eyes, and not her ears, told her. Her theme was apathy. Notice how her lead *shows* the reader there was public apathy.

PROVIDENCE—About half of the candidates for state general office and Congress attended a "Meet the Candidates" night at Rhode Island College last night, and they almost outnumbered the audience.

Every Republican candidate attended except James G. Reynolds, the Senate candidate. According to Doris McGarry, president of the Rhode Island League of Women Voters, his press secretary said he

Story Types

was ill. The league sponsored the event.

The only Democrats who attended were Robert Burns, the incumbent secretary of state, Dennis Roberts, candidate for attorney general, and Sen. Claiborne Pell. Neither independent candidate showed up.

About 30 persons, many of them students, attended the 2½–hour session in the lounge of Browne Hall. Mrs. McGarry said she didn't know whether to blame the low turnout on "illness or general apathy."

The format consisted of two-minute statements and questions from the audience, with the candidates each giving an answer and sometimes rebutting another's answer.

Only two candidates got to meet their incumbent opponents face-to-face. The livelier of those exchanges occurred between Burns and his opponent, Michael Murray, a Warwick city councilman. The Republican and Democratic candidates for attorney general, William A. Dimitri and Roberts, had just come from a live television debate on Channel 36 and they appeared a bit talked-out.

Reynolds' absence was particularly noted because of his charge last week that Pell had refused to face him head-on. At that time, Pell said he planned only two such confrontations, and one of them was last night's.

Burns said the first thing he will do when he is re-elected is to work to reform recently-passed election laws.

The absentee and shut-in ballot law, which allows voters to have their ballots sent to the headquarters of a candidate who delivers it to their homes, is "wrong, wrong, wrong," Burns said.

News Conferences

The news conference has two scenes. Scene 1, the curtain-raiser, consists of the statement by the person calling the conference. The press politely hears out the message. Then Scene 2 begins, the questioning of the subject. Occasionally, but not often, a source will have an important announcement to make and not allow any questions. News can be made during both scenes.

The potential candidate for his party's nomination for governor announces he is pulling out of the race:

State Sen. Jack Felton said today he is withdrawing from the race for the Republican nomination for governor.

He pulled himself out of the contest at a press conference at the Simcoe Hotel.

"My plans now are to seek re-election to the legislature," he said. Felton's withdrawal clears the way for Ben Appleman, the only remaining announced candidate for the GOP nomination. . . .

Most often, the news comes out of the question-and-answer period when reporters try to dig out comments about pressing issues. At a presidential press conference, Ronald Reagan discussed general issues in an opening statement. The big news was made in answer to a reporter who asked how the United

States could be sure a super-secret airplane Reagan wanted to sell to Saudi Arabia might not fall into the hands of unfriendly countries if the Saudi government were toppled.

Reagan replied there was "no way" the United States would stand by and let that government be overthrown.

The president's remark seemed casual, almost an aside, and the reporters went on to other issues. As the importance of his remark struck one reporter, he asked another question, and the president's reply was, again, brief.

All told, Reagan's comments on this issue occupied about a twentieth of the time of the news conference. Yet because of its importance—the United States implicitly warning all nations not to step into Saudi Arabia—it became the lead of the story. Because the reporters had only seven sentences from the president to back up their lead, they called a White House spokesman for comments and checked with a variety of sources. They also included considerable background.

The Boston Globe led its account this way:

> President Ronald Reagan said yesterday that the United States would defend Saudi Arabia against any threat to take over the kingdom and cut off the flow of oil to the West.
>
> Reagan's remark, which his aides acknowledged afterward constituted a major foreign policy pronouncement, was delivered as an aside to a question. . . .

News Conference Essentials

- Major point of speaker
- Name and identification of speaker
- Purpose, time, location and length of conference
- Background of major point
- Major point in statement; major points in question-and-answer period
- Consequences of announcement

Speeches

The speech story is almost always based on the answer to the question: Who said what?

Who: The speaker

What: The major theme of the speech

The key to writing speech stories is to isolate the major point the speaker is trying to make and then to select direct quotes that amplify this point. The major point goes into the lead, in the writer's own words. The quotes go into the body of the story.

Since speeches are often long and may include several themes, the reporter has to be choosy. A speech story should not include more than three or four of the speaker's points. There are exceptions—a major policy speech will be covered in detail—but the usual, everyday talk can be covered in a few hundred words.

Gates urges homeowners association to support death penalty, '8,500 plan'

By Nicole Szulc
Herald Examiner staff writer

Los Angeles Police Chief Daryl Gates told some 300 Los Feliz residents last night they could contribute to stemming crime by supporting the death penalty.

At a monthly meeting of the Loz Feliz Improvement Association, which claims to be the largest and oldest home improvement association in Los Angeles County, Gates reminded the audience that two seats on the California Supreme Court recently had been vacated by two justices who favored capital punishment.

"You can help put a stop to crime by letting Governor Brown know how you want those Supreme Court vacancies filled," Gates said.

The police chief had been invited to speak to residents concerned about skyrocketing crime in their neighborhoods who are anxious to organize neighborhood watches or private security patrols. He outlined for them a three-fold plan to put a stop to violence.

Gates said the first point was to change the criminal sentencing structure, so "we can return to a system where if you commit a crime, you get punished."

Secondly, Gates pointed to the so-called "8,500 tax plan," which would provide funds to increase the city's police force to that number.

Next, Gates said, citizens have to learn to "become their brother's keepers," so neighbors know each other and can be "each other's eyes and ears" in trying to cut down neighborhood crime.

Neighborhood watches and security patrols are positive steps in the direction of crime prevention, Gates said, and he pledged the full support of the LAPD in bringing such organizations about.

Finally, Gates told the audience they must look into themselves in order to be able to defend themselves.

"If we hadn't won World War II, we probably wouldn't be here tonight discussing this," he said. "But now the greatest danger we face is from within."

Here is a speech story by Nicole Szulc of the *Los Angeles Herald Examiner*. Szulc selected the death penalty as the major point of the speech and placed it in the lead.

The second paragraph gives the name of the organization sponsoring the meeting. The third paragraph has a direct quote that amplifies the speaker's point, and the fourth paragraph contains background.

Notice that the other points made by the police chief are placed near the end of the story.

Sometimes, something that **happened** provides the main element for the story. During a political campaign in Wisconsin, the Republican candidate for senator was reciting the failings of his opponent and closed with, "I challenge him to deny these charges."

Suddenly, from the back, his opponent rose and shouted, "I deny every one of those charges," and he made his way to the stage. The **happening** obviously became the lead, and the confrontation between the two made up most of the story.

Speeches and speakers come in as many varieties as the offerings of a boardwalk ice cream parlor. There is the Kiwanis Club luncheon talk given by a member of the local chapter of the Audubon Society who discusses the need to save saltwater marshlands, and the recollections of a dentist before the county dental society about the early days of dentistry when Painless Parker cruised city streets in a horse-drawn wagon and extracted molars for 50 cents each.

Whatever the topic, whoever the speaker, the story must include certain essentials.

Speech Essentials

- Name, identification of speaker
- Major point of speech
- Quotes to support main point
- Purpose, time and place of speech
- Nature of audience; prominent people in audience
- Audience reaction
- Background of major point
- Speaker's dress, mannerisms, if important
- Speaker's comments before and after speech, if any
- Additional points made in speech
- Material from question-and-answer period, if any

Writing the Lead

As we've said, the lead of the speech story generally answers the question: Who said what? It does so in S-V-O fashion, the speaker's name or identifying label first and what he or she said next.

Some editors prefer the lead reversed: What was said by whom.

> Rural Americans are not going to let high-voltage lines crisscross their homes, farms and ranches, two Carleton College faculty members said today.

The theory behind this structure is that often what was said is more important than who said it. For broadcast news writing, and increasingly for newspaper usage, the S-V-O structure is preferred.

The identification of the speaker is essential. This gives him or her the credentials to merit our attention. The identifying label usually establishes the speaker's credentials at once in the lead. We use a label when the name of the speaker will mean little to readers or listeners. With widely known people, the name alone usually establishes the person's authority to speak:

Identifying label

> The owner of a chain of fast-food restaurants in the Midwest told a convention of food handlers here today that in 10 years a home-cooked meal will be unusual.

Identifying label

> A University of Wisconsin historian said today that mass culture is a means through which men and women are manipulated.

Widely known name

> Gov. William Blair said today his administration plans to increase aid to the state's colleges and universities that have suffered from federal cutbacks.

In addition to identifying the speaker and stressing the speaker's major point, two other essentials may be placed in the lead:

- Where the talk is given—location
- To whom the speech is given—audience

It is not always possible to jam location and audience into the lead and still make it crisp:

> The head of a local architectural firm told members of the Engineers and Architects Club at their monthly meeting in the Miller Hotel last night that the proposed city hall may prove too costly to build.

To shorten such leads, drop the location and audience to the second or third paragraph:

> The head of a local architectural firm said last night that the proposed city hall may prove too costly to build.
> Preston Wilcox told the Engineers and Architects Club that the cost is estimated at $22 million. He spoke at the Miller Hotel.

The Audience

In our list of essentials, the word *audience* refers to those directly addressed. In Wilcox's talk, the audience is a local club. Audience can also mean the people the speaker hopes to reach through the press. Many speakers have the general public in mind when they speak. Wilcox obviously was intent on warning the public about the costs of constructing a new city hall.

The writer handled this aspect of Wilcox's talk by including background:

```
    Wilcox's talk comes in the midst of a controversy over
whether to go ahead with construction. The increased cost
of labor and supplies has sent costs soaring.
    Taxpayer organizations oppose the construction that
was authorized by the city council in 1984. But local
unions and the administration of Mayor Fred Partell favor
going ahead.
```

Sometimes, as we have seen, the audience may provide the lead element. An unusually small audience for a presidential candidate's major speech can merit the lead, unless the candidate says something extraordinary. An unexpectedly large audience can be the basis of the lead as well, as can the use of a small hall to make the audience seem to be a crowd.

Heckling or boredom at political speeches may be lead material. Significant questions from members of the audience may reveal more newsworthy information than the speech itself.

Constructing the Story

As in all the types of stories in this chapter, the speech story is built on direct quotes, the words of the speaker. Careful: The sign of the beginner is using a direct quote in the lead. A great orator is able to reach out and grab the audience and shake it with ringing sentences worthy of a lead. Such a speaker comes along once in a decade. Name one.

Most of the time, the writer begins with a paraphrase of the speaker's major point. This is followed closely by a direct quote that best makes the point.

The speech story is a blend of direct and indirect quotes, of the speaker's exact language and the writer's paraphrasings.

Caution Sometimes a writer is tempted to take a clever or flashy quote and put it high in the story to attract the readers' interest. This can create problems. Often, the quote is only the speaker's way of getting attention and may not relate to the news point. Placed high in the story, the quote may mislead the reader. The same caution should be taken with the anecdotes speakers sometimes use to spice their talks. Unless they lead directly to the news point, they should not be used high in the story.

Finding the proper material for the lead can be difficult. Some speakers dart from one subject to another, like a trout moving upstream, now here, now there.

A tipoff to the theme can be the title of the talk, if there is one. Watching the speaker's demeanor can indicate the emphasis of the speech. When the words come slowly and deliberately, the speaker is trying to stress his or her point. When the arms wave or a finger points, listen closely or follow the prepared text, pencil ready to underline.

When in doubt about the speaker's theme, ask the speaker. Post-speech interviews can sometimes turn up better leads than the speech itself.

Occasionally, the writer will find the lead in a point the speaker did *not* emphasize. The manager of a local television station may be speaking to a women's club about the merits of programming for the mass audience. In passing, he may say that his station is cutting back on public affairs programming because "nobody watches those shows anyway."

The writer knows that the change in local programming is of greater interest than a generalized defense of situation comedies and quiz shows. To gather more details, the reporter may stop the speaker on his way out or call him at the station.

When a speaker does not explain a point adequately or the reporter needs additional information, the speaker should be interviewed after the presentation or telephoned. The story should state how the information was obtained. If this cannot be done, the story may have to include a sentence or two saying that the point was not clarified. The writer should not hesitate to do this. Otherwise, the reader will presume the writer neglected to explain something important.

An AP reporter covering a speech at an Asian population conference quoted a member of the Islamic Consultative Assembly as saying that the regime in Iran had eliminated 114,000 prostitutes "who were the products of the disgraceful, satanic domination of America and lived at the highest level of wretchedness." To this, the AP reporter added his own comment, "She did not say how this was done."

Follow-Up

The texts of important speeches are often distributed to the press ahead of their delivery. Examination of the prepared text gives reporters time to study the material and to write without pressure. It also allows newspapers and broadcast stations to use the material before the talk is given—unless it is embargoed (restricted for use) until after delivery.

When prepared texts are used before delivery, the writer places in the lead or high in the story the phrase "In a speech prepared for delivery. . . ."

Reporters always cover important speeches with eyes on the text and ears on the speaker. News can be made by last-minute insertions to or deletions from the prepared speech.

Prepared Texts

The basics of writing the types of stories we have examined in this chapter are:

1. Catch the meaning or the significance of the event and put it in the lead.
2. Place the quotations that amplify and buttress the lead high in the story.
3. Give the setting of the event—location, nature of audience and time.
4. Include the possible consequences of what was said.

Summary

From the Office and On the Beat

The essential elements of 14 kinds of stories are described in this chapter.

Accident stories focus on the names of the dead and injured.

Fire stories center on two themes: human casualties and physical damage.

Crime, detection and **arrest** stories usually are written from police reports. Additional reporting gives these stories human interest. Coverage of the **courthouse** beat emphasizes large damage suits and trials for major crimes.

Obituaries give the name, age, address, major accomplishments and survivors of the deceased.

Sports stories are most effective when the writer knows the sport and the players and coaches and when the writer makes the action, rather than supercharged language, propel the story. Game stories require the names of the teams, score, decisive play(s), strategy of players and coaches and the effect on standings.

Briefs or **shorts** include **precedes,** or **advances, personals** and other short items that run no more than five or six sentences. **Folos** are stories that follow up on a theme taken from another story. **Sidebars** emphasize an aspect of the main story printed nearby. **Roundups** combine two or more stories into one by finding a theme common to the stories and using that theme in the lead.

Weather forecasts and stories about unusual or extreme weather include data from official sources and are enhanced by human interest.

Many editors assign their new reporters to the police beat as a way of introducing them to the community. Although at first glance this seems to be the way to see the city from the underside, the beat does give the reporter a quick overview of the city since accidents, fire and crime strike widely and at all levels of society.

Let's look at the traffic accident story first. The accident story is a staple of journalism. More than a million people are killed or injured every year in traffic accidents, and all but the largest newspapers carry stories of these accidents. Only the most minor—the so-called fender benders—are ignored or written in summary form in a column of briefs.

Accidents

In all accident stories, the names of the dead and injured must be reported. The victims are identified by age, address and occupation. The extent of the injuries and the condition of the injured are also given.

Accident Essentials

- Names and identification of dead and injured
- Time and location of accident
- Types of vehicles involved
- Cause (Quote official sources.)
- Source of information
- Names and identification of drivers and of others in vehicles if relevant
- Where dead and injured were taken
- Extent of injuries
- Condition of injured
- Funeral arrangements, if available
- Arrests or citations by officers

If the accident merits a long story because of its severity, add the following:

- Damage to vehicles
- Speed, origin and destination of vehicles
- Unusual weather or highway conditions
- Accounts of eyewitnesses and investigating officers

Caution Do not try to fix blame, to give the cause of an accident, or to give information about excessive speed or drinking by a driver unless the information comes from an official source.

For minor accidents, only the first six essentials are included, as in this story about a car striking a pedestrian:

Auto Hits Man, Breaks His Legs

James Oates, 46, of 447 Dartmouth Ave. suffered two broken legs Thursday evening when struck by a car while crossing Bailey Avenue near LaSalle Avenue, police said.

He is reported in serious condition in the Erie County Medical Center.

Police reported that John Rinzel, 24, of 211 Doat St., driver, said the man stepped into the path of his vehicle from a parked car. He was not charged.

—*Buffalo Evening News*

For fatal accidents, background about the victim is given, as is information about survivors and funeral arrangements:

Bullitt Man Dies in KY 61 Crash

A 34-year-old Bullitt County man, Jackie L. Boone, was killed Monday in a car-motorcycle accident near Lebanon Junction.

According to state police at the Elizabethtown post, Boone, of Route 1A, Lebanon Junction, was killed when the motorcycle he was riding was struck from the rear by an auto about three miles north of Lebanon Junction on KY 61.

Deputy Coroner J. B. Close said Boone died at the scene of a broken neck.

The driver of the auto, Marla Seay of New Albany, was not injured. No charges were filed.

Boone, formerly of Louisville, was a maintenance machinist for Naval Ordnance Station and a Navy veteran.

Survivors include his wife, the former Janice Goeing; a son, Jackie L. Boone; his parents, Mr. and Mrs. Witt Boone; four sisters, Miss Juanita Boone, Mrs. Norbert Carey, Mrs. Colleen Gipson and Mrs. Beth Lehner; and a brother, Robert Boone.

The funeral will be at 10 a.m. Friday at O.D. White & Sons Funeral Home, 2727 S. Third St., with burial in Resthaven Memorial Park.

Visitation will be at the funeral home after noon tomorrow.

—Louisville Times

Despite the frequency of vehicular accidents, the news writer can often find an interesting fact to begin the story with instead of leading with the name and identification of the dead and injured and the location. Look at how a *Miami Herald* writer started a fatal accident story:

James D. Robinson of Opa-locka was driving in the proper lane when he died.

The car that killed him and seriously injured his wife and two small children was not.

In the next few paragraphs the writer gave full identification of those involved in the fatal collision, the location, where the injured were taken, and the extent of their injuries. The story ended with this paragraph.

Charges are pending, Broward Sheriff's Deputy Hal Samuels said. Altieri's blood was tested to determine if he had been drinking while driving, Samuels said.

Death or serious injury are not always necessary for an accident story to make the news. Massive traffic tie-ups, with the usual dented fenders and broken brake lights, also interest readers. So do the accident stories that have a humorous twist, as this AP story does:

> MUSKOGEE, Okla. (AP)—A woman who stopped on a slick bridge here to scrape off her windshield drove off without a scratch, leaving 36 dented cars behind her.

Fires

Stories about fires usually are given good play. Fire stories interest readers, possibly because of our fear of fires. Whatever the reason, the beginner will likely find himself or herself handling a fire story within days, whether it is a farmhouse fire that causes $20,000 in damage or an apartment house fire that kills eight people:

> HARRISBURG—A farmhouse six miles northeast of Harrisburg was badly damaged Sunday evening by a fire that began when the occupants of the dwelling were away.
>
> Harrisburg Fire Chief Sonny Hanf said the two-story frame house, at 24661 Rowland Rd., sustained a loss of about $20,000. The building is owned by George Turney of Dallas and rented by Jim and Patsy Rosenberg, Hanf said.
>
> According to Hanf, Jim Rosenberg returned to the house about 7 p.m. Sunday and found a bedroom in flames. Firefighters from Harrisburg and Halsey responded to the alarm.
>
> Hanf said fire damage was confined to the bedroom area, although the rest of the house sustained smoke and water damage.
>
> —*Eugene* (Ore.) *Register-Guard*

> PATERSON, N.J. (AP)— Eight people died in a predawn tenement fire and 11 were missing yesterday after a man who had been spurned by a female resident allegedly set the building ablaze with a can of gasoline, authorities said.
>
> Two dozen others were injured, "many of them jumping from windows," said police Sgt. Edward Hanna.
>
> "The firemen were inside the building, crawling around on their hands and knees, feeling for people," he said. "Twenty minutes after I got there, they carried out three kids while the fire was really going. I never saw anything like it in my life."
>
> Paterson Fire Chief Harold J. Kane said the bodies were found after firefighters gained control of the blaze that left more than 100 people homeless.
>
> "We just hope it ends here. But we're waiting on a crane to help us go through what's left of the building,". . . .

Burned Out. When someone is injured or killed, or the damages are large, this information goes into the lead. Home fire stories also center on the consequences to the residents—homeless, clothing gone, perhaps a valuable stamp collection or library gone up in smoke.
Susan Plageman, *The Berkshire Eagle*

Fire Essentials

- Deaths, injuries
- Full identification of victims
- Location
- Type of structure
- Official cause
- Source of information
- How victims were injured or killed
- When and where fire started, and how and when it was brought under control
- Rescue attempts
- Where injured, dead taken
- Extent of injuries
- Investigation of cause
- Damage to structure, cost, insurance coverage
- Number of units and firefighters; amount of water used
- Name(s) of fire company(ies) responding
- Quotes of eyewitnesses, firefighters, residents of structure
- Human interest details
- Time of first alarm; who called fire department

Go back to the fire story datelined HARRISBURG that began this section. One of the essentials is missing—the cause of the fire. If the cause of the fire was unknown at the time the story was written, say so.

Fires are frequent in large cities, especially in winter, but they are not covered unless there is considerable damage, loss of life, traffic congestion, or a large amount of equipment is called out. In small and medium-sized cities, fires are usually covered even when there is no loss of life and damage is minor.

When a wooden grain elevator burst into flames one Saturday morning in downtown Hays, Kan., *The Daily News* sent reporters and photographers to cover the fire. Although the fire was brought under control in three hours and no one was hurt, the newspaper devoted almost all of the front page to the story and to a large picture. An inside page carried five photos and the continuation of the page one story.

In rural communities, fire is a great enemy, and coverage is thorough. The fire companies that answer the call are identified and the chief's quotes usually are used.

A farm fire that destroyed a feed barn, a tractor, a hay baler and 3,000 bales of hay received front page play in the *Georgetown News,* a weekly newspaper in Kentucky. The fire was caused by lightning. Ed Moore, chief of the Scott County Fire Department, was quoted in the story as saying:

"We just call this kind of thing an act of God. I've seen farms with lightning rods go up in smoke. Once the lightning flash causes a dust explosion in the hay, there's just nothing you can do to save the barn."

Quotations add human interest to the stories. In the following story, a quote is used in the second paragraph and the names of the cities from which firefighters were dispatched is also included.

Brush fire threatens homes

WAVES—A brush fire driven by northeast winds scorched 12 acres near this Hatteras Island village Wednesday night, threatening several homes, before it was brought under control.

"Everyone on the island was involved," said Bert Austin, Dare County's chief deputy sheriff.

Firemen from Waves, Rodanthe, Salvo, Avon, and Buxton answered the alarm about 7 p.m. National Park Service, Coast Guard, and N.C. Division of Forest Resources personnel assisted.

Austin said the flames reached within 50 feet of one home before the dry swamp grass was doused by firemen.

The fire started when an electric wire fell in the grass. The wire apparently had been damaged by the accumulation of salt, a common problem for utility companies in Dare County.

—*The Virginian-Pilot*
(Norfolk, Va.)

When there are deaths or many injuries—as in the AP story from Paterson, N.J.—the lead must focus on this essential. When property is the only casualty—as in the Harrisburg farmhouse fire—then that usually is the basis of the lead.

Fires sometimes threaten homes in areas plagued by forest fires and brushfires, and this often provides the lead material, as in the story from Waves.

Dennis Love of *The Anniston* (Ala.) *Star* describes how he heard about an unusual fire in a rural area and tells how he gathered the information for his story.

"While on weekend duty one Saturday night, I got a tip while calling funeral homes throughout our seven-county circulation area. An employee said he was handling funeral arrangements for a 76-year-old man who died in a school bus fire the night before.

"An accidental death alone merits a brief story, but this man's age and obvious questions about why he was in the bus required further checking. I called the coroner, the sheriff's department and the fire department—all of which were represented on the scene—and pieced together the basic information.

"The old man, who lived with his brother in a rural part of the county, often slept in an old school bus he had converted into a camping vehicle. On this night he had apparently fallen asleep while smoking and was unable to escape the flames that rapidly engulfed the old vehicle. The coroner said there was no evidence of foul play."

Then Love began to try to reach relatives of the dead man to piece together the details. The coroner supplied the name of one relative who gave Love the telephone number of the family home, which he had not been able to find in the directory. He reached the victim's brother. This was a vital call.

"He gave me a first-hand account of what had happened, and he testified to his brother's love of cigarettes, which they were convinced caused the fire. He also said his brother recently had moved in with him from a nursing home and was not in the best of health and often needed assistance in moving around. I wrote down his comments and was ready to write the story."

Here is Love's story, and alongside it his comments about how he wrote it:

I had some colorful quotes from the brother about his brother's smoking habits, and since that had emerged as the consensus as to the cause of death, I decided to emphasize that angle in my lead paragraph. His age was also significant, as was the school bus setting, so I incorporated all of it in what I consider a somewhat clumsy lead. But it seemed to work.

FRUITHURST—Seventy-six-year-old Tom Jenkins' penchant for chainsmoking has been blamed for the fire which engulfed the old school bus in which he slept early Saturday and in which he died.

Next, the sequence of events was in order so I used the clearest and most official source I had—that of the coroner. I let him give the basic facts in the next three paragraphs, throwing in an aside about the victim's health in the third graf.

Cleburne County Coroner Hollis Estes said he and the Heflin Fire Department were summoned to the Coldwater community near Fruithurst shortly after 4 a.m. Saturday to find the old bus—converted into a camping vehicle—ravaged by flames.

The bus was parked in the front yard of the home of the victim's brother, Hubert Jenkins. Tom Jenkins was living with his brother while he recovered from a stroke he suffered earlier this year, according to family members.

Estes said the bedding in the rear of the bus apparently caught fire from a burning cigarette and spread rapidly throughout the vehicle. The coroner said there was no evidence of foul play and no autopsy would be performed.

Then I came back to the smoking angle, using my best quote from the victim's brother. I let him describe the chainsmoking habits, tell about the camper and the events leading up to his discovering the fire in progress.

"Lord, he (the victim) was always careless with his cigarettes," said Hubert Jenkins Saturday night. "He would just smoke one right after the other. Only thing we can figure is he got out there in the camper and fell asleep or something with one lit."

Jenkins said his brother, who left Golden Springs Nursing Home in April, spent a great deal of time sitting in the bus, which was equipped with a stove, refrigerator and other appliances.

"Friday afternoon, he said he was going out for some fresh air, and I watched him make a beeline for the bus," Jenkins said. "I checked on him later on and he was just sitting on the side of the bunk bed, said he wanted to stay out there a while longer."

Jenkins said his brother later told his daughter "he wanted to spend the night out there."

Around 4 a.m., Jenkins said he awoke to the sound of "something popping. It sounded like his old walking cane he used—I thought he was tapping on the side of the bus to get my attention. Before I could get to the door I could see the trailer" on fire. Jenkins said he believes the popping sound that woke him was .22-caliber cartridges exploding in the bus.

Jenkins said his brother needed some help in "getting around" after the stroke, but was at a loss to explain why the victim was unable to escape the flames.

He said the bus had a front and rear entrance, but the back door was blocked by the bed on which Jenkins slept. Estes said, however, that the body was found on the floor of the bus.

I closed the story with his brother's explanation.

"It just looks like when he woke up he tried to get out, but just didn't make it," said Hubert Jenkins.

Love said his story lets "the people who were involved answer the obvious questions: How and why did Jenkins die where he did, and why couldn't he avoid his death? My last phone call to the family of the deceased brought all that together, and helped to take the story a bit beyond the level of a routine police item."

Crime Stories

The main job of the police reporter is handling crime—reports of violent and property crimes, investigations and detection, and arrests. The police reporter may also cover the police and municipal or criminal courts to follow up the arrests he or she reports.

Almost everyone knows someone who has been a victim of a crime, or has himself or herself been a victim. A third of all households in the United States were affected by burglary or a violent crime in the 1980s. In towns where people never locked their doors, there is now a thriving business in burglar alarm systems. Automobile owners search for the switch, wiring or siren that will keep a thief from taking off with their Toyotas and Fords. In some cities, women are advised not to wear necklaces or earrings on the streets. Around college and university campuses, the number of rapes has doubled and tripled in recent years.

During the 1970s, the number of crimes reported to law enforcement officials increased by 50 percent. In the 1980s, the number of crimes plateaued. The FBI reports a property crime is committed every three seconds and a violent crime every 24 seconds. A rape occurs every six minutes and a murder every 23 minutes.

Almost every community in the country has contributed to these figures. This means that police reporters have had to be more discriminating in their reporting. If they did not, they would not have enough time to report the most newsworthy crimes in their cities and towns.

To help clear the way through this flood of police information, the police reporter usually concentrates on violent crimes and spends less time on property crimes.

Violent Crime refers to events that may result in injury to a person. **Property Crimes** are unlawful acts with the intent of gaining property that do not involve the use of or threat of force.

Violent Crimes	**Property Crimes**
Murder	Burglary
Rape	Larceny
Robbery	Motor vehicle theft
Aggravated assault	

Crime Reports

Few police reporters have ever seen a crime committed. Yet they write about crimes every day, often with the intensity and drama of an eyewitness. Most of their information comes from crime reports. These are the forms filled out by officers who have investigated the crime. The reporter supplements these reports with interviews with the officers or their superiors and with those who witnessed the crime or were its victims.

Reporters determine the nature of the crime from the code number at the top of the crime report. The code number tells the reporter whether the crime is serious or minor.

Crime Essentials

- Victim(s), full identification
- Nature of crime
- Date, time, location of crime
- Violent crime: official cause of death or injury; weapon used; motivation; background of victim, if relevant
- Property crime: value of loss; method of theft or entry
- Suspects (no names unless charges filed), clues
- Unusual circumstances
- Quotes of witnesses, victim(s), police
- Source of information

The following story about a violent crime was taken from a crime report. It begins with the nature of the crime and the victims. In the second paragraph, the victims are identified and their injuries described. The third paragraph describes the possible weapon and the questioning of two suspects.

Man, Woman Shot During Fracas in Field

A man and woman were shot about 10:40 p.m. Monday when gunfire erupted during what police called a "neighborhood-type" argument in a field at 34th and Forest.

The victims were identified as Tony Simmons, 20, of 5117 Woodland, who was listed in critical condition with a gunshot wound to the forehead, and Ms. Debra Williams, 21, of 3327 Tracy, in fair condition with a gunshot wound to the left hand. Both were admitted to the Truman Medical Center.

Police, who said they heard different accounts of the shooting at the scene, said they were questioning two persons in connection with the incident. A pump shotgun believed to have been used in the shooting was recovered on the porch of a home at 3329 Tracy, police said.

—*Kansas City Times*

Robbery

Beginning reporters sometimes confuse robbery, a violent crime, and burglary, a property crime. The difference is this: Robbery is a crime against a person. Burglary is a crime against property.

Robbery involves taking or attempting to take something of value from a person by force or threat of force or violence. The writer approaches robbery stories from two avenues—the value of goods stolen and the prominence of the person involved. Usually, the value of goods taken is the element chosen for the lead, but when a widely-known person is robbed, that is the lead, regardless of the amount taken from the person.

Here is a typical robbery story:

A lone gunman held up the Thrifty Liquor Store at 42 First St. this morning and got away with $1,780 in cash, police said.

The owner, Martin Nolan, said that he was closing the store when a man in his thirties bought a bottle of wine. As Nolan opened the register, the man took a revolver from his jacket pocket and told Nolan to hand over the day's receipts.

On leaving, he warned Nolan against following him. But Nolan told police he managed to see the tall, thin man drive off in a 1979 blue compact car with Arkansas plates.

Burglary

Burglary is the unlawful entry of a structure to commit a felony or a theft. (A felony is a crime that is punishable by a year or more in a state or federal penitentiary.) In the case of burglaries, state law usually defines the dollar amount of stolen goods at which the theft passes from a misdemeanor to a felony. In some states, it is $250, in others $500, and so on. (A misdemeanor is a crime punishable by a fine or a term of less than one year in a city or county jail or prison.)

When the loss in a burglary is considerable, the lead focuses on the value of the stolen goods:

Jewelry and personal items worth $50,000 were reported missing from the home of Victor Sewell, 560 Eastern Lake Ave., last night.

Police said Sewell told them he and Mrs. Sewell returned from a visit to friends about 11 p.m. and discovered the window to a bedroom at the rear of the house had been forced open.

Sewell, an attorney, told police he had purchased a matching diamond bracelet and necklace last week in London where he attended a law seminar. He said he had told no one of the purchase.

Police said the bedroom was the only room in the house that had been entered.

Detection

Police are understandably close-mouthed during the investigation of a serious crime, which makes it hard for the reporter to obtain material for a story during the detection-investigation stage.

Sometimes, the police will seek help from the press in locating a suspect and will provide information. Now and then a reporter will learn something the police want to keep confidential. Most police reporters will keep the material under wraps. They risk antagonizing their sources if they use it. In the larger cities, the unwritten code is that a reporter may use anything he or she can learn. If the department cannot keep its people quiet, so be it.

Early information about suspects may compromise not only the investigation but the court case. A reporter must weigh all this before running any but officially sanctioned material.

Detection Essentials

- Progress of investigation
- Suspects
- Additional clues
- Personnel assigned to case
- Summary of crime

Caution   Only the most serious crimes are investigated by most big-city police departments. Generally, the greater the public interest, the more likely the police are to push an inquiry. The murder of a prominent person or a police officer will be investigated. But in large cities, the murder of a drug dealer or a drifter may be closed quickly. Burglaries and car thefts have, for all practical purposes, been decriminalized in large cities, unless the criminal is caught in the act. There is almost no follow-up investigation of these crimes.

Some of the best crime stories are of arrests. Again, the information usually comes from a report, in this case an arrest report, which the reporter examines on his or her rounds of the police department. For arrests in serious crimes, the police or district attorney may call a news conference to make the announcement for all the media.

Usually, charges are filed on arrest, but sometimes a suspect is held for investigation. A suspect may be detained for a limited period until formal charges are filed. In the arrest story, the writer must be certain that the charges mentioned have actually been filed.

Arrest Essentials

- Name, identification of person arrested
- Crime person is charged with
- Details of crime, including name and identification of victim
- Circumstances of arrest
- Officers involved in arrest
- Source of information

For serious crimes, add these:

- Investigation
- Background of suspect
- Motive
- Circumstances of arrest announcement
- Booking, arraignment, any other procedures

The Arrest Lead Generally, the lead to the arrest story is based on the name and identification of the person arrested and the crime that the person is accused of committing.

If the arrest is the result of extraordinary police detection or unusual circumstances, a delayed lead may be put on the story, with the arrest coming as a climax.

Here are some leads that emphasize different essentials:

Name, identification of person arrested

Two teenagers are in the Dade County jail, charged with first degree murder in the robbery and execution of a meat truck driver whose truck they hijacked. Robert Borton, 18 of 1981 NW 37th Ct., and his longtime friend, Carlton Derly, 19, of 2149 NW 24th Ct., were arrested Wednesday night.

Arrests

Only a Third to a half of those arrested are formally charged with a crime. For most arrests, the prosecutor decides not to draw up a charge because the evidence is inadequate, witnesses will not testify, or additional information makes prosecution inadvisable. This has led newspapers, such as the *St. Louis Post-Dispatch,* to withhold the names of most of those arrested until a charge is drawn.

The police arrested three brothers and accused them of breaking into a church yesterday in the suburb of Brookline.

The police identified the men as. . . .

Circumstances of arrest

HOUSTON—A one-armed busboy captured a fleeing gunman, tripping him twice and holding him in a headlock for police, after the gunman held up a restaurant and shot a cook, authorities said today.

Detail of crime

BALTIMORE—A suspect has been arrested in the weekend slaying of a department store manager who was found shot to death with his 3-year-old son standing over him, police said.

Investigation

Eleven South Americans were in custody today after a four-month investigation by the Sheriff's Department, Narcotics Bureau and U.S. Customs resulted in the seizure of $750,000 worth of cocaine, $139,500 in cash, a rifle, three handguns and a sizeable amount of gold jewelry, Undersheriff Sherman Block said yesterday.

What's Newsworthy? The size of the community and the amount of its crime determine what kinds of arrests become news. In Miami, Detroit, Chicago, Los Angeles and cities of similar size, the arrest of a murder suspect may merit a few lines, if that, unless the victim is prominent or the crime had been given attention.

But in smaller cities and towns even the theft of some jeans and the arrest of a suspect is worth a story:

A Dress Barn employee was arrested Wednesday on a warrant charging him with stealing 49 pairs of blue jeans.

Joseph Scapella, 40, of 95 Trudy Lane was charged with second degree larceny in connection with the theft of the jeans valued at $1,302 and taken from a Dress Barn warehouse March 26, police said.

This story appeared in *The Advocate* in Stamford, Conn. The story is as long as a piece about an arrest for attempted murder in Chicago, which was carried by the newspaper only because of the grisly nature of the crime:

A resident of a West Side halfway house was charged Monday with shoving his roommate out of a third-floor window, then rushing downstairs and stabbing him 11 times as he lay in the alley where he landed.

The police charged Allen Taber with attempted murder. The victim, Fred Krumpe, was in critical condition with multiple fractures.

Analyzing the Arrest Story Here is an arrest story with the list of arrest essentials alongside it:

Circumstances of arrest, crime committed

A special burglary detail yesterday chased and caught a suspect the officers believe responsible for a rash of house burglaries in the Tacoma Avenue area.

Charges, name and identification of person arrested

Karl Vogt, 31, of 967 Eastern St., was charged with burglary and possession of burglary tools.

Police said that Vogt was spotted by a detective in the special unit going from house to house along Tacoma Avenue. When he saw the man enter 98 Tacoma Ave. he radioed for the rest of the detail. Vogt awoke a tenant, John Strong, and then tried to flee but was arrested a block from the building.

Circumstances of arrest elaborated

The detail was set up for round-the-clock surveillance of the neighborhood after several house burglaries were reported.

Officers making arrest

Detectives who made the arrest included Ray Miller, John Hazar and Bill Smith.

Crime is handled by a variety of law enforcement agencies. Local crime is under the jurisdiction of the municipal police force. More than 90 percent of all cities with a population of 2,500 or more have their own police forces. At the county level, sheriff's departments handle duties similar to local police for unincorporated areas and in municipalities with no local police force. The sheriff often operates the county jail. State police and highway patrols handle traffic on state highways and provide assistance to local police and sheriff's departments.

Law Enforcement Agencies

At the federal level, there are more than 50 law enforcement agencies. Those with the largest work loads are:

Department of Justice	**Internal Revenue Service**
FBI	Customs Service
Drug Enforcement Administration	Bureau of Alcohol, Tobacco and Firearms

The Secret Service is under the jurisdiction of the Department of the Treasury, and the Postal Inspection Service is within the U.S. Postal Service.

State Judicial System

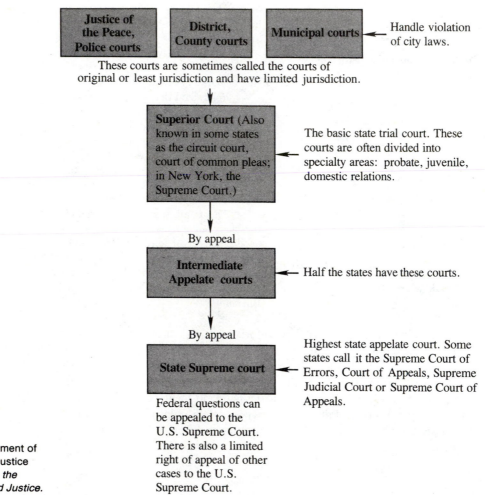

Justice of the Peace, Police courts

District, County courts

Municipal courts ← Handle violation of city laws.

These courts are sometimes called the courts of original or least jurisdiction and have limited jurisdiction.

Superior Court (Also known in some states as the circuit court, court of common pleas; in New York, the Supreme Court.) ← The basic state trial court. These courts are often divided into specialty areas: probate, juvenile, domestic relations.

By appeal

Intermediate Appelate courts ← Half the states have these courts.

By appeal

State Supreme court ← Highest state appellate court. Some states call it the Supreme Court of Errors, Court of Appeals, Supreme Judicial Court or Supreme Court of Appeals.

Federal questions can be appealed to the U.S. Supreme Court. There is also a limited right of appeal of other cases to the U.S. Supreme Court.

Source: U.S. Department of Justice, Bureau of Justice Statistics, *Report to the Nation on Crime and Justice.*

Figure 15.1 This chart shows the sequence of events in the criminal justice system following a crime. The court system consists of three main stems: juvenile, misdemeanor and felony. Although systems differ from state to state, all states require certain steps because of constitutionally guaranteed due process for those accused of a crime. Source: Adapted from *The Challenge of Crime in a Free Society.* The President's Commission on Law Enforcement and Administration of Justice, 1967.

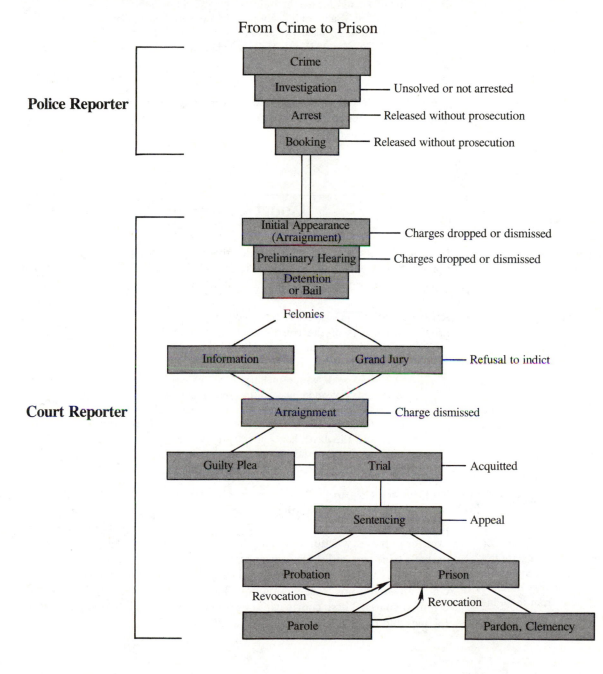

From Crime to Prison

Booking

After an arrest, the suspect is **booked** at the police station on the arrest charge:

A 23-year-old prison parolee, the object of a statewide manhunt, surrendered in San Luis Obispo County and was booked Tuesday in the murder of a teen-age Hollywood girl, Los Angeles police said.

Mauricio Rodriguez Silva was being held without bail in the Hollywood Division jail. He is expected to be arraigned on a murder charge Thursday, authorities said. . . .

—Los Angeles Times

The police reporter usually will cover the booking at the police station. The court reporter will take over for the arraignment, which is the beginning of the court process.

Court Coverage

Criminal Law

Criminal law procedure can be roughly divided into two areas for coverage—the pretrial appearances by the accused and the trial. Both areas are given considerable coverage in the case of a major crime.

Pretrial

Arraignment The suspect is arraigned in a local court soon after arrest. The procedure consists of the court's advising the suspect of the charge and in hearing the suspect's plea. Bail is sometimes set at the arraignment.

The Federal Courts have held that the time between arrest and arraignment can be no longer than 24 hours. Many states have laws stipulating that an arraignment and bail hearing must be held without unnecessary delay.

A 19-year-old West Roxbury man yesterday pleaded innocent to a second-degree murder and assault and battery charges in connection with the death last winter of a Boston College student.

The case of Scott O'Leary was continued one month for a pretrial conference following his arraignment before Suffolk Superior Court Judge James P. Donohue. . . .

—The Boston Globe

Note: Criminal and civil law varies from state to state. The descriptions in this section may differ somewhat from those in your state.

Preliminary Hearing This hearing is sometimes called a probable cause hearing. The judge reviews the facts and may hear testimony. The judge then decides whether there is reasonable and probable cause to bind the suspect over for grand jury action—to hold the suspect in jail or to set him or her free on bail. A person without a lawyer may have one assigned.

Arraignments and preliminary hearings are held in what are known as courts of original or least jurisdiction. These are municipal, police, city and criminal courts. These courts can try misdemeanors. A higher court must try felonies and can impose sentences for convictions.

Grand Jury A jury, usually of 23 persons, hears the evidence presented by a prosecutor and decides whether to issue an indictment (true bill) or to dismiss the charge (no bill):

> A Cobb County grand jury returned murder indictments Thursday against two men and a woman accused of causing the death of a Marietta woman who took an overdose of cocaine in February. . . .
>
> *—The Atlanta Constitution*

In some states, an **information,** which is a formal written accusation, is submitted to the court by the prosecutor instead of an indictment being returned by a grand jury.

Re-arraignment The defendant is informed of the charge in the indictment or information, is advised of his or her rights and is asked to plead to the charges. If the plea is guilty and the judge has jurisdiction, the defendant may be sentenced. If the plea is not guilty, the case is set for trial.

Pretrial Hearings A number of different hearings may be held before the case goes to trial. Some are:

> *Suppression*—Consideration of the admissibility of evidence or a confession.
> *Sanity*—Determination of the fitness of the defendant to stand trial.
> *Jurisdictional*—Determination of whether the court has jurisdiction over the case.

Plea Bargaining

During any of these steps in the pretrial procedure the defendant may plead guilty. Often, the defendant is allowed to plead to a lesser charge than the one on which he or she has been indicted. This negotiation of a plea is called **plea bargaining** and is used in most courts to help to clear the calendar of the enormous number of cases before them. A study of 13 cities showed that plea bargaining occurred in from 81 percent of the cases in Louisville to 97 percent in New York City.

> A 26-year-old man described by authorities as a Marine deserter has been sentenced to life in Walpole state prison after pleading guilty to second-degree murder in the Oct. 12 death of concert pianist Mary Louise Sellon, 30, of Medford.

> The guilty plea last Tuesday of Steven Ballway came less than a week before he was scheduled for trial in Suffolk Superior Court on first-degree murder and rape charges.
>
> *—The Boston Globe*

Sometimes, a deal will be worked out with a defendant in return for his or her willingness to cooperate with authorities:

PHOENIX—A Boulder man charged with seven others in a 56-count indictment has been placed on four years' probation for possessing cocaine and selling marijuana.

Dennis J. Cimmino, 31, was sentenced by Judge Cheryl Hendrix of Maricopa County Superior Court after pleading guilty to the two drug charges and agreeing to help prosecutors. . . .

Should no plea bargain be made—which often happens when the defendant is a frequent offender—the case moves to trial. In many cities, district attorneys concentrate their sparse resources in prosecuting what is known as the career criminal, the defendant with a long record of felony arrests and convictions.

The Trial

Jury Selection A jury is chosen from a **wheel** or jury box that contains the names of all registered voters in the jurisdiction. A defendant may waive the right to trial by jury and ask the judge to hear the evidence.

Trial The trial begins with opening statements by the prosecutor and the defense attorney. The reporter usually learns the outline of the case from these statements. They are followed by the prosecutor's presentation of the state's witnesses. (In criminal trials, the state, not an individual, brings the charges.)

The defense then may cross-examine the prosecutor's witnesses, after which the prosecutor may question the witnesses in redirect examination.

The defense then presents its case by calling its witnesses:

The Leonia police officer who answered the first call for help from the Crawbuck home, where Bill Battista lay dying, testified yesterday that the family failed to cooperate and withheld information that might have led him to handle the case differently.

In the first day of defense testimony in the wrongful-death suit being heard in Hackensack, police Cpl. Carmey Cross told the jury. . . .

—*The Record* (Hackensack, N.J.)

CLAXTON, Ga.—Annette Moore sat in Evans County Superior Court and read from a pocket-size Bible while her son testified for more than an hour as the sole witness in his own defense.

Before 18-year-old Michael Moore was arrested Feb. 1 and charged with murder in the bludgeoning and stabbing death of his girlfriend's mother, Rebecca Futch, he was his own mother's hope for the future.

Now, in the third and last day of testimony before Judge John R. Harvey, he was staring a possible death sentence in the face and blaming his girlfriend for the crime.

Moore's girlfriend, Sherri Futch, is white. Her mother did not like her seeing Moore, Miss Futch said, because he is black. Moore testified that on the evening of Feb. 1 he and Miss Futch, 17, planned to tell her mother that she was pregnant. . . .

The prosecutor may cross-examine defense witnesses, and the defense is allowed then to make redirect examination of its witnesses.

Both sides are allowed to present rebuttals to testimony. The last step in the trial procedure is the final argument by both sides.

Charge to Jury The judge charges or instructs the jury about the law involved in the case.

The Jury

Jury Deliberations and Verdict The jury retires to a jury room to decide the facts of the case. The jurors must reach a unanimous verdict in all states but Louisiana, Montana, Oklahoma, Oregon and Texas. The jury may ask the judge for further instructions about the law, and it may request that testimony be read to it from the transcript. Since jury deliberations are secret, these occasional requests may tip the reporter to what the jury is considering.

RIVERSIDE—Douglas Neslund, the 40-year-old founder and director of the Los Angeles-based California Boys Choir, was convicted by a Riverside Superior Court jury of molesting several of his choirboys.

The jury deliberated almost three full days before finding Neslund guilty on four felony counts and one misdemeanor count of child molestation. . . .

—*Los Angeles Times*

Sentence If the jury returns a verdict of guilty, the judge will sentence the defendant at once or may await a probation report or schedule a pre-sentence hearing at which evidence of aggravating or mitigating circumstances may be considered. In some states, the jury decides the sentence for capital offenses such as murder.

Eddie L. Green was sentenced Wednesday to a five-to-15-year prison term in the bludgeoning death three years ago of a Buffalo man who, Green claims, had made advances to his girlfriend.

—*The Buffalo News*

Stories can be written at any stage of the process. If the crime is notorious or involves a prominent person, a reporter may be assigned to stay with the event from arraignment through sentencing.

Criminal Trial Essentials

- Identification of defendant
- Original charge
- New charge if plea bargain
- Nature of crime, details

- Status of proceeding
  What happened today
  Review of trial
  Next steps
- Name of judge, title of court
- Courtroom scene

Trials are often dramatic, and the reporter should seek to reflect the drama. They are also complex, frequently complicated by legal jargon and technical procedures. The reporter must look beyond the technical points to the human interest, the tale that is unfolding.

Civil Law

Damage Suit Filed

Alvin Kellogg of St. James, Minn., checked into a Rochester motel room on Sept. 13, 1985, planning to have his annual checkup the next day at the Mayo clinic.

That night he suffered a stroke in his room. He claims in a suit filed in Olstead County Court that he was not found until three days later. He is suing the Chambers Corp., which owns the motel, for $500,000.

Kellogg, 67, alleges that the company was negligent because its employees at the Phillips Downtown Motel failed to discover him for three days. Medical reports filed with the suit state that Kellogg was severely dehydrated when he was found. . . .

We have been discussing criminal law procedures. In this area of law, the government is the accuser. In the other major area of law, civil law, the action is usually brought by an individual or a group. Civil law is not seen by the press as having the drama of criminal law, and consequently coverage of the civil courts is spotty, usually confined to the suits brought in what is called **actions at law.** These suits seek the recovery of property and damages for personal injury and breach of contract.

The county courthouse reporter has the responsibility for checking the court clerk's records daily to ferret out the most interesting and significant suits filed. A guide to making judgments is the sum sought by the person filing the suit. But be careful: Lawyers sometimes seek huge sums for the damage allegedly done their client, then agree to a much-reduced figure in pretrial bargaining. In fact, most suits never reach the trial stage.

When a settlement is reached, the story must contain the amount awarded by the jury, the name of the person bringing the suit and the damage inflicted, the defendant, the title of the court in which the suit was heard, the incident leading to the suit:

A 20-year-old Wyckoff woman who was injured in February 1981 yesterday won a $405,000 jury award in Superior Court in Hackensack from the friend who was driving the car.

Megan McMurtrie of 402 Meer Ave. was semiconscious for eight days of a month-long hospitalization after Kathryn Gallant lost control of the Mercedes Benz in which Ms. McMurtrie was riding, causing the car to strike a tree in Franklin Lakes. . . .

—*The Record*

The other area of civil law is called **equity proceedings.** Here, an individual or a group seeks to have the court compel an individual, the government, or an organization to do something or to refrain from an action.

Here is the beginning of a story about the court's issuance of a temporary restraining order:

> Dr. John H. Lambette's attorney obtained a court order Friday barring state health officials from suspending the heart specialist's medical license.
>
> State Superior Court Judge Karl Krane granted the order and scheduled a hearing next Tuesday to determine whether the temporary restraining order should be made permanent. . . .

Injunctions are usually issued pending a hearing to determine whether they should be made permanent.

There are two judicial systems, federal and state. Most coverage is of the state system. In cities where federal courts are located, the newspaper usually assigns a full-time staff member to cover the federal court.

Federal courts hear a wide variety of cases that involve the violation of federal laws—immigration cases, constitutional issues, interstate car theft, drug shipments from outside the country into the country, tax cases, civil rights.

> NEW YORK (UPI)—The largest tax fraud case in U.S. history has ended with the conviction of four Wall Street executives and a hung jury in the case of a fifth defendant.
>
> The nine-man, three-woman jury considering the complex trail of $130 million worth of phony tax shelters reached a partial verdict. . . .

> DETROIT—One white man was found guilty and another was acquitted in federal court yesterday in a civil-rights trial stemming from the 1982 killing of Vincent Chin, a 27-year-old Chinese-American.
>
> A jury of 11 whites and one black found Ronald Ebbens, 45,
>
> guilty on one count of violating Chin's civil rights. Chin had been bludgeoned to death with a baseball bat after a barroom brawl in what U.S. Department of Justice prosecutors said was a racially motivated slaying.
>
> —*Los Angeles Times*

The federal court system has three tiers: the district courts, where most trials are held; the courts of appeal in 12 circuits to which cases may be taken by appeal, and the final court of appeal, the United States Supreme Court, to which cases are taken by writ of certiorari.

Obituaries

The Washington-based political reporter had finished his talk to the journalism class and asked for questions. He had just completed a five-state tour of the Midwest to sound out political feelings about the president.

"What was the strongest impression you got from your trip?" a student asked.

The reporter paused a moment before answering. "This isn't really a political matter," he said. "But when I was interviewing a woman in her kitchen in Iowa, I glanced over to the wall where she had some things clipped to a wallboard. At the top was a newspaper clipping behind a piece of clear plastic.

"It was the story of President Kennedy's funeral. The paper was yellow and frayed. It told me something about the woman's politics. But it also told me something about journalism. Here was the most basic journalistic story of all, an obituary, and it had been saved for all these years."

Obituaries are among the most frequently read items in newspapers. A third to a half of the readers regularly read them.

The Kentucky Post in Covington for years carried an obituary for everyone who died within the newspaper's circulation area. The *Post* would take special pains to obtain material. Every morning, reporters would call hospitals in the area for death reports, and funeral directors were expected to call the newspaper with material.

After a while, the obituaries began to take too much space. The newspaper decided to reduce the type size of its obituaries from eight points to seven.

"We got all kinds of complaints," says David Brown, the managing editor. "Since then, we haven't fooled with them much."

For the *Post,* obituaries must include all the basic information and be tightly written.

Unlike the *Post,* the *Knoxville News-Sentinel* runs obituaries only of people prominent in the community or of those whose achievements merit attention. "To get a good death story, we stress trying to make the person live. We want it to be a personality piece of sorts about a person who had a family and friends and achievements," says Wade Saye, assistant managing editor of the *News-Sentinel.*

"Our goal is to really catch the personality of the person in the story."

For *The Cincinnati Post,* a person need not be prominent to be a good subject for an obituary. "We did an obit once on a bus driver whose name meant nothing to most people," says Leon Hirtl, managing editor of the *Post.* "But we discovered that many people knew him as the bus driver who sang."

For those newspapers that run most or all deaths in their obituary columns, most obituaries are written tightly as follows:

BATCH, FRED J., 83, of 5623 80th St. N, died Thursday (June 21, 1984). Born in Boston, he came here in 1969 from Framingham, Mass. and was a retired musician. He was a member of Boston Musicians Protective Association. Survivors include his wife Nell; two sisters, Beatrice Carlson, Randolph, Mass., and Mildred Villa, Manchester, Mass., and several nieces and nephews. National Cremation Society.

BAUER, ALICE T., 84, of 219 Fourth Ave. N, died Thursday (June 21, 1984). Born in Poland, she came here in 1982 from Shenandoah, Pa. and was a seamstress. She was a member of Sacred Heart Catholic Church. Survivors include two sons, Thomas P. Cosky Sr., and Joseph J. Civrkowski of Pinellas Park; four grandchildren, and three great-grandchildren. R. Lee Williams Funeral Home.

Some newspapers provide this service with the paid death notice and will run staff-written obituaries only for the people the newspaper considers newsworthy.

But newsworthiness is sometimes an elusive guideline for an obituary. If the president of a local highway equipment firm is worth seven or eight paragraphs, why not the bookkeeper in his firm who emigrated from Hungary as a youth 50 years ago? What made him leave home and family, and how did he fare on arrival? What were his struggles to educate himself? Did he struggle alone, or did he have help? Friends and relatives would know.

"There are a lot of missed opportunities for good stories with obituaries," says Jim Adams, city editor of *The Cincinnati Post*. "It's my philosophy that you treat the obituary the same as any other news story—get quotes and talk to people and try to give a face to the person you're writing about."

Obituary Essentials

- Name, age, address and occupation of the deceased
- Time and place of death
- Cause of death
- Date and place of birth
- Survivors
- Funeral and burial arrangements

These are the bare essentials. For the longer obituary, add:

- Accomplishments and achievements
- Memberships in organizations
- Armed forces service
- Anecdotes of friends and relatives

Usually, the basic material is made available by the mortuary handling the death. Material may be available from the advertising department, which may receive a paid death notice from the funeral home. Occasionally, an obituary is called in by a person identifying himself or herself as a friend or relative. Be careful. Unless you know the person well, always verify the information by telephoning a relative or a mortuary. Some people call in phony death reports for the kick they get in seeing an obituary of someone who is very much alive.

Personal Details

Obviously, the obituaries of John Kennedy and John Lennon attracted readers. Readers are also interested in stories about the deaths of local people. Here, in capsule form, is the biography of someone we know or have heard about. We can read that the local Chevrolet dealer grew orchids as a hobby and had won prizes at local shows, or that the retired music teacher had set a national collegiate record for the 100-yard dash 50 years ago.

Obituaries balance these personal details with the obvious necessities—name, age, address, occupation, survivors, funeral arrangements.

The following obituary from the *Lexington* (Ky.) *Herald-Leader* includes the kind of detail that reveals, in just a few paragraphs, the story not only of a local businessman but of a class of people who pulled themselves up from humble beginnings:

Store Founder 'Al' Wenneker Dies at Age 76

Alex "Al" Wenneker, a prominent Lexington businessman, died here yesterday. He was 76.

With a rented storefront on Main Street measuring only 12 feet by 30 feet, eight kitchen chairs, empty boxes used as shelves and a relatively small stock of shoes, Wenneker and his wife Mary opened for business back in 1935. The business, located at 155 East Main Street until 1979, was called Wenneker's Sample Shoe Store.

Although no longer at the Main Street location, Wenneker's Shoe Stores have become a very successful business chain here with locations at three of Lexington's shopping malls.

Wenneker was a member of Temple Adath Israel.

A native of St. Louis, Mo., he was the son of William Wenneker, a Russian immigrant, and Libby McDowell Wenneker.

Besides his wife, survivors include two sons, James E. Wenneker and William R. Wenneker, both of Lexington; four sisters; and three grandchildren.

The funeral will be at 3 p.m. Tuesday at W.R. Milward Mortuary — Broadway. Burial will be in Lexington Cemetery. Visitation is from 3 to 5 and 7 to 9 p.m. today.

Light Touch

The obituary does not have to be written in somber tones of black. If the deceased was known to be genial and easygoing, why not write an obituary to match his or her life? Here is the beginning of such an obituary from *The Milwaukee Journal:*

Services for Paul W. LaPointe, widely known Milwaukee restaurateur who was better known as "Frenchy," will be at 11 a.m. Tuesday at the Wittkopp Funeral Home in Plymouth. Burial will follow in St. John's Cemetery in Elkhart Lake.

LaPointe, 72, died Saturday, apparently of a heart attack, at his summer home on Elkhart Lake. He lived in Milwaukee at 2629 N. Summit Ave.

A self-described workaholic, LaPointe owned and operated Frenchy's Restaurant at 1827 E. North Ave. from 1945 until he retired in 1975. In February 1979 he decided retirement was not for him and opened Paul's Small Cafe at 1854 E. Kenilworth Place, just around the corner from his old restaurant.

In an interview in 1980, LaPointe spoke of his futile attempt at retirement.

"Just wait until you get to be 65 or 70 and you're just looking at four walls," he told a reporter. . . .

Death of a Pilot

Joseph D. Robins was a popular man in his home town of Dalton, Mass. Everyone knew Joe. When he died in an airplane accident, the local weekly, the *Dalton News-Record,* carried his obituary as its number one news story following his burial. The obituary was written by Avice Meehan, the managing editor of the newspaper.

"I called Joe's two closest friends to find out what Joe was like," Meehan said. The nearby daily newspaper had carried a news story about the airplane crash, but by making several calls Meehan was able to reconstruct the accident in detail. She knew that her readers—Robins' friends and neighbors—would want to know just how Robins, a veteran pilot, had been killed.

She also knew that obituaries in the *Dalton News-Record* are read closely and carefully. Here is how she began the Robins obituary:

Lead based on his accomplishments

DALTON—Joseph D. Robins, a well-known flier and the most senior member of the Dalton Police Department, was buried Saturday in Ashuelot Street Cemetery following a Liturgy of Christian Burial at St. Agnes' Church.

Burial and funeral service

Age, cause of death

His death at the age of 59 in a plane crash last week at the North Adams Airport has left this community shaken.

Anecdote about Robins' popularity

"This is a small department," said Police Chief Anthony Calabrese. "We are like a family here."

Since his death, officers have worn black bands on their badges. The flags at Town Hall and at Crane & Co. have flown at half mast. . . .

Meehan began her story with the latest material, the burial. She went on to describe in detail the funeral, the members of the honor guard and the burial service before she turned to the event that took Robins' life.

As we have said, the basic techniques explained in the writing chapters are used in all these story types. Here, Meehan uses her best quote up high, in the third paragraph, to show the loss felt by Robins' colleagues, and she uses a good observation, the black bands on the badges, in the next paragraph.

The Obituary Lead

Generally, a person's occupation, accomplishments or distinctive contribution to the community is placed in the lead to identify him or her:

Occupation

Raymond T. Baron, former president of Paxton and Baron Co., book publishers, died yesterday in his home at 75 Arden Lane. He was 78 years old.

Accomplishment

Mortimer Heineman, an advertising executive who helped create the slogan "Promise her anything, but give her Arpège," died yesterday following a heart attack. He was 74 years old.

Contribution

Florence Gable Cerrin, long active in the local chapter of the American Red Cross, died yesterday at her home at 65 Eastern Parkway at the age of 94.

Funeral and **burial arrangements** can also be the basis of the lead. Some newspapers will try to vary their leads so that instead of every lead beginning with the report of someone's death, an occasional obituary will begin with the date, time and place of the funeral and burial.

Services for Albert D. Scott, 79, of 156 W. Central Ave., will be held tomorrow at 11 a.m. in the Boulder Funeral Home.

Burial for the retired pharmacist will follow in the Piedmont Cemetery in Oberlin.

Scott died yesterday at his home after suffering a heart attack. . . .

When the death has occurred a few days before, the lead usually will be based on the funeral and burial arrangements.

Delayed leads are rarely used for obituaries. If the delayed lead is in good taste, it is acceptable:

Margaret Wilson did get her last wish.

When she was told she had terminal cancer, the 73-year-old former high school teacher asked

that she be buried in her ancestral family plot in Ireland.

Next Tuesday, her ashes will be. . . .

An obituary should capture an important aspect of the person's life. If the deceased was an actor, the obituary emphasizes that from the beginning:

HOLLYWOOD, Calif.—Stage and film actor Arthur O'Connell, nominated twice for the best supporting Oscar, died here Monday. He was 73.

O'Connell made his American film debut with a small part in

Orson Welles' "Citizen Kane." He went on to work with many of Hollywood's top stars, including Jimmy Stewart, Bette Davis, Marilyn Monroe, Elvis Presley and William Holden. . . .

A man who made his fame as an expert on reptiles was described this way in his obituary:

LAKE CITY, Fla.—Widely known snake handler Ross Allen, who planned to enliven this sleepy North Florida town with a tourist

attraction called Alligator Town U.S.A., has died of cancer.

Mr. Allen, 73, had been ill for several weeks. . . .

When the author William Saroyan died, *The St. Petersburg Times* carried this lead on his obituary:

FRESNO, Calif.—William Saroyan, the boisterous, brilliant and reclusive American bard of Central California whose prize-winning books and plays underscored the

dreariness of life—and who readily admitted he was as great a writer as his admirers said he was—died Monday of cancer in Fresno. He was 72.

Cause of Death

The cause of death is included in the obituary. Sometimes, a family will request that a terminal illness not be mentioned in the obituary. Some families feel that cancer-related deaths should remain private, and obliging newspapers use the euphemism a "long illness" to refer to such diseases. A "brief illness" is often used to describe a heart attack. The best guideline is to include the cause of death and let the editor decide whether to use it.

The St. Petersburg Times began one of its obituaries this way:

> CLEARWATER—Anita Bilgore, a 35-year resident of Clearwater and the founder of Girls Clubs of Pinellas County, died Monday at Medical Center Hospital after a brief illness.

Nowhere was the cause of death given, but immediately beneath this obituary was another that began:

> NEW PORT RICHEY— Twelve-year-old Kathy Kruzlic, who battled terminal cancer for more than a year, died Monday at All Children's Hospital in St. Petersburg with her parents at her bedside.

Almost all newspapers and stations will give the cause of death when the deceased is a child or the death was the result of an accident.

Some newspapers go behind the immediate cause of death. When Thomas Schippers, a well-known orchestra conductor, died of cancer, *The New York Times* received several letters asking whether Schippers had been a smoker. The information should have been included in the obituary, the *Times* admitted. The newspaper had included this information in the obituaries of heavy smokers who died of lung cancer, an editor stated.

Sudden Death When death strikes a young or middle-aged person suddenly, the story can be as much news story as obituary, as we saw with fatal accident stories. With sudden death stories, the cause of death is essential and must go into the lead. Here is how Rick Hampson of the AP began his story about the shooting of John Lennon:

> NEW YORK--(AP)--JOHN LENNON, THE SINGER-SONGWRITER WHO HELPED MAKE THE BEATLES MUSICAL SUPERSTARS AND POP-CULTURE LEGENDS IN THE 1960S, WAS KILLED IN A LATE-NIGHT SPRAY OF GUNFIRE OUTSIDE HIS LUXURY APARTMENT BUILDING.

```
HE WAS THE CO-AUTHOR WITH PAUL MCCARTNEY OF
SUCH FAMOUS SONGS AS ``I WANT TO HOLD YOUR HAND,''
``YESTERDAY'' AND ``LET IT BE.''
     MINUTES AFTER THE SHOTS RANG OUT, POLICE TOOK A
SUSPECT INTO CUSTODY. EARLY TODAY, THEY CHARGED
MARK DAVID CHAPMAN, 25, OF HAWAII, WITH MURDER. NO
MOTIVE WAS KNOWN IMMEDIATELY.
```

Written under pressure shortly after Lennon was shot, the reporter had
to balance the facts about the slaying and Lennon's background, which was
obtained from the AP library.

Here is the beginning of the story about the death of Elvis Presley written
by Les Seago of AP soon after the death was reported:

```
     MEMPHIS, TENN.--(AP)--ELVIS PRESLEY, THE
MISSISSIPPI BOY WHOSE ROCK 'N' ROLL GUITAR AND
GYRATING HIPS CHANGED AMERICAN MUSIC STYLES, DIED
TUESDAY AFTERNOON OF HEART FAILURE. HE WAS 42.
     DR. JERRY FRANCISCO, MEDICAL EXAMINER FOR
SHELBY COUNTY, SAID THE CAUSE OF DEATH WAS
``CARDIAC ARRYTHMIA,'' AN IRREGULAR HEARTBEAT. HE
SAID ``THAT'S JUST ANOTHER NAME FOR A FORM OF HEART
ATTACK.''
     FRANCISCO SAID THE THREE-HOUR AUTOPSY
UNCOVERED NO SIGN OF ANY OTHER DISEASES, AND THERE
WAS NO SIGN OF ANY DRUG ABUSE.
     PRESLEY WAS DECLARED DEAD AT 3:30 P.M. 4:30
P.M. EDT AT BAPTIST HOSPITAL, WHERE HE HAD BEEN
TAKEN BY A FIRE DEPARTMENT AMBULANCE AFTER BEING
FOUND UNCONSCIOUS AT HIS GRACELAND MANSION.
```

When a widely known person dies, a local follow-up is sometimes possible.
The person may have been born or gone to school in town. Here is how a
Springfield paper handled the death in another state of a former resident:

Localizing the Obituary

> Robert Cowan, who served as
> governor from 1956–60, died today
> in a retirement home in St. Augus-
> tine, Fla. Cowan was born in
> Springfield and attended school
> here before moving to Gulfport in
> 1915. . . .

Sometimes, the local connection is less specific, as when the nation
mourned the death of President John F. Kennedy. Then, local observances
were the subject of many stories.

Sports

A sportswriter once asked Carl Furillo, the great outfielder for the Brooklyn Dodgers, how he learned to play the tough right-field wall in Ebbetts Field.

"I worked, that's how," Furillo replied.

And that, says the writer, Roger Kahn, is how a reporter learns to write sports stories. The first efforts may be as fumbling as the lead that a high school correspondent called in to a newspaper after his high school team had won a no-hit game:

> In the best-pitched game these
> old eyes have ever seen. . . .

Or the sport being covered may be as confusing as it was to Becky Teagarden, a sportswriter for the *Columbus* (Ohio) *Citizen-Journal* when she covered her first basketball game.

"I didn't know what was going on," she recalls. But she had the good sense to corner the coach after the game. She asked him, "Tell me, what happened out there?"

The high school reporter learned, too. His first task was to learn to keep himself out of the story. The reader is interested in the athletes and the game, not in the writer.

For most beginning sportswriters, the important lesson is that good sports writing is good writing. This means getting to the point quickly, stressing human interest, avoiding sports jargon and clichés, and giving the reader some insight into the game or the personality being described.

In other words, sports writers follow the principles of good writing that have been described in previous chapters.

School Sports

Sports writers who aspire to cover the Cleveland Indians, Dallas Cowboys or Golden State Warriors break in on school or non-professional sports. Although many people follow professional sports, many more are fans of the local high school or regional college teams. These fans expect the same quality of reporting and writing the fans of professional teams are given.

Look at the beginning of a story about a game between two Colorado high school baseball teams:

> Longmont pitcher Tim Fobes was in trouble in the seventh inning of the Trojans' 5–4 home-field win over Thompson Valley Friday afternoon. But coach Joe Brooks was not about to pull him out.
>
> "I walked out and told him we were going to win or lose with Tim Fobes," Brooks said after the game. Fobes survived the ordeal, but a game that Longmont appeared to have in its pocket suddenly became interesting.

John Gunn of the *Times-Call* in Longmont, Colo., is informative and entertaining in this lead. He gives the final score, and he provides the reader with a human interest detail. In just two sentences in his lead, Gunn has included several of the essential elements of the game story.

Game Story Essentials

- The score
- Names of teams, type of sport
- When and where the game took place
- Key incident or play
- Outstanding player(s)
- League
- Scoring
- Effect of game on league standings
- Strategy
- Crowd size; behavior, if a factor
- Statistics
- Injuries
- Winning or losing streaks
- Duration of game
- Record(s) set
- Postgame quotes

As we said, any of the essentials can be the major element that is placed in the lead of the story. Let's look at a Monday newspaper that carried the results of Sunday's professional football games. None of the stories began with the score alone. All used an incident, a play, an outstanding player, or an injury along with the score:

The Sports Lead

Injury

Notice that the score is not in the lead but in the second paragraph. The writer, Norm Miller of *Daily News,* concentrates on the injury angle and its consequences in the first three paragraphs of the story.

LOS ANGELES—For all practical purposes the champion Raiders' second victory of the new season was clinched on the sixth play after the opening kickoff yesterday when the Packers' starting quarterback, Lynn Dickey, was kayoed by a back injury.

With a pea-green rookie named Randy Wright at QB for Green Bay, the bullying Raiders defense had a laugher while the 46,265 paying customers sat through a rather boring 28–7 Los Angeles win.

Dickey, one of the more highly-regarded NFC quarterbacks, was forced out of the game after 2½ minutes when he caught a knee in the back during a blitz-sack by Mike Davis, the Raiders' 205-pound safety. At the time, the contact did not appear rough enough to cause a serious injury.

Behind the Score. Scores are remembered for a few hours, says a sports writer. But the emotions endure. By capturing the human element in the game, the writer may tell a story that moves beyond the athletic field. This picture by Morris Berman of the *Pittsburgh Post-Gazette* captured the moment that a battered Y. A. Tittle of the New York Giants sensed his career as a quarterback was at an end.

Morris Berman, *Pittsburgh Post-Gazette*

Record and Outstanding Player

CHICAGO—Walter Payton ripped off a 72-yard touchdown run and rushed for 179 yards in 20 carries yesterday, breaking Jim Brown's NFL combined yardage record and leading the Chicago Bears to a 27–0 victory over the Denver Broncos.

Payton also caught two passes for seven yards for a combined total of 186 yards giving him a career total of 15,517 to Brown's mark of 15,459.

—Associated Press

Key Play

Effect on the league standings

The second and third
paragraphs follow up the
lead angle with quotations
from a postgame interview.

ATLANTA—Ed Murray drilled
a 48-yard field goal 5:06 into overtime
yesterday to give the Detroit Lions a
27–24 victory over the Atlanta Falcons.

NEW YORK—The Giants, who
had not begun a season with two victo-
ries since 1968, upset the Cowboys,
28–7, yesterday at Giants Stadium to
stay on top of the standings as the only
unbeaten team in the NFC East.

The oldest Giant, Dave Jennings,
searched his memory for the last time
this team was all alone in first place.
"Darn, maybe 1929?"

"I could get used to it," said
George Martin.

When writing for a weekly newspaper or when the game is a few days
old before it reaches the newspaper's columns, the lead will emphasize a personality or perhaps the consequences of the home team's victory or loss—injuries for the next game, change in standings, changes in starting players.

Imagination is vital to the sports story. There are so many sports, such a mul-
titude of games that after a while the sports pages seem to swim in team names
and numbers. Sports is the story of men and women straining mind and body
to reach beyond their limits, of unusual people and strange events. The stories
should reflect this.

Be Imaginative

When Nolan Ryan pitched his record fifth no-hit baseball game, the
story was as much his nonchalance as the accomplishment. When a team, the
Montreal Expos, cannot win a game against the Los Angeles Dodgers in their
home park, the story of still another loss is the story of jinxes and superstitions.

"People forget about game scores in one hour," says T. J. Simers of *The
Commercial Appeal* in Memphis. "But a story about emotion may stick with
them for two hours." Simers is being sarcastic about the durability of a news
story, but he does have a point.

The writer who captures the human dimension of the event creates a
story the reader will remember, and this is what we all strive for in journalism—the story that makes the reader sit up and take notice.

Leads can focus on the small details unseen by fans in the stadium or
watching on television:

Paul Williams leaned a foot too
far to his right last night, and that
was the ball game.

This was the beginning of a story about a baseball team trailing 1–0 in the bottom of the ninth with two out. Williams had walked, the next batter had two balls and no strikes. And suddenly the game was over because Williams was picked off first base by the pitcher.

Structuring the Sports Story

When possible, the sportswriter tries to match the drama of the game with his or her account of it. The difference between the fans' observations and the sports story is the knowledge that the sportswriter takes to the game. This insight must be shown in the story. For this reason, sportswriters often like to begin their stories with the little things that are the turning points of the game, such as the base runner's too-long lead that abruptly ended a possible ninth-inning rally.

Increasingly, delayed leads are put on sports stories. The first paragraph or two may contain an incident, anecdote, a key play or a strategic move. Then, in the second or third paragraph, the writer gives the score. Next, a few paragraphs are devoted to the important points of the game—the scoring, significant substitutions, injuries, or changes in the standings.

If most fans already know the result of a game, it is a good idea to focus on a key play or turning point in the game:

Some clutch free-throw shooting by Paul Threet and a lucky bounce helped Park School clinch the co-championship of the Independent Athletic Conference basketball league. Threet made both attempts in a one-and-one situation Thursday with seven seconds left in overtime as Park defeated visiting St. Mary's for the Deaf 62–61 in a game here. . . .

—*Buffalo Evening News*

Another technique is to use the comments and observations of the players or coaches involved in key plays or strategy. Most quotes are obtained in locker-room interviews after the game, a necessity for game coverage.

Restraint Essential

Sportswriters are enthusiasts. Sometimes they write as though they are covering the end of the world, not a game. This kind of enthusiasm leads to these excesses:

Shrillness This is a common ailment, especially of some television announcers. In football, every other play is accompanied by a rise in the voice. A writer can be shrill, too. A story written with high-pitch intensity from lead to end irritates the reader. Every game has pauses, lulls, even dull periods. The story should not be dull, but it should not scream at the reader.

Advice for the Novice Sports Writer

Here are some do's and don'ts suggested by experienced sportswriters:

Avoid commenting in straight game stories. Often, comments reflect lazy reporting.

Use good quotes that reveal important aspects of the game. Avoid inane quotes.

Watch out for the coach who has the same quotes every season, every game.

Be in touch with the reader. Too often, sportswriters write for each other.

Don't sacrifice information for style. First, give the information. The style will come naturally.

Don't use war references, such as "battling," or "troops being sent in." You're covering a game, not a war.

Overstatement is the sign of the beginner. If anything, understate.

Don't use sports jargon—*netminder, pigskin, hoop, horsehide.*

Athletes are human, not gods. Avoid making them into heroes.

Overstatement Games sometimes are made into battles of titans, and the language of the story is exaggerated and pumped up. Writing of this sort often flows shamelessly in stories about the games of traditional rivals—Green Bay Packers–Chicago Bears, Stanford–University of California at Berkeley, New York Knicks–Boston Celtics, Kansas–Missouri, Iowa State–University of Iowa.

Mindless Emotionalism Fans do become excited by games. They have even been known to hurl beer cans at players and officials. Some fans become so involved with the action that it becomes a life-and-death conflict for them. Sportswriters should reflect the intensity and the seriousness of sports, but they must also keep their distance. These are, after all, only games.

Extra Dimension

Most of those who turn to their newspapers to read of yesterday's games already know the results. They might have seen one game on television and heard the scores of others on television or radio. The reporter's task is to add an extra ingredient.

Emery Filmer, a sports reporter for *The Advocate* in Stamford, Conn., was covering a local team in the state baseball playoffs. On Tuesday, the team, the Stamford Catholic High School Crusaders, had upset the defending state champions, 2–1. Then, on Wednesday, Stamford lost 7–2 in the semifinal.

Filmer was writing for the Thursday newspaper. *The Advocate* is an afternoon newspaper, which meant that most fans following the local team already knew it had lost.

How would you handle this situation? A story that begins this way would be barely adequate:

```
Andrew Warde High School defeated the Stamford
Catholic High School Crusaders yesterday in the
semifinal state baseball playoffs by a score of 7-2.
```

There is nothing wrong with this lead, except that it repeats what many readers already know. How about this one:

```
The Crusaders from Stamford Catholic High School hung
up their gloves yesterday and will have to wait another
year before trying for the state high school baseball
championship. The Crusaders lost to Andrew Warde 7-2 in a
semifinal playoff game yesterday.
```

Although this lead is also adequate, it says little more than the previous lead. All it does is add a picturesque but trite phrase, "hung up their gloves."

Filmer was able to write an effective lead because he understood the key to the Crusaders' loss, the absence of their leading pitcher. He added a dimension to his story because of his knowledge of the team and the game. Here is how Filmer's story begins:

Warde eliminates Catholic, 7-2

by Emery Filmer
The Advocate

Here are the two sides of the Stamford Catholic High School Crusaders:

On Tuesday night, they played a near-perfect game in upsetting the defending state champion Westhill Vikings, 2-1, in an FCIAC first-round playoff game. But on Wednesday, they fell behind 5-0 in the first inning and ended up on the short end of a 7-2 score against Andrew Warde, a club they had beaten 8-3 last month

So, what's the difference?

Roger Haggerty perhaps. After all, he wasn't pitching Wednesday.

"Knowing that we did not have to face Haggerty tonight was a definite factor in our favor," admitted Warde coach Ed Bengermino after his team had qualified for its first appearance in the FCIAC championship game.

Haggerty pitched a brilliant two-hitter against the heavy-hitting Vikings on Tuesday to vault the Crusaders into Wednesday's semifinal against the Eastern Division champions, Warde. It was Haggerty's sixth victory of the year and lowered his ERA to 1.82.

But, unfortunately, he can not pitch every day. And therein lies the difference in the Stamford Catholic Crusaders.

Wednesday, Catholic manager Mickey Lione tabbed lanky righthander Matt Reed to start against Warde. Now Reed has had a better-than-average season (3.95 ERA), but his three wins were the second most on the team.

The difference was apparent immediatly. The first five Crimson Eagle batters to face Reed all reached base, and all scored.

"Reed just didn't throw strikes," said Lione. "He was constantly falling behind

2 and 0 and 3 and 0 on everybody. So he had to come in with a lot of fat pitches."

Although he only walked one batter, Reed was never ahead of a hitter through the first five batters.

John Martin led off with a double and Mark Carlson followed with run-scoring single. So after two batters, Reed had allowed one run and two hits, which were the seven-inning totals for Haggerty a night earlier.

After a walk and a Greg Cantwell single, Joe Braun singled in the second run. After Reed retired the next man on a ground out which made it 3-0, Dan Schettino closed out the first-inning onslaught with a two-run single.

Before half of the crowd had arrived, Warde led, 5-0.

"We got beat by Haggerty last year and this year and both times he just blew us away," Bengermino admitted.

(Please turn to Page 32)

Story Types

In the Newsroom

When the reporter arrived at his desk early one morning he could tell he would not be out on his beat for at least two hours. On his desk were a batch of papers, a couple of notes from the city editor and a telephone message. Without taking time for his usual chat with the reporter at the next desk, he set to work.

First, he looked through the papers. Several were announcements and press releases. One was about a regional history conference that would be held on the campus of the local college. Another concerned a skating party to be held Sunday for a charity. The third was about a speech to be given by the governor next week. He put these in one pile, took a slip of paper and wrote *advances* on it and clipped the works together.

Another sheet contained a release from an army base about the promotion of a local soldier. He scribbled the word *personal* across the top of the press release.

He knew that he could handle these releases quickly. The others would take a little more time. One was an obituary, another required some calls to localize a wire story, and the third necessitated a call to the weather bureau for a weather story the city editor wanted for the newspaper's early edition.

Better get the easy ones out of the way first, he decided. He turned to the advances and the personal item. These would require short pieces. In fact, these tightly written pieces are called **briefs** or **shorts**.

Briefs

The trick to writing briefs, he had been told his first day on the job, is to give the reader the basics. "No frills, no ornamentation. The Five W's and an H and get out of there fast," an experienced reporter had told him. No more than two or three paragraphs, unless the advance is about a big meeting of the city council that is coming up, or the personal is about the appointment of a new minister to the largest church in town, or the marriage in town next month of the 72-year-old senior U.S. senator.

Precedes

The reporter then looked over the seven-paragraph press release from the local college that detailed the history conference to be held next week. He wrote a precede:

The eighth annual Midwestern Conference of History Teachers will be held on the Hampden College campus next Thursday and Friday.

Registration will take place in McGuire Auditorium Wednesday afternoon and Thursday. The fee is $5. Sessions will be held in the Liberal Arts building.

The main speaker will be Professor Felix S. Woodward of Oxford University. He will speak Thursday evening on "Breaking the Plains."

The smaller the newspaper, the longer the precede. Here is how the skating benefit story was written:

A fund-raising skating party to assist the Norwalk Community Hospital will be held Sunday at the Wheels Roller Skating Center at 61 Converse St.

There will be two sessions, from 7 to 9 p.m. and from 9:30 to 11:30 p.m. Music will be provided by "Soul Sounds." Admission is $3.

The income will be used to furnish a children's playroom in the hospital.

Here is an advance from *The Berkshire Eagle,* a daily newspaper with a circulation of 31,000 that stresses local news. The *Eagle* has room for stories like this:

A talk on bobcats in Massachusetts, part of the Berkshire Sanctuaries predator series, will be given tonight at 7:30 in the members room at Pleasant Valley Wildlife Sanctuary in Lenox.

Chet McCord, who is in charge of research for the state Division of Fisheries and Wildlife, will be the speaker.

While a graduate student at the University of Massachusetts, McCord studied bobcats on the Prescott Peninsula near Quabbin Reservoir in central Massachusetts. Using collars with radio transmitters, he studied the bobcats' movements and habitat preferences.

Fee for the talk is $1 for Massachusetts Audubon Society members and $2 for non-members.

The precede, or advance, tells people about events they may want to attend or at least want to know about. Knowing that the local school board will be considering a change in the busing policy, parents may call or write board members to express their opinions if they cannot attend the meeting. A family may not want to go roller skating but might send a donation to the community hospital after reading the short item about the benefit.

Precede Essentials

- Event or activity planned
- Date, time, place of activity
- Purpose
- Sponsor
- Fee, admission charge, if any
- Background, if a significant event

Names make news. In big cities, the names that make news are those of public figures—television personalities, the wealthy, politicians, athletes, the social set. In smaller towns, the names are those of neighbors, and their comings and goings are recorded in detail. These news items are called **personals.**

Here is the beginning of a personal item from "Notes on People" in *The New York Times,* daily circulation 950,000:

> There were people who looked like George Burns, Goldie Hawn, Woody Allen and Katharine Hepburn. And there were quite a few who looked like Prince Charles and Lady Diana Spencer.
> The party Tuesday night at Ted Hook's Backstage restaurant. . . .

Here are two personal items from the Hinsdale correspondent on the weekly *Dalton News-Record:*

> Airman First Class Edward G. Barrett and Mrs. Barrett have returned to their home in Hampton, Va., after spending a week with their grandparents, Mr. and Mrs. Richard Boker.
>
> The Ladies Aid Society will have a food sale during the annual town meeting this Saturday. Ethel Perth and Julia Anderson are in charge of the event. Nancy Jenkins is in charge of the snack bar where homemade doughnuts and coffee will be available. Hours are 1 p.m. to 5 p.m.

Births, engagements and weddings, awards, retirements, promotions, confirmations, bar and bat mitzvahs, appointments—all are duly recognized.

"Small is beautiful," says Avice Meehan, managing editor of *The News-Record.* "Mainly we concentrate on the little things—items about the Boy Scouts, the high school junior that the Lions Club has selected to represent the club in the All-State Band at the district convention, the names of officers of the local Historical Commission."

The personal cements communities. It tells people about the successes, and sometimes the tribulations, of the family down the street, around the block and at the edge of town.

Some newspapers use personals imaginatively. When Waconah Regional High School held its graduation, *The News-Record* ran a paragraph about the plans of each of the graduates for colleges and careers.

> Frank Availe, son of Frank and Karen Availe, County Road, Becket. Undecided.
>
> Debra Wuinee, daughter of Mr. and Mrs. Robert Wuinee of 32 East Deming St., Dalton. BCC to study accounting.

Personal Essentials

- Name, identification
- Newsworthy activity
- Connection of individual(s) to activity
- Special or unusual activities in connection with the event

Personals are usually handled in a straightforward manner. If there is a special or unusual activity connected to the event, that can become the lead—the wedding held on the lawn of a summer home, the birthday party celebrated atop a mountain.

For weddings, the names of the bride and groom and the location of the wedding are carried in the lead. Also essential to the story are the background of the couple and the names of the parents:

> Ann Margarita Poray and Marvin Abercrombie were married yesterday in St. John's Church.
>
> The bride is a teacher in the Fairfield Junior High School. She was graduated from Weston College. Abercrombie is with the First National Bank in Fairfield. He is a graduate of Brown University.
>
> The bride is the daughter of Mr. and Mrs. Phillip Poray of 62 Antonio St. The bridegroom is the son of Dr. and Mrs. Albert Abercrombie of Boston.

For engagements, the parents of the bride-to-be usually make the announcement and this is placed in the lead:

> Mr. and Mrs. Burton V. Carroway announced the engagement of their daughter, Faye Elizabeth, to Robert Becker, son of Mr. and Mrs. Stanley Becker.
>
> The wedding is planned for Sept. 21.
>
> Ms. Carroway, 435 Eastern St., is a librarian with the state legislative service. Becker is a salesman for Reed Chevrolet and lives at 67 Marion Ave.

Small town newspapers carry stories about the celebration of wedding anniversaries (usually 25th, 35th, 40th and 50th).

> Mr. and Mrs. W. J. Stagg were honored by their children in celebration of their golden wedding anniversary Saturday in the Reorganized Church of Jesus Christ of the Latter Day Saints. At the celebration, they renewed their wedding vows.
>
> Mildred Forrest and William J. Stagg were married on July 25, 1935, in Lawrence, Kan. They have three married children and five grandchildren.

Most briefs can be handled quickly because few require additional information. The material that has been included in the announcement or press release usually is sufficient. Two points to remember:

1. If there is any indication of an unusual situation or circumstance in the material, check it out. There might be a good story hidden there.
2. Avoid running the press releases in the form given to you. They should be rewritten after the facts are checked.

There are other stories that can be written from the office but require reporting and checking. Let's begin with a story that needs to be **localized.**

Localizing the News

The logic of localizing news stories is simple. As we learned in chapter 3, readers prefer to read about people and events close to them. Proximity, we learned, is a basic news determinant.

A reporter is handed a wire service story that lists the names of 11 people who were killed in Ohio when the bus they were riding in collided with a truck. Two of those who died were local residents.

The reporter calls the AP to ask if anyone from the local area was injured. He also makes a few calls to gather background information on the two people who were killed and the funeral arrangements.

An essential task is to make sure that the names are spelled correctly. They are often garbled in wire stories in such situations. Another is to verify that the people involved are actually from the home community. Mistakes do happen.

Here is the wire story:

```
    YOUNGSTOWN, OHIO--ELEVEN PEOPLE WERE KILLED
WHEN THE CHARTERED BUS IN WHICH THEY WERE RIDING
COLLIDED WITH A TRUCK ON U.S. 80 LAST NIGHT.
    THE DRIVER OF THE TRUCK AND 15 PASSENGERS WERE
INJURED. THE BUS HAD BEEN RENTED BY A CHURCH GROUP,
THE PRESBYTERIAN FELLOWSHIP LEAGUE, THAT WAS
HOLDING A CONFERENCE IN AKRON.
    WITNESSES TOLD INVESTIGATING OFFICERS THE
TRUCK SEEMED TO VEER INTO THE BUS AS THE BUS TRIED TO
PASS IT.
    NAMES OF THE DEAD ARE:
    ALVIN BAILEY, 59. . . .
```

The localized version began this way:

Two local residents were killed last night when the bus in which they were passengers collided with a truck on U.S. 80 near Youngstown, Ohio.

The dead are: Alvin Bailey, 59, of 12 Belford Place and Charlene Dearborn, 21, of 68 Topper St.

The Associated Press reports they were attending. . . .

News writers can localize major national and international events, as Ingrid Peritz did for *The Gazette* in Montreal. The Islamic revolution in Iran caused a rift among Iranian students studying abroad. Some became followers of the fundamentalist Ayatollah Khomeini, the aged absolute ruler of the country, and some opposed his rule, which they described as tyrannical. The students at the university Peritz was attending often had heated debates, and this gave her an idea for a story for an anniversary of the revolution in Iran.

Here is how her story began:

The famous scowl and penetrating eyes of Iran's leader dominate Mohammed Abbaszadeh's sparsely furnished living room in his Montreal West apartment.

It is as though Ayatollah Ruhollah Khomeini, the 81-year-old patriarch of Iran's Islamic revolution who seized power three years ago yesterday, watches over Iranians in Montreal as carefully as he does his countrymen at home.

"I support Khomeini with all of my power," says Abbaszadeh, 27, a devout Moslem who has lived in Montreal for three years. "His is the only way."

Yet that "way" stabs through the very heart of Montreal's 2,000-member Iranian community, dividing the Iranians into two camps: Abbaszadeh's Khomeini followers pitted against an anti-Khomeini majority.

A bitter student rivalry between the two Khomeini factions in the city has been fuelled by anti-Khomeini charges that the Iranian government is tampering with student allowances, and claims the Iranian embassy is cancelling student passports in acts of political persecution. For their part, the Khomeini followers in Montreal brand the anti-Khomeini students as terrorists and agents of the U.S. Central Intelligence Agency.

After this general overview, Peritz tells individual stories, beginning with Reza:

Reza, 25, shuffles nervously in his plaid shirt and rumpled jeans, clutching his chemistry books under one arm. His jet black hair is dishevelled, his large eyes weary and bloodshot, as though the pressures of exams have worn him out.

But it is not exam time at Concordia—Reza is beset by worries that most students never dream of.

"They (Iranian authorities) know who we are," he says in a whisper, his eyes darting back and forth. "They know everybody against the regime . . . they take our passports and force us back to Iran. But if we return, they will execute us at the airport."

Under no circumstances will Reza reveal his last name—his family will be persecuted in Iran, he warns, if his words reach the authorities back home.

Reza says his fears are matched by dozens of Iranian students. Like him, many were drawn to Montreal by its promise of a coveted university degree. Some followed cousins and brothers; others were lured by our universities' one-time relaxed admission policies. . . .

Localizing Essentials

- Name of local person or situation that justifies localizing
- General situation or background
- Source of information—name of wire service or organization.

A **folo** is a story that follows up on a theme in another story. If a national educational organization reports that a growing percentage of high school graduates is putting off college, the enterprising reporter who sees the wire story hits the telephone to call area high schools, junior colleges and four-year schools. Folos usually run the day after the original story appears.

When President Reagan sent Congress a budget that would have cut back on services to the needy, reporters sought to determine the local consequences. Here is how one newswriter began her follow-up story:

Follow-up Stories

> Needy local residents would be severely hurt by Reagan administration proposals in Congress that would cut and restrict many federal programs.
>
> This was the opinion of officials of several public and private organizations concerned with social, economic and health services for the poor here. Margaret Murtagh, executive secretary of the Family and Children's Services agency, a private organization, said:
>
> "Half of the proposed reductions affect the poor. The budget seems to single these people out."
>
> Another local agency, the Hospital and Home. . . .

Some people sit at home and paste stamps into albums, while others fly model airplanes. Most hobbies are perfectly safe. But some people climb mountains. Why?

This question occurred to several editors after an icefall entombed 11 mountain climbers under 70 feet of ice on Mount Rainier one Sunday in June, and just a few hours later five others died after a climbing party plummeted 2,000 feet down Mount Hood.

Reporters were told to find some local mountain climbers. Their answers made an interesting folo to the wire stories of the tragedies. Here is one local folo:

> Contrary to the view of one well-known mountain climber, climbers do not attempt to scale mountains just because they are there.
>
> "First, you have the beauty," said John Simac, 78 Harper Ave., who has climbed Mount Rainier in the state of Washington a dozen times, as well as other mountains.
>
> "Then you have the challenge. Sometimes, it is almost too great," Simac said.
>
> Then the challenge defeats the climber with frostbite and frustration. But sometimes the loss is greater. Last Sunday, 11 men climbing Mount Rainier were entombed when. . . .

Notice the insertion in the fourth paragraph of the **news peg,** the reason for the folo.

Reaction stories are folos. When the mayor of Boston described the city as "a racist city," the *Boston Herald American* followed up his accusation with reactions from various people. Here is how the folo by Greg O'Brien begins:

News peg—Reaction

> Mayor Kevin H. White yesterday called Boston "a racist city," touching off a wave of reaction from politicians, church leaders, union officials and businessmen.

News peg elaborated

> White, who has consistently rejected charges that racism is widespread in Boston, spoke extemporaneously yesterday to a group of 75 persons attending a Greater Boston Civil Rights Coalition conference. He concluded last winter, he said, that blacks and other minorities in Boston did not have equal access to "institutions around town."

Reaction elaborated

> Reaction to the mayor's remarks differed widely. Lt. Gov. Thomas P. O'Neill III said that racism wasn't confined to Boston, but was a statewide problem.
>
> "It's not just the city," he said. "We've had a racial problem statewide. Kevin White takes it on the chin when everything is thrust on one city. We have real serious problems statewide. Government is supposed to provide a brand of leadership that provides access, and that means everybody."

Folo Essentials

- Reaction, response, local aspect of an event
- Event that gives the folo its news peg

These are the absolute minimum essentials of the folo. The rest of the story should include the elaboration and buttressing of these essential elements.

The *Herald American* jumped on another story involving the city administration. This time the story was about a dress code that city hall employees were supposed to adhere to. The dress code contained the following provision for female city employees:

> Wearing apparel must be clean, neat and of a "business look" nature. Pants suits, dungarees, slacks or shorts will not be permitted at any time.

As soon as the code was issued, the *Herald American* assigned reporters to do a story on the new code. The newspaper also assigned a reporter to ask fashion designers for their reactions.

If the reaction story had appeared the next day, it would have been a folo. But since the reporter was able to report and write the story so quickly, the reaction appeared alongside the story about the code. The accompanying story about the comments of fashion designers became a **sidebar.**

Sidebar

A sidebar is a story that emphasizes an aspect of another story that is printed nearby. When Bonnie Britt did a series of articles for the *Houston Chronicle* on the dangers of insulation used in the construction of mobile homes, she wanted to get the reaction of the mobile home industry, which was being sued by a number of Texas mobile home owners.

Britt sought out the attorney for the industry. Although he was unwilling to comment, Britt dug into his background for the following sidebar that appeared alongside one of her articles in the series:

> One of the ironies in the formaldehyde story is the involvement of former Atty. Gen. John Hill, who while in office obtained 440 injunctions and $5 million in civil penalties against polluters.
>
> Hill is the lead attorney hired to defend the Texas mobile home industry in the 70 or so lawsuits filed by mobile home buyers irritated by indoor pollutants.
>
> The second irony underlying Hill's defense of the industry is that formaldehyde irritation struck close to home. In this case, his grandchildren's home. Hill's grandchildren (ages 1 and 4) became sick after exposure to urea formaldehyde foam insulation in their parents' brick home, according to plaintiff attorneys Robert Bennett and Andy Vickery.
>
> When asked why he would take so prominent a role in the cases if this were true, Hill would only say "No comment." . . .

The essentials for the sidebar are the same as those for the folo. The news peg of the original story and the reaction or response are placed high up and close together.

Roundup Stories

The **roundup** is frequently used to combine several stories into one. The roundup is based on finding an element common to two or more events and then writing a lead that reflects the common element.

When a heavy fog covered the East Coast there were ship collisions in New York harbor and off Virginia. The AP put the two stories together. The common element in the lead was the fog:

The Staten Island ferry collided with a freighter in New York harbor and two freighters collided off Virginia Wednesday morning, as dense fog cloaked the East Coast. More than 80 persons were injured in the accidents, none seriously, and all four ships were damaged.

In New York, the ferryboat American Legion, carrying 2,500 rush-hour commuters, was near the Statue of Liberty when it collided with the freighter Heogh Orchid at about 7:20 a.m. injuring 83 persons, officials said.

"It looked like a large gray shadow coming out of the fog," said ferry passenger Matthew Bendix, 17.

Four of the 83 injured were hospitalized in satisfactory condition, and the others were treated and released, hospital officials said.

A Greek cargo vessel, the Hellenic Carrier, was taking on water and leaving a trail of diesel fuel as it limped toward Norfolk, Va., after it collided with another ship at about 7:20 a.m., said spokesmen for the 5th Coast Guard District headquarters at Portsmouth, Va.

The Greek ship's crewmen huddled in lifeboats for more than two hours before being rescued, Coast Guard officials said. Two were slightly injured, one suffering a sprained ankle and another treated aboard a Navy destroyer with a tetanus shot for cuts.

Mahfooz Hussain, who was at the wheel of the Hellenic Carrier when the two ships crashed, said there was a heavy blanket of fog over the area.

Notice that the lead includes both incidents. The body of the story amplifies each accident separately, one after the other.

Roundups are frequently used for traffic accident stories. You can spot them after a weekend or a holiday, or when bad weather has caused a number of accidents:

Crews in North Dakota found the bodies of two people yesterday who died in a blizzard that dumped up to 25 inches of snow. The same blizzard paralyzed northeastern Wyoming, where it claimed three lives. Further east, thunderstorms raged over Tennessee, leaving one man dead and another critically injured after they were struck by lightning.

—Associated Press

Roundup Essentials

- Lead focuses on a common element
- Body takes each incident or event and elaborates it in turn
- Causes, consequences, quotes may be inserted high in story if they explain the situation

Weather Stories

The spectators in the large auditorium were filing out after having watched the second round of competition for Miss Iowa. The lines moved slowly, and people were chatting. But they weren't talking about Miss Muscatine's chances of making it to the finals, or the fact that Miss Dubuque seemed embarrassed about parading in front of a few thousand people in a skimpy bathing suit.

They were looking out the windows of the auditorium watching a hailstorm gather force, and the talk was about the weather.

"It'll tear up the beans pretty bad," one man said. "Wind like that is worse than hail when you come down to it."

Everybody talks about the weather, and every reporter takes a turn at doing the weather story. The television weather people have made the nation even more conscious of weather. The mobility of the population has made people interested in weather outside their immediate vicinity. The traveler going to California wonders what the weather is like in San Francisco, and the Florida-bound family checks to see whether their Christmas holiday will be spent under blue skies in 80-degree weather.

Most of us have friends or relatives in other cities and states. When a windstorm hits Washington, a flood strikes the midwestern states or a drought wilts crops and people in the Southwest, we sympathize and might even write or call our relatives or friends.

In short, weather is news.

Locally, people want to know what the forecast is, every day, and when there is anything out of the usual, they want a full story. If it is turning warmer, people will put on lightweight clothing. If rain is forecast, umbrellas and overshoes come out of the closet. If the weekend looks grim, the sports fans stock up on beer and snacks for a weekend of television sports.

Weather stories are often routinely written, but they need not be. When a heavy snowfall hit New York City, Meyer Berger, a gifted writer who covered local news for *The New York Times,* wrote that the storm "left tremendous drifts in the countryside, and in main urban avenues it veiled skylines, tufting skyscrapers and steeples with enormous white caps."

Cooling Off. Human interest is an essential part of all news stories, even those about the weather. When the temperature flirted with the 100 degree mark, children in Baltimore took to the fire hydrants, and youngsters on a Kentucky farm cooled off in their mother's washtub.
Top, Richard Childress, *The Baltimore Sun; bottom*, Stewart Bowman, *The Courier-Journal*

The daily weather forecast was taken out of the routine by H. Allen Smith of the *New York World-Telegram* who wrote what may be the best one-liner in all of journalism:

Snow, followed by small boys on sleds.

As you can see, there are two types of weather stories, the daily forecast and the longer piece for unusual or extreme weather. Here are the essentials for both types:

Weather Essentials

- Forecast for next 24 hours
- Long-range forecast
- Most recent temperatures, humidity and precipitation
- Record highs and lows, if any

When weather is severe, the writer must consider the consequences. The effects are included along with the basics:

- Deaths, injuries, property damage
- Amount of precipitation (or drought)
- Strength of wind
- Any record(s) set
- Predicted duration of severe weather
- Consequences:
  Traffic—roads blocked, accidents
  Travel—air, bus, rail, local travel curtailed or stopped
  Public services—power, water and telephone outages
  Business—crops, tourism affected; business shut down temporarily
  Schools—closings or changed hours

Writers try to show the consequences of unusual weather by introducing human interest, the effect of the weather on people. When unusually warm weather settled over western Massachusetts, *The Berkshire Eagle* reporter wrote that "large numbers of baby carriages blossomed forth on North Street and mopeds were seen put-putting about."

When the temperature reached 99 degrees in Baltimore one June day, a reporter for *The Baltimore Sun* had a novel idea for his story. He talked to youngsters at the zoo, and this became his lead. The desk then put the national weather roundup in the body, and the story ended with a local reference.

Summary

Different as they may seem at first glance, these 15 types of stories have much in common. All are written in anticipation of the reader's or viewer's questions. This means: All persons in the story are fully identified, the events reported are backgrounded, and the possible consequences of the event or situation are presented.

The best sources are used, and they are quoted when possible. Drama and human interest are essential.

Underlying all news writing is the knowledge and the competence in craft that the news writer takes to the task. You can write good stories only if you know what you are writing about and if you have control of the writing techniques that make up the craft of journalism.

PART FIVE

Photojournalism

Dorothea Lange, The Library
of Congress

Visual Reporting

The photojournalist uses the camera to give us pictures that provide information, insights and revelations about people, events and ideas. The photojournalist sees and portrays the world in visual terms.

Good news and feature photos are truthful, informative, interesting and have significance or impact. They may be educational, entertaining. They are technically sound.

Photojournalists know people, how they live, work and play. Their photographs reflect this sensitivity and understanding. The picture-storyteller also is a master of his or her equipment, knowing just which lens, shutter speed and aperture are appropriate for each shot.

From earliest times, people have used pictures to make a record of their thoughts and experiences—the hunt etched on the walls of caves, mourning women scratched on pottery, ceremonies painted on wood and canvas. Modern man and woman make pictures, too, millions of them. We also place them on our walls. And we send them off to speak to distant friends and relatives. Pictures tell our stories. They are a universal language.

Pictures extend our reach. They allow us to see events that have passed into history, to travel to places we will never visit, to experience the emotions of others. They communicate feelings, set moods. Dorothea Lange's photo of the mother and children of a migrant labor family takes us back half a century to the depression to show us the haunting face of a young mother, aged by adversity, looking into a future that seems without hope.

Today's picture-storytellers work for newspapers, magazines and television stations. Called photojournalists, they combine the skills of journalist and photographer. The news writer seeks to capture the essence of the event in words; the photojournalist uses his or her camera to capture the essence of the event in visual terms. On small dailies and weekly newspapers, reporters usually are expected to take photographs to illustrate their stories.

The Picture Is Universal

U.S. Navy Photograph

Arthur Rothstein, Courtesy of
the Library of Congress

Courtesy of Morris Berman
and *Pittsburgh Post-Gazette*

Photographs provide insights, revelations and information. They let us live with people different from ourselves, experience events half a world away and those too small and too fast for the eye and brain to capture in their natural state. They hold for us the leap of the ballet dancer, the fetus in the mother's womb, the finish of a close race.

The photojournalist's picture enables us to understand and emotionally identify with the event. By using scene or setting and the expression, gesture and body language of those in the picture, the photojournalist communicates with us at a personal level. Sometimes, a news photograph comes to symbolize the issues and the problems of a period in history.

Some photographs reach us in the same way that a song or symphony, a novel or short story touch us. The news photo of the death throes of the battleship *Arizona* at Pearl Harbor portrays a humbled United States and the beginning of a struggle for survival with a powerful adversary.

Arthur Rothstein's picture of a farmer and his sons making their way through swirling sands became a symbol of the struggle of the country's farmers when the dust bowl ravaged the Southwest. The barefoot boys, the younger one shielding his eyes against the stinging sands, the father's shapeless clothing and the hopelessness of his slouch tell the story. Photographs like this one made the public aware of the need for rehabilitation of rural areas and led Congress to adopt new farm legislation.

Morris Berman's sports photo of the sacked quarterback transcends the game and the season. Here is the downed battler, come to the end of a career. The sagging body and the agonized face tell us the athlete knows his speed and agility are gone, that the body will no longer respond.

These photographs and the others in the textbook tell us something about what makes a good picture, and they reveal something about what it takes to be a good photojournalist.

A good picture is first a truthful portrayal of an event. It is a pictorial record of the event the photojournalist is reporting. Beyond this, the good photograph can be described as interesting, informative, educational. It may be entertaining.

Topping Off. Chris Stephens of *The Plain Dealer* had several purposes in mind when she positioned herself 45 stories up in the Sohio Project. She wanted to show the last beam being put in place and to capture the workers in their precarious positions. She also wanted to include the Terminal Tower, the city's tallest building and its most recognizable landmark. Stephens used a 35mm lens wide-angle so that she could include the beam and the workers around it. The photo was shot with a fast film that allowed her to stop down to get plenty of depth of field so that beam, workers and the Tower are sharp. Notice the way the two beams on the side frame the final beam and direct the reader to it.

Chris Stephens, *The Plain Dealer*

The good photograph has impact; it has a message. It is technically sound and aesthetically right. The good picture makes proper use of light and dark, the horizon, curves and diagonals. There is logic and rhythm in the picture. It has a point of interest.

Clearly, the photojournalist has to be able to recognize the news and to freeze in visual form the point of the event.

The student thinking of a career in photojournalism should have a creative streak, Rothstein says. But he or she must have a practical bent as well.

Reporting Visually

Anguish. Sometimes the photographs of a disaster scene do not tell us as much as does the portrait of one human being's response to the tragedy. Here is a face in the crowd of scores of friends and relatives who waited at the mine entrance after an explosion trapped more than a hundred miners. The toll was 111 dead. Taken in 1947 by Sam Caldwell of the *St. Louis Post-Dispatch,* today the photo would probably be cropped, says Claude Cookman, to eliminate the faces to the left of the principal subject, or they would be "burnt down" in the printing process to make them less noticeable.
Sam Caldwell, *St. Louis Post-Dispatch*

    The photojournalist has to know something about photographic equipment in order to be able to make minor repairs. A knowledge of light, optics and the chemistry of photography are indispensable.
    Rothstein, former technical director of *Look* magazine and a renowned photographer, says the photojournalist must have the talent and ability to portray events and ideas in "unusual visual terms."

"Most important," he says, "is the knowledge of human beings and how they live, work and play."

That knowledge must be built on a sensitivity, the capacity to identify with what is being photographed. "Every photographer in each situation becomes a vicarious participant in the event," says Michael Geissinger of the photography faculty at the Rochester Institute of Technology. The news photo of the woman awaiting word about the men trapped in a Centralia, Ill., mine shaft, is "an example of the emotion a photographer must experience in order to produce a profound picture," Geissinger says.

The photograph portrays the grief and tension of one woman. But it represents all those who look fearfully into the unknown. The harsh and cutting light, the "pitiful hands that don't seem to know what to do with each other," as Claude Cookman says, the eyes focused on some awful scene as much in her mind as in front of her—all these prepare us for the awful news of death underground. The explosion took the lives of 111 miners.

Cookman, a picture and graphics editor with AP Wirephoto and *The Louisville Times* and *The Miami Herald,* says, "Every photo incorporates at least two aspects, content and pictorial treatment." For newspapers, the content must be significant.

Pictorial treatment involves "training the eye and mastering the technical side of the medium in order to organize reality into a visually interesting photograph," Cookman says. This process involves the photojournalist in selection—choosing what is significant, paring away the extraneous. Using light, composition, camera angle and space, the photojournalist is able to help the reader to recognize the significant.

The starting point for the photojournalist is the same as it is for the news writer: Know what you want to say and use the techniques and craft to say it. That is, the photojournalist must be clear about the point he or she is trying to make in the photograph and must have command of the technical aspects of photography.

Helping the Reader

Just as the news writer has the help of modern technology to speed his or her thoughts from fingertips to printed form, the photojournalist has versatile cameras, lenses of amazing diversity, an array of film and a modern laboratory to help tell the story in picture form.

"But these techniques are used only to obtain more freedom, to make the mechanics of taking a picture so simple that they (photojournalists) can concentrate on the subject, the idea and the event," says Rothstein.

Techniques and technology are not ends in themselves. Fritz Lang, the movie director, declared as a moral of technique, "Every camera movement must have a motivation, a reason."

Concentrate on Subject

Feature. Jim Greenwood took this photo while on feature assignment for *The Indiana Daily Student*. The picture was taken from the top of the university football stadium on a late fall afternoon while the bicyclist was riding laps in preparation for the Little 500 bike race on campus. The long shadow makes for a dramatic shot. Greenwood used a Nikkor 43-86 zoom on his Nikon F3, motorized camera. The film was Tri-X.

Jim Greenwood

News. A few days after Jesse Jackson announced his candidacy for the presidency in 1984, he spoke on the campus of California State University at Northridge. David Blumenkrantz was assigned to photograph the event for his school newspaper. "When Jackson went on stage there were several photographers crowding around the podium," Blumenkrantz says. "It's at times like this that concentration on simple things like focus become important." With the light augmented by television lights, Blumenkrantz did not have to use his flash. Jackson is giving the sign for "I love you" to a group of deaf students. To catch this, Blumenkrantz shot Jackson at 125th of a second, f2.8. He used a Nikkor 105mm lens. The telephoto and the wide opening gave him a shallow depth of field, causing Jackson's hand to be out of focus. The face, the focal point, is sharp.
David Blumenkrantz

Photos can be divided into two types, feature and spot. The feature photograph shows us a person or event of interest, creates a mood, or interprets an event or situation. The spot photo records a timely subject.

Describing his ability to handle spot and feature assignments, an experienced midwestern photojournalist said:

"I have trained and dedicated myself to being on the scene. I never miss. When it happens, I'm there. I am a street photographer when things break fast, and a professional journalist, warm and sensitive, with a creative eye for special arrangements."

Social Document. Some pictures do more than supplement the news story. They give the reader new insights, new ways of looking at the world. The photograph can capture a face or a scene with the arresting impact that only the most gifted writer can match. Lewis Hine's photograph of a child at work in a southern cotton mill is simple, yet devasting. At first, says Cookman, there is nothing so terrible about the scene depicted. ''The factory does not seem particularly dangerous, and we cannot see the girl's face closely enough to tell whether she is fatigued, malnourished or otherwise ravaged by her experience,'' he says. But what is not shown is important: ''Our associations of what a good childhood should be like—education and play and freedom from drudgery.'' The picture was taken in 1908, when children labored in mines and factories. This knowledge combines with our emotional reaction to the picture to make it a powerful statement.

The photo is pictorially simple. The long loom directs the eye to the picture's focal point, the girl. The strong light from the window not only sets up an interesting pattern but reminds us of the world outside, where children play. The narrow corridor seems to imprison the child.

Hine, a documentary photographer who took pictures of immigrants at Ellis Island and children and adults laboring in American industry, is considered by some to be the country's greatest photographer. His social commentaries on film of children in factories helped lead to changes in child labor laws. Hine took 15,000 pictures from 1900 to 1940. Recognition came too late. He died a pauper in 1940.

Lewis Hine, International Museum of Photography at George Eastman House

Prep and Shoot. The photojournalist is able to hit it off with people quickly, to gain their trust so they are willing to be photographed. Photojournalists say they combine the talents of the psychologist and the sociologist. Here, Karen Leff, a young freelance photographer, chats with a merchant, gains her confidence, then shoots her picture. Leff graduated from Boston University School of Public Communication in photojournalism and works in New York City as a freelancer. Her photos have appeared in *Women's Sports Magazine, The New York Times, USA Today,* and *Tennis Magazine,* and she has done assignments for AP. "Since freelance photography is not consistent enough to pay the rent, it means working in a job, usually not related to photography, part-time," Leff says. "One of the reasons I stick with freelance photography is that each assignment means a new adventure and a new set of personalities, locations and events."
Karen Leff

For the beginner, the task of learning begins not with shooting yards of film and spending hours in the darkroom. The starting point is internal—thinking, feeling and looking before the shutter is snapped. Know what it is you want to show, the experts say, and then examine what you have done with that in mind. Ask yourself, what is the print saying?

"Simplicity is a virtue in any type of communication," Cookman says. "It's also a good place to start in photography. Begin by recording what you see that interests you, and most often that will be people.

Advice for the Beginner

"After you've learned to get them to relax and to stop worrying that your camera will make them look ugly or ridiculous, then concentrate on telling as much about them as you can through expression, body language, setting, clothing and other props."

After practicing on one person, capture the interaction of two or more people, Cookman suggests. Try to record a range of emotions and experiences.

"To tell a complete story, make sure there is action in all your pictures. For every subject let there be a visual verb," Cookman recommends.

After some experience with recording people and events, try to interpret them. "Don't just show the reader what happened; help him or her to feel what it's like. By selecting significant details and by carefully choosing your lighting, framing, camera angle and shutter timing, take the reader into the events.

"When you can constantly make photos that allow the viewer to empathize with what's happening, to put himself or herself into the picture and thereby gain a vicarious understanding of the event and of humanity, then you've earned the title—photojournalist."

The Photo Editor

Photographers are assigned by the picture editor, who tries to select the photographer who will do the best job on the particular assignment. Some photographers specialize in sports; others do their best work on feature assignments. On special assignment, the photographer may accompany the reporter. If they have time, the two will discuss picture possibilities before leaving the office. On the scene, they may also exchange picture ideas, though the reporter often is too busy reporting and the photographer too involved in shooting.

Back in the office, the photo editor looks over the negatives or prints. The final decision as to which shots are used, how they are cropped and printed is the editor's.

If it is true that journalism is history in a hurry, then it follows that sometimes the historical or universal is overlooked in the rush to deadline. This is the backdrop to an interesting story about Berman's photograph of Y. A. Tittle, the New York Giants quarterback.

Berman was standing near the Giants' 35-yard line when Tittle dropped back to pass. It was the second game of the 1964 season, against the Pittsburgh Steelers. "It had been a dull contest," Berman recalls. "But since Tittle had a reputation as a great passer, I trained my lens on him." As Tittle let the ball go, a 270-pound defensive end slammed into him. Tittle crumpled to the ground, unable to see his pass snared by a Steeler defender, who ran into the end zone.

"I just kept shooting Tittle," Berman says. "He was bleeding, and his helmet had been torn off. He was unable to stand. Then he just bowed his head as if something very serious had happened."

The photo, made with a 200mm lens at f8 at 1/1000, was passed over by Berman's photo editor. "I couldn't believe it," Berman recalls thinking. "For some reason he preferred the shots of Tittle surrounded by his teammates and being carried off the field." The photograph won many awards and hangs in the Football Hall of Fame.

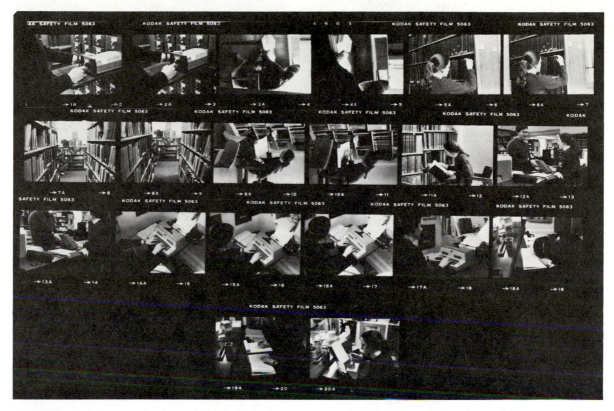

Proof Sheet. Photographs for newspapers and magazines are selected from a proof sheet like this one, which was submitted for a picture story on a student preparing a term paper. The photo editor indicates on the sheet which shots will be used, their size and how they will be cropped. You might want to select several shots from this sheet for a page that you plan. Indicate how they should be cropped, the size of each and write cutlines or captions.

Photo Essay

The photo essay or picture story is a series of pictures with a common theme that documents an event or tells a story about a person or a place. While single photos are effective, the series can reveal subtleties and make distinctions that one photograph cannot.

Usually, the picture story is built around the strongest single photo, the picture that describes or defines the theme. The photographer keeps this in mind while shooting, as well as the necessity to take pictures that will make the display interesting and exciting. A wide-angle lens may be used for one

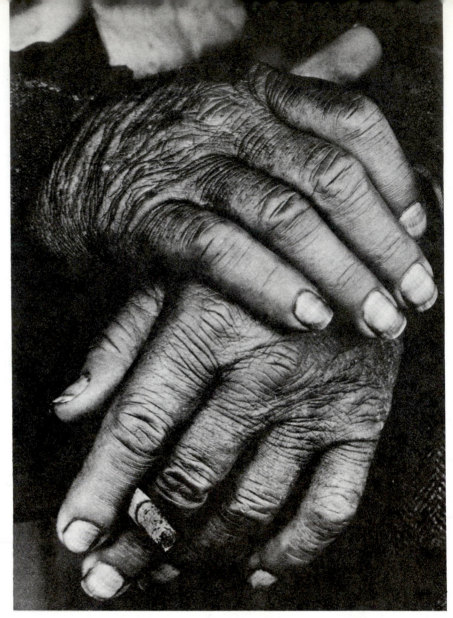

Detailing. For a series of photos of an elderly transient, Blumenkrantz made this close-up of his hands with a 105mm lens, 1/250, f5.6.
David Blumenkrantz

shot, a telephoto for another. Pictures are taken from a variety of positions. Close-ups that focus on a single aspect of the subject vary the perspective. Called detailing, these close-in shots give the viewer an intimate relationship with the subject, and in some cases provide a view that would be difficult if not impossible otherwise.

The essay may use various lighting techniques—the light from windows, room light, silhouette.

The film is printed and the pictures cropped according to a layout that emphasizes the theme and presents the photos in varying sizes and shapes. The theme photo is placed in a dominant area and is surrounded by supporting photographs.

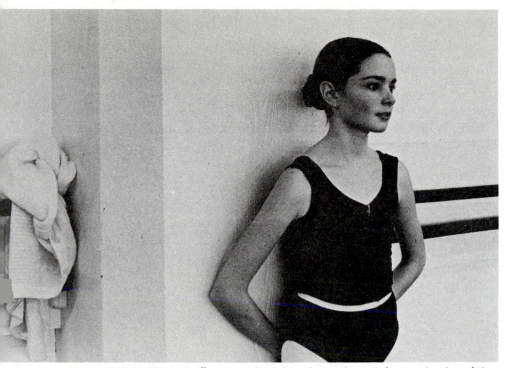

Natural Light. Karen Leff was assigned to shoot pictures for a calendar of the Boston Ballet Company. She wanted to show the largely unseen side of ballet, classes, practice, rehearsals. She spotted this girl watching, and dreaming, as other dancers practiced. "I felt that the soft, diffused window light of the studio fit the young dancer in its softness," Leff said. "I think the picture could have worked without the sweater, but it had an appealing shape and texture and worked well with the freshness of the girl." She used a 50mm lens because she was close to the subject and wanted to capture the sweater on the barre, which she felt she could crop later. Since the subject was not moving, she could shoot at 1/60. The opening was f5.6.
Karen Leff

Most photojournalists use the 35mm camera, a single-lens reflex (SLR) with a fast lens. The same lens is used for viewing the scene and exposing the film; what you see in the viewfinder is what you will see in the print. The camera usually has a built-in exposure meter that measures the light on the scene and allows the photographer to determine how to expose the film. Some cameras are automated so that the proper amount of light is automatically let in.

The Camera

The lens opening or aperture affects the amount of light reaching the film. The lens opening is measured in numbers preceded by the letter "f," called f-stops. The smaller numbers have the wider apertures, letting in more light

Aperture

than the larger numbers: f1.4 lets in twice as much light as f2. Each lens setting on the camera indicates half the light of the preceding setting: f1.4, 2, 2.8, 4, 5.6, 8, 11, 16, 22, 32, 45.

The other element that controls the amount of light that strikes the film is the shutter speed.

Shutter Speed

The shutter speed affects the length of the exposure, the amount of time the shutter is open. The shutter openings are measured in fractions of a second. The markings of 15, 30, 60, 125, 250, 500, 1000 refer to 1/15, 1/30, etc. of a second. The B marking allows the photographer to keep the shutter open as long as the shutter release is pressed down.

The correct exposure is a combination of lens opening and shutter speed. Since much of the photographer's work involves action in poorly lit areas, the shutter speed usually is 125 or less and the lens opening is wide, f2.8 or f4. The shutter speed may not stop the action, and the wide lens opening cuts down on the depth of field, the area of sharpness. Compromises and adjustments are always being made.

Freezing Action.
Blumenkrantz took this shot for a layout on a scuba expedition off Catalina Island. The picture was taken at a 500th of a second, f16. The fast shutter speed stopped the action, and the small lens opening allowed a deep depth of field so that the gull, the man's hand and face are sharp. Blumenkrantz said anticipation of the proper moment to snap the shutter was essential. The original photo was tightly cropped for the layout.
David Blumenkrantz

One of the adjustments photojournalists are always making uses the concept of reciprocity. Since the apertures (f-stops) double or halve the amount of light reaching the film and the shutter speeds do the same thing, they can be adjusted together to accomplish the purpose the photographer has in mind. If the reading is f4 at 125th of a second and the photographer must stop high-speed action, the shutter speed will be set at 250, which lets in half the amount of light at 125. To compensate for this, the lens is opened one stop to f2.8, which lets in twice as much light as f4.

But f2.8 has a narrower depth of field than f4, and if depth of field is essential for the photo, the f-stop will have to be left at f4 and the shutter speed at 125, which may result in a blurred image of the action.

Depth of field refers to the area between the nearest and the farthest points in the picture that are in sharp focus. Depth of field is affected by three factors that the photographer can control:

Lens opening: Smaller the f-stop number, shorter the depth of field.
Focal length: Shorter the focal length, deeper the depth of field.
Lens-to-subject distance: Farther away, deeper the depth of field.

In Berman's photo of the football player, the viewer's eye is directed to the player because the background is purposely out of focus. At the same time, the background is clear enough to tell us we are at a game.

Most cameras have a depth of field scale on the lens that tells the photographer the extent of the area of sharpness at each f-stop. By using this scale, the photographer can deliberately put areas out of focus, such as a distracting background, or make sure some parts of the scenes are sharp.

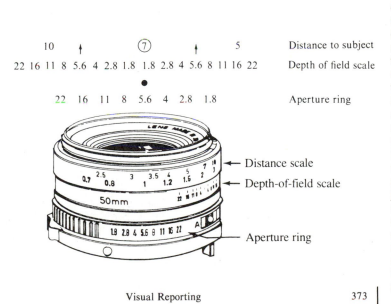

Figure 16.1 The limits of depth of field (area of sharpness) can be determined for different apertures by reading the depth of field scale on the lens barrel. Here, the aperture is f11. Reading the depth of field scale, we can see that the area of sharpness will cover an area from seven feet from the camera to almost 20 feet. For action photos, the photojournalist can preset the aperture for the desired depth of field. In this diagram, a picture taken at f5.6 at a distance of seven feet will be in focus from six feet to eight feet. (Note arrows.)

Don Ultang, a Pulitzer Prize-winning photojournalist and a photography instructor at Drake University, suggests using the "one-third rule" to make a quick determination for the point of focus so that the various elements in a picture are sharp.

1. Estimate the distance between the nearest and farthest subjects.
2. Take one-third the difference between the two figures.
3. Add the one-third figure to the nearest distance and set this figure on the distance scale.

Sharp. By focusing at f16, the photographer was able to keep in focus the foreground and background.

Mike McClure

For example: To take a picture where the nearest subject is five feet away and the farthest 20 feet, the difference is 15 feet. One third of 15 is five. Add the difference (five) to the distance to nearest subject (five) and set the camera at 10 feet.

For grab shots in quick-shooting situations, Ultang often will preset his distance scale at 12 or 13 feet. (The one-third rule does not work in low-light situations with wide-open apertures.)

In the photo of a moose foraging on a bright winter day, Mike McClure has pinpoint sharpness from the brush in the foreground to the Tetons miles away. McClure was able to close his lens to f16 because of the bright light. He used a film with a speed of ASA 125 and made the print on Oriental Seagull grade 4 paper.

Lenses

Focal Length

Lenses are usually described in terms of focal length—normal, long and short. The 50mm lens is considered the normal lens because it most nearly duplicates human vision. The long lens, 100mm and up, is known as the telephoto lens. This lens brings distant objects close and compresses the scene. The longer the lens, the greater the magnification and the narrower the angle of coverage. The short lens is known as the wide-angle lens. It takes in more of the scene than the other lenses.

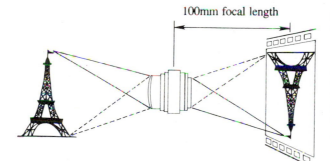

100mm focal length

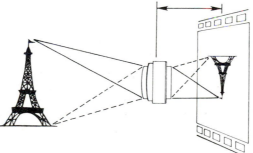

50mm focal length

Figure 16.2 Focal length affects the magnification of an object. As the focal length increases, the size of the object on the film increases. A 100mm lens—telephoto lens—produces an image twice the size that a 50mm lens—normal lens—produces.

Figure 16.3 As the focal length increases, the angle of view narrows. A 100mm lens makes an image twice as large as a 50mm lens. This diagram shows what happens when lenses with different focal lengths are used. (Focal length is measured from the optical center of the lens to the image it forms on the film.)

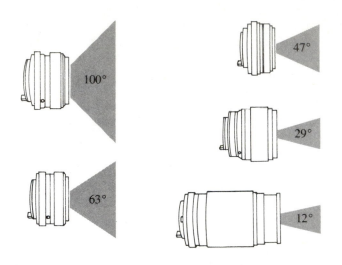

The shorter the focal length, the greater the area that can be photographed and the smaller the objects will appear. The photographer can move the camera toward or away from the scene, or he or she can change lenses to bring about the effect desired. Sometimes, the simplest step is to change the lens. But each lens has limitations as well as advantages.

Limitations

Normal   The normal lens is usually designed with large maximum lens openings, which permit photos in low-level light situations. Distant objects are small; objects outside the area directly ahead, 47 degrees in the angle of view, are not registered on the film.

Long   Distant objects are increased in size, but the area photographed is smaller the longer the lens that is used: 85mm, 29 degrees; 200mm, 12 degrees; 1000mm, 2.5 degrees. Also, the longer the focal length the shallower the depth of field. Since the larger image magnifies slight hand movements, a fast shutter speed is necessary when the camera is hand held. (A practical guide: Use a shutter speed at least as fast as the reciprocal of the focal length—with a 200mm lens, shoot at 1/250 or faster.)

Short   This lens is useful in crowded areas where the photographer is close to the scene. The shorter the focal length the greater the depth of field. The photographer can preset the wide-angle lens and be sure distant and close subjects will be in focus. However, wide-angle lenses when used close to the subject will make the subject disproportionately larger than objects of the same size in the background.

Lenses. The fisherman on the left was photographed with a 28mm, wide-angle lens. The shot on the right was made with a 135mm, telephoto lens. The photo with the wide-angle lens shows the loneliness of the winter fisherman. The one shot with the telephoto tells another story—the uninviting weather that brings out only the most intrepid angler.

Short Lens. This photo, says David Blumenkrantz, shows the importance of not being reluctant to move close to the subject. "I must have been less than three feet from the saxophone player when I snapped this frame," he says. Blumenkrantz used a 35mm lens, which allowed him to capture the dancer and the drummers. The three men are in focus.
David Blumenkrantz

Medium-long Lens. When Blumenkrantz pointed his camera at this transient, the man covered his face with his arm and accused Blumenkrantz of using him to make money. "I talked with Bob for nearly 45 minutes," says Blumenkrantz. "As so often happens, when you lend a kind and interested ear, people open up." Blumenkrantz used a 105mm lens to take this picture; 1/250, f5.6, Tri-X film.
David Blumenkrantz

Other lenses:

Zoom: Combines a range of focal lengths in one lens. Zoom lenses have the advantage of eliminating the need to change lenses. They are not practical in extremely low light conditions.
Micro: Is used for close-ups. This lens is corrected to eliminate the distortion of subjects close to the lens.
Fisheye: Has an extended wide angle of view; some of them extend to 180 degrees. Objects close to the lens and those far away are distorted. The image appears as a circle instead of the usual rectangle.

Different situations call for different lenses. Since the long lens compresses space, a telephoto lens is often used to convey a sense of cramped space. To photograph a person's face, the normal lens on a camera close to the subject would make the person's features nearest the camera (nose and forehead) disproportionately large. A medium-long lens (85–135mm) would give better results. Also, the longer lens would allow the photographer to be further away from the subject, which would lessen the person's discomfort.

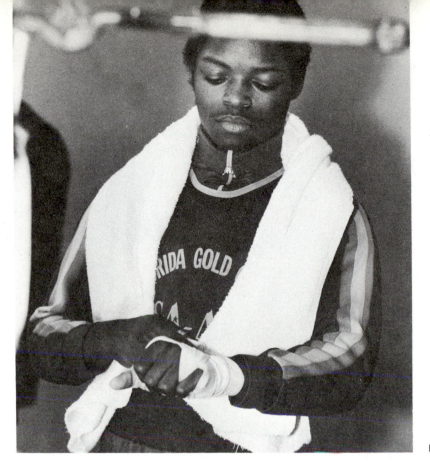

Karen Leff

Film is described by its speed—its sensitivity to light. Fast films have speeds of ASA 400 and up. The faster the film, the less exposure or light needed to produce an image. A medium-speed film would be ASA 125; slow film, ASA 32. Fast films allow the photographer to take pictures in dimly-lit areas, but there is an increase in graininess and a decline in the contrast and in the sharpness of the image in the print. Fast film makes large prints grainy, even mottled. The slow or medium fast film shows more detail.

In some situations, even ASA 400 is not fast enough. Photographers can "push" a film to as much as ASA 1600 by using a high-energy developer for their film. When Karen Leff was photographing boxers at a gymnasium where the lighting was dim, she pushed her film to 1600 so that the hands of the boxers would not be blurred. She shot the picture of the boxer taping his hands at 1/125th of a second at f2.8. Had she used the film at its normal speed, 400, she would have had to use a shutter speed of 1/30th, too slow to stop the motion. If she wanted to retain the shutter speed of 1/125th, she could have opened the lens to let in more light. But that would have meant an aperture of f1.4, which was not available on the 100mm telephoto lens she was using.

Film

Joel Kilthau

The photographs on these two pages, made by a student, Joel H. Kilthau, at the Rochester Institute of Technology, illustrate the solutions—one successful, the other a failure—to problems faced by photographers.

The photograph above was made at a competition among volunteer fire companies in which the task was to fill a container at the top of a ladder from buckets passed by the firemen. The job demanded speed, strength and teamwork. Geissinger, Kilthau's instructor, says the photo shows these elements, with the additional information that not all the water was deposited in the container. Notice the upward thrust of the hands that lead the viewer to the focal point, the bucket being passed upward.

Joel Kilthau

The photograph on this page has all the elements necessary for a successful photo, says Geissinger, but they are assembled awkwardly. The photograph was intentionally designed to illustrate several failures by the photographer:

Background The automobile next to the youngster's head is distracting. Failure to notice the background is a common mistake among beginning photographers, Geissinger says. The bright street also distracts.

Composition There is too great a gap between the primary subjects. The viewer, attracted by the youngster's upward glance, has to work too hard to find the adult. Once located, the adult is too near the top of the photo and the viewer's eye continues off the page.

Cropping

The point or intent of a picture can be shifted or emphasized by cropping the print or enlarging a section of the negative. The cropping—cutting away unwanted parts of the picture—can be done on the photo editor's desk or in the darkroom.

Look at the picture from chapter 3 of the black man being kicked. Cookman suggests that cropping the photo just inside the left edge of the utility pole would strengthen it "by not allowing our eye to escape from the central message to the area to the left." The pole would then force a solid border on the left side of the picture.

Compare the photos here. In the cropped photo, the reader's attention is concentrated on the downed man as well as on the clenched fists of the man to the left and the fighting stance of the man at center.

Taking this shot, says Cookman, required considerable courage. Some of the journalists covering the civil rights struggle were beaten. This photograph shows the intensity of feeling, not only in the overt blow to the man's stomach but in the barely restrained aggression of the bystanders. The cropped photo enhances that intensity.

Wilmer Counts, *The Arkansas Democrat*

Lifeless . . . Lively. As with stories, pictures improve with human interest. The photo on the left lacks this essential quality. By placing a person in this scene the photographer was able to make the photograph more interesting, more likely to catch the eye. Also by placing a person in the photo on the right, the photographer gives the reader a sense of scale.

Chapter 2: All Kinds The photograph of the railroad worker here and the close-up in chapter 10 (**The Right Word**) were taken as "wild art," says Joseph Noble, of *The Stuart News*. There is no story or assignment; the photographer finds subject matter on his or her own and is responsible for writing the cutline.

Examples

Chapter 3: Conflict The photograph of the farmer and his boys struggling in a dust storm is one of the most frequently reproduced photographs by a U.S. photographer. It was taken by Arthur Rothstein for the photographic section of the Farm Security Administration, founded in 1935 by Roy Emerson Stryker, whose concept of the documentary photograph permanently influenced photojournalism. In the decade that FSA photographers worked, they took 270,000 pictures that had news as well as historical value. The photographs not only recorded those who worked the soil but carried an eloquent message of social significance—change was essential to give these people dignity.

Timeliness The sheriff's department used a helicopter and tracking dogs to locate this man. Noble followed some of the officers into the brush and was nearby when they flushed the man out of the palmettos. Noble used a 180mm lens to focus on the fugitive's face as he was handcuffed.

Chapter 7: Attribution The car in which this woman was riding was far from where Noble was standing with his camera. When the divers brought her body to the surface, he could barely see the figures. The shot was taken with a 400mm lens and the film was processed in a high-energy developer. "The negative revealed more of the event than I was aware of while taking the photo," Noble said.

The photograph of the sheet-draped body was one of 30 taken by Marc Ascher. Most were rejected because they focused too closely on the body of the woman, who was slain by her husband of 50 years. For this shot, Ascher says he framed the scene to show the kind of suburban home in which the domestic crime occurred. Note the two-car garage, the neat, brick-patterned walk. He also wanted to include the address and the family name. He included the madonna to show the family's religious devotion.

Chapter 10: The Right Word The close-up of the worker was one of a pair of "wild art" shots by Noble. The photograph at the water's edge was made on a bright day with a 135mm telephoto lens. To prevent overexposure from the sunlit water, the aperture was f22, which caused the silhouette effect of the figure that provides the white-and-black contrast. The Civil War photo of Matthew Brady could not be used in newspapers or magazines at the time because it was not possible then to use halftones. They were exhibited and copied in drawings and were a powerful influence on the documentary photographers who followed. The lounging men is an FSA photo by Rothstein taken in the summer of 1939 in Butte, Mont., a mining town where unemployment was high during the depression.

Chapter 11: Exact Detail Karen Leff, the photographer, says she was intrigued by the animation of the sculptor's works, which Leff photographed for a photo-exhibition "Women and Work." To capture the artist at work, Leff stood on a chair to provide an angle from which the sculpted figures seemed to come to life, pulling each other in a circle. To include most of the studio, she used a 28mm lens. The picture was shot at 1/60th at f8.

Part 4: Tennis Player Leff says the four key ingredients in shooting sports are timing, framing, follow focus and concentration. To master these, a knowledge of sports is essential, as it enables the photographer to visualize the shots he or she wants to take. It also helps, says Leff, to anticipate the typical movements in a game. As Leff watched this match she noticed that the player "had an exceptionally graceful way of lunging for the ball at the net, almost as if he were a dancer or a fencer." To capture this movement, she selected a 100mm lens. The 50mm lens would not have concentrated her shot sufficiently, she felt. In looking back, though, she says an 80mm lens would have been better, as it might have allowed her to catch the ball as well as the player and racket. She shot at 1/500th, the average speed for most sports pictures, and f4, which cut down the depth of field, an advantage in that distracting background was eliminated.

Grieving Mother The mother was photographed after her drowned child was placed in an ambulance. Noble was 20 feet away and used a 180mm lens for a close-up. "I felt extremely uncomfortable and made only one exposure," he said. The newspaper received several complaints about insensitive journalism, and the newspaper replied in an editorial: "What if one mother's grief could spare another, but no one knew of her loss?" The editorial in *The Stuart News* went on to say that the photo "tells a tragic story that poignantly and graphically depicts every parent's worst fear."

PART SIX

Laws and Codes

Bottom, Hank Reichard,
Columbus Citizen-Journal;
top left, Editor & Publisher;
top right, Harry Baumert, *The*
Des Moines Register

Libel, Ethics
and Taste

The laws of libel and privacy, codes of ethics and guidelines on matters of taste place limits on the journalist.

Libel is the publication of false and malicious material that damages a person's reputation. A person who can prove he or she has been injured by a story or photograph can collect damages in a libel suit. Stories that are based on facts and are thorough, fair and impartial do not cause libel suits.

Privacy is the right of the individual to be left alone. A reporter cannot invade a person's home or use listening or recording devices to intrude on a person's privacy.

Ethics are not enforced by laws. They are understandings among journalists as to what is proper behavior for the practice of journalism. Some of these agreements are contained in codes. Others are the personal beliefs and commitments of journalists.

Taste—what society considers proper in the use of language and subject matter—changes with time, the nature of the audience and the nature of those involved in the event. Generally, material that may be vulgar, obscene, profane, or offensive is permissible if it is absolutely essential to the news story.

Looking Ahead

- The news story was like a dozen others that the newspaper had printed—a local resident had been arrested for drunk driving. But this one led to a libel suit.
- For several months, the reporter was underground. He had used a false identity to work his way into membership of the Ku Klux Klan for a series of articles on the organization that preaches hatred of blacks, Jews and Catholics. Some journalists questioned the methods he used to gather information for his articles.
- On their 6 p.m. news broadcasts, two Cleveland television stations reported that a coroner's examination of a 69-year-old woman murdered in a parking lot determined that the body was actually that of a man. The victim was Stella Walsh, a former women's Olympic track champion and a well-known member of Cleveland's Polish-American community, which assailed the news reports of the two stations.

What was wrong, if anything, with these news stories? In this chapter, we will be looking at (1) libel laws, (2) journalistic ethics and (3) guidelines for matters of taste to find the answers to this question. First, to libel.

Libel

The news story reported that L. D. Sylvester of 536 Western Ave. had been arrested for drunk driving the night before and had posted bond. Several weeks later, Sylvester's lawyer sued the newspaper for libel. Sylvester said he had never been arrested. In fact, he had been out of town the evening that the newspaper had him careening down the center of town.

An error had been made, the editor learned on a quick check. There was nothing to do but settle out of court for several thousand dollars. The newspaper had no defense.

What had happened was simple, but devastating. In his haste at the police station, the police reporter had scribbled the man's name and address on his note pad. Drunk driving stories are not major events, and the reporter had been hurrying to get on to more important arrests.

Back in the office, the reporter could not read the scribbled address and looked in the telephone book for the address of L. D. Sylvester. He found the address as 536 Western Ave., which went into the story.

Actually, the arrested person was T. D. Sylvester of 561 Eastern Ave.

The incident reveals the cause of most libel suits: sloppy reporting and careless writing, the failure to check or verify potentially dangerous material.

Definition of Libel

Libel is the publication of material that injures a person by causing:

1. Financial loss.
2. Damage to reputation.
3. Humiliation, mental anguish or suffering.

Newspapers do publish stories that cause people to lose their jobs and that damage their reputations. The Ohio congressman who put his mistress on his Washington payroll in a do-nothing job was exposed by reporters and defeated for re-election. No job and a tarnished reputation. Even so, the congressman did not sue for libel because the story was true. He knew a suit would be hopeless. The reporters had the sworn statement of the woman and proof from the payroll records.

The true story can be printed or broadcast without fear. When the story is untrue, however, there is trouble. In the Sylvester incident, the story of his arrest was the only one of a dozen arrest stories that weekend that was erroneous. The other persons undoubtedly were humiliated by the news of their arrests. Unlike Sylvester, they had no grounds for a libel suit. The printed reports were accurate.

Sylvester, however, could prove that he was the victim of an error. Errors can be costly. Here is one that proved costly.

On March 2, 1976, the *National Enquirer* carried this item in one of its gossip columns:

The *Enquirer* and Carol Burnett

> At a Washington restaurant, a boisterous Carol Burnett had a loud argument with another diner, Henry Kissinger. She traipsed around the place offering everyone a bite of her dessert. But Carol really raised eyebrows when she accidentally knocked a glass of wine over one diner—and started giggling instead of apologizing. The guy wasn't amused and "accidentally" spilled a glass of water over Carol's dress.

A month later, the weekly newspaper published a retraction admitting its report was wrong. But Burnett sued for libel. The television star testified that despite the retraction, the item had caused her great anguish and diminished reputation.

Burnett's lawyer claimed she had been the victim of defamation. One definition of libel is that it is published defamation, that is, written material that exposes a person to public hatred, contempt or ridicule, or injures the person in his or her business occupation.

The jury hearing the Burnett case felt that she had been so seriously defamed and had suffered such humiliation that it awarded her $300,000 in compensatory damages (for injuries actually suffered) and $1.3 million in punitive damages (to punish the *Enquirer*). The award was later lowered to $200,000 by a California appeals court.

There are three basic defenses against libel suits:

Libel Defenses

1. **Truth**   If the reporter can show that the defamatory material is true, the offended person may sue but the case usually cannot be won. It is not enough for the reporter to say he or she thought the material was truthful or that someone else said it was true. There must be proof of its truth. Truth is almost always an absolute defense in a libel suit.
2. **Privilege**   Anything said in a **public and official** legislative or judicial situation—whether it is true or false—can be reported. Legislative bodies include the city council, county commissions, state legislature and congress. In the courts, statements by attorneys, the judge and witnesses and any documents filed with the court are privileged.
3. **Fair Comment and Criticism**   Critics who assess the work of artists, authors, performers, sports figures and others who offer their services to the public may comment on the work or performance. The criticism must be based on facts and must not attack the personal life of the individual whose work is being assessed. The comment must not be malicious.

Anita and Elvis—The Reunion that Never Happened

The story in *The Commercial Appeal* in Memphis, Tenn., was a sensation to his fans: Elvis Presley had held a reunion in Las Vegas with Anita Wood Brewer, who at one time was Presley's "No. 1 girl." Brewer had divorced her husband, the newspaper said, and joined Presley.

The story was dead wrong, and the newspaper printed a retraction. But the Brewers sued. In its defense, the newspaper claimed that both husband and wife were public figures—she was a well-known singer and he was a famous football star. (Brewer had been a college football star at the University of Mississippi and then played with the Cleveland Browns and the New Orleans Saints.)

A federal district jury court disagreed with the newspaper's defense and awarded each of the Brewers $400,000 in damages. The newspaper appealed to the circuit court of appeals.

This time, the newspaper won. The circuit court agreed that the Brewers were public figures despite the passage of time. If they wanted to sue, the court said, they had to prove actual malice, not negligence or carelessness. The U.S. Supreme Court refused to review the case.

In all of these defenses, the reporter is on safe ground if the report is a full, fair, impartial and accurate account of the event. If the story is so one-sided that it could be proved that the reporter intentionally singled out the critical or defamatory material, the reporter could be in trouble if sued.

The Sullivan Ruling

In 1964, the U.S. Supreme Court granted reporters some leeway for their mistakes. In a famous case, *The New York Times* v. *Sullivan,* the Court ruled that if a **public official** is the victim of a libelous story, the official must prove that the account was published with "actual malice." To prove actual malice, the official must prove in court that the material was published with:

1. The knowledge that it was false, or
2. The reckless disregard of whether the material was true.

The Sullivan decision took away from the individual state courts their control over libel actions. In its ruling, the Court said that a constitutional issue was involved—freedom of the press. This is why so many libel decisions are appealed to federal courts.

For a while, the Court's ruling about "actual malice" was extended to public figures and to private individuals involved in public or official matters.

However, recent court decisions have restricted the definition of a public figure, so that now some public figures and most private individuals need only prove that the defamatory material was published or broadcast because of carelessness or negligence.

Public Officials

Elected officials—mayor, governor, members of congress, legislators, city council members, etc.

High-level appointed officials—supervisors, inspectors, medical examiners, cabinet members, etc.

Police officers

Judges

Careful: Not all public employees are public officials.

Public Figures

People with power and influence—newspaper columnists, authors, radio and television personalities, popular performers, union officials

People involved in important public controversies who seek to influence the outcome—a person who vigorously and publicly opposes or supports a referendum, bond issue, candidacy

---

Any story that contains material that might injure someone's reputation should be treated carefully. Hasty, careless reporting and writing are dangerous. Some suggestions:

Avoiding Libel

Confirm and verify all defamatory material. A reporter should double-check anything that:

1. Questions a person's fitness to handle his or her job.
2. Alleges a person has committed a crime or has performed some act that constitutes a crime.
3. Implies or directly states that a person has a mental illness or a loathsome disease.

Make sure that questionable material can be proved true.

Be especially careful of arrest reports, damage suits and criminal court hearings. These stories cause more libel suits than all others, and almost all are the result of careless reporting or writing. Check names, addresses; make sure the defendant and plaintiff are properly identified.

Watch out for charges, assertions, claims. Just because someone says something and you quote the person accurately does not mean you have avoided libel. If a district attorney tells you he is investigating a business with a long string of lawsuits and you quote the official, you may lose a libel suit if the owner proves he has never been sued. If the district attorney makes the same statement in a court proceeding, or if he files charges and makes any allegations in them, the material may be used because it is protected by the defense of privilege.

Don't try to sneak in defamatory material by suggestion with such words as allegedly, *or* reported. These are not protections against libel.

When charges and accusations are made in a privileged situation, it is a good idea to check with the person being defamed. This demonstrates your fairness.

Watch out for words that a court may hold to be libelous. Some of these words and their context:

Subject	Dangerous Words
Commission of a crime	Swindler, thief, loan shark, shoplifter, bigamist, gangster, ex-convict
Performance in job or profession	Incompetent, failure, quack, shyster, hack, bribery, slick operator
Diseases that could cause a person to be ostracized	Wino, leper, sickie
Damage to a person's credit	Unreliable, bankrupt, gambler, cheat, failure
Lack of chastity	Loose, B-girl, hooker, seducer, immoral, street-walker, adultery, prostitute
Lack of mental capacity	Screwy, nutty, strange, incompetent, out-of-it
Incite ridicule or contempt	Phony, coward, hypocrite, communist, fascist

Don't color the article with opinions. Watch out for personal enthusiasms that cause you to lose control of the writing.

Be careful of statements by police or court officials outside court.

Truth is a defense, but good intentions are not. You may not have meant to defame someone, but when your well-intended writing proves to be untrue, your intention is no defense.

A retraction of an error is not a defense. It may lessen damages and could eliminate punitive damages.

Careful journalists have no trouble with libel. The careless writer and the writer who stretches facts do get into trouble. The reporter who wants to impress an editor or readers by going beyond what can be proved sooner or later tumbles. Some lose their jobs. Others cause their publishers to lose money.

A reporter for a Cleveland newspaper who invented quotes from a widow in an interview had a fascinating story. But it proved costly when the widow sued and won.

Another danger area for reporters is the private lives of individuals. Reporters cannot indiscriminately pry, peek and probe into the personal affairs of anyone they choose to single out.

Privacy

In their search for news, reporters gather material about the personal lives of people that can be embarrassing or unpleasant to those involved. Newspapers routinely carry hospital admissions, divorce actions, arrests and traffic violations. Reporters search out and interview the parents of children killed in automobile accidents and fires. Sunday supplements and magazines detail the sex lives of the stars and the drug habits and alcoholism of athletes. Television carries the shame and the grief of those involved in tragedy and crime into millions of living rooms.

These stories can be published and broadcast because the people are involved in legitimate news events. The drunk driver has no claim to privacy when he or she is arrested. The details of a divorce case may be published. The horrors of a nursing home fire and the sorrow of relatives may be shown on television.

A Florida newspaper published the picture of a scantily clad woman being led by police from an apartment house where she had been held captive. The woman sued, claiming the picture had embarrassed and humiliated her. Her lawyer told a jury that there was no argument about the truth of the incident but that the picture had invaded her privacy. The jury agreed and awarded the woman $10,000 in damages.

The verdict was appealed and the appeals court reversed the decision. It found that the photograph was part of a legitimate news story and that its publication was not so outrageous as to show intentional "infliction of emotional distress."

However, when the press digs into private acts that are of no public interest or that are of no legitimate concern to the public, there can be trouble, even when the account is accurate. The law of libel protects a person's reputation and character. The right of privacy gives the person the right to be left alone, unless the person is involved in a legitimate news event.

The right to privacy protects people from several kinds of activities that journalists engage in:

1. **Publicizing private matters**   Public disclosure of private facts and acts of an individual that are considered offensive can lead to legal trouble. Sensational material about a person's love life, health, business affairs or social activities can constitute invasion of privacy. If the acts are private and of no legitimate concern to the public, the material is dangerous.

   If a rock star talks about his drug habit, or an athlete discloses he is struggling with alcoholism, the information can be used. The courts have also ruled that personal material can be used if it concerns a **newsworthy person,** is of **public concern** and **is not "highly offensive to a reasonable person, one of ordinary sensibilities."**

   If the activity takes place in public or the information is in a public document—no matter how sensational or offensive—it can be used.

2. **Intrusion**   If the reporter forces himself or herself into a private area to gather news, this is intrusion. The intrusion need not be physical. The use of tape recorders, hidden microphones, cameras and any other kind of electronic equipment without the person's permission is intrusion, even if the material is not used.

   When a reporter misrepresents his or her identity to gain entrance, eavesdrops on personal affairs or trespasses, this is intrusion.

3. **Publicizing false material**   When a reporter tries to dramatize an event by inventing material, or when a television station produces a docudrama—a fictionalized account of an actual person or event—and defamatory material is used, the person may be placed before the public in what the law calls a "false light." A person may also be placed in a false light when he or she is linked to a defamatory situation. For example: A documentary on drug dealers operating on a city street may inadvertently show an innocent pedestrian walking down the street.

4. **Appropriation**   Use of someone's name or picture for advertising or for commercial purposes or for one's own use constitutes appropriation, unless consent is given. Legitimate news events can be covered, and no permission is needed. However, a feature story that uses the name and activities of a well-known person can be the cause of problems if the purpose of the story is to promote the newspaper's sales. In this situation, a court may rule that the story was designed to exploit the commercial value of the person.

An excellent guide to the laws of libel and privacy is *Synopsis of the Law of Libel and the Right of Privacy* by Bruce W. Sanford, published by Scripps-Howard Newspapers. The paperback edition is distributed by World

Almanac Publications, 200 Park Ave., New York, N.Y. 10166. Sanford is with the law firm that represents Scripps-Howard and has lectured and written extensively on libel and privacy.

Journalistic Ethics

- A reporter for the Oceanside, Calif., *Blade-Tribune* wrote a column for the newspaper that was almost a word-for-word copy of a column by Art Buchwald. He was asked to resign.
- A columnist for the *Daily News* in New York invented characters and quotes in a story about a street clash between British soldiers and a gang of youths in Belfast, Northern Ireland. He was forced to resign.
- A sports writer for *The Evening Tribune* in San Diego wrote a piece that contained material that had been published in *Inside Sports*. For using "certain phraseologies" from the magazine, he was suspended from his job.
- A *Washington Post* reporter who won a Pulitzer Prize in 1981 for her moving story about an 8-year-old heroin addict was fired when it was discovered that her story was fiction. The *Post* returned the prize.
- Walter Cronkite accepted an appointment to the board of directors of Pan American World Airways after he stepped down from his long tenure as the anchor man of the CBS "Evening News." Cronkite became a special correspondent for the network, and some of his work was to involve coverage of space programs with which Pan American had contracts. Cronkite was criticized for accepting the post on the ground it was a potential conflict of interests for him to accept money from an enterprise he would be covering. Six months after joining the Pan American board, Cronkite resigned from it.

These situations involve matters of journalistic ethics. Each is an example of a violation of one of the underlying rules of conduct for the journalist.

The journalist is expected to be truthful, to do his or her own work, to avoid pursuing any activity that would raise questions about his or her integrity. These and other ethical principles are outlined in various codes that newspapers, broadcast stations and national journalism organizations have adopted.

The codes prescribe responsibility to the reader or listener, accuracy, fairness and compassion. The code of the Society of Professional Journalists, for example, states that "the duty of journalists is to seek the truth." The code also states that "gifts, favors, free travel, special treatment or privileges can compromise the integrity of journalists and their employers. Nothing of value should be accepted."

Newspaper Code of Ethics

The following guidelines are excerpted from the code of ethics of *The Des Moines Register:*

An individual's own good judgment and integrity are the keystones of this code because it would be impossible to spell out every single question that might arise. . . .

Our management and employees must remain free of obligation to any special interest . . . avoiding all possible conflicts of interest or even the appearance thereof. . . .

MEALS—This code will continue the present company policy of having staff members pay for their own meals. . . . When it [is] impossible to pay for a meal beforehand or at the time . . . appropriate payment [shall be] sent later.

TRAVEL— . . . There are times when staffers ride with sports teams on chartered aircraft or with public officials on military aircraft or in chartered private aircraft with a political figure. On such occasions, the company will send a check covering our staffer's share of the transportation.

TICKETS—It shall be our policy that no staffer accept any free ticket to any event. . . .

OUTSIDE EMPLOYMENT AND ACTIVITIES— . . . No employee will hold membership on boards of directors of corporations, or assume leadership or activist roles on boards or organizations about which this employee might be called upon to write stories, take pictures, edit copy or make editorial judgments.

. . . Working for a political candidate or party would be a clear conflict of interests for almost any staff member. . . . There is a flat rule against any employee producing publicity material for any public official, politician, government agency or sports team. . . . [No staff member shall] make public statements of opinion that will compromise that staff member's credibility on the job.

In its code, the American Society of Newspaper Editors sets out six major categories:

1. **Responsibility**   The task of the journalist is to serve the general welfare by informing people so they can make judgments about the issues confronting them. Journalists should not abuse their power for selfish motives or unworthy purposes.
2. **Freedom of the press**   Freedom belongs to the people, and journalists must make sure public business is conducted in public. They must be vigilant against those who exploit the press for their purposes.
3. **Independence**   Journalists must avoid conflicts of interest. They should accept nothing from sources nor engage in any activity that compromises or might seem to compromise their integrity.
4. **Truth and accuracy**   The journalist must seek to keep the good faith of readers by assuring them that the news is accurate, free from bias, and that all sides are presented fairly.

5. **Impartiality** News reports and opinion should be clearly distinct. Opinion articles should be clearly identified as such.
6. **Fair play** Journalists should respect the rights of people in the news and be accountable to the public for the fairness and accuracy of their reports. Persons accused in the news should be allowed to respond.

(The Code of Ethics of the Society of Professional Journalists is included in Appendix D.)

Personal Code

Most of us know right from wrong. Our moral sense might have been influenced by our parents, schools or religious training. Some of our guidelines come from reading. For some young men and women, friends exert a powerful influence in establishing what is right and wrong.

For two days, a 16-year-old student at Milpitas High School in California bragged to his classmates he had raped and strangled his 14-year-old girlfriend. He then led several friends to a remote spot in the foothills near San Jose and showed them her body.

Eight youngsters saw the body of the girl. Some covered it with leaves to hide it. One dropped a rock on her head to make sure the corpse was really that of a human.

Not one of the youngsters informed the police.

An assembly-line worker, who had heard from friends that "a corpse was up in the hills," was shown the body by a student who had been taken to the scene by the 16-year-old. The worker called the police.

When word got out that the body had been recovered, some of the high school students criticized the worker for notifying the police. One described him as a "snitch . . . a fucking narc." The worker said that he had been hassled for his action. "I don't know if I'd do it again," he said.

Sheriff's Sgt. Gary Meeker wondered, "What the hell has happened to these kids?"

Sgt. Ron Icely of the Milpitas Police Department thinks he knows. "Usually when people are witnesses to a homicide, they come forward right away," he said. "But you have this code of honor (that says) forget about the girl on the side of the ravine and let's protect our buddy."

Although loyalty to friends is an honorable quality, at times we must respond to a greater demand on our loyalty, and this is our responsibility to society. Journalists can use their social responsibility as a basis for establishing a personal code of behavior.

Responsibility and Independence

Journalism is a public service. Its purpose is to serve all the people by providing information gathered by men and women who are independent of commitments or obligations to any special group. The journalist places responsibility to the public above and beyond loyalty to an employer, a political party or friends.

The journalist is committed to the free and open flow of information. Passing on information is the journalist's duty. Thus, if a source or a friend asks that something be withheld from print or broadcast, the journalist must weigh the request against his or her commitment to inform the public.

If an editor, publisher or news director kills a story or removes information from a story on the ground that it will hurt business, advertising or friends of the newspaper or station, the journalist again must confront the situation from a moral perspective.

In both cases, the action the journalist must take is clear: See that the information reaches readers and listeners. As a result, some journalists have lost sources and some have quit their jobs rather than be a party to a cover-up.

Sometimes, this independence can be strained almost to the breaking point, as it is when reporters learn about something that the government wants kept secret because of "national security." In such cases, the reporter is confronted by a dilemma. In a democracy, the public is entitled to know what its government is doing. At the same time, revealing this information endangers security, according to the government.

Watching Power

This brings us to a second basic point in the formulation of a personal code of ethical behavior. The point is that journalists serve their readers and listeners by checking on power. They maintain an adversary relationship to power. The power may be held by a dean, a corporation president, the mayor, or the president.

The founding fathers of this country made sure that journalists would be free of government interference or supervision so that the press could be a check on power.

If we go back to the first part of this chapter where we discussed libel, you can see the willingness of the federal courts to grant journalists wide freedom, even the freedom to make mistakes that libel officials. In the Sullivan ruling, the Supreme Court said that the press needed to be free of restrictions so that it can provide "the opportunity for free political discussion to the end that government may be responsive to the will of the people. . . ."

Reporters and their newspapers have confronted power at the highest levels, even at the risk of compromising what officials have said is "national security."

Given such power, the press can be an unchecked power itself. If government has no control over the press, what then is to protect the public from a free-wheeling, irresponsible press? Very little. And this is precisely why codes and guidelines—whether they are written and handed to reporters along with a stylebook, or are the reporter's personal beliefs—are so important.

Search for Truth

We have discussed two essentials for a personal code of ethics—responsibility to the public and independence from power. There are others for the young journalist to consider. A third is the mission to seek truth.

Most reporters understand that they should be truthful. But what is truth? At one level, it is the accurate reporting of what a source says in an interview. But the truth-seeker must do more. On important stories, the reporter is obligated to dig into the background, the causes, the underlying layers of the event.

A tenement burns down. Three people are killed. The reporter quotes the investigators about the cause—faulty wiring. The reporter makes still another check, an independent check. Has the city any record of violations of fire laws against the building? Was the building actually a death trap for its occupants?

A reporter who notices a pattern of fires in the area may even dig further and discover an arson ring, as a young woman working for a New Jersey newspaper did.

Not content with the official version, she checked records, looked at property transfers, examined insurance claims. She found that most of the fires were listed as being of suspicious origin, that the buildings had been heavily insured, and that they were owned by local police officers. Several people had been hurt in the fires, and one person had been killed.

Reporters have little tolerance for any person or any action that hurts people. This is the fourth point in our personal code. Journalists are concerned with the victims of unfair, illegal, discriminatory actions. They identify with the unfairly afflicted.

At the beginning of this chapter, mention was made of the reporter who adopted an identity to expose the Ku Klux Klan in his state. The use of poses and disguises is an old device frequently used by investigative reporters. A *Wall Street Journal* reporter obtained a job in a factory in Texas and then revealed the company's harsh personnel practices and anti-union bias. A reporter for *The Washington Post* feigned mental illness and was admitted to a large mental hospital. She described the inadequate care given patients.

Poses and Disguises

Lately, newspapers are questioning the use of this technique. They do not feel free to criticize others for illegal and underhanded actions in business and public life if they are themselves using questionable tactics to gather news.

Spies, snoops and informers are not respected in our society. Yet the newspaper whose reporters use poses and disguises do spy and snoop and then tell the story. It seems unethical, and it is. But it can be justified, under certain circumstances.

The reporter who is trying to formulate a personal ethical code might want to consider this point: When a critical condition exists in which people are endangered by a person or an organization, the journalist may use a tactic or a technique that otherwise would be considered unethical.

If the tactic will remove or publicize the danger, then the reporter may find justification for purposely misleading people from whom he or she intends to elicit information.

Guidelines for a Personal Code of Ethics

Here are some additional points for the beginning journalist to consider for a personal code of ethics:

The willingness to admit errors.

The determination to follow the facts, even if they lead in a direction you personally dislike or disagree with.

A commitment to make yourself improve as a journalist so that you can better serve those who rely on you as their eyes and ears.

Resistance to praise, the attractions of money, popularity and power—if any of these should stand in the way of writing the truth.

An identification with those who suffer.

The desire to make your community a better place to live in for all its people— youngsters in school, the sick in hospitals, the poor without jobs, the elderly without hope, the victims of discrimination.

A helpful booklet about journalistic ethics is published by the American Society of Newspaper Editors: *Playing It Straight: A Practical Discussion of the Ethical Principles of the American Society of Newspaper Editors.* The author is John L. Hulteng.

The journalist has a responsibility to the general society to serve as its watchdog, and sometimes this requires the warning bark of a brief story. At other times, it may be necessary to bite deeply into the situation. We punish the dog who bites unnecessarily, but we reward the watchdog that grabs the gunman by the arm, or threatens the thief's throat.

In the case of the Klan, its members have advocated violence against minority groups, and some Klansmen have been sentenced to prison for murder and conspiracy. The reporter who joined the Klan by using a pose may be thought of as providing a public service.

When such techniques are used, they should be described to the reader or listener. A tactic or technique used by a reporter that he or she is ashamed to admit in print or on the air should not be used in reporting.

Self-examination

One last word on developing a personal code. Each of us knows when he or she is giving the best possible effort. Sometimes we cannot do our best because we have not pushed ourselves.

Only the journalist knows when he or she is not doing the best he or she can. To accept anything of ourselves but the best is unethical because the journalist's duty is to inform, and only the best effort informs fully.

In other words, the student and the professional journalist must always be checking themselves: Is this story telling people all they need to know about the event? Should I make one more telephone call, check another document before I let it go? Is this the precise word in this sentence, or should I try harder to find a word that describes the situation more accurately? Am I being honest with the reader in the way I've structured this story, or have I emphasized a secondary element because it is more dramatic?

The Obscene, the Indecent and the Profane

Go back a few pages to the section on journalistic ethics. Reread the part that is titled "Personal Code." Was there something in this material that offended you, some word or reference that bothered you, that you would have preferred not to have read?

Flip the pages back still further. Look at the photographs in chapter 2. Were you uncomfortable when you looked at any of them?

In both places there is material that some people may consider offensive, a word and some photographs that are in questionable taste. The word is used in a quotation from a youth who condemned the worker who called the police to report the body in the foothills. He describes the worker as a "snitch . . . a fucking narc." The photographs are the grim, if not horrifying, pictures of the execution of members of Liberia's old guard.

Unquestionably, most people are bothered by obscene language and by explicit representations of death. Why, then, was the material used? Why did some newspapers that ran the story of the youngsters in Milpitas make the quote read: "f------ narc," whereas others used the actual language of the youth? And why did the Pulitzer Prize jurors think so much of the execution pictures they awarded the photographer a prize, while others turned away from the photographs in horror and condemned their use as another example of journalistic bad taste and sensationalism?

Because such questions are easier to raise than they are to answer, many people, and even some editors, have declared: Nothing obscene, profane or indecent should be published or broadcast. One example of how different newspapers chose to treat questionable material is shown in figure 16.1.

If the news is supposed to give the public a picture of reality, then a head-in-the-sand attitude deprives the public of essential information. Not only that, it is hypocritical. At the same time that some readers and listeners (and some editors as well) condemn the gossip columnist and are appalled by the picture of the dead child lying in the street, they applaud the movies and soap operas that routinely parade incest, adultery, murder and nudity.

Death and Its Aftermath.
The Dover, N.H., newspaper, *Foster's Daily Democrat,* ran this picture of a University of New Hampshire student being pulled from the water after the university rowing shell was swamped by a gale. Readers objected to the picture, saying it was in poor taste. Managing Editor Rod Doherty replied: "We used the photo because it was explicit in its depiction of the event. It showed the conclusion of a tragedy that need not have occurred. Our obligation is to collect and print the news."
Tim Lorette, *Foster's Daily Democrat*

Here is a summary of a week's activities on a few of the TV soaps:

ANOTHER WORLD: Jerry, who was Clarice's caller, raped Clarice while in a schizophrenic fit. James accepted Steve after Steve revealed his identity to all at a posh whing-ding.

AS THE WORLD TURNS: Eric and Sofia got spaced out on joints laced with PCP. Lydia, Miranda's sister, arrived. Len was arrested in a gambling raid. James and Nick became restaurant part-ners, but Steve was quietly aware that James planned to use the eatery as a dope front.

THE DOCTORS: Billy sacked with Nola after seeing Greta and Theo doing the town. Maggie suffered pregnancy complications.

THE YOUNG AND THE RESTLESS: Karen lied to Jill saying that Andy sleeps around. Barbara, under the name Bobbie Smith, rented April's old room from Dorothy and Wayne.

Many viewers do their housework—and homework—with one eye on these daily dramas. College students schedule their classes around their favorite soaps. And vacationers insist that their cottages come equipped with color TV sets so they can follow "All My Children," "The Guiding Light" and "Search for Tomorrow."

Clearly, there are words, subject matter and pictures that should be off-limits. But how do we determine what they are? Do we refrain from using

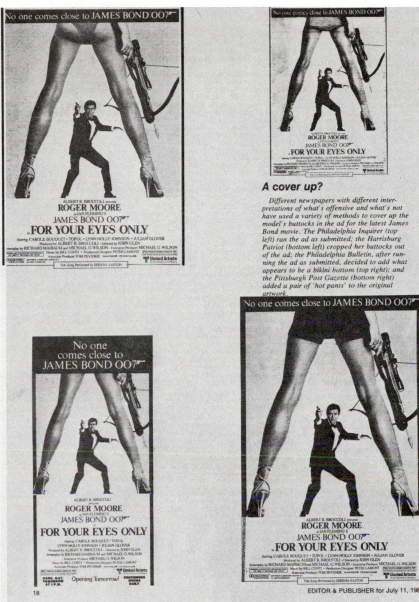

Figure 17.1 Cover-Up. Newspapers are sensitive to the possibility of offending their readers, as this display page from *Editor & Publisher* illustrates. After the advertisement for the movie ran untouched in *The Patriot Ledger* in Quincy, Mass., a group calling itself Morality in Media in Massachusetts complained the ad was vulgar and added to the "decivilization of society." *Editor & Publisher*

A cover up?

Different newspapers with different interpretations of what's offensive and what's not have used a variety of methods to cover up the model's buttocks in the ad for the latest James Bond movie. The Philadelphia Inquirer (top left) ran the ad as submitted; the Harrisburg Patriot (bottom left) cropped her buttocks out of the ad; the Philadelphia Bulletin, after running the ad as submitted, decided to add what appears to be a bikini bottom (top right); and the Pittsburgh Post Gazette (bottom right) added a pair of 'hot pants' to the original artwork.

EDITOR & PUBLISHER for July 11, 1981

any material that would offend someone? Benjamin Franklin had no use for such a resolution to the problem:

> If all printers were determined not to print anything until they were sure it would offend nobody, there would be very little printed.

These days, when so much of what is newsworthy does involve unsavory matters, a great deal of news would be eliminated if we sought to offend no one. Crime is a major problem in our society, and many of the crimes are unspeakably violent and vicious. Do we refrain from running the brutal rape, the beheading of a five-year-old, the robbery gang that drove ballpoint pens through the ears of helpless patrons of a supermarket?

We need guidelines for the use of frank language, subject matter that is offensive and pictures that are gruesome.

Vulgar Language

The New York Times permits the use of obscenity or vulgarity "only when the printing of the objectionable word or words will give the reader an obviously essential insight into matters of great moment—an insight that cannot be otherwise conveyed."

Language that is obscene and profane is offensive to many people. They find words that refer to the sex act or to bodily functions to be unsavory. Many also have deep resentments against words that profane the deity.

Much of the hostility to such language stems from the desire to keep this kind of language from becoming acceptable speech. Taste is the sum of many value judgments about what is acceptable language or behavior. If such language is seen and heard frequently by young people, it becomes a part of their language and, possibly, will influence their behavior. Thus, adults—who are responsible for establishing values for their children—are anxious to hold the line against obscenity and profanity.

On the other hand, such language is part of everyday life. How do newspapers, radio and television stations tread the thin line between the extremes without falling on either side—offending well-intentioned people or cutting readers and listeners off from reality?

Let's start with the quote from the youngster angry at the man he described as a "snitch." *The Miami Herald,* which carried the quote as "f----- narc," tried to walk the line. It did not run the obscenity, but by using the first letter and the exact number of dashes it was obvious to nearly all readers what the youngster actually said. I used the word *fucking* in this section. Why? Primarily to convey the intensity of the youth's feeling, but also because of the audience, the readers of this book. The *Herald's* readers range from grade school students to senior citizens. Some of the adults have strong feelings about obscenities. The newspaper prefers not to risk offending them.

The readers of this book are men and women who know the language of youth. To have used dashes instead of the actual word would have been, it seemed to me, insulting, condescending. If there is a young man or woman reading this book who has never heard the word, that is a rare person indeed these days. In addition, students are entitled to know the precise details of subjects they are studying. To sum it up, the word was used because it was **essential to the situation,** because the **nature of the audience** was such that the word would not be considered offensive, and because this is a textbook. Two concepts are put in boldface because they are important guides in deciding whether to use certain kinds of language in newspapers.

When Mark Patinkin and Christopher Scanlan of the *Journal-Bulletin* in Providence, R.I., interviewed the director of a job-training agency about unemployment among blacks, the official was frank, firm and forceful. This was reflected in his language. They quoted him as saying:

"It's a deep, deep problem," he said. "People don't realize it's an American problem. They say it's a black problem. It's a goddamn American problem and it requires the best energies of everybody to jump in and try and resolve it."

The profanity undoubtedly offended some readers of the newspaper. However, the writers chose to use it because of the intensity of feeling it revealed. The word was essential to the interview, they felt.

Some words are offensive in certain contexts, not in others. What do you think of this headline and lead from *The St. Petersburg Times?*:

Marie Osmond Says She Is a Virgin

Saying, "I have just as many passions as any other woman," Marie Osmond declares she is a virgin and a "square lady" in February's issue of *Ladies Home Journal.*

Celebrities raise the shades on their personal lives to allow journalists and the public to peek in. But that does not mean that every scene in every room need be described. Osmond has no objection to talking about her virginity, but what purpose does it serve in a newspaper? It adds nothing we need to know about the world.

So, what's the point? Marie Osmond's virginity is used to titillate readers, to give them the kind of excitement other media apparently dangle in front of their readers and viewers. In this sense, such stories do meet the competition—magazines, soap operas, movies.

If the editor desires to set a news policy in this direction, then editors and news writers must follow the policy. We now have a third guideline for determining what should be used—**the policy of the newspaper or station.**

Up to this point, we have been assuming that everyone agrees on what is offensive. The material we have used is clearly offensive to most people. But what is in poor taste to one person may be acceptable to another. The 16-year-old gang member and the Episcopal minister probably do not share the same definition of what is profane and what is obscene.

The truth is that there is no agreement on taste. There never will be. Just as some like licorice and others find it abominable, and just as some people will stand in the rain all night to buy tickets for a football game or a Bette Midler concert while others consider this a form of madness, so there can be no consensus on matters of taste.

However, we can say that opinions are changing, that overall there is a greater tolerance for what had been considered tasteless and offensive in what we read and see.

In 1905, the Brooklyn Public Library decided to ban from the children's room *The Adventures of Huckleberry Finn* and *Tom Sawyer* by Mark Twain. The librarians decided that the books were "bad examples" for children. The guardians of public morality often contend that their actions are intended to protect the young from contamination.

When Twain heard about the action of the librarians, he was contrite, and he made a public statement of his contrition.

"I wrote *Tom Sawyer* and *Huck Finn* for adults exclusively, and it always distresses me when I find that boys and girls have been allowed access to them," he wrote.

"The mind that becomes soiled in youth can never again be washed clean. I know this by my own experience, and to this day I cherish an unappeasable bitterness against the unfaithful guardians of my young life, who not only permitted but compelled me to read an unexpurgated Bible through before I was 15 years old.

"None can do that and ever draw a sweet breath again. . . ."

Twain was poking fun at the zealous guardians of public morality. *Huckleberry Finn* and books by J. D. Salinger, Kurt Vonnegut and others are constantly under attack by these zealots. Those who seek to ban books have been taken to the courts, which have held that book-banning is unconstitutional.

If we look at the subject matter of the stories that newspapers and newscasts carry we can see similar changes in the attitudes toward journalistic subject matter.

Subject Matter

Subject matter as well as language that were once deemed unfit for readers' consumption are now their daily fare. Even the most conservative newspapers carry the unsavory details of trials and the sordid aspects of crime. *The New York Times,* which promised at its founding that it would not "soil the breakfast table," has carried stories about teenage prostitution (male as well as female) and some of the bizarre antics of celebrities.

The details of the rape of a 7-year-old child by two 6-year-olds and an 8-year-old were carried by the AP and were printed by many newspapers. Here is the beginning of this sordid story:

SYRACUSE, N.Y. (AP)—Two 6-year-old boys and an 8-year-old boy are accused of raping a 7-year-old girl in the back of a school bus and again in an apartment building, police say.

"If they're not the youngest, then they are certainly among the youngest" rape suspects in the state, Syracuse police investigator Rod Carr said.

The incident allegedly occurred Monday afternoon when the four children were riding home from school.

After allegedly raping the girl on the back floor of a moving city school bus, the three boys forced her into an apartment building where they attacked her a second time, according to a report issued by Carr.

Police were vague on the details of the alleged rape, and some medical experts said Wednesday a rape by boys so young would be physically "unusual." Dr. Gerald Nathanson, a pediatrician at Montefiore Hospital in New York City, said rape involving boys aged 6 to 8 would be "highly improbable."

But Carr said doctors at Crouse-Irving Memorial Hospital here confirmed the girl had been raped. The girl was taken to the hospital after her mother discovered her crying in bed, he said.

"We just received the medical reports, and, as unlikely as it may seem, it indicates that a rape took place."

The mother of the girl, whose name was withheld, said her daughter used to play alongside the three boys. . . .

This is a horrible story, clearly offensive to almost anyone. Why run it? Most of the newspapers that used it were not trying to peddle papers. They were, rather, trying to call attention to something terrible about the society we live in, to cry out that something must be very wrong if children can behave this way.

This leads to another guideline for our consideration: **Material that warns us or serves as a deterrent** may be used despite its tastelessness. Indeed, it is the shock value of the offensive material that drives home the point.

The Sex Industry

When Charles Bernsen of *The Commercial Appeal* was assigned to do a series of articles on the commercial sex industry in Memphis he had to see just what was being sold.

He says he went out to see his first peep show:

I remember coming out of the place, pausing to blink away the bright sunlight, and thinking: "How in the hell am I going to put what I just saw in the newspaper?"

The dilemma only got worse. I visited 12 more peep shows during the next eight weeks, including two that had "live show" booths in which patrons were urged to masturbate while they watched a naked woman writhe in feigned sexual ecstasy on the other side of a glass partition.

I went to 17 nightclubs that featured topless and/or bottomless dancers. In addition to watching the stage show, a patron could pay $5 for a four-minute "table dance" during which he often did more than just simulate the sex act with the naked waitress dancing between his outstretched legs.

I subscribed to a Memphis firm's obscene phone call service. (Pay them $20 and they send you a telephone number. Call the number and a woman will tell you what she'd like to do to you if only you were there with her.)

I subscribed to the same company's referral service for "swingers." (Pay them $20 and they send you the names and telephone numbers of folks in your area who are interested in getting together for a little mate swapping or group sex.)

I went to a public swingers club that said it offered "twosomes, threesomes, foursomes and moresomes" and did.

Bernsen and the newspaper were trapped in a dilemma. The commodity being peddled was bound to repel many readers, but the story had to be told because of the consequences of commercial sex. Much of it, Bernsen found, was controlled by organized crime, and its activities included "murders, beatings and attempted bombings." Also, it was big business in Memphis, grossing about $10 million a year.

"A business that big needs to be covered," Bernsen said. "That doesn't mean propriety should be tossed out the window.

"It doesn't do any good to write a story if your readers are going to gag on their orange juice and refuse to read it. But the business of selling sexual titillation can be reported fully and accurately without being titillating."

The policy that was adopted for the series was this: "If it was important to understanding how a part of the sex industry operated, we described or explained it in as much detail as possible. If it was superfluous, we avoided explicit detail that might be offensive."

This brings us to another guideline: **Explicit details of tasteless matters are avoided unless absolutely relevant to the story.**

Man or Woman?

Just what is relevant? This question came up with the story that we mentioned at the beginning of this chapter: the murder of Stella Walsh, the Olympic track champion and a prominent member of Cleveland's Polish-American community.

After the two television stations reported the coroner's finding that the examination revealed the body of 69-year-old Walsh was that of a man and not a woman, the community became angry and hostile. People called and wrote to protest against the station's revelation.

The only local television station that did not mention the result of the autopsy was WJKW-TV, whose news director said that although the station knew of the sex angle it did not use it because: "We didn't think it was germane to the story. It was essentially a story of crime and violence."

Cleveland's two daily newspapers agreed with the news director's sentiments. An editor of the *Plain Dealer* said that the paper "felt there should be dignity in death."

To these objections, the assistant news director of WEWS-TV said that the coroner's findings were the story.

The full story was run by *The Philadelphia Inquirer, The Boston Globe* and *The New York Times.* Only then did the Cleveland papers use the details.

Unquestionably, the coroner's findings were relevant. On the other hand, the local newspapers and WJKW were undoubtedly sensitive to their audience, the Polish-American community, many of whom wrote angry letters to the stations. WKYC-TV received 200 calls the night it used the story and 100 calls and letters over the next week, almost all critical of the reporting.

Legitimate or Irresponsible? When the *Columbus Citizen-Journal* ran this picture of the body of a nine-year-old girl who had been struck by a car, readers wrote and called to protest. They described it as tasteless and irresponsible journalism. Many readers said that such realism is unnecessary. The newspaper replied that the photo was a stark reminder to parents and to children of the dangers of city streets.
Hank Reichard, *Columbus Citizen-Journal*

The picture was stark and tragic: A child's body, half covered by a blanket, lay in the street where she had been struck and killed by a car.

Photographs

As soon as the newspaper arrived in the homes of readers, the complaints began. Callers, then letter writers, complained that using the picture was irresponsible, that it was sensational journalism. Richard R. Campbell, editor of the *Columbus Citizen-Journal,* said "the most common accusation was that the picture was tasteless.

"One reader called us coldhearted and tasteless and urged us not to forget discretion and compassion." Another reader said, "You have won first prize in the journalistic bad taste contest. Your prize for achieving this distinction is an all-expense paid trip to 'Sensational City' for the photographer and the editor who saw fit to print the picture."

Campbell said that the decision to run the photograph was his. His reasons, he said, were these:

> There could be no more dramatic way to point out to mothers and fathers and children, to drivers and pedestrians, the danger of carelessly stepping into the street. The proverb says one picture is worth more than 1,000 words. Here was such a picture.
>
> Secondly, it was part of our role of writing history.
>
> One father who appreciated our reason for using the photo said he showed it to his small sons, separately, and took the time to explain to each what happened to the little girl and why. That is what we expected the reaction to be.

If we look back at the guidelines for using material that may be in questionable taste, we can see that one of the reasons editors used the picture was that they hoped it would serve as a warning, a deterrent. The horror of the picture might register, as no written warnings can, the dangers to youngsters of playing in the street or darting out into the street.

Campbell also mentions the fact that this was part of local history. Of course, not every incident and accident is recorded by newspapers. The newspaper is, as historians are, selective. The editor chose to run this picture because it was a graphic demonstration of a part of every community's history—the appalling toll of traffic deaths.

"We gave our readers a slice of Tuesday's life in Columbus that they did not want to see," a reporter said about the protests. "Hank Reichard took the image of that broken little girl and hurled it in our faces so that we would have to look at her, too.

"Hank made us care that a little girl had died when she should not have died, in a place that was terribly wrong for a child's death. He made us suffer."

Some of the same reasons can be given for the other photographs in this book that might have offended readers—the pictures by Larry C. Price of the execution on the beach in Liberia. These pictures did indeed show us history in the making.

Sports pictures do not usually provide problems of taste. But Harry Baumert's photograph of an angry basketball coach caused problems for editors at *The Des Moines Register*. The photograph was of Iowa State University coach Johnny Orr gesticulating toward a referee—the "finger photo," as it was dubbed. (See the picture in the photo display that opens this section.)

Heckling the Hecklers. Nelson Rockefeller, then vice president, responds to hecklers at a political rally. Many newspapers ran the picture— obviously of an obscene gesture—on page one. Don Black, *Press and Sun-Bulletin*

Although the editor of the newspaper approved the picture for publication, the sports editor killed it. "While it was a dramatic photo, it was clearly obscene. I didn't feel there was sufficient news value to risk alienating the bulk of our readers," the sports editor concluded.

Drake Mabry, associate editor of the *Register* decided to ask editors over the country whether they would have used the picture. The result: 129 said no; 31 said yes, and 61 said perhaps.

Of those who would have turned it down, 32 said they had used the photograph of Nelson Rockefeller, then vice president, making the same gesture to heckling students. AP Newsphotos ran the Rockefeller picture, but not the Iowa State shot. Why?

Rockefeller was widely known, his actions covered by the press. The coach, says Hal Buell, AP assistant general manager for Newsphotos, is hardly in that class. Buell says, ". . . a picture of nobody giving nobody the finger is still a picture of nothing. So we wouldn't carry it, basically because it lacks news value."

Summary

Here are some guidelines for questionable language, subject matter and photographs:

The material must be essential to the story being told. Without the material, the point would not be made or would be diluted.

The audience must be taken into consideration. If the great majority of readers or listeners would be offended, the material should not be used.

If the material serves as a warning, then it may be used despite its offensive nature.

Details of crimes, sex acts and other shocking actions should not be used unless absolutely relevant.

If the event has historical significance, it should be used.

Preparing Copy

1. Use copy paper, newsprint or some other non-glossy paper. Triple space. Use large margins left and right.
2. Make a carbon of all your work. Keep the carbon.
3. In the upper left-hand corner of the first sheet of all assignments, place your name, slug of story, news source and date. Thus:

Chamberlain
PHA-attended
10/7/85

4. On the first page, begin one-third down the page. Write on one side of the paper only.
5. If the story consists of more than one page, write and circle *more* at the bottom of the page that is being continued. On the next page, put your name, "2" and slug at top left of page. Thus: Chamberlain-2-PHA. For the next page, make it 3, and so on.
6. End each page with a complete paragraph, not in the middle of a sentence.
7. Do not correct mistakes by backspacing and typing over. Cross out and retype. Never write over.
8. For simple errors, use copy editing symbols. (See fig. 10.1.) Do not confuse these with proofreading marks.
9. Never divide words at the end of a line. Hit the margin release and continue or cross out and begin word anew on the next line.
10. Keep copy clean. Retype hard-to-read sections and paste over, preferably with rubber cement.
11. Do not write more than one story on each sheet of paper.
12. End stories with an end mark: 30, #, or END.
13. Follow the stylebook. (See Appendix B.)
14. When finished, fold all pages together, in half, copy on the outside, reporter's name showing in the upper left.

Preparing Copy on a Typewriter

Preparing Copy on a Video Display Terminal

Most newspapers have traded in their typewriters for electronic equipment that has eliminated the costly and time-consuming process of typesetting a newspaper with hot metal.

The video display terminal (VDT) consists of keyboard and screen. The keyboard is used much like a typewriter, although it also has keys with special instructions for setting the type, moving copy around and editing.

The screen displays the copy as it is typed. Depending on the terminal model, 14 to 30 lines of copy can be seen on the screen.

The copy may be stored on a magnetic disk, a magnetic card or in some other storage device. It can then be called up for copy editing, which is also carried out on the screen of the terminal.

The edited version is sent to the phototypesetter, which sets the story according to the instructions of the news writer or editor. The story is produced on photosensitive paper that is placed in a processor.

In the processor, the paper is developed and a positive image or print is produced. The printed material is proofread and then placed on sheets for makeup.

For the news writer, keyboarding a story is faster and easier than using the typewriter. Since the system has a programmed set of instructions that justifies lines and hyphenates words, the writer does not have to return the carriage but types in an endless line. Corrections and other changes are made with the use of a cursor, a patch of light that can be moved anywhere on the screen.

On newspapers whose terminals connect to a large storage computer, news writers can call up various reference materials, such as the newspaper's clippings on a subject. Reporters also can store their notes or partially completed stories, and with the use of their personal code numbers can call these up.

When the story is finished, it is read on the screen by a copy editor who also puts into the terminal a number of instructions about how the copy is to be set. These instructions are called *formats* or *parameters*.

A list of computer terms is included in the glossary at the end of the book.

Appendix B

Stylebook

The purpose of this stylebook is to set standards of consistency for abbreviations, capitalization, punctuation and other usage on which there may be differences of opinion. The stylebook makes the rules. This brief stylebook is based on common practices adopted by the AP and UPI for their stylebooks.

Addresses, months, states and titles are often abbreviated.

Abbreviations

Addresses   Abbreviate *Avenue, Boulevard, Street* with specific address—1314 Kentucky St. Spell out without specific address—Kentucky Street, Fifth Avenue.

Months   Abbreviate month with specific date—Jan. 25, 1927. Spell out when month stands alone or is followed by a year—January 1927.

States   Abbreviate all states but the following when used with a city, in a dateline, or with party affiliation—Alaska, Hawaii, Idaho, Iowa, Maine, Ohio, Utah. Do not use Postal Service abbreviations. Spell out all states when standing alone.

Ala.	Fla.	Md.	Neb.	N.D.	Tenn.	Wyo.
Ariz.	Ga.	Mass.	Nev.	Okla.	Tex.	
Ark.	Ill.	Mich.	N.H.	Ore.	Vt.	
Calif.	Ind.	Minn.	N.J.	Pa.	Va.	
Colo.	Kan.	Miss.	N.M.	R.I.	Wash.	
Conn.	Ky.	Mo.	N.Y.	S.C.	W. Va.	
Del.	La.	Mont.	N.C.	S.D.	Wis.	

Titles   Abbreviate titles before a name, except academic titles—professor, dean, chairman. When standing alone, spell out—The governor vetoed the bill.

Addresses	Use figures for the address number—3 Third Ave.; 45 Main St. Spell out numbers under 10 as street names—21 Fourth Ave.; 450 11th St.

Age

Infant Under one year of age.

Child The period between infancy and youth, ages one to 13.

Youth 13–18.

Man, Woman Over 18.

Adult Over 18, unless used in specific legal context for crimes such as drinking.

Middle-aged 35–55.

Elderly Over 65. Avoid when describing people.

Capitalization

Generally, follow a down style.

Proper nouns Use capitals for names of persons, places, trademarks, titles when used with names; nicknames of persons, states, teams; titles of books, plays, movies.

President Make it a capital when it precedes the name; lowercase in all other uses—President Hoover. The president.

False titles Generally avoid false titles—right fielder Tommy Jones; television star Babs Buchin. Put some titles after person's names with commas—Tommy Jones, right fielder, struck out. Lowercase the title if used to precede name.

Contractions

Avoid unless used in direct quotes or to set an informal tone to story.

Courtesy Titles

Miss, Mrs., Ms., Mr. usually are not used on first reference with the full name. Use *Mrs.* on first reference for clarity when a woman requests that her husband's first name be used or her own first name cannot be ascertained—Mrs. Bruce Berning. On first reference, use the woman's first name. Do not use *Mr.* in any reference.

Use the courtesy title for a woman on second reference, following the woman's preference: If married, use *Mrs.* unless she prefers *Ms.* If married and she prefers to be known by her maiden name, use *Miss* or *Ms.*, if she prefers. If unmarried, use *Miss* on second reference unless the woman prefers *Ms.* For divorced women or women whose husbands have died, use *Mrs.* on second reference unless the woman prefers *Ms.*

Note: A number of newspapers drop *Mrs., Miss* and *Ms.* as well as *Mr.* on second reference—A Norfolk woman, Frances Savage, accused the judge of running a "three-ring circus." Savage made her charges in a letter to the editor. In 1985, the AP stylebook added: If the woman says she does not want a courtesy title, refer to her on second reference by last name only.

Punctuation   July 6, 1957, is her birth date. (Use commas.) She was born in July 1957. (No comma between month and year.)   **Dates**

Abbreviation   Abbreviate month with specific date—Feb. 19. Spell out all months when standing alone. With dates, use abbreviations: *Jan., Feb., Aug., Sept., Oct., Nov., Dec.;* spell out *March, April, May, June, July.*

Spell out one through nine; use figures for 10 and above.   **Numerals**

Spell out a number when it begins a sentence—Fifteen members voted against the bill. Use figures when a year begins a sentence—1980 began auspiciously.

Use figures for percentages and percents.

For amounts of $1 million and more, use the $ sign and figures up to two decimal places with the *million, billion, trillion* spelled out—$1.65 million. Exact amounts are given in figures—$1,650,398.

When spelling out large numbers, separate figure ending in "y" from next number with a hyphen–Seventy-nine; one hundred seventy-nine.

A pronoun should agree with its antecedent in number, person and gender.   **Pronouns**
The most common fault is a shift in (1) number or (2) person.

1.   The organization added basketball and hockey to their winter program. (Wrong.)
      The organization added basketball and hockey to its winter program. (Right.)
2.   When one wants to ski, you have to buy good equipment. (Wrong.)
      When one wants to ski, he or she has to buy good equipment. (Right.)

If the antecedent is singular, it is referred to with a singular pronoun. A singular pronoun is preferred with these antecedents: each, every, either, neither, someone, somebody, anyone, anything, anybody, everyone, no one, nobody.

A common error is to give teams, groups and organizations the plural pronoun:

> The team played their best shortstop. (Wrong.)
> The team played its best shortstop. (Right.)
> The Police Department wants recruits. They need 1,500 applicants. (Wrong.)
> The Police Department wants recruits. It needs 1,500 applicants. (Right.)

The nouns in the above examples are called collective nouns. If the noun is plural in idea, use the plural pronoun:

> The family enjoyed their vacations.

Punctuation   Keep a good grammar book handy. No stylebook can adequately cover the complexities of the 13 punctuation marks: apostrophe, brackets, colon, comma, dash, ellipsis, exclamation point, hyphen, parentheses, period, question mark, quotation marks, semicolon. The following is a guide to frequent problems and usages:

Apostrophe   Use for (1) possessives, (2) to indicate omitted figures or letters and (3) to form some plurals.

1.   *Possessives:* Add apostrophe and *s* (*'s*) to the end of common nouns or the indefinite pronoun unless it begins with *s* or *z* sound:
>   The woman's coat. The women's coats.
>   The child's toy. The children's toys.
>   Someone's pistol. One's hopes.
     If the word is plural and ends in an *s* or *z* sound, add apostrophe only:
>   Boys' books. Joneses' farm.
2.   *Omitted figures or letters:* Use in contractions—Don't, can't. Put in place of omitted figure—Class of '86.
3.   *To form some plurals:* When figures, letters, symbols and words are referred to as words, use the apostrophe and *s*.
>   Figures: She skated perfect 8's.
>   Letters: He received all A's in his finals.
>   Symbols: Journalists never use *&'s* to substitute for the *ands* in their copy.

Caution: The pronouns *ours, yours, theirs, his, hers, whose* do not take the apostrophe. Its is the possessive pronoun. *It's* is the contraction of *it is.*
Note: Compound words and nouns in joint possession use the possessive in the last word:

Everybody else's homes.
His sister-in-law's book.
Carter and Kennedy's party.

If there is separate possession, each noun takes the possessive form:

Mondale's and Kennedy's opinions differ.

Brackets Check whether the newspaper can set them. The wire services cannot transmit brackets. Use to enclose a word or words within a quote that the writer inserts—"Happiness [his note read] is a state of mind." Use for paragraph(s) within a story that refer to an event separate from the datelined material.

Colon The colon usually is used at the end of a sentence to call attention to what follows. It introduces lists, tabulations, texts and quotations of more than one sentence.

It can also be used to mark a full stop before a dramatic word or statement—She had only one goal in life: work. The colon is used in time of day, 7:45 p.m.; elapsed time of an event, 4:01.1, and in dialogue in question and answer, as from a trial.

Comma The best general guide for the use of the comma is the human voice as it pauses, stops and varies in tone. The comma marks the pause, the short stop:

1. He looked into the hospital room, but he was unable to find the patient.
2. Although he continued his search on the floor for another 20 minutes, he was unable to find anyone to help him.
3. He decided that he would go downstairs, ask at the desk and then telephone the police.
4. If that also failed, he thought to himself, he would have to give up the search.

Note that when reading these sentences aloud, the commas are natural resting points for pauses. The four sentences also illustrate the four principles governing the use of commas:

1. The comma is used to separate main clauses when they are joined by a coordinating conjunction. (The coordinating conjunctions are: *for, nor, and, but, or.*) The comma can be eliminated if the main clauses are short—He looked into the room and he froze.
2. Use the comma after an introductory element: a clause, long phrase, transitional expression or interjection.

3. Use the comma to separate words, phrases or clauses in a series. Also, use it in a series of coordinate adjectives—He was wearing a long, full cape.
4. Set off non-essential material in a sentence with comma(s). When the parenthetical or interrupting non-restrictive clauses and phrases are in the middle of a sentence two commas are needed—The country, he was told, needed his assistance. Other uses of the comma:

Use a comma with full sentence quotes, not with partial quotes—He asked, "Where are you going?" The man replied that he was "blindly groping" his way home.

To separate city and county, city and state. In place of the word *of* between a name and city—Jimmy Carter, Plains, Ga.

To set off a person's age—Orville Sterb, 19, of Fullerton, Calif. In dates—March 19, 1940, was the date he entered the army.

In party affiliations—Bill Bradley, D-N.J., spoke.

Caution: The comma is frequently misused by placing it between two main clauses instead of using the period or semicolon. This is called the comma splice:

The typewriter was jammed, he could not type his theme. (Wrong.)
The typewriter was jammed. He could not type his theme. The
typewriter was jammed; he could not type his theme. (Right.)

Dash Use a dash (1) to indicate a sudden or dramatic shift in thought within a sentence, (2) to set off a series of words that contains commas and (3) to introduce sections of a list or a summary.

The dash is a call for a short pause, as are the comma and the parenthesis. The comma is the most often used and is the least dramatic of the separators. The parentheses set off unimportant elements. The dash tends to emphasize material. It has this quality because it is used sparingly.

1. He stared at the picture—and he was startled to find himself thinking of her face. The man stood up—painfully and awkwardly—and extended his hand in greeting.
2. There were three persons watching them—an elderly woman, a youth with a crutch at his side and a young woman in jeans holding a paperback—and he pulled her aside out of their view.
3. He gave her his reasons for being there.
   —He wanted to apologize;
   —He needed to give her some material;
   —He was leaving on a long trip.

(*Note:* This third form should be used infrequently, usually when the listing will be followed by an elaboration.)

The dash is also used in datelines.

Ellipsis Use the ellipsis to indicate material omitted from a quoted passage from a text, transcript, play, etc.—The minutes stated that Breen had asked, "How many gallons of paint . . . were used in the project?" Put one space before and one space after each of the three periods. If the omission ends with a period, use four periods, one to mark the end of the sentence (without space, as a regular period), three more for the ellipsis.

The ellipsis is also used by some columnists to separate short items in a paragraph.

Do not use to mark pauses, shifts in thought, or for emphasis.

Exclamation point Much overused. There are reporters who have gone through a lifetime of writing and have never used the exclamation point, except when copying material in which it is used. The exclamation point is used to indicate powerful feelings, surprise, wonder. Most good writers prefer to let the material move the reader to provide his or her own exclamation.

When using, do not use a comma or period after the exclamation point. Place inside quotation marks if it is part of the quoted material.

Hyphen The hyphen is used (1) to join words to express a single idea or (2) to avoid confusion or ambiguity.

1. Use the hyphen to join two or more words that serve as a single adjective before a noun—A well-known movie is on television tonight. He had a know-it-all expression.
   Caution: Do not use the hyphen when the first word of the compound ends in "ly" or when the words follow the noun—He is an easily recognized person. Her hair was blond black.
2. Avoid (a) ambiguity or (b) an awkward joining of letters or syllables by putting a hyphen between prefixes or suffixes and the root word. Follow the dictionary usage.

   a. He recovered the chair. He re-covered the chair.
   b. Re-enter, shell-like.

Parentheses Generally, avoid. They may be necessary for the insertion of background or to set off supplementary or illustrative material.

Use period inside closing parenthesis if the matter is a complete sentence.

Period Use the period at the end of declarative sentences, indirect questions, most imperative sentences and most abbreviations.

The period is placed inside quotation marks.

Question mark The question mark is used for direct questions, not indirect questions.

Direct: Where are you going?
Indirect: He asked where she was going.

The question mark goes inside quotation marks if it applies to the quoted material—He asked, "Have you seen the movie?" Put it outside if it applies to the entire sentence—Have you seen "Guys and Dolls"?

Quotation marks Quotation marks set off (1) direct quotations, (2) some titles and nicknames and (3) words used in a special way.

1. Set off the exact words of the speaker—"He walked like a duck," she said. He replied that he walked "more like an alley cat on the prowl."
2. Use for book and movie titles, titles of short stories, poems, songs, articles from magazines and plays. Some nicknames take quotation marks—Sen. Henry "Scoop" Jackson. Do not use for nicknames of sports figures.
3. For words used in a special sense—An "Indian giver" is someone who gives something to another and then takes it back.

Punctuation with quotation marks:

The comma—Use it outside the quotation marks when setting off the speaker at the beginning of a sentence—He said, "You care too much for money." Use inside quotation marks when the speaker ends the sentence—"I just want to be safe," she replied.
The colon and semicolon—Always place outside the quotation marks—He mentioned her "incredible desire for work"; he meant her "insatiable desire for work."
The dash, question mark and exclamation point—inside when they apply to quoted matter only; outside when they refer to the whole sentence—She asked: "How do you know so much?" He asked himself, what's the meaning of "know so much"?

For quotes within quotes, use single quote mark (the apostrophe on typewriter) for the inner quotation— "Have you read 'War and Peace'?" he asked. Note that no comma is used after the question mark.

Semicolon Usually overused by beginning reporters. Unless there is a special reason to use the semicolon, use the period.

Use the semicolon to separate a series of equal elements when the individual segments contain material that is set off by commas. This makes for clarity in the series—He suggested that she spend her allowance on the new series at the opera, "Operas of the Present"; books of plays by Shaw, Ibsen and Aristophanes; and novels by Tolstoy, Dickens and F. Scott Fitzgerald.

Sexism

Avoid stereotyping women or men. Be conscious of equality in treatment of both sexes.

In writing of careers and jobs, avoid presuming that the wage-earner is a man and that the woman is a homemaker.

> The average worker with a wife and three children. . . . (Wrong.)
> The average family of five. . . . (Right.)

Avoid physical descriptions of women or men when not absolutely relevant to the story.

Use parallel references to both sexes—the men and the women, not the men and the ladies; husband and wife, not man and wife.

Do not use nouns and pronouns to indicate sex unless the sex difference is basic to understanding or there is no suitable substitute. One way to avoid such subtle sexism is to change the noun to the plural, eliminating the masculine pronoun: Drivers should have their licenses.

Personal appearances and marital and family relationships should be mentioned only when relevant to the story.

Spelling

When in doubt about spelling, consult an accepted dictionary. Use the first spelling listed. If the word is not listed, do not use it unless it is a direct quote.

Time

Exact times are often unnecessary. Last night and this morning are acceptable substitutes for yesterday and today, if appropriate. Use exact time when pertinent, but avoid redundancies—8 a.m. this morning should be 8 a.m. today or 8 o'clock this morning.

Use figures except for noon and midnight.

Separate hours from minutes with a colon—3:15 p.m.

Complete Stories

Without Heat: It's a Way of Life for Them

Chapter 2

by Mary Ann Giordano

It is warm and bright in Marie Walker's kitchen. Four flames glow on the aging stove as a pot of water boils steadily. The door of the oven is open, and she sits in front of it, her sock-covered feet propped on the door as the gas heat warms her toes.

It is the only hot spot in the apartment, the only place in the entire building where warm breath does not send puffs of vapor into the air.

A thermometer in a front room, where the sun shines through a window, registers 52 degrees. That is warm, the Walker family says. Saturday it reached a high of 39 degrees inside.

It is so cold the pipes burst in the four-story apartment building at 587 Gates Ave. in Bedford-Stuyvesant and the seven members of the Walker family must take turns drawing water from a hydrant on the street.

Water from hydrant

None of the Walkers like that chore. They say it "embarrasses" them to have to use the wrench on the hydrant in front of their apartment to draw enough water for their cooking and washing needs. Sometimes they fight over "whose water" it is. They say they never appreciated water so much in their lives.

But that is not their only hardship. When the pipes burst, their toilet stopped working, and the bowl remains filled with water. Their friends have been startled in answering the door to find one of the Walkers out of breath in the rush to a workable toilet.

The Walkers— 60-year-old Marie; her daughter Sarah and Sarah's three children; and another daughter Ethel and Ethel's son—had thanked God every morning this winter for the mild weather. They thanked God because they knew they faced cold weather without any heat. Last week, their prayers ran out.

Still hasn't lost her smile

"We got very religious this winter," says Ethel Walker, a 28-year-old marketing student who manages to keep a constant smile on her face as she tells of her struggle for decent housing.

"I mean very religious," she says. "Every morning we would wake up and say, thank God. It's warm again today."

It is not the only time the Walkers have prayed for such things. For more than three years, they have been the only tenants in their eight-apartment building. They have prayed to keep the junkies out, prayed the rats will have enough to eat elsewhere and will stay away from them, and prayed that they will soon be able to move.

Marie Walker has lived at 587 Gates Ave. for 20 years. It was a nice building when she moved in, she says. Then the landlord abandoned it and the city took it over. It was sold then to another landlord who more than quadrupled the rents.

Rent control and more than 15 years in that building saved Marie from a substantial rent increase.

High rents drive tenants out

When the other tenants could not afford to pay the high rents and moved out, she was left alone. She's been alone with her family in the building ever since. Only the junkies who populate the lower floors at night and the rats who seem to own the place are there to keep them company.

Since then, the building—like the neighborhood around it—has continued to deteriorate. Last winter, after many nights without heat, the boiler broke for good.

The Walkers learned to live without hot water, heating small amounts on the stove and visiting friends for baths. They accepted things when their new landlord told them the building wasn't profitable enough for her and she was pulling out. It wasn't until the water stopped completely that things became unbearable.

"It's bad enough when you can't get no hot water, but when you can't get no water . . ." Marie Walker says, her voice trailing off as she shakes her head.

Chill affects her arthritis

She rubs her swollen right knee from time to time, trying to massage the arthritis out of her joints. The cold and the broken windows in her rear bedroom—covered only by sheets of heavy plastic—do not help her soreness during the night. The stove burning steadily and the heaps of blankets only take the stinging chill from the air.

Ethel and Sarah and Sarah's 2-year-old daughter, Crystal, share two twin beds pushed together in the front room. Harry, 11, and Tyrone, 9—Sarah's sons—and Jamel, 7—Ethel's son—sleep together in a nearby room.

The Walkers do not sleep soundly. Ethel and Sarah leave a light burning in their room through the night to let would-be arsonists know someone lives there.

"All someone has to do is set a match to this place," Sarah says sadly.

They sleep with a prayer that the meager lock on the front door will discourage the junkies from coming in, they say, and they address the rats as "Mr." and "Mrs."

"We have to ask them, can we sleep tonight, is it okay if we sleep?" Sarah jokes.

Hopes to get city housing

No lack of enterprise has contributed to the Walkers' situation. They have tried to get out. Ethel has been approved for Section 8 housing and is simply awaiting a vacancy that can offer her better conditions than she has. Sarah is trying to get into city housing with her mother, and has been on the phone constantly to get help.

It has not been easy for them. After almost four years, Ethel lost her job as secretary with an engineering firm in cutbacks. The job loss eliminated a substantial source of income for the family, and is also making it difficult for Ethel to move into a Section 8 apartment. It is also making it difficult for her to study, as she pursues a goal of becoming a broadcast journalist.

Sarah says she and her mother simply waited too long to get out. They kept waiting for better, but things kept getting worse.

"We're past scared," Ethel says. "We're at the bottom now and the only way to go is up."

"There ain't nothing left but for us to die," Marie Walker said. Then, shuffling off her slippers, she pulled her legs up over the oven door, pushed her feet back inside, and leaned back in the warmth.

—The *Daily News* (N.Y.)

A Family Still Asks for Home

Chapter 2

by Mary Ann Giordano

The plumbing is still broken, the heat is still out, the junkies and rats still roam freely through the lower floors, and the Walker family of Bedford-Stuyvesant is still looking for decent housing.

Three weeks after an article appeared in *The Daily News* detailing the plight of the seven members of the Walker family, they are still trekking through the maze of housing regulations—cruel realities that confront New Yorkers searching for livable housing.

A vacancy notice was posted on their building at 587 Gates Ave. last week after the housing code inspectors found the place uninhabitable. Now, 60-year-old Marie Walker, her daughters, Sarah and Ethel, and the daughters' four children, are on waiting lists for other apartments.

Meanwhile, they are still drawing all their water from the fire hydrant in front of their apartment and storing it in bottles kept over the unworkable sink.

They still must run to the apartments of friends and neighbors to find a workable toilet.

Warmed by sun

The boiler remains broken and they are still gathering in a frontroom of the house to be warmed by the sun when it streams in through the window.

The gas stove is lit often to provide heat to the rear of the house, and last month the Walkers paid $85 for gas and electricity. That price was estimated, however. The meter readers could not enter the basement to get the true readings because it has remained flooded with several feet of water from when the pipes burst.

20-year residents

There is housing available for the Walkers, housing authorities said. But the Walkers are looking for better than they have. They are looking for the security they thought they had for most of the 20 years they lived at 587 Gates Ave.

But a change in landlords and hefty rent increases drove all the tenants out of that building, and for the last two years, the Walkers have been the only tenants in the four-story building.

Protected by rent control, they continued to pay their $49.12 a month until early fall, when the landlord stopped purchasing oil and told them she was abandoning the building.

Their attempts to get out of the building have not been easy, they said. It took until earlier this month for housing inspectors to arrive, and they did not post the vacate notice until last Thursday.

Then, Sarah Walker was counseled by the Department of Relocation, who took her application for emergency housing. Sarah said the counselor told her he could place her, her two sons, her toddler daughter, and her mother, in temporary housing. She said he told her it would be three to five months before she could place them in permanent housing.

"I was very upset," Sarah said. "We really don't want to move into the hotels, either, because they're trouble, too. But we can't stay here for three to five months."

Sarah said she is hoping to get into public housing but, knowing there is a lengthy waiting list for such apart-ments, she is hoping to get any apartment with better conditions than those in which her family is living.

Meanwhile, Ethel Walker is looking for a Section 8-subsidized apartment for herself and her son. A broadcast major at New York City Community College in Downtown Brooklyn, she has been trying to look for apartments in between studying and attending classes. She is also looking for a job.

"You try to do better. You try to get out of it," Ethel said. "I'm just trying to make it out here."

—The *Daily News* (N.Y.)

Chapter 4

Old Hitler: A Shark Hunter's Obsession

by Jeff Klinkenberg

Ron Swint moaned in the dark about the shark called Old Hitler, the largest shark in Tampa Bay, as traffic roared by on the Skyway Bridge. Somebody in a car shouted and Swint automatically winced. He has been hit by beer cans thrown from passing cars. A huge truck rumbled by so fast the bridge shook. Diesel fumes hung in the air.

The first shark to come along was not Old Hitler, but it was a big one, a shark Swint later estimated at 500 pounds, a shark that swallowed a three-pound live ladyfish bait and swam toward the lights of Tampa. The shark almost killed Swint.

Swint was pulling on the shark rod with all his strength when the line snapped. His own momentum carried him into the lane of traffic. The truck never slowed down, but Swint was quick enough to scramble back onto the side-walk with his expensive rod and reel.

Shaken, he said: "That's why I never drink when I'm out here. You need all your faculties to fish for sharks. If I'd had a few beers tonight, I may not have been quick enough to get out of the way. I've almost been pulled in the water by sharks, but this was the first one that al-most got me killed by the traffic.

"And that wasn't even Old Hitler."

Four times Ron Swint has hooked the shark he calls Old Hitler and four times it has escaped. "Last year I wasn't even a challenge," Swint said. "Old Hitler ripped me off." Last time Swint was ready. "Old Hitler took 1,500 yards of line and I turned him. I thought I had him. Then my line broke."

Swint is obsessed by Old Hitler, the most intimidating shark in the bay. Old Hitler, Swint says, is a 22-foot hammer-head. Its head is 5½ feet wide. Old Hitler, Swint says, weighs 1,500 pounds, easy. If Old Hitler is indeed that large, it is twice the size of the biggest hammerhead ever taken on rod and reel. The world record, captured off Jacksonville in 1975, weighed 703 pounds and was 14 feet long. Swint intends to catch Old Hitler and break the record. "That SOB is mine," Swint said, voice, rising in the night. "I'm gonna get him."

It was 11 p.m. near the main span of the Skyway, the bridge from which Swint fishes nightly for sharks, and he was prepared for another titanic tussle with Old Hitler. His face now illuminated by the eerie glow of a gasoline lantern, Swint said with reverence: "Old Hitler has attacked boats. They've had to close beaches a couple of times. Old Hitler is . . ." His narration was interrupted by the clicking drag of his enormous fishing reel filled with 2,500 yards of 80-pound test line. Something large had picked the bait from the bottom and was swimming away.

Swint, who had recovered from his near miss with the truck, picked up his rod and harnessed it to his chest. With one hand he tied a rope to a hole in the sidewalk. A big shark could pull him from the bridge. Occasionally, Swint ties himself to the structure with the rope.

The shark swam slowly away from the bridge. "Old Hitler hits softly," said Swint, a 32-year-old St. Petersburg resident who says he retired from Ohio so he could fish for sharks in Florida. "Old Hitler," Swint said, "will take line out so my reel makes five or six clicks. Then he takes off against the full drag. It's the most amazing thing you'd ever want to see."

But this shark wasn't Old Hitler. It was probably a pup, a shark that weighed less than 200 pounds, because it didn't even swallow the bait. It mutilated it, then abandoned it on the bottom.

"Even when I don't catch a fish, having a run is the most exciting thing in the world," Swint said.

Three years ago, Swint got it in his mind to devote the rest of his life to catching sharks. He had a good job in Columbus, Ohio, he says, as the product manager for a pollution firm. He made a good salary, he traveled, he was unmarried, "and I read in some books that Tampa Bay was the second best place for sharks in the world, second only to Australia. And shark fishing was about the only thing I'd never done. And I'd seen people retire at 65 and drop dead eight days later, so I figured it was a good time to retire. At 29." And so he did.

He works part time now, for The Tackle Box, a fishing store on U.S. 19. He repairs rods and reels. He is good at the work. Sometimes he does a little bartending for a friend. He has a lot of time to fish, on the Skyway at night, for sharks. "I think there's a lot of sharks in the bay because they follow the ships in from the Gulf," said Swint, a tall, muscular man who wears a necklace made from shark cartilage. "Those ships throw their garbage overboard and the sharks must follow it in."

There's a fortune to be made from sharks, Swint says enthusiastically, and he is just now looking into that prospect. A world record shark, he says, will be worth $1.5 million from endorsements from tackle businesses. A nine-foot shark, he says, is worth $5,000 if correctly processed.

A 200-pound shark will yield 190 pounds of delicious meat, he says. "But the trouble is nobody does it right," he said. "Lot of guys shoot sharks before they land them. Even from the Skyway. You kill a shark and you ruin it. Their bladders explode and the flesh will be contaminated by urine."

Swint lands sharks alive and immediately removes internal organs. He says he sells the flesh to private parties for $1 a pound. He also tans the hides, he says, and sells them to people who use them to make women's apparel, belts and wallets. From the jaws of a large shark he can make 300 necklaces, which sell for $9 each, he says. He can make five canes, at $40 each, from the backbone cartilage.

But Swint has more than a mercenary interest in sharks. "I would rather fight a shark then any other fish," he said. "There's something special about them."

The shark expeditions begin before dark, when Swint drives his aging, odiferous station wagon—he transports dead sharks on the roof—to the Skyway. He stops the car near the main span—"This is dangerous and illegal. I've been fined $25 for doing it"—and unloads four fishing rods, a large tackle box, two buckets, rope, a bridge gaff, pads, a jug of Kool-Aid and two gasoline lanterns. He unloads his car in less than a minute. Then he drives to the end of the bridge, parks, and walks a mile back.

When it gets dark, Swint ties a lantern to the bridge and dangles it six inches above the water. The light attracts small fish, which Swint catches on a spinning rod. He uses the small fish for bait to catch ladyfish, which in turn are used to entice the sharks on his big outfit, a size 16/0 reel that sits on a rod as thick as a broomstick. The rod and reel, which Swint bought after eight months of studying sharks, weighs 25 pounds. He says he paid $1,200 for it.

To get his bait away from the bridge, he ties a balloon to the line with thread. The balloon drifts with the tide away from the bridge. When the bait is carried a sufficient distance, Swint pulls hard on his fishing rod and the balloon breaks loose. The bait sinks to the bottom.

"It's never boring out here," Swint said. "I can catch ladyfish all night while I wait for a shark run. Sometimes I catch tarpon. I've caught tarpon, boy. I've gotten exactly 72 this year. They swim right under my lantern sometimes. But

I break off tarpon, or cobia, or grouper, or snook—whatever I might have on—if I hear my big rod going out. There's nothing like a shark."

The hardest part of catching a big shark from the bridge is landing it. The fight, Swint says, is often short. He lets sharks tire themselves out, then reels them in. But when he pulls them to the bridge, the work begins.

He first drops a rope around the tail of the shark—that often takes some nifty maneuvering; the shark won't cooperate—and hoists it from the water. When he can't lift it higher, he ties the rope to the bridge. Then he loops another rope around the head of the shark and lifts. When he can't pull that any higher, he lifts the tail rope. "It works like a winch," Swint said. "I've pulled 300-pounders in by myself."

Last September 24 he caught a shark he couldn't work himself. But he was lucky that night. He was fishing from the jetty of Pass-a-Grille. It took him 45 minutes to reel in the tiger shark, estimated to weigh 970 pounds. Swint tied it to the jetty, but he wasn't strong enough to bring it in.

Swint phoned a towing service for help, he says. The first three towing services did not believe him. "I told the fourth service that my car was broken down," Swint said. "When the guy arrived, I told him my car was okay but I needed some help down on the jetty. He pulled up my shark."

Last summer Swint says he lived four days on the Skyway. He slept during the day on the sidewalk. Old Hitler never touched his baits.

—St. Petersburg Times

Disco Does Wonders For Radio Station

by Geoff Walden

New York—Last July 24th, at 5:59 p.m., WKTU-FM, "Mellow 92," was playing Neil Young's soft-rock song, "It's Over."

At 6:00 p.m., WKTU-FM, "The new, Disco 92," was playing Donna Summer's "The Last Dance."

For Donna Summer, the song went on to win this year's Oscar for Best Original Song, for the movie, "Thank God It's Friday." For the radio station, the song was the start of the all-disco format that has made WKTU the most-listened to station in America, with an average of 275,000 people tuning in every quarter hour.

As Mellow 92, WKTU had about a 2 percent share of New York's radio audience according to Michael Ellis, who selects the station's music. That meant that 20 stations in New York alone had more listeners than WKTU, Ellis said.

As of February (the latest figure), Disco 92's New York audience share was 10.3 percent, higher than the country's perennial radio leader, New York's all-top-40 station, WABC-AM.

"It was the first double-digit share for a New York station in several years," Ellis said.

Six months after WKTU went all-disco, its ad rates had more than quadrupled, from $60 to $280 per minute.

Other stations around the country have caught "Saturday Night Fever," too, but "their results have been uneven," Ellis said. He believes that "New York is the disco capital of the world," and there are many reasons for the music's failure to beat as loudly in other cities. He thinks a city has to be fast-paced, heavily urbanized and ethnic for disco to command a large share of its radio market.

"The Sun Belt is less receptive to disco than the Snow Belt, with the exception of Miami, which is probably one of the two or three biggest disco markets," he said. Miami, he explained, has a large Cuban population, which like New York's Puerto Rican community, is keeping time to disco's pulse.

But Ellis cautioned against looking upon disco as an ethnic phenomenon. "Disco crosses race, class and age," he said, adding that older people like disco better than rock. He thinks WKTU is the number-one station among listeners as old as 50.

Ellis sees the origin of disco's popularity as a rebellion from rock's increasing sophistication.

"Rock was exciting when it was new in the '60's, and you had superstar groups," he said. "But when it matured, it got artistic and esoteric. It was higher-quality music, but it was losing its common touch.

"Punk and disco broke with rock. They were throwbacks to simpler beats, and they were more accessible. But punk didn't catch on, because it was too anti-social. Disco never threatened anybody."

Disco has become so popular in New York that two other major stations besides WKTU are thriving by pumping out disco refrains (one is WABC, which has changed its format to majority disco).

Ellis foresees more disco stations arising nationwide, and he advocates WKTU's setup for them.

The format is relaxed and informal. The disc jockeys avoid "radio" voices, and they trade banter with the newscasters. Newscasts are held to 92 seconds. DJ's occasionally announce, "You're listening to America's No. 1 station," but on the air WKTU generally understates its success. The setup is almost diametrically opposite to the frantic, jingle-filled style of WABC.

Also, WKTU plays no commercials from midnight to 5:30 a.m., and from 12:30 p.m. to 1:30 p.m., every day.

David Rapaport, the station's general manager, says that WKTU has the fewest ads of any successful commercial station in New York. "We believe too many commercials can lose your audience," he said. "We could be making considerably more money if we took more ads."

Marc Cichon, WKTU's operations director, says that the station's rise reflects the general ascendancy of FM. "Originally, FM was heard only in homes and only by a limited audience,"

he said. "Now, more or less every new car has FM."

Cichon said that AM stations are as much concerned over the decline of their whole radio band, as they are over the fall of individual stations. He said that AM is going to test stereo transmission (it has always delivered monaural sound).

The question for WKTU, stereo FM, is, will disco keep in step with changing times?

Ellis answers, "I think disco will continue to be popular through the '80s. It's been growing since '73, and it has yet to peak."

—Columbia News Service

Chapter 15

New York Fights Youth Crime With Tough New Offender Law

by Richard Higgins

New York—Rafael Torres and Hector Valdez sat at the brown wooden table, playing Superman coloring books, combing their hair, waving and occasionally shouting to friends in the room.

It could have been a scene out of the South Bronx junior high school where they are enrolled in the eighth grade. But it was the beginning of an arson and multiple murder trial in the Bronx Criminal Courthouse and the two skinny, squirming boys were not there to learn; they were the defendants.

At night, the boys are taken to a special, isolated section of the city's sprawling jail on Rikers Island, where three dozen others await court appearances on charges from robbery to murder. They are all 13-to-15-year-old

juveniles, children of the city's ghettos who have become symbols of New York's new effort to crack down on juvenile crime.

Their presence at Rikers is just one dramatic result of a new state law that sends 13-to-15-year-old juveniles accused of certain serious crimes directly into the adult court system. Until Sept. 1, 1978, when the new juvenile offender law took effect, youths under 16 were handled exclusively in Family Court. More than 600 juveniles have been arrested under the new law, one of the strictest in the nation.

The new law allows 13-year-olds charged with murder and 14- and 15-year-olds charged with murder and several other serious felonies—such as rape, arson, aggravated assault and robbery—to be tried as adults. Thus youths who are too young legally to buy liquor, vote, drive or even quit school can be sentenced to life in prison if convicted of murder.

Under the old law, the most Rafael Torres and Hector Valdez could have received in Family Court was 18 months in a secure facility of the State Division for Youth and three and one half years of supervision.

New York's new law is in step with a trend toward toughness in juvenile justice systems across the country. As violent youth crime increasingly disturbs the public, the 1960s quest for rehabilitation is giving way to strident demands for punishment. Two dozen states in recent years have enacted measures to beef up the punitive power of their juvenile courts or to permit the waiver of youths from juvenile to adult courts. Connecticut is now considering a bill similar to the New York law.

The juvenile offender law has sharply divided the state's criminal justice system since it was hastily passed in the wake of two brutal murders committed by 15-year-olds. In the midst of his then-faltering re-election campaign, Gov. Hugh Carey reversed his stand and embraced the law.

The city's district attorneys and police say the law was needed because youths under 16 were becoming heavily engaged in serious crime—even in heroin traffic and murder contracts—on the assumption that they had virtual "immunity" against significant punishment in Family Court.

State Sen. Ralph J. Marino, a Long Island Republican and staunch backer of the new law, believes it was needed to halt "rampant youth crime" because the therapeutic orientation of Family Court wasn't working. "If these hoods commit adult crimes, let's treat 'em that way," he said. "It'll probably be good for 'em."

But civil libertarians and children's advocates have denounced the law as "Draconian" and "brutalizing," and charged that it particularly victimizes poor and minority youths.

"It's a demoralizing regression," commented Carol Sherman, a lawyer for the juvenile rights division of the New York Legal Aid Society, the chief defender of youths in court. "The notion that the city is being run rampant by murderous youths is a myth being exploited by politicians."

She pointed out that police arrests of juveniles for murder decreased from 110 in 1974 to 44 in 1978.

Under the juvenile offender law, youths whose cases start out in Criminal Court may be transferred at any point to Family Court, if the judge and prosecutor agree it "serves the interest of justice."

One reason the law has stirred so much controversy is that more than three-fourths of the juveniles arrested under it have had their cases transferred to Family Court or had charges against them dropped. The reason for this, say Legal Aid lawyers and, privately, some judges, is that police are bringing inflated charges.

"Typically, we're defending kids involved in schoolyard brawls, such as a 14-year-old beating up and stealing a radio or skateboard from a 13-year-old classmate," said Charles Schinitsky, attorney-in-charge of Legal Aid's juvenile rights division. Because such cases involve weapons or the use of force, they may be prosecuted as first degree robbery.

Schinitsky said such "nonsense cases" comprise about 80 percent of the juvenile offender cases. He charged that hundreds of youths were being unnecessarily exposed to the adult court system, where, he said, they are "stigmatized as criminals."

City prosecutors hotly deny the charge. John J. O'Donnell, chief juvenile prosecutor in the Manhattan District Attorney's office, said many "so-called schoolyard brawls" involve vicious attacks and serious injuries. "Is it less criminal if the victim is another youth?" he asked.

Several Family Court judges have said they support a proposed amendment to the juvenile offender law that would start all youth cases in the Family Court, but allow only the most serious to be waived up to the Criminal Court. "It makes more sense that way," said Judge Edith Miller of the Manhattan Family Court.

Since Family Court remains confidential, youths whose cases do not belong in Criminal Court would be protected, Miller said. Other judges said such a move would save the state time and money.

The response of anti-crime Republicans in Albany to such a move is likely to be cool. Sen. Marino's reply to such a change was terse: "Over my dead body. If anything, we'll beef it up." To the anxiety of Legal Aid lawyers that youths are being brutalized in court, Marino answers, "It's brutalizing to be stabbed."

Although New York prosecutors, like Bronx District Attorney Mario Merola, think that the new law is having a deterrent effect because "word has gone out on the streets that the old, easy days are over," many judges are not so sure. One Brooklyn Family Court judge said, "Either youth crime will decrease, or we'll start seeing 12-year-old drug runners and hit men."

—*Columbia News Service*

Code of Ethics

The following is the code of ethics of the Society of Professional Journalists (Sigma Delta Chi, 1973):

The Society of Professional Journalists, Sigma Delta Chi, believes the duty of journalists is to serve the truth.

We believe the agencies of mass communication are carriers of public discussion and information, acting on their Constitutional mandate and freedom to learn and report the facts.

We believe in publishing the truth as part of the public's right to know truth.

We believe those responsibilities carry obligations that require journalists to perform with intelligence, objectivity, accuracy, and fairness.

To these ends, we declare acceptance of the standards of practice here set forth:

RESPONSIBILITY: The public's right to know of events of public importance and interest is the overriding mission of the mass media. The purpose of distributing news and enlightened opinion is to serve the general welfare. Journalists who use their professional status as representatives of the public for selfish or other unworthy motives violate a high trust.

FREEDOM OF THE PRESS: Freedom of the press is to be guarded as an inalienable right of people in a free society. It carries with it the freedom and the responsibility to discuss, question, and challenge actions and utterances of our government and of our public and private institutions. Journalists uphold the right to speak unpopular opinions and the privilege to agree with the majority.

ETHICS: Journalists must be free of obligation to any interest other than the public's right to know the truth.

1. Gifts, favors, free travel, special treatment or privileges can compromise the integrity of journalists and their employers. Nothing of value should be accepted.
2. Secondary employment, political involvement, holding public office, and service in community organizations should be avoided if it compromises the integrity of journalists and their employers. Journalists and their employers should conduct their personal lives in

a manner which protects them from conflict of interest, real or apparent. Their responsibilities to the public are paramount. That is the nature of their profession.

3. So-called news communications from private sources should not be published or broadcast without substantiation of their claims to news value.

4. Journalists will seek news that serves the public interest, despite the obstacles. They will make constant efforts to assure that the public's business is conducted in public and that public records are open to public inspection.

5. Journalists acknowledge the newsman's ethic of protecting confidential sources of information.

ACCURACY AND OBJECTIVITY: Good faith with the public is the foundation of all worthy journalism.

1. Truth is our ultimate goal.

2. Objectivity in reporting the news is another goal, which serves as the mark of an experienced professional. It is a standard of performance toward which we strive. We honor those who achieve it.

3. There is no excuse for inaccuracies or lack of thoroughness.

4. Newspaper headlines should be fully warranted by the contents of the articles they accompany. Photographs and telecasts should give an accurate picture of an event and not highlight a minor incident out of context.

5. Sound practice makes clear distinction between news reports and expressions of opinion. News reports should be free of opinion or bias and represent all sides of an issue.

6. Partisanship in editorial comment which knowingly departs from the truth violates the spirit of American journalism.

7. Journalists recognize their responsibility for offering informed analysis, comment, and editorial opinion on public events and issues. They accept the obligation to present such material by individuals whose competence, experience, and judgment qualify them for it.

8. Special articles or presentations devoted to advocacy or the writer's own conclusions and interpretations should be labeled as such.

FAIR PLAY: Journalists at all times will show respect for the dignity, privacy, rights, and well-being of people encountered in the course of gathering and presenting the news.

1. The news media should not communicate unofficial charges affecting reputation or moral character without giving the accused a chance to reply.

2. The news media must guard against invading a person's right to privacy.

3. The media should not pander to morbid curiosity about details of vice and crime.

4. It is the duty of news media to make prompt and complete correction of their errors.
5. Journalists should be accountable to the public for their reports and the public should be encouraged to voice its grievances against the media. Open dialogue with our readers, viewers, and listeners should be fostered.

PLEDGE: Journalists should actively censure and try to prevent violations of these standards, and they should encourage their observance by all newspeople. Adherence to this code of ethics is intended to preserve the bond of mutual trust and respect between American journalists and the American people.

The codes have come about because of the realization that the press has enormous power and that this power can be abused, misused and misdirected. The codes are helpful, but no code can force a reporter or news writer to do anything. The choice between right and wrong is up to the individual.

Glossary

These definitions were provided by the press associations and working reporters and editors. Most of the brief entries are from the *New England Daily Newspaper Study,* an examination of 105 daily newspapers, edited by Loren Ghiglione (Southbridge, Mass.: Southbridge Evening News Inc., 1973).

Print Terms

add An addition to a story already written or in the process of being written.

A.M. Morning newspaper.

assignment Instruction to a reporter to cover an event. An editor keeps an assignment book that contains notations for reporters such as the following:

> Jacobs—10 a.m.: Health officials tour new sewage treatment plant.
>
> Klaren—11 a.m.: Interview Ben Wastersen, possible Democratic congressional candidate.
>
> Mannen—Noon: Rotary Club luncheon speaker, Horlan, the numerologist. A feature?

attribution Designation of the person being quoted. Also, the source of information in a story. Sometimes, information is given on a not-for-attribution basis.

background Material in a story that gives the circumstances surrounding or preceding the event.

banger An exclamation point. Avoid. Let the reader do the exclaiming.

banner Headline across or near the top of all or most of a newspaper page. Also called a line, ribbon, streamer, screamer.

B copy Bottom section of a story written ahead of an event that will occur too close to deadline for the entire story to be processed. The B copy usually consists of background material.

beat Area assigned to a reporter for regular coverage. For example, police or city hall. Also, an exclusive story.

body type Type in which most of a newspaper is set, usually 8 or 9 point type.

boldface Heavy, black typeface; type that is blacker than the text with which it is used. Abbreviated bf.

break When a news development becomes known and available. Also, the point of interruption in a story continued from one page to another.

bright Short, amusing story.

bulldog Early edition, usually the first of a newspaper.

byline Name of the reporter who wrote the story, placed atop the published article. An old-timer comments on the current use of bylines. "In the old days, a reporter was given a byline if he or she personally covered an important or unusual story, or the story was an exclusive. Sometimes if the writing was superior, a byline was given. Nowadays, everyone gets a byline, even if the story is a rewrite and the reporter never saw the event described in the story."

caps Capital letters; same as uppercase.

caps and lower case Initial capital in a word followed by small letters. See lowercase.

clip News story clipped from a newspaper, usually for future reference.

cold type In composition, type set photographically or by pasting up letters and pictures on acetate or paper.

column The vertical division of the news page. A standard-size newspaper is divided into five to eight columns. Also, a signed article of opinion or strong personal expression, frequently by an authority or expert—a sports column, a medical column, political or social commentary, and the like.

copy Written form in which a news story or other material is prepared.

443

copy desk The desk used by copy editors to read copy. The slot man is in charge of the desk.

copy flow After a reporter finishes a story, it moves to the city desk where the city editor reads it for major errors or problems. If it does not need further work, the story is moved to the copy desk for final editing and a headline. It then moves to the mechanical department.

correction Errors that reach publication are retracted or corrected if they are serious or someone demands a correction. Libelous matter is always corrected immediately, often in a separate news story rather than in the standard box assigned to corrections.

correspondent Reporter who sends news from outside a newspaper office. On smaller papers often not a regular full-time staff member.

crony journalism Reporting that ignores or treats lightly negative news about friends of a reporter. Beat reporters sometimes have a tendency to protect their informants in order to retain them as sources.

crop To cut or mask the unwanted portions, usually of a photograph.

cut Printed picture or illustration. Also, to eliminate material from a story. See trim.

cutline Any descriptive or explanatory material under a picture.

dateline Name of the city or town and sometimes the date at the start of a story that is not of local origin.

deadline Time at which the copy for an edition must be ready.

dirty copy Matter for publication that needs extensive correction, usually because the reporter has made indecipherable markings on copy.

edition One version of a newspaper. Some papers have one edition a day, some several. Not to be confused with issue, which usually refers to all editions under a single date.

editorial Article of comment or opinion usually on the editorial page.

editorial material All material in the newspaper that is not advertising.

enterprise copy Story, often initiated by a reporter, that digs deeper than the usual news story.

exclusive Story one reporter has obtained to the exclusion of the competition. A beat. Popularly known as a scoop, a term never used in the newsroom.

feature Story emphasizing the human or entertaining aspects of a situation. A news story or other material differentiated from straight news. As a verb, it means to give prominence to a story.

file To send a story to the office, usually by wire or telephone, or to put news service stories on the wire.

filler Material used to fill space. Small items used to fill out columns where needed. Also called column closers and shorts.

flag Printed title of a newspaper on page one. Also known as logotype or nameplate.

free advertising Use of the names of businesses and products not essential to the story. Instead of the brand name, use the broad term camera for Leica or Kodak.

futures calendar Date book in which story ideas, meetings and activities scheduled for a later occurrence are listed. Also known as a futures book. Kept by city and assignment editors and by careful reporters.

good night Before leaving for the day, beat reporters check in with the desk and are given a good night, which means there is nothing further for the reporter from the desk for the day. On some newspapers, the call is made for the lunch break, too. Desks need to know where their reporters are in case of breaking stories.

graf Abbreviation for paragraph.

Guild Newspaper Guild, an international union to which reporters and other newspaper workers belong. Newspapers that have contracts with the Guild are said to be "organized."

handout Term for written publicity or special-interest news sent to a newspaper for publication.

hard news Spot news; live and current news in contrast to features.

head or headline The display type over a printed news story.

head shot Picture featuring little more than the head and shoulders of the person shown.

HFR Abbreviation for "hold for release." Material that cannot be used until it is released by the source or at a designated time. Also known as embargoed material.

identification Personal data used to identify a person: name, title (if any), age, address, occupation, education, race, religion, ethnicity. The identifying characteristics used are those relevant to the story. Generally, we use name, age, occupation, address. To lend authority to the observations or statements of sources, we give their background. Use race, religion, national origin only when relevant to the story. In obituaries and crime stories, the readers want as much identification as possible. In general news stories, logic should indicate relevancy: Toledo readers are not interested in the home address of the North Carolina senator who collapses in a hotel and dies. But the newspaper in his home town of Raleigh will insert the address in the press association copy.

insert Material placed between copy in a story. Usually, a paragraph or more to be placed in material already sent to the desk.

investigative reporting Technique used to unearth information sources often want hidden. This type of reporting involves examination of documents and records, the cultivation of informants, painstaking and extended research. Investigative reporting usually seeks to expose wrongdoing and has concentrated on public officials and their activities. In recent years, industry and business have been scrutinized. Some journalists contend that the term is redundant, that all good reporting is investigative, that behind every surface fact is the real story that a resourceful, curious and persistent reporter can dig up.

italics Type in which letters and characters slant to the right.

jump Continuation of a story from one page to another. As a verb, to continue material. Also called runover.

kill To delete a section from copy or to discard the entire story; also, to spike a story.

lead (pronounced leed) First paragraph in news story. A direct or straight news lead summarizes the main facts. A delayed lead, usually used on feature stories, evokes a scene or sets a mood.
Also used to refer to the main idea of a story: An editor will ask a reporter, "What's the lead on the piece?" expecting a quick summary of the main facts. Also: A tip on a story; an idea for a story. A source will tell a reporter, "I have a lead on a story for you." In turn, the reporter will tell the editor, "I have a lead on a story that may develop."

localize Emphasizing the names of persons from the local community who are involved in events outside the city or region: A local couple rescued in a Paris hotel fire; the city police chief who speaks at a national conference.

lowercase Small letters, as contrasted to capitals.

LTK Designation on copy for "lead to come." Usually placed after the slug. Indicates the written material will be given a lead later.

makeup Layout or design. The arrangement of body type, headlines and illustrations into pages.

masthead Formal statement of a newspaper's name, officers, place of publication and other descriptive information, usually on the editorial page. Sometimes confused with flag or nameplate.

morgue Newspaper library.

mug shot See head shot.

new lead See running story.

news hole Space in a newspaper allotted to news, illustrations and other non-advertising material.

obituary Account of a person's death; also called obit.

offset Printing process in which an image is transferred from a printing plate to a rubber roller and then set off on paper.

off the record Material offered the reporter in confidence. If the reporter accepts the material with this understanding, it cannot be used except as general background in a later story. Some reporters never accept off-the-record material. Some reporters will accept the material with the provision that if they can obtain the information elsewhere they will use it. Reporters who learn of off-the-record material from other than the original source can use it.
No public, official meeting can be off the record, and almost all official documents (court records, police information) are public information. Private groups can ask that their meetings be kept off the record, but reporters frequently ignore such requests when the meeting is public or large numbers of persons are present.

op-ed page Abbreviation for the page opposite the editorial page. The page is frequently devoted to opinion columns and related illustrations.

overnight Story usually written late at night for the afternoon newspapers of the next day. Most often used by the press services. The overnight, or overnighter, usually has little new information in it but is cleverly written so that the reader thinks the story is new. Also known as second-day stories.

play Emphasis given to a news story or picture—size and place in the newspaper of the story; typeface and size of headline.

P.M. Afternoon or evening newspaper.

pool Arrangement whereby limited numbers of reporters and photographers are selected to represent all those assigned to the story. Pooling is adopted when a large number of persons would overwhelm the event or alter its nature. The news and film are shared with the rest of the press corps.

press release Publicity handout, or a story given to the news media for publication.

proof Reproduction of type on paper for the purpose of making corrections or alterations.

puff or puffery Publicity story or a story that contains unwarranted superlatives.

quotes Quotation marks; also a part of a story in which someone is directly quoted.

rewrite To write for a second time to strengthen a story or to condense it.

rewrite man Person who takes the facts of stories over the telephone and then puts them together into a story and who may rewrite reporters' stories.

rowback A story that attempts to correct a previous story without indicating that the prior story had been in error or without taking responsibility for the error.

running story Event that develops and is covered over a period of time. For an event covered in subsequent editions of a newspaper or on a single cycle of a wire service, additional material is handled as follows:

New lead—Important new information.
Add and insert—Less important information.
Sub—Material that replaces dated material, which is removed.

sell Presentation a reporter makes to impress the editor with the importance of his or her story; also, editors sell stories to their superiors at news conferences.

shirttail Short, related story adapted to the end of a longer one.

short Filler, generally of some current news value.

situationer Story that pulls together a continuing event for the reader who may not have kept track as it unfolded. The situationer is helpful with complex or technical developments or on stories with varied datelines and participants.

slant To write a story so as to influence the reader's thinking. To editorialize, to color or misrepresent.

slug Word or words placed on all copy to identify the story.

source Person, record, document or event that provides the information for the story.

source book Alphabetical listing, by name and by title, of the addresses and the office and home telephone numbers of persons on the reporter's beat and some general numbers—FBI agent in charge in town, police and fire department spokesmen, hospital information, weather bureau.

split page Front page of an inside section; also known as the break page, second front page.

stringer Correspondent, not a regular staff member, who is paid by the story or by the number of words written.

style Rules for capitalization, punctuation and spelling that standardize usage so that the material presented is uniform. Most newspapers and stations have stylebooks. The most frequently used is the common stylebook of the United Press International and the Associated Press.

stylebook Specific listing of the conventions of spelling, abbreviation, punctuation, capitalization used by a particular newspaper, wire service. Broadcast stylebooks include pronunciations.

sub See running story.

subhead One-line and sometimes two-line head (usually in boldface body type) inserted in a long story at intervals for emphasis or to break up a long column of type.

text Verbatim report of a speech or public statement.

thumbnail Half-column-wide cut or portrait.

tight Full, too full. Also refers to a paper so crowded with ads that the news space must be reduced. It is the opposite of the wide open paper.

tip Information passed to a reporter, often in confidence. The material usually requires further fact gathering. Occasionally, verification is impossible and the reporter must decide whether to go with the tip on the strength of the insider's knowledge and reliability. Sometimes the reporter will not want to seek confirmation for fear of alerting sources who will alter the situation or release the information to the competition. Tips often lead to exclusives.

titles Mr., Mrs., Miss, Ms., Secretary of State, Police Chief, Senator are formal designations and may be used before the person's name. Usage depends upon the station's or newspaper's policy. False titles—Vietnam war hero, actress, leftfielder—are properly used after the name: For instance, Nate Thurmond, the center . . . instead of Center Nate Thurmond. . .

trim to reduce or condense copy carefully.

update Story that brings the reader up to date on a situation or personality previously in the news. If the state legislature appropriated additional funds for five new criminal court judges to meet the increased number of cases in the courts an update might be written some months later to see how many more cases were handled after the judges went to work. An update usually has no hard news angle.

VDT Video display terminal, a part of the electronic system used in news and advertising departments that eliminates typewriters. Copy is written on typewriter-like keyboards and words appear on attached television screens rather than on paper. The story is stored on a disk in a computer. Editing is done on the terminals.

verification Determination of the truth of the material the reporter gathers or is given. The assertions, sometimes even the actual observation, do not necessarily mean the information is accurate or true. Some of the basic tools of verification are: the telephone book, for names and addresses; the city directory, for occupations; *Who's Who,* for biographical information. For verification of more complex material, the procedure of Thucydides, the Greek historian and author of the

History of the Peloponnesian War, is good advice for the journalist: "As to the deeds done in the war, I have not thought myself at liberty to record them on hearsay from the first informant or on arbitrary conjecture. My account rests either on personal knowledge or on the closest possible scrutiny of each statement made by others. The process of research was laborious, because the conflicting accounts were given by those who had witnessed the several events, as partiality swayed or memory served them."

wire services Synonym for press associations, the Associated Press and the United Press International. There are foreign-owned press services to which some newspapers subscribe: Reuters, Tass, Agence France Presse.

Broadcast Terms

actuality An on-the-scene report.
audio Sound.

closeup (broadcast) Shot of the face of the subject that dominates the frame so that little background is visible.
cover shot A long shot usually cut in at the beginning of a sequence to establish place or location.
cue A signal in script or by word or gesture to begin or to stop. Two types: incue and outcue.
cut Quick transition from one type of picture to another. Radio: a portion of an actuality on tape used on broadcast.
cutaway Transition shot—usually short—from one theme to another, used to avoid jump cut. Often a shot of the interviewer listening.
dissolve Smooth fading of one picture for another. As the second shot becomes distinct, the first slowly disappears.
dolly Camera platform. Dolly-in: move platform toward subject. Dolly-out: move platform away.
dub The transfer of one video tape to another.

FI or **fade in** A scene that begins without full brilliance and gradually assumes full brightness. **FO** or **fade out** is the opposite.
freeze frame A single frame that is frozen into position.

graphics All visual displays, such as art work, maps, charts and still photos.

jump cut Transition from one subject to a different subject in an abrupt manner. Avoided with cutaway shot between the scenes.

mix Combining two or more sound elements into one.
montage A series of brief shots of various subjects to give a single impression or communicate one idea.

O/C On camera. A reporter delivering copy directly to the camera without covering pictures.
outtakes Scenes that are discarded for the final story.

pan or **pan shot** Moving the camera from left to right or right to left.

remote A taped or live broadcast from a location outside the studio. Also, the unit that originates such a broadcast.

segue An uninterrupted transition from one sound to another; a sound dissolve. (Pronounced seg-way.)
SOF Sound on film. Recorded simultaneously with the picture.
SOT Sound on tape. Record simultaneously with picture on tape.

trim To eliminate material.

V/O Reporter's voice over pictures.
VTR Videotape recording.

zoom Use of a variable focus lens to take closeups and wide angle shots from a stationary position. By using a zoom lens an impression can be given of moving closer or farther away from the subject.

Computer Terms

These definitions were provided by Merrill Perlman of *The New York Times.*

busy light or working light Tells the user that the computer is working on the function requested. Most computer systems prevent any other functions being performed while the light is on.

change case Usually a key that allows a lowercase letter to be turned into an uppercase letter. The function is particularly useful when the user has forgotten to unlock the shift key.

control, command, supershift Usually a key that allows an extra function to be programmed onto a single key. For example, an x will yield a lowercase x with no extra key pressed, an uppercase x when the shift is pressed and perhaps a + mark when the supershift key is pressed. The control key also may act as a safety key that must be pressed simultaneously with another function key to, for example, erase an entire story.

crash The system "locks up" and the terminals stop functioning. This is the bane of computerized newsrooms, since in most cases all the copy that was on the screen when the system crashed is either lost or frozen. Most computer systems have a key or function that allows the user to protect or save copy from crashes by taking it off the screen for a moment so it can be entered into computer memory.

CRT Cathode ray tube.

cursor The square of light that indicates the place in the copy where the changes will be made. The user positions the cursor using directional keys before adding or deleting matter.

delete Just that. Most computer systems have keys for deleting characters, words, sentences, lines, paragraphs or blocks of copy that are defined by the user.

directory, file, basket Designations for the storage of stories, notes, memos, etc. The computerized equivalent of a file holder. Each reporter will have a file or directory; the copy desk will have another, etc.

film Terminology on some computer systems for setting a story into type.

format A specific set of instructions telling the computer to do something. Many systems have common formats built in; others require the user to format each story individually. The formats usually consist of the type size, the leading, the type face, the column width and any special instructions, such as cut-ins for the copy, to allow for half-column graphics or other special typographical set-ups. In some systems, formatting is called styling.

home In most systems, a single key allows the user to return the cursor "home" to the top left-hand corner of the screen, or to the start of the text, depending on how the system is programmed.

hyphenate and justify Usually a function key on most systems, this takes the story, removes it from the screen for a bit and returns it to the screen with the words lined up and hyphenated in the proper column width, just as they will appear in type.

keystroke Pressing one key one time. Functions are often expressed in terms of a keystroke.

load When the computer terminal is being programmed, either by the user or by the systems people, this is called loading.

program To give instructions to the computer. Keys on various systems are programmable as well, so often-used functions or phrases can be entered into them. For example, a programmable key may have "By The ASSOCIATED PRESS" programmed into it, so the person working at the terminal can press just the programmed key to get all those characters.

scope Jargon for video display tube or terminal.

scroll To move the text on the screen up or down, to bring the next lines into view. Most computer systems allow users to scroll through the entire story; some limit scrolling to a certain number of characters.

terminal An individual work station.

tube Jargon for video display tube or terminal.

VDT Video display tube or video display terminal.

Credits

Stories on pp. 5, 6, 7 Reprinted by permission from the *Associated Press.*
Story on pp. 9, 10 Reprinted by permission from *United Press International.*
Story on p. 15 Reprinted by permission from the *Dalton News-Record.*
Stories on pp. 21, 22 Reprinted by permission from *The Providence Journal-Bulletin.*

Chapter 1

Story on p. 28 From *Daily News.* Copyright © 1980 New York News, Inc. Reprinted by permission.
Story on p. 34, 35 Reprinted by permission from *The Providence Journal-Bulletin.*
Story on p. 36 Reprinted by permission from the *Hollywood Sun Tattler,* a Scripps-Howard newspaper.
Story on p. 38 Reprinted by permission from the *Cincinnati Post.*
Story on p. 39 From Charles M. Young, in *Rolling Stone #266,* June 1, 1978. © 1978 by Straight Arrow Publishers, Inc. All Rights Reserved. Reprinted by permission.

Chapter 2

Story on p. 54 Reprinted by permission from *United Press International.*
Story on pp. 62, 63 Reprinted by permission from *The Anniston Star.*
Figure 3.1 Reprinted by permission from *The Free Press* (Mankato, Minn.).

Chapter 3

Story on p. 78 Reprinted by permission from *The St. Petersburg Times.*
Story on pp. 79, 80 From *New York, New York,* edited by Donald H. Johnston.
Copyright © 1981 Arno Press, New York City. Reprinted by permission.

Chapter 4

Story on p. 99 Reprinted by permission from the *Associated Press.*
Story on p. 100 Reprinted by permission from *The Blade.*
Stories on pp. 104, 105 From *Newsday.* Copyright © 1981 Newsday, Inc. Reprinted by permission.

Chapter 5

Story on p. 121 Reprinted by permission from *The Gazette* (Montreal).
Story on p. 126 Reprinted by permission from the *Lexington (Ky.) Herald-Leader.*

Chapter 6

Story on p. 147 Reprinted by permission from *The Miami Herald.*
Excerpt on p. 147 Copyright © 1981 by the Dow Jones Co., Inc. Reprinted by permission from *The Wall Street Journal.*
Story on p. 147 Reprinted by permission from *The St. Petersburg Times.*
Story on p. 150 Copyright © 1981 by *The Courier-Journal.* Reprinted by permission.
Story on p. 151 Reprinted by permission from *The News Tribune.*
Story on pp. 151–153 Reprinted by permission from *Columbus Citizen Journal.*
Quotation on p. 157 Copyright © 1982 by the New York Times Company.
Reprinted by permission from *The New York Times Manual of Style and Usage.*
Quotation on p. 157 Copyright © 1982 by The New York Times Company. Reprinted by permission from *Winners and Sinners.*

Chapter 7

Chapter 8

Story on pp. 171, 172 Reprinted by permission from *The Blade*.

Story on p. 173 Reprinted by permission from the *Associated Press*.

Articles on p. 174 Reprinted by permission from *New York, New York*, edited by Donald H. Johnston. Copyright © 1981 Arno Press, New York City.

Story on p. 181 Reprinted by permission from *The Houston Chronicle*.

Chapter 9

Story on pp. 192–194 From Cary B. Willis, in *Daily News*. Reprinted by permission.

Story on pp. 196, 197 Reprinted by permission from *Buffalo Evening News*.

Story on p. 198 Reprinted by permission from *The Advocate* (Stamford, Conn.).

Story on pp. 201, 202 Reprinted by permission from the *Associated Press*.

Story on p. 205 Reprinted by permission from *The Blade*.

Story on p. 207 Reprinted by permission from *The News and Observer* (Raleigh, N.C.).

Excerpt from story on p. 208 Copyright © 1981 by the Dow Jones Co., Inc. Reprinted by permission from *The Wall Street Journal*.

Chapter 11

Story on pp. 234, 235 Reprinted by permission from *The Philadelphia Bulletin*.

Story on p. 240 Reprinted by permission from *Working: People Talk about What They Do All Day and What They Think of While They Do It,* by Studs Terkel. Copyright © 1972 by Pantheon Books, a Division of Random House, Inc.

Story on pp. 244–248 Reprinted by permission from *Birmingham Post-Herald*.

Chapter 12

Story on p. 256 Reprinted by permission from *United Press International*.

Figure 12.1 Reprinted by permission from CBS.

Part 4

Stories on pp. 269, 270 Reprinted by permission from the *Associated Press*.

Chapter 13

Figure 13.1 (p. 274) Reprinted by permission from *The Hays Daily News*.

Story on p. 277 Reprinted by permission from *The Providence Journal-Bulletin*.

Story on p. 284 Reprinted by permission from *The Virginian-Pilot* (Norfolk, Va.).

Article on pp. 285, 286 Reprinted by permission from *New York, New York*, edited by Donald H. Johnston. Copyright © 1981 Arno Press, New York City.

Chapter 14

Story on p. 291, 292 Copyright © 1981 by *The Courier-Journal*. Reprinted by permission.

Story on p. 295 Reprinted by permission from *The Lexington-Herald*.

Story on pp. 296, 297 Reprinted by permission from *The Providence Journal-Bulletin*.

Story on p. 299 Reprinted by permission from *The Los Angeles Herald Examiner*.

Chapter 15

Story on p. 306 Reprinted by permission from the *Buffalo Evening News*.

Story on p. 307 Reprinted by permission from *The Louisville Times*.

Story on p. 308 Reprinted by permission from *Eugene Register-Guard*.

Story on p. 308 Reprinted by permission from the *Associated Press*.

Story on p. 310 Reprinted by permission from *The Virginian-Pilot* (Norfolk, Va.).

Article on pp. 311–313 Reprinted by permission from *The Anniston Star*.

Story on p. 315 Reprinted by permission from the *Kansas City Times*.

Article on p. 323 Reprinted by permission from *The Atlanta Constitution*.

Excerpt on pp. 330, 331 Reprinted by permission from the *Lexington Herald-Leader*.

Story on p. 331 Reprinted by permission from *The Milwaukee Journal*.

Story on p. 332 Reprinted by permission from *The Dalton News Record*.

Stories on pp. 334, 335 Reprinted by permission from the *Associated Press*.

Story on p. 342 Reprinted by permission from *The Advocate*.

Story on p. 344 Reprinted by permission from *The Berkshire Eagle*.

Story on p. 348 Reprinted by permission from *The Gazette* (Montreal).

Stories on pp. 349, 350 Reprinted by permission from the *Boston Herald American*.

Story on p. 351 Reprinted by permission from *The Houston Chronicle*.

Material on p. 398 Reprinted by permission from *The Des Moines Register and Tribune*.
Figure 17.1 Copyright © 1981 by *Editor and Publisher Co., Inc.* Reprinted by permission.
Story on pp. 408, 409 Reprinted by permission from the *Associated Press*.
Story on p. 409 Reprinted by permission from *The Commercial Appeal*.

Stylebook: Reprinted from *News Reporting and Writing* by Melvin Mencher. Copyright © 1981 Wm. C. Brown
Publishers, Dubuque, Iowa. All Rights Reserved. Reprinted by permission.

Stories on pp. 429–432 From the *Daily News*. Copyright © 1980 New York News, Inc. Reprinted by permission.
Story on pp. 432–434 Reprinted by permission from *The St. Petersburg Times*.
Article on pp. 435, 436 Reprinted by permission from *New York, New York,* edited by Donald H. Johnston, director of Columbia News Service. Copyright © 1981 Arno Press, New York City.
Article on pp. 436–438 Reprinted by permission from *New York, New York,* edited by Donald H. Johnston, director of Columbia News Service. Copyright © 1981 Arno Press, New York City.

Index

Ultang, Don, 374–75
United Press International, 54, 60, 160,
        212, 219, 256–57, 327
    policy of, on attribution, 141
    "World in Brief," 258–59
U.S. Navy Photograph, 49, 360

Vachon, John, 118
Van Gilder, Bonnie, 79–80
Verification, 158–61
Vincent, Mal, 278–79, 284–85
Voboril, Mary, 147, 164
Vonnegut, Kurt, 247

Walden, Geoff, 173–74, 435
Walker, Stanley, 235
Wall, Maryjean, 126
Wall Street Journal, 209–10, 401
    human interest in stories in, 154
Washburn, Lindy, 3–7, 23, 30, 57, 101,
        102, 164
Washington Post, 212, 235, 257, 397, 401
    employment of women by, 44
    policy of, on attribution, 141
Weather stories, 353–55
    essentials for, 355
Weiner, Timothy, 285–86
Weinraub, Bernard, 142
Werner, Perry, 81

WEWS-TV (Cleveland), 410
Whipple, Ed, 204
Widener, Jeff, 82
Williams, Joseph M., 249–50
Willis, Cary B., 192–94
WIND (Chicago), 110–11
Wire services
    rewriting for broadcast, 259–61
WJKW-TV (Cleveland), 410
WKYC-TV (Cleveland), 410
WLS (Chicago), 159
Wolfe, Tom, 199, 201, 202
Wong, Jan, 93, 94–95, 107, 121, 146
Woodward, Bob, 109
Worcester, Wayne, 37
Word usage, 214–15
WRC-TV (Washington, D.C.), 159–60
Writing style, 129–33
    active voice, 132
    implied opinion in, 132–33
    and nature of story, 131, 244–48
    passive voice, 132

Young, Charles M., 39

Zagoria, Sam, 124
Zimmerman, Fred, 97–98, 250

Melvin Mencher is professor of the Graduate School of Journalism at Columbia University. He joined the Columbia faculty in 1962 after teaching at the University of Kansas. He worked for the United Press, was the statehouse correspondent for *The Albuquerque Journal*, handled investigative reporting for *The Fresno* (California) *Bee* and covered political and social developments in Central America for *The Christian Science Monitor*. He was a Nieman Fellow at Harvard University. He is the author of *News Reporting and Writing* (also published by Wm. C. Brown).

About the Author